Religion, Politics, and the Law

Commentaries and Controversies

PETER SCHOTTEN
Augustana College

DENNIS STEVENS
Augustana College

Wadsworth Publishing Company
I(T)P ® An International Thomson Publishing Company

Belmont • Albany • Bonn • Boston • Cincinnati • Detroit • London • Madrid
Melbourne • Mexico City • New York • Paris • San Francisco • Singapore
Tokyo • Toronto • Washington

For Bernice and Bonnie

Philosophy Editor: Tammy Goldfeld
Editorial Assistant: Kelly Zavislak
Production Editor: Jennie Redwitz
Managing Designer: Stephen Rapley
Print Buyer: Karen Hunt

Permissions Editor: Jeanne Bosschart
Copy Editor: Donald Pharr
Compositor: Christine Pramuk
Cover Designer: Andrew Ogus
Printer: Malloy Lithographing, Inc.

COPYRIGHT © 1996
By Wadsworth Publishing Company
A Division of International Thomson Publishing Inc.
I(T)P The ITP logo is a registered trademark under license.

Printed in the United States of America
1 2 3 4 5 6 7 8 9 10—01 00 99 98 97 96

For more information, contact Wadsworth Publishing Company.

Wadsworth Publishing Company
10 Davis Drive
Belmont, California 94002
USA

International Thomson Editores
Campos Eliseos 385, Piso 7
Col. Polanco
11560 México D.F. México

International Thomson Publishing Europe
Berkshire House 168-173
High Holborn
London, WC1V 7AA
England

International Thomson
Publishing GmbH
Königswinterer Strasse 418
53227 Bonn
Germany

Thomas Nelson Australia
102 Dodds Street
South Melbourne 3205
Victoria, Australia

International Thomson Publishing Asia
221 Henderson Road
#05-10 Henderson Building
Singapore 0315

Nelson Canada
1120 Birchmount Road
Scarborough, Ontario
Canada M1K 5G4

International Thomson Publishing Japan
Hirakawacho Kyowa Building, 3F
2-2-1 Hirakawacho
Chiyoda-ku, Tokyo 102, Japan

Library of Congress Cataloging-in-Publication Data

Schotten, Peter M.
   Religion, politics, and the law : commentaries and controversies / Peter Schotten, Dennis Stevens.
     p. cm.
   Includes bibliographical references and index.
   ISBN 0-534-19488-5 (paperback)
   1. Religion and state—United States. 2. Religion and politics—United States. 3. United States—Politics and government. 4. United States—Politics and government—1993- 5. United States—Religion. 6. United States—Religion—1960- I. Stevens, Dennis G.
BL2525.S335 1996
322'.1'0973—dc20

95-16439

Brief Contents

Contents

III   RELIGION AND EDUCATION

IV   RELIGION AND MEDICAL CARE

Preface

Religion is a source of guidance and comfort for people around the world, yet many countries face a daily challenge of deep religious division and conflict. Religious differences today, as in the past, have often led to war or have been a major contributing factor to tensions that have led to war. Bosnia, India, Israel, Ireland, and the Sudan (to name only a few examples) have all faced serious conflicts over religion in recent years. The conflicts have been bloody, and the resolutions—when they have come—have rarely brought different religious groups together in anything approaching lasting harmony. There are also tensions among religious groups in the United States, but these tensions until now have been moderated by the influence of political and legal institutions and the ideas established by our Founders. Will we continue to reap the benefits that religious tolerance has made possible in our country? Our hopes for the future are dependent on what is referred to as "separation of church and state."

But we cannot preserve something we do not understand. This book is designed to encourage thought and provoke discussion about the relationship of religion and politics. To illustrate what we have identified as the fundamental issues, we have generally relied upon controversies that have ended up in court, either in the Supreme Court or in lower venues. We believe that this approach has allowed us to present what are complicated issues in a clear and well-defined form. This book, in other words, makes use of court cases without attempting to be any sort of comprehensive manual on the current state of the law. It does not pretend to be a complete sourcebook of recent cases. Rather, it is our hope that the cases we have chosen—some major and some minor—will introduce students to the wide variety of questions that emerge from the dynamic relationship between religion and politics in the United States. The many questions raised within this book's chapters—some that reflect our opinions and some that do not—are presented for the purposes of reflection and discussion. We believe that such questions provide an indispensable beginning for developing any coherent understanding of the connections among religion, politics, and the law.

This book is organized so that it can be used easily in the classroom. The first five chapters address historical and philosophical issues, and often present arguments about the relationship of religion and politics. These are the chapters in which we offer our interpretation of the issues behind the current debate. We do, of course, attempt to treat fairly the areas of disagreement within the debate. These chapters are argumentative in the classical sense of the term; they present an argument. But they are not polemical. Since the issues are controversial, not all readers will necessarily accept our conclusions or perhaps even our way of presenting them. The remaining chapters are "issue chapters." They are designed to raise questions rather than to answer them. Each of these chapters has the same format: the title of the chapter is a question; the problem behind the question is posed; a series of short case summaries is presented to illustrate the complexity of the problem; each case is discussed briefly (and questions raised by it are posed); and the issues are clarified in a short conclusion. We cannot claim that our views about religion and politics do not surface within the issue chapters, but we have attempted to eliminate them as much as is humanly possible.

There are, then, really two ways to use this book. For those who want to strengthen their understanding of the historical and philosophical background of the contemporary debate on religion and politics, the first five chapters will be particularly useful. For those who want to focus on contemporary issues, the issue chapters can be emphasized. Whichever approach to the book is used, it will have fulfilled its purpose if it helps foster critical thinking about these difficult issues.

We would like to thank Augustana College for its assistance; much of the work on this book was made possible because of its leave policy and grants to us from the Augustana Research and Artists Fund. The quality of the book was greatly enhanced by Daniel Dreisbach of The American University, Frank Guliuzza of Weber State University, Steven Monsma of Pepperdine University, Julia Stronks of the University of Maryland–College Park, Graham H. Walker of the University of Pennsylvania, and Paul J. Weber of the University of Louisville. Their expertise in the field was invaluable. Donald Pharr's careful editorial work was thorough and insightful. Finally, the Wadsworth team made the project a success. Tammy Goldfeld organized the entire project admirably, helping us through every stage, and Jennie Redwitz's professional and kind attention to the production phase helped bring the book to life.

❖

PART I

Historical and Philosophical Background

1

European Roots

Religion and Politics in the Western Tradition

Until the sixteenth century, it was generally believed that justice could not be defined without reference to the divine.[1] Therefore, the political community did not understand itself in merely human terms. In ancient Athens, for example, public worship of the many gods of the city—part divine, part human—was a unifying force for political life and constituted a very specific kind of civic religion.[2] In the Greek *polis* there was no distinction between the religious and secular spheres. The purpose of the political community was thought to be primarily moral, and the development of good character (virtue) was its first responsibility. In other words, justice in politics was thought to flow from a morality that was linked to the divine.[3] One could say that the political community considered it a sacred duty to "legislate morality."[4] And by deriving its legitimacy from its participation in divine justice, the political community established a firm connection between piety and obedience to the law. Disobedience was seen as an act of impiety, and questioning the justice of the political community was the same thing as doubting the gods. In the ancient world, religion and politics were part of an organic whole.

Significantly, many of the most important and enduring criticisms of ancient political communities were also cast in religious or quasireligious terms. In Plato's *Republic,* Socrates presented a view of the best regime as a standard for all politics, and this best regime was founded on reasoning about the divine and hence eternal and unchanging ideas.[5] The biblical tradition also offered a perspective for understanding politics. The Jews and Christians of the ancient world developed different views of justice, but both held fast to the belief that justice is the gift of God and that politics must be judged by trans-political standards.[6]

Traditionally, the political community in the West was indebted to these different views of the divine for justice itself, but the clash over these different views inevitably led to political conflict. For example, Athens came to see Socrates as subversive and finally put him to death because he called the traditional gods into question.[7] Similarly, Jesus was regarded as subversive by the Romans for openly challenging the authority of the Roman gods (including the divinity of the Emperor). Nor was religious persecution the preserve of regimes based on polytheism. It is ironic that Christianity, which was initially the victim of repression, became repressive once it came to power in Rome. As Leo Pfeffer says,

> The Church, which until so recently had been the victim of persecution and oppression, now welcomed such persecution and repression by the state of nonconformists and the unorthodox.... Deviation from orthodoxy was made a crime against the state, often punishable by death. Heretics were forbidden to build churches, hold religious assemblies, or teach their doctrines even privately. Pagans were required to hear instruction in the churches, were subject to exile if they refused baptism, and to death if, after receiving baptism, they lapsed into pagan rites. The partnership between church and state was not an easy one.[8]

Following the sacking of Rome by barbarians, St. Augustine offered a religious explanation of why Rome could have suffered such a defeat even though it had embraced Christianity a generation before. Augustine contended that Christianity could neither preserve the Empire nor cause its decline; the community of Christian believers (the true City of God) was not to be confused with earthly (and flawed) political communities. Jesus died for salvation of individual souls, not for the preservation of politics, and "true justice has no existence save that republic whose founder and ruler is Christ, if at least any choose to call this a republic...."[9] It is important to understand that Augustine did not favor anything like a separation of church and state in the modern sense. He clearly and unequivocally championed the Christian political community. He believed that politics could foster citizen morality only if it was grounded in Christianity. In the event that the political community would lack this specific religious orientation, he argued that only the Christian church, not the political community, could make human beings moral.[10]

Augustine is an important historical figure because of his perception of the relationship of religion and politics. His writings provide the key to understanding many medieval political disputes. With the rise of the Christian church, political conflict often focused on the extent to which regimes advanced religious principles; later, it focused on the extent to which the nascent form of the modern state could act independently of the church. For example, this was the character of the dispute between the twelfth-century king of England, Henry II, and his appointed archbishop of Canterbury; they struggled to determine the acceptable boundaries of jurisdiction between the secular and ecclesiastical courts. This conflict illustrates the strong drive toward creating an independent secular power, while revealing at the same time the continuing importance of the religious realm.[11]

During the Middle Ages, the Christian church played a key role in the organization and structuring of civic life. Even until the late sixteenth century, European monarchs based their claim to rule on divine right—on the doctrine that they were God's representatives on earth and answerable to God alone. As one thoughtful historian has written, "Despite all that distinguished the great monotheistic religions from the polytheism dominant in ancient times, it nonetheless remained the case that every polity within Christendom and the House of Islam rested on the authority which was grounded in divine right."[12]

The ancient and medieval world in the West was in one way or another grounded in religion. The idea of a politics independent of religion had not yet emerged. The divine foundation of the political community was, in other words, the source of both meaning and conflict in politics.

RELIGION FROM A SECULAR PERSPECTIVE: BITTER FRUITS, IMPORTANT LESSONS

The legacy of Christianity's influence in the West is nothing if not controversial. To begin, it is fair to say that Christianity and the church were responsible for many of the best and most enduring contributions to Western history from the decline of Rome to the sixteenth century. During this period, Christianity and its church decisively influenced virtually every part of human life. Love and benevolence, inspired by the piety taught by Christianity, led to many commemorations of the divine, including churches, hospitals, beautiful music, orphanages, and the advancement of numerous good and humane doctrines. The church was also responsible for preserving, transcribing, and editing important philosophic and literary texts that would have otherwise been lost forever.

However, Christianity specifically, and revealed religion generally, also exhibited some unfortunate tendencies. To an influential number of secular Enlightenment philosophers, it appeared that revealed religion's influence in history could be defined primarily in terms of these negative attributes. These philosophers regretted and feared the extreme fanaticism, the intellectual censorship, the persecution of nonbelievers and other-believers, and the warfare inspired by zealously held religious beliefs. Such occurrences were to be regretted and condemned, partially because they threatened the very enterprise of philosophy and free thought. Three phenomena in particular stood out: the Crusades, the Spanish Inquisition, and numerous religiously based European wars. Each profoundly influenced the lives of tens of thousands of people. That religion would lead people to a firm conviction that their beliefs were true and that their understanding of God's ways were certain was hardly surprising.

More than any other belief or set of beliefs, religion gave meaning, purpose, and direction to human life, both individually and collectively. That fanaticism, hatred, and violence could so closely be associated with revealed religion may not have been utterly shocking (given prior history), but it still proved to be constantly disappointing and frightening. This realization decisively influenced those political thinkers who would undertake to legitimize the newly emerging political state on a secular, rather than a religious, basis.

Conflict based upon religious disagreement found unfortunate expression in the Crusades. Sometimes portrayed as a glorious era, the Crusades were also tragic. They were actually a series of campaigns from 1096 to 1291 in which Christians fought to take Jerusalem away from the Muslims. Muslims had originally taken Jerusalem by force because the land there was holy to them as well. Thus, Christians retaliated by waging sporadic wars against Muslims for over three hundred years. The campaigns were almost all badly organized, as Chaim Potok suggests in his description of the First Crusade:

> They were responding to the Command of God. It was the start of the promised second coming of Jesus. The day of Judgment was close at hand. All through the spring and summer peasants from the north gathered up their belongings and moved through the land. Families joined together into groups; groups became bands; soon a vast swollen pious superstition-ridden host was marching toward the Rhine. Some had visions. One group was led by a knight, another by a nobleman, a third by a goat with magical powers. They filled the roads and fields and forests of the Rhine.[13]

Jewish communities were particularly hard hit. About eight hundred Jews were killed in the city of Worms, more than a thousand died in Mainz, and thousands more were killed in Cologne after the synagogue was destroyed. When one of the campaigns finally reached Jerusalem in 1099, the soldiers attacked the city and massacred the inhabitants. Muslims and Jews were killed and mutilated, and the few who were not killed were sold into slavery. All of this was done in the name of God. Sadly, profound religious belief encouraged the shedding of innocent blood and caused incalculable suffering.

Persecution of minority religions was also practiced in Europe throughout the Middle Ages.[14] Jews and Muslims in Europe were often forced to live in special areas (ghettos) and to accept only certain jobs—that is, to perform necessary tasks such as moneylending, which Christians found essential to their communities yet found personally abhorrent or religiously forbidden. This, of course, is the tense situation portrayed in Shakespeare's *Merchant of Venice*. But Christians in Europe took even more forceful measures to deal with despised minority religions. In 1290 the Jews were expelled from England, in 1400 they were expelled from France, and in 1492—the same year Columbus sailed for the New World—Ferdinand and Isabella expelled them from Spain. In 1502 these Spanish rulers also exiled all Muslims who refused conversion. Also, throughout Europe during this time, there were many instances of localized violence and bloodshed against religious minorities. In a number of instances, Christians perceived their response to be defensive or retaliatory. For instance, numerous bloody excursions by Muslims into Europe, especially in the Iberian peninsula, led to intermittent hostilities between Christians and Muslims.

A high level of religious intolerance and persecution was evident in the Spanish Inquisition, which began in 1478. During the next decade, the Inquisition grew in scope, branching out into the whole of the country and continuing spasmodically thereafter in Spain as well as in other European countries. The church had established courts of inquisition in the twelfth century for the purpose of identifying, examining, and punishing heretics, who were frequently burned at the stake. In Spain, and elsewhere throughout Europe, these courts prosecuted nonbelievers and alleged nonbelievers, including all varieties of non-Christians and Christian religious converts. But of all the European countries, Spain was the most severe. Muslim and Jewish converts were its initial and most brutalized victims. The following account details what happened to Jews, who suffered considerably, but not uniquely:

> From the outset, the Spanish Inquisition moved with thoroughness and brutality, its use of secret confessions extorted under torture considered the ideal way to ensnare the maximum number of Jews. During a period of grace, people were invited to come forth to confess and inform upon one another; those who informed would later share in the confiscated property of the accused. Because accusations were made in secret and hearsay was acceptable, the circle of intimidation widened swiftly, as did the practice of blackmail. The accused never met his accuser. Practically overnight, the Holy Office was flooded with hundreds, then thousands, of files packed with detailed testimonies about secret Jewish activities. Those who did not confess during the official grace period but were later implicated in Judaizing faced extreme punishment after long and painful interrogation. The Inquisition became infamous for its diabolical use of water tortures and ropehanging, later depicted so movingly by Goya. In theory, the purpose of the torture was to extract a confession in order to save the soul of the accused.[15]

In countries such as Spain, intolerance and persecution resulted from a combination of factors. Simple hatred of Jews, Muslims, and nonbelievers was one important impetus for oppression. But it is also important to remember that the political community at that time was, by definition, intolerant. Justice was understood as God's justice; it demanded that orthodoxy be enforced in religious matters because the properly ordered soul was the focus of political action, and the soul could not be properly ordered by a pluralistic community (that is, by a community informed both by religious truth and religious error). Thus, from the perspective of the persecutors, strong actions were necessary for the sake of the community and even for the good of the persecuted. It is revealing that the harshness of the Inquisition had its roots in both the highest and lowest of motives.

As if the Crusades and the Inquisition were not sufficiently horrible, there is one more unhappy story to be told—that of religiously motivated European wars. It is not surprising that as Christianity fragmented, Christians would begin to view religious differences among themselves as intolerable. The Protestant Revolution—which began in 1517 when Martin Luther posed his 95 theses on a church door in Wittenberg—helped shatter the unity of Christendom by denying the church's supreme authority on scriptural matters as well as the Pope's ultimate religious supremacy. As a consequence, two interrelated historical forces were unleashed. First, in the wake of accelerating religious turmoil, a number of tensions that had simmered below the surface of Christianity now came to the fore. Consequently, Christianity became formally divided into a number of hostile sects: Lutherans, Calvinists, Anabaptists, Anglicans, Puritans, and others. Next, these competing religious sects became thoroughly embroiled in politics, and more than a century of religious warfare ensued. From 1559 to 1689, religious warfare was the norm: The French civil wars of 1562–1595, the Dutch revolt against Philip II, the Scottish rebellion against Mary Stuart, the Spanish attack on England in 1588, the Thirty Years' War in Germany between 1618 and 1648, the Puritan Revolution of 1640–1660 and the Glorious Revolution of 1688–1689 were all primarily, or at least partially, religious wars.[16]

These events were breathtaking in scope, affecting every part of western and central Europe. Wanton bloodshed was a constant theme. In France, the struggle between Catholics and Protestants assumed the character of a civil war. It reached something of a low point in the slaughter of thousands of Calvinists, known as Huguenots, beginning on St. Bartholomew's Day, August 24, 1572. The Huguenots fought back, although a number of years would pass until an uneasy truce would be reached. Still later, Germany was decimated by the Thirty Years' War (1618–1648), fought primarily by mercenary armies. According to one historical account,

> The immediate effect of the Thirty Years War on Germany was disastrous. For three decades hostile German and foreign armies had tramped back and forth across Germany, killing, raping, and looting defenseless inhabitants. In the wake of Wallenstein's army of 50,000, for instance, swarmed 150,000 camp followers bent on plunder. To the usual horrors of war was added religious fanaticism. Many years would be required for Germany to recover from these wounds.[17]

In England, Henry VIII broke with the Catholic Church in the early 1530s, when he had himself declared the head of the newly proclaimed Protestant Church of England in order to obtain an annulment of his marriage, which the pope had not been willing to grant. Henry did not have a male heir and believed that a new wife was necessary for him to get one. The break with Rome was, of course, controversial, and anyone refusing to accept the new Church of England was put to death. Thomas More, whose story is dramatized in playwright Robert Bolt's *A Man for All Seasons*, was the most illustrious victim of Henry's form of religious persecution.

England well illustrates Europe's religious-based turbulence throughout this era; it was not safe to be either a Catholic or a Protestant in England. As the Church of England (the Anglican Church) moved further from or closer to Catholicism, various groups in the country were embraced or persecuted. When Mary took the throne in 1583, she once again recognized the pope as supreme and had hundreds of Protestants executed (hence her name "Bloody Mary"). Later, when Charles I alienated the Puritans (dissenters from the Church of England who had become powerful in Parliament), full-scale civil war erupted from 1642 to 1649.

Oliver Cromwell, a Puritan, was victorious over Charles and had him beheaded. Cromwell took power and attempted to rule England without the monarchy. This new form of rule proved unsuccessful. After Cromwell was dead (and after his son had attempted to continue his father's rule), the monarchy was restored under Charles II. After the Restoration, religious tensions and conflict continued, complicated by the struggle for authority between the king and Parliament. For example, the Clarendon Code was passed by Parliament in 1662. Directed against Catholics and Protestant nonconformists, the Code declared only Anglican religious meetings legal and forbade any preachers who were not Anglican from coming within five miles of any city.[18]

Charles, however, seeking to make an alliance with the French King Louis XIV and the Catholic Church, suspended the Code in 1672, only to encounter popular resistance so substantial that he subsequently rescinded the suspension. Charles II was succeeded by his brother, James II, who openly proclaimed himself a Catholic and had a son by a Catholic wife. This infuriated the strongly Anglican Parliament, and a number of political opponents of the king invited William and Mary to take power away from James, who was driven out of England in 1688. William took the throne with the understanding that Parliament, not the monarch, would reign supreme. The Glorious Revolution, as it is called, did not end religious persecution in England, where the Anglican Parliament continued to suppress both Catholics and Protestant nonconformists, forcing some—for example, Puritans—to leave England for the New World in order to worship in their own way.

These religious conflicts had a profound effect on European society and politics. The Protestant Reformation unleashed powerful ideas by freeing the individual from the authoritative scriptural interpretations of the church. Over time, historians have contended that the Reformation advanced individualism and human equality, unleased individual creativity, and eventually led to progress in the arts and sciences. Yet it was also, in the words on one historian, "an age of crusaders and martyrs, of plots and assassinations, of fanatic mobs and psalm-singing armies."[19] It was, in other words, a time of irrational hatred, violence, and fanaticism, all proclaimed in the name of religious truth. Consider the following testimony about the Protestant religious wars in France during the seventeenth century:

> I personally heard the proposition made and defended by a well-known Catholic ... that there was less danger [in the hereafter] by eating a child, in such circumstances [during the siege of Paris by the Protestant Henry of Navarre], than by recognizing [supporting] a heretic ... and that all the best theologians of the University were of this opinion.[20]

Nor were such opinions without political effect. It was not uncommon for rulers and would-be rulers to invoke God's name to suit their particular purposes.[21] God was invoked by Calvinists to support rebellion, constitutionalism, and limited government; by Jesuits to support deposing heretical rulers and returning to papal authority; by an assorted number of princes who grounded their absolute monarchical rule in divine right; and by radicals of every stripe who invoked God's sanction on behalf of republicanism, democracy, and even a kind of communism. It seems that government, God, and unmitigated human brutality not only coexisted together but also reinforced one another. People of different religious faiths were not able to live together in peace. This appalling state of affairs could not be allowed to continue. A solution to the political–religious problem was required, and it was precisely this issue that drove some of the best minds of Europe to begin to reflect on ways of resolving this conflict.

POLITICS AND RELIGION:
REASSESSMENT AND REDEFINITION

Religiously rooted violence, persecution, and warfare had profoundly important human consequences, not the least of which were the enormous amounts of pain and suffering inflicted upon innocent people. In addition, these disputes rendered civic peace impossible. Nations appeared forever consigned to fight each other in the name of religion. Such disputes could assume a variety of forms; however, in any form, they threatened the stability and, indeed, the very idea of the emerging nation state. Like Germany during the Thirty Years' War, nations might become a battleground for foreign armies fighting over religious differences. Or like France and England, states might face the constant threat of religiously motivated civil war. Not simply injury and death, but the constant companions of warfare—hatred, fanaticism, and irrational fear—threatened to become the political norm of human relations.

Furthermore, there was another problem associated with the confluence of religion and politics at this time. Even during periods of relative peace and stability, religiously based political regimes frequently suppressed unorthodox or critical ideas. During the fifteenth and sixteenth centuries, censorship was frequent. Writers, philosophers, and scientists faced the unappealing prospect of not only having their work censored, but also of having their lives endangered. This proved to be an intolerable state of affairs.

Modern political philosophers thus undertook two great efforts, each of which was at least partially designed to lessen the dangerous zeal of religious fanaticism. The first was to reformulate the ultimate basis of politics in secular political terms—that is, to establish a nonreligious foundation for politics. The second was to reinterpret religion and to render it more benign. Each effort was successful as well as profoundly important, and each would heavily influence the way that people thought about politics and religion for hundreds of years.

In order to understand the modern philosophical effort to reformulate the basis of politics in secular terms, it is important to reemphasize that fact that there simply were no secular states in the fifteenth and sixteenth century. The boundary between church and state was a matter of dispute. The division between the "city of God" and the "city of man" was often clearer in principle than in practice.[22] But the important fact was that the rulers of both church and state understood themselves in religious terms; political rulers traced their authority to divine right. They did not base claims for allegiance or obedience on secular authority alone. Thus, the legitimacy of government—its right to rule as well its reason for ruling—was fundamentally religious.[23] Although the Protestant revolution did create a new spirit of independence for political communities, it was initially manifested by independence from the Catholic Church, not independence from religion itself.[24] Individual princes began to define religion within their own political communities, but they were anything but independent secular rulers. It was not until modern political philosophers had developed a new foundation for politics—a secular foundation—that church and state could be different enough to make radically different claims from different authorities.

The sixteenth-century Italian philosopher Machiavelli began the great revolt against religion (and against the classical political philosophy represented by Plato and Aristotle) in the name of the secular state. He argued that human beings should not define themselves in terms of moral virtue, and he rejected the old view that divine justice must guide the political community. He states in *The Prince* that politics guided either by biblical or classical standards always aims too high. Human beings should not try to live by divine standards.[25] These utopian tendencies—as he understood them—were harmful to politics. For example, he believed that Christianity as well as the institution of the church played an important role in fostering Italian disunity.[26] Christianity weakened the human spirit, and the Catholic church used the promise and threat of the afterlife to lessen citizens' allegiance to temporal states. Machiavelli was especially concerned about the dangerous political excesses caused by religious fervor. As an authoritative interpreter of Machiavelli has pointed out,

> Concern with the salvation of men's immortal souls seemed to permit, nay, to require courses of action which would have appeared to the classics, and which did appear to Machiavelli, to be inhuman and cruel: Machiavelli speaks of the pious cruelty of Ferdinand of Aragon, and by implication of the inquisition, in expelling the Marannos from Spain. Machiavelli was the only non-Jew of his age who expressed this view. He seems to have diagnosed the great evils of religious persecution as a necessary consequence of the Christian principle, and ultimately of the Biblical principle.[27]

Of course, Machiavelli was not opposed to cruelty under some circumstances, but cruelty in the name of salvation was, in his opinion, unnecessary and destructive of good political order.

During the next century, building upon Machiavelli's critique of religion and classical political philosophy, the English philosophers Thomas Hobbes and John Locke developed an influential secular understanding of human nature and politics. They argued that the proper foundation for politics was a nature that was not under the authority of God (hence rejecting the Bible) and that lacked order and moral meaning (hence rejecting the teleological view of nature offered by Plato and Aristotle). Specifically, Hobbes and Locke argued that politics should be grounded in the doctrine of natural rights.[28] According to this doctrine, human beings are by nature apolitical and amoral, concerned with maximizing their power or comfort and governed by one primary desire: to preserve their own lives.[29] Both Hobbes and Locke argued that a right to life exists because the desire for self-preservation is so great that it cannot be denied. (For Locke, the rights to liberty and property follow from the right of self-preservation.) Where no government exists, people live in what these philosophers called a "state of nature," where life and human well-being are constantly endangered and the passion for self-preservation predominates. In such a place, existence is, according to Hobbes, "solitary, poor, nasty, brutish and short."[30]

The deep and powerful desire for self-preservation naturally leads to conflict in the state of nature, but it can also be channeled to provide a basis for peace. This paradox is the key to understanding the new theory of civil society and government. Hobbes and Locke believed that people could best preserve their lives (and, in Locke's case, their liberty and property as well) if they banded together and agreed to limit their own individual power in favor of public and political power. This agreement to limit personal power for the purpose of self-preservation is usually referred to as the social contract.

According to the political understanding advanced by Hobbes and Locke, justice and morality comprise the formal and informal rules necessary to support the social contract. This understanding of the modern secular state, informed by the doctrine of natural rights, has goals that are completely different from those of the political communities that had been inspired by religion or classical political philosophy. The state was no longer concerned with the salvation of the soul or with its proper ordering. Its purpose was no longer to emulate divine justice. Politics was now designed to achieve the much more modest ends of public peace and prosperity—goals that previously had been endangered by religious warfare and persecution. Hobbes and Locke offered a less-exalted vision of politics, yet their concept of the secular state was potentially far less volatile.

As Machiavelli, Hobbes, and Locke tried to found the political state upon a solid, secular footing, a second effort by philosophers designed to promote civil peace and freedom of thought was also under way. That was the attempt to reinterpret the essential meaning of religion in order to render it benign. Although Hobbes,[31] Locke,[32] and other thinkers contributed to this project, the seventeenth-century philosopher Benedict Spinoza is most commonly associated with it. Proclaiming himself to be a friend of religion, Spinoza undertook a lengthy examination of the Bible.[33] He thought it should be understood as a recounting of historical events interpreted in the light of reason (as opposed to the divine word of God, to be accepted on the basis of faith). He pointed to the contradictions within the Bible, and he argued that reason could not distinguish the accurate from the inaccurate. Therefore, such sections of the Bible had to be set aside, for they had no discernible meaning. Furthermore, where miracles were described, they were to be interpreted in light of the natural (that is, a scientific, mathematical law, which Spinoza declared God had formulated and which had been imperfectly understood in previous ages). The effect of Spinoza's interpretation of the Bible was that it eliminated its most supernatural elements, namely revelation and miracles. What remained was a common morality—teachings about loving one's neighbor as oneself. As Thomas Jefferson would later strive to emulate in his book of biblical stories, religion would be reduced to a set of moral conventions that promoted social harmony. Such a religion could pose no danger of religious persecution for philosophers or scientists whose findings contradicted established religious teachings. A reformulated religion could at last be reconciled with the increasingly powerful secular desire for peace.

JOHN LOCKE'S
PLEA FOR TOLERANCE

In addition to attempting to reformulate both the basis of politics and the very nature of revealed religion, a number of leading thinkers during this period also began advocating an important social and political virtue: liberty of the mind. Applied to religious matters, freedom of the intellect implied toleration of different religions (as long as they did not endanger the political order or other religions). Toleration was defended as derived from right reason as well as from religious precept, properly interpreted. Frequently, toleration constituted a liberal principle affecting both secular and religious expression, resulting in an advocacy of both freedom of the intellect and freedom of worship. However, most thinkers who championed a greater realm for intellectual freedom did not necessarily advocate unlimited religious toleration. Thus, the seventeenth-century writer Milton, who argued for expanded freedom of press and against prior restraint and censorship, nonetheless rejected toleration of different religions (particularly Catholicism).[34] Even John Locke, in arguably the most influential work on religious toleration ever written—the famous *Letter Concerning Toleration*—did not write what by present-day standards would be considered a liberal document.[35] Nonetheless, Locke's work was an extraordinarily influential document, so it needs to be understood. Elsewhere (in his famous *Essay Concerning Human Understanding*), Locke asserted that even the most dogmatically held opinions need to be open to scrutiny, for error, self-deception, and passion frequently lead human beings astray. Civil peace, Locke noted, requires the widespread, mutual recognition of the frailty of human opinions.[36] This was an essential point for understanding *religious* opinions, and it was advanced by Locke in his *Letter Concerning Toleration*. As in his *Second Treatise,* Locke also intended here to strengthen the secular foundation of the political state, for he believed that it was only when the state's legitimacy was based on the secular basis of natural rights (and especially the right to liberty) that tolerance could be achieved.

Locke pointed out that religion and religious opinion had produced baneful results; the church had been a "pernicious seed of discord and war" and a "powerful provocation to endless hatreds, rapines, and slaughters."[37] Religion had been a source of conflict because people did not adequately understand that the purposes of the church and state are fundamentally different.[38] The church is properly concerned with the saving of souls, but the state exists to protect individuals' natural rights to life, liberty, and property. In a well-ordered civil society, church and state should confine themselves to their separate spheres of activity. Locke argued that this basic separation of church and state is good for both, but his primary goal was to foster public peace and thereby to strengthen the state, not to strengthen or protect religion or the church. To this end, Locke stated in the first part of the *Letter* that all force belongs to the civil magistrate, and in the second half of the *Letter* he carried the argument even further. He wrote that there are two important elements of every church: its outward form and rites of worship, and its doctrines and articles of faith. Yet, as we shall see, each of these important elements was subordinated to civil authority.

To Locke, the primacy of civil authority is not readily apparent, especially regarding the form and rites of worship. At first glance, Locke seems to limit the power of the magistrate when he writes that "the magistrate has no power to enforce by law, either in his own church or much less in another, the use of any rites or ceremonies whatsoever in the worship of God."[39] But if this is a limitation, it is a rather unimpressive one, because it forbids government only from dealing with inconsequential matters. Thus, Locke observes that "the greatest part of these ceremonies and superstitions consists in the religious use of such things as are in their own nature indifferent."[40] Here and elsewhere, Locke's language is cautious and is intended to be inoffensive to church authorities, religious officials, and practitioners, although his meaning is not difficult to discern. Hence, while admitting that the magistrate does not have the power to "forbid the use of such rites and ceremonies as are already received, approved, and practiced by any church; because, if he did so, he would destroy the church itself," he actually means that civil authorities should not forbid such rites unless necessity dictates otherwise.[41] Violations of the law cannot be tolerated by the magistrate even if they are incorporated into a religious rite; no church may sacrifice infants or encourage people to "lustfully pollute themselves in promiscuous uncleanliness," because such things are not allowed by law.[42] Locke's statement on the relationship between civil authorities and religious rites begins to look something like this: whatever is lawful in the civil society shall not be prohibited by the magistrate, but the magistrate shall be the judge of what is lawful.

Locke attempted to reassure his readers that his doctrine would not harm religion by declaring that "the magistrate ought always to be very careful that he does not misuse his authority to the oppression of any church, under pretense of public good."[43] This is an important point, yet the fact remains that the civil magistrate possesses the power to judge what is lawful. Although the magistrate is forbidden to oppress a church in order to achieve a nonsecular goal, the *effect* of any secular decision can still be oppressive to religion. In other words, the church can be hurt as an institution even though civil authorities are not guilty of religious persecution. For example, civil authorities could, for completely secular reasons, forbid the drinking of any wine, even though wine is an essential part of worship services for a number of religious groups. According to Locke's standards, these groups could not claim a right to be exempted from this decision. In practice, then—despite Locke's seeming assurances to the contrary—civil authorities could make decisions that adversely affect religion.

Like its ritual, a church's articles of faith could also be regulated by civil authorities. Locke divided articles of faith into two parts: the speculative and the practical (that is, beliefs that have no bearing on social relations and beliefs that have social consequences, respectively). The church may preach any speculative opinion "because they have no manner of relation to the civil rights of subjects."[44] For example, the opinions of Jews regarding the New Testament or the opinions of Catholics regarding the Mass may be mistaken or misguided, but they are not punishable under law. Toleration of such speculative opinions is possible because "the business of laws is not to provide for the truth of opinions, but for the safety and security of the commonwealth, and of every particular man's goods and person."[45] But practical opinions—those that affect behavior—are another matter. They concern both the church and the state, and if a conflict arises between these two, Locke says that civil authority must prevail.

Locke outlines four kinds of practical opinions that the state could regulate or forbid.[46] First of all, he writes that "no opinions contrary to human society, or to those moral rules which are necessary to the preservation of civil society, are to be tolerated by the magistrate."[47] There are, in other words, important, secularly rooted limits to tolerance.[48] Second, civil authorities may regulate opinion that one sect may consider special prerogatives (for example, a sect that arrogated to itself special or supreme secular authority). Third, a belief that one must be loyal to a foreign prince (for example, the Pope) may also be regulated by law. Fourth, atheism may be outlawed. Thus, the state becomes the final authority regarding which religious opinions will be allowed in civil society, although Locke emphasized that decisions on these matters must be made for secular reasons only.

With the benefit of historical hindsight, it is tempting to see Locke's doctrine of tolerance as being overly restrictive. Particularly, his seemingly narrow interpretation of tolerance, which excluded Catholics and atheists, appears to us today hardly tolerant at all. Yet, before coming to such a conclusion, it is essential to see Locke's writing within the context of its time. First, regarding Locke's exceptions to the doctrine of tolerance (for instance, regarding atheists), it is important to remember that Locke wrote in a time when thinkers (like himself) were still punished for heretical or subversive opinions.[49] Freedom of the mind, liberty of thought, and respect for the private religious beliefs of others simply had no sanction before the treatises written by Locke and such fellow thinkers as Spinoza and Milton. Therefore, it is significant that Locke advocated the idea of tolerance at all—and in so doing still managed to preserve a substantial realm of religious liberty and individual freedom of conscience divorced from governmental interference. This was Locke's revolutionary project, and he succeeded remarkably well.[50]

WHITHER RELIGION?

Although Locke's doctrine of toleration allowed for significant regulation of religion for secular reasons, Locke did not want religion to be destroyed by civil authorities. It was not religion, but the zealous political power wielded by revealed religion, that Locke opposed. By contrast, a calmer, less politically influential religion provided a useful support for morality in civil society. Although Locke did not believe that it was the business of the state to foster morality, he also held that it would be foolish for civil authorities to destroy the religions that support morality in the private sphere. Locke writes in his *Reasonableness of Christianity* that religion is helpful as a foundation for morality because unaided reason, in this area, proves weak; experience, on the other hand, "shows that the knowledge of morality by mere natural light (how agreeable soever it be to it) makes but a slow progress and little advance in the world."[51] Here Locke focuses his attention upon the frailty of human opinion by presenting two reasons that philosophy had failed to provide an adequate support for morality. First, there are some matters that reason alone is not capable of proving and that must be left to the realm of faith. Second, even if it were possible for reason to prove all things, Locke argued that there would be very few people who would be so capable of reason that they would obey a morality discovered by it:

> ...it is too hard a task for unassisted reason to establish morality in all its parts upon its true foundation with a clear and convincing light. And it is at least a surer and shorter way, to the apprehensions of the vulgar and mass of mankind, that one manifestly sent from God and coming with visible authority from Him, should, as a king and lawmaker, tell them their duties and require their obedience....[52]

Even if all the duties of morality could be clearly demonstrated with mathematical precision, Locke would still conclude that the method of teaching human beings their duties through reason would be proper for only the few who had the time and capacity for such a difficult undertaking: "The greatest part cannot know, and therefore they must *believe*."[53]

As long as morality rests upon a mere human foundation, it will easily be dismissed by most people. Earlier philosophers had demonstrated the beauty of virtue, but human beings still refused to practice it. "Before our Savior's time," noted Locke, "the doctrine of a future state, though it was not wholly hid, yet it was not clearly known in the world."[54] It was Jesus who brought the idea of immortal life into the world and "[h]ow has this one truth changed the nature of things in the world, and given the advantage to piety over all could tempt or deter men from it!"[55] Thus, Locke teaches that only a morality with a divine sanction could prove to be successful. Christianity is not the only religion that can serve this purpose; other religions can provide adherents with a sound morality, and Locke's doctrine of toleration ensures them a place in civil society. However, most of Locke's attention is devoted to Christianity. The devout will notice that Locke's praise of religion is directed only toward its usefulness to civil society; Christianity is important because the morality it teaches will be followed more faithfully than the morality of philosophers.

Locke begins his *Letter* by telling us that church and state have separate spheres, but the subsequent argument modifies this simple view. In practice, religion will be affected significantly by secular law. Also, as we learn from the *Reasonableness of Christianity*, religion can be useful to civil society, for it can provide a strong foundation for morality. The state should not attempt to "legislate morality" in the way that classical or Christian political communities did, but it should value institutions like the church that exist in the private sphere. Locke's doctrine of toleration was designed to promote public peace in order to protect rights; it was not designed to serve religion. In many ways, however, this doctrine would also protect religion. Insofar as the doctrine of toleration is successful in discouraging the bitter religious conflict that ravaged Europe for centuries, religion will benefit commensurately.

THE POLITICAL AFTERMATH

The political efforts of Machiavelli, Hobbes, Spinoza, and Locke proved to be successful and extraordinarily influential. As will be demonstrated in the next chapter, the United States—the first great republic of modernity—was conceived in accordance with many of their ideas. Thus, this nation would be founded upon a secular basis: the purpose of government would be to safeguard individual rights. Religion, as practiced within the nation at the time of its founding, was increasingly tempered and fragmented among different Christian sects. Toleration of different religious opinions, though not total, had become sufficiently widespread that the Constitution prohibited religious oaths as a precondition for holding political office. Although there are many causes for these developments—Tocqueville saw democracy advanced by the inexorable march of equality[56]—the importance of philosophers' ideas in such matters should not be entirely deprecated or dismissed. Undoubtedly, there is a great deal of truth in the observations of the twentieth-century economist John Maynard Keynes regarding the gradual yet profound influence of ideas on ordinary life:

The ideas of economists and political philosophers, both when they are right and when they are wrong, are more powerful than is commonly understood. Indeed the world is ruled by little else.... I am sure that the power of vested interests is vastly exaggerated compared with the gradual encroachment of ideas. Not, indeed, immediately, but after a certain interval; for in the field of economic and political philosophy there are not many who are influenced by new theories after they are twenty-five or thirty years of age, so that the ideas which civil servants and politicians and even agitators apply to current events are not likely to be the newest. But, soon or late, it is ideas, not vested interest, which are dangerous for good or evil.[57]

The ideas of political philosophers, the egalitarian force of historical events, and the American political example all have profoundly influenced contemporary developments in Western European nations (and, increasingly, some non-Western nations as well). However, the dangers posed by fanatical religion remain an ever-present threat in today's world, as can be seen by the religious (and ethnic) warfare that endures in Eastern Europe (particularly in the former Yugoslavia), in Asia (particularly in the former Soviet Union), in some parts of Africa, and in the Middle East.[58] Still, the depoliticization of religion within liberal democracies in Western Europe has proven impressive. Religion still plays an important, although diminished, role in the public life of such nations. England has retained its established church, although the influence of both Protestantism and Catholicism has been significantly lessened; only in Ireland has the legacy of religious conflict refused to disappear. Similarly, although the Catholic Church in Spain (while disestablished in 1978) still plays a powerful role in Spanish politics, it is not a threat to civil peace. In both France and Germany, even though there exists no established church, religion (particularly in the educational realm) continues to play a far more important role there than it does in the United States. Yet, despite this more substantial influence of religion in public life, these nations remain largely free from the divisive influence of religion-based politics. Democratic European regimes that recognize the rights of their citizens are grounded in the idea of fostering mutual respect of citizens for one another; they are not actively engaged in policies of religious oppression. It would seem that the legacy of Spinoza and—most emphatically—of Locke, endures.

Yet their happy legacy does not survive completely unscathed. Some would argue that in certain respects, the legacy has been challenged by moral nihilism. In this sense, while the language employed by Locke and similar thinkers has endured, the meaning has not remained. Thus, *tolerance*, which for Locke had a precise meaning of respecting the religious practices and speculative religious opinions of fellow citizens, has come to mean—especially in cultural anthropology, much of psychology, and, frequently, lay usage—being nonjudgmental. Such nonjudgmentalism in turn sometimes implies (cultural) relativism, a distant cousin of Locke's idea of toleration, but with radically different assumptions and consequences. Thus, while Locke's doctrine of religious toleration was advocated for the purpose of promoting civil peace and advancing a common morality, the contemporary rationale for toleration is that people ought to be tolerant of all (or almost all) moral, social, religious, and behavioral differences, and this current attitude posits no common morality or truth about morality except the value of tolerance.[59] Whether one ought to be tolerant of such differences (or whether some are dysfunctional, dangerous, or unhealthy) and whether any civil society can exist without a common morality supported by tradition or authority remain difficult questions.[60]

Another contemporary departure from the understandings of Hobbes, Spinoza, and Locke relates to the very idea of religion. At least since Nietzsche's influential proclamation that God is dead (by which he meant that there was no moral order in the universe, so all transcendent standards of religion and truth had become irrelevant),[61] it has become increasingly fashionable to see human beings as free to decide important moral questions for themselves and to see religion, social reality, and moral judgments as all humanly constructed. Having lost all transcendent power, God appears reduced to a construct of the human mind, to some abstract formulation about what is best within us. Thus, while thinkers like Spinoza and Locke sought to purge religion of its supernatural power, retaining it as a system of common human morality ultimately supported by divine sanction, contemporary thought increasingly sees religious belief as radically individualistic and humanly constructed. At a societal level, this makes a common morality difficult to accept or achieve.[62] At the level of politics, the attack on transcendent standards undermines the idea of basing political regimes upon the idea of natural rights (as Locke did). Political regimes, like individual morality, increasingly can be justified in whatever terms we choose. Might makes right and a faith in a metaphysical entity called the people become equally valid justifications for the exercise of any kind of political power.[63] According to this point of view, religion, as traditionally understood or even as reformulated and modified by Enlightenment thinkers, no longer supports or even hinders political power; it has simply become irrelevant.

Thus, the modern political and philosophical enterprise, which began by recognizing that the secular state's survival would be enhanced by religious belief and with the recognition that unfettered religion too quickly allowed politics to degenerate into warfare and persecution, has passed down an ambivalent legacy. In one sense, it has been wildly successful, for the modern democratic state has increasingly justified itself by the idea of protecting secular, individual rights, including the right to liberty in general and religious liberty in particular. Furthermore, religion itself has been tamed, largely shorn of its fanaticism. Religious tolerance, understood as the need to respect the private religious beliefs of fellow citizens (and even of citizens in other nations and different cultures), has been instrumental in serving public peace in the United States and elsewhere. On the other hand, the reigning intellectual climate of the age has radicalized earlier understandings and criticisms of religion. It encourages a definition of tolerance that may in fact serve as a foundation for intolerance, and it leads to a new vision of God, not as a supernatural deity who judges humanity, but as a construct of the human mind. Such opinions have served to enfeeble the foundations of religion, rendering it far weaker than even many of its earlier critics desired. The ultimate solution of the religious–political problem remains out of reach, although the nature of the problem seems to have shifted significantly.

Recognizing this problem is important, and it informs the remainder of our discussion in this book. Indeed, the many specific and narrow dilemmas in religion, politics, and law that we will examine cannot ever be completely divorced from their larger philosophical contexts.

NOTES

1. Since this book is concerned with detailing the relationship among politics, law, and religion in the United States, this chapter focuses upon Western history, which profoundly influenced the American tradition.

2. The fact that classical regimes had their own religions helps explain why religious wars were not fought in the ancient world; it was when religion claimed universal authority and became influential that such wars were fought. Note Rousseau's discussion of this topic in "On Civil Religion" (Book IV, Chapter VIII, *On the Social Contract).*

3. However, it is noteworthy that Aristotle's *Nicomachean Ethics*, the most famous discussion of developing moral virtue as the proper end of politics, does not mention piety as a virtue.

4. It is worth noting that ancient regimes often did not live up to (or in accordance with) their oft-proclaimed lofty goals. It was one thing for people to believe that the purpose of the political community was to foster virtue; it was an entirely different matter for them to actually lead virtuous lives.

5. Plato, *The Republic,* trans. Allan Bloom (New York: Basic Books, 1968), p. 157 (477a–b); p. 189 (508d–509b). Socrates' ideas were presented as divine, although their relationship to the gods is ambiguous. At the very least, one can say that Socrates argued that the ideas are not human creations or constructs; they are transcendent and can inform human understanding and action.

6. See Moses Maimonides, *"The Guide of the Perplexed"* in *Medieval Political Philosophy,* ed. Ralph Lerner and Muhsin Mahdi (Ithaca, NY: Cornell Univ. Press, 1963) p. 1911. See also Thomas Aquinas, *Political Ideas of St. Thomas Aquinas,* ed. Dino Bigongairi (New York: Hafner, 1953), pp. 3–57.

7. However, it is significant that Socrates never denied the principle that religion and politics are inseparable; he accepted the authority of Athens to enforce religious orthodoxy.

8. Leo Pfeffer, *Church, State and Freedom* (Boston: Beacon, 1953), p. 13.

9. St. Augustine, *The City of God*, trans. Marcus Dods (New York: Modern Library, 1950), Bk. II, chapter 21, p. 63.

10. See Frederick Copleston, *A History of Philosophy,* trans. Marcus Dods (Garden City, NY: Modern Library, 1950), Volume 2, Part I, p. 104.

11. This struggle is highlighted in Becket, Jean Anouih's famous play.

12. Paul Rahe, *Republics: Ancient and Modern* (Chapel Hill, NC: Univ. of North Carolina Press, 1992), p. 356.

13. Chaim Potok, *Wanderings,* (New York: Knopf, 1978), p. 305.

14. Significantly, Jews and Christians were systematically discriminated against in Middle East Muslim nations, but since this study concentrates upon Europe, discussion of this issue is beyond this book's scope.

15. Jane Gerber, *The Jews of Spain: A History of the Sephardic Experience* (New York: Free Press, 1992), pp. 130–31.

16. Richard Dunn, *The Age of Religious Wars, 1559–1689* (New York: Norton, 1970), p. ix. Much of the subsequent discussion relies upon Dunn, and we acknowledge our reliance upon his work.

17. John Harrison and Richard Sullivan, *A Short History of Western Civilization* (New York: Knopf, 1978), p. 361. Wallenstein, an ally of the staunchly Catholic Holy Roman Empire ruler Ferdinand II, was a soldier of fortune who led his own army throughout the conflict.

18. Harrison and Sullivan, p. 384.

19. Dunn, p. ix.

20. Quoted in Philip Hallie, *Cruelty* (Middletown, CT: Wesleyan Univ. Press, 1982), p. 101.

21. This paragraph follows Dunn, p. 11.

22. The language is, St Augustine's, which is rooted in Jesus's admonition to render to Caesar and God what is due each. See Matt. xxii, 21.

23. See p. 1.

24. Harold Berman, *Law and Revolution: The Formulation of the Western* Legal *Tradition* (Cambridge: Harvard University Press, 1983), p. 29.

25. Niccolo Machiavelli, *The Prince*, ed. Mark Musa (New York: St. Martin's, 1959), p. 44.

26. Niccolo Machiavelli, *Discourses on the First Ten Books of Titus Livius* (New York: Modern Library, 1940), p. 152.

27. Leo Strauss, *What Is Political Philosophy?* (Glencoe, IL: Free Press, 1959), p. 44.

28. Although Hobbes and Locke differed on a number of key points, including the kind of government they advocated, they also agree in many important respects, and in this abbreviated discussion we will treat them together.

29. Thomas Hobbes, *Leviathan* (London: Collier, 1962), chapter xiii. Also see John Locke, *Two Treatises of Civil Government*, ed. Peter Laslett (New York: New American Library, 1960), pp. II, 13, 123, 127.

30. Note Strauss's observation regarding Hobbes' discussion of the state of nature: "The state of nature became an essential topic of political philosophy only with Hobbes, who still almost apologized for employing that term. It is only since Hobbes that the philosophic doctrine of natural law has been essentially a doctrine of the state of nature. Prior to him, the term 'state of nature' was at home in Christian theology rather than in political philosophy. That state of nature was distinguished especially from the state of grace, it was subdivided into the state of pure nature and the state of fallen nature. Hobbes dropped the subdivision and replaced the state of grace by the state of civil society. He thus denied, if not the fact, at any rate the importance of the Fall and accordingly asserted that what is needed for remedying the deficiencies or the 'inconveniences' of the state of nature is, not divine grace, but the right kind of human government." Leo Strauss, *Natural Right and History* (Chicago: Univ. of Chicago Press, 1965), p. 184.

31. Thus, according to two perceptive authors, in the *Leviathan* "Hobbes in his biblical exegesis … attempts to transform Christianity from a transcendent faith into a civil theology, cutting out the core of the religion while preserving its rhetorical skin to give the appearance of divine imprimatur to the authority of the sovereign." See Richard Sherlock and Roger Barrus, "The Problem of Religion in Liberalism," *Interpretation*, vol. 20, no. 3 (Spring 1993), pp. 292–93.

32. See Sherlock and Barrus, p. 297. They write about Locke's extensive writings on religion as follows: "Christianity for Locke is a purely moralistic religion, a collection of simple homilies fit even for the common lot of mankind, represented by the illiterate and credulous men chosen by Jesus as his apostles. Locke very carefully avoids the argument that divine revelation is necessary for the elaboration of the true morality. He does admit that the assertion of revelation is necessary in order to teach the true morality to the 'vulgar and mass of mankind.' "

33. Benedict Spinoza, *Tractatus Theologico-Politicus*, in *Works of Spinoza*, ed. & trans. R. H. M. Elwes (New York: Dover, 1955), vol. I.

34. Compare Milton's *Aeropagitica* with his *True Religion, Heresie, Schism, and Toleration*.

35. For a good discussion of the great influence exerted by John Locke's *Letter* on Thomas Jefferson's thought regarding the relationship between the secular and the religious realms, see Michael Malbin, *Religion and Politics: The Intentions of the Authors of the First Amendment* (Washington: American Enterprise Press, 1978), pp. 29–37.

36. According to Locke, "to maintain peace, and the common offices of humanity, and friendship in the diversity of opinions... We should do well to commiserate our mutual ignorance, and endeavor to remove it in all the gentle and fair ways of information; and not instantly treat others ill, as obstinate and perverse, because they will not renounce their own, and receive our own opinions, or at least those we would force upon them, when it is more than probable that we are no less obstinate in not embracing some of theirs. For where is the man that has uncontestable evidence of the truth of all that he holds, or of the falsehood of all he condemns; or can say that he has examined to the bottom all his own, or other men's opinions? The necessity of believing without knowledge, nay often upon very slight grounds, in this fleeting state of action and blindness we are in, should make us more busy and careful to inform ourselves than contain others. *An Essay Concerning Human Understanding* (New York: Dover, 1959), vol. II, bk. IV, ch. 16, pp. 372–73.

37. John Locke, *A Letter Concerning Toleration* (New York: Bobbs-Merrill, 1955), p. 27.

38. Locke, *Letter,* p. 17.

39. Locke, *Letter,* p. 35.

40. Locke, *Letter,* p. 37.

41. Locke, *Letter,* p. 39.

42. Locke, *Letter,* p. 39.

43. Locke, *Letter,* p. 40.

44. Locke, *Letter,* p. 45.

45. Locke, *Letter,* p. 45.

46. This paragraph on the four types of practical opinions is based upon Malbin's thoughtful analysis of Locke's *Letter.* See Malbin, p. 32.

47. Malbin, p. 50.

48. The conclusion is, as Leonard Levy puts it, that Locke "drew the line at seditious libel." And, in this area, religion afforded no special exemption from the law. See Leonard Levy, *Freedom of Speech and Press in Early American History: Legacy of Suppression* (New York: Harper, 1963), p. 103.

49. Walter Berns points out that Locke contended that the proof of Jesus' authority was attested to by miracles, yet Locke's understanding of miracles was "suggested in the fact that he specified that it should not be published until after his death." See Walter Berns, "Religion and the Founding Principle," *The Moral Foundations of the American Republic,* ed. Robert Horwitz (Charlottesville: Univ. of Virginia Press, 1986), 3d ed., p. 220, n. 43. Perhaps of equal interest is the fact that Locke's *Two Treatises of Government* were originally published anonymously in 1609 and were subsequently acknowledged by Locke only in his will.

50. According to Paul Rahe, "In repudiating divine right, in asserting that magistrates have no business enforcing outward piety or suppressing the propagation of heresy, and in intimating that the public authority should concern itself with virtue and vice only to the degree necessary for the material welfare and preservation of mankind, Locke turns his back on nearly all previous regimes—pagan, Jewish, Christian, and Muslim alike. In contending that absolute monarchy is 'inconsistent with Civil Society,' he denies the legitimacy of virtually every polity that existed on the European continent and elsewhere." Rahe, p. 520.

51. John Locke *On the Reasonableness of Christianity* (Chicago: Regency Gateway, 1965), p. 271, para. 241.

52. Locke, *Reasonableness,* p. 170, para. 241.

53. Locke, *Reasonableness,* p. 179, para. 243.

54. Locke, *Reasonableness,* p. 181, para. 244.

55. Locke, *Reasonableness,* p. 182, para. 245.

56. According to Tocqueville, social, economic, and religious forces all moved in this direction, for "there is hardly an important event in the last seven hundred years which has not turned out to be

advantageous for equality." Tocqueville's list was impressive and not unrelated to this chapter's previous discussion: "The Crusades and the English wars decimated the nobles and divided up their lands. Municipal institutions introduced democratic liberty into the heart of the feudal monarchy; the invention of firearms made villein [sic] and noble equal on the field of battle; printing offered equal resources to their minds; the post brought enlightenment to hovel and palace alike; Protestantism maintained that all men are equally able to find a path to heaven. America, once discovered, opened a thousand new roads to fortune...." Alexis de Tocqueville, *Democracy in America,* ed. J. P. Meyer (Garden City, New York: Doubleday Anchor, 1969), vol. I, p. 11.

57. John Maynard Keynes, *The General Theory of Employment, Interest, and Money* (New York: Harcourt, no date), pp. 383–84.

58. Foremost, here, is Hitler's Holocaust, which resulted in the death of five to six million Jews. An additional problem in present-day Western Europe is prejudice against foreign workers, many of whom have non-Christian, (most often Moslem) religious beliefs.

59. On the logical problem inherent in advancing tolerance as an objectively true value while denying the possibility of objective truth, see Henry Veatch, *Rational Man: A Modern Interpretation of Aristotelian Ethics* (Bloomington, IN: Indiana Univ. Press, 1962), pp. 37–46.

60. On the extent to which cultural relativism blinds us from making judgments that certain societal beliefs and practices are destructive and maladaptive, see Robert Edgerton, *Sick Societies Challenging the Myth of Primitive Harmony* (New York: Free Press, 1992).

61. Note Veatch's observation (which concludes by paraphrasing Nietzsche): "'God is Dead.' This was Nietzsche's proclamation, and nowadays, it is something that nearly everyone accepts without question.... We don't even bother to proclaim it any more; we just act on it. For the import of Nietzsche's proclamation is simply that there is no objectively grounded moral order anywhere in the universe: morality can appeal neither to God nor to nature nor to reality of any kind as sources from which it may derive its basis and its justification. And 'if the belief in God and in an essentially moral order of things is no longer tenable' why not accept the consequence, viz., 'the belief in the absolute immorality of nature and in the utter prurposelessness and meaningless of our psychologically necessary human impulses and affections?'" See Veatch, pp. 180–81.

62. An excellent critique of this position is Philip E. Johnson, "Nihilism and the End of Law," *First Things* no. 32 (March 1993), pp. 19–25.

63. This statement represents an abbreviated and simplified, although essentially accurate, explanation of why it is sometimes said that Nietzsche's philosophy lies at the core of Nazi Germany's political ideology.

2

A New American
Direction

I n the last chapter, we saw that the Founders were concerned with the European history of government persecution, political strife, individual fanaticism, and societal intolerance that seemed to flow from religion. They wanted to avoid the European example, for they believed that religions and free governments alike required an atmosphere of mutual respect among citizens. For the United States' experiment in popular government to succeed, a new political solution to this political–religious problem was required. Thus, in 1787, the following question challenged the Founders: How could the devastating problems caused by religious fervor be solved in the new United States?

Few historical questions have been so widely debated as those regarding the Founders' understanding of religion in the Constitution and how they fashioned a workable relationship between government and religion. There does exist general consensus on one point of crucial importance: the American approach to the political–religious problem was novel for its day. An alliance between church and state had been the reigning pattern in the Western world *for over fourteen centuries,* in England (even if one excludes the earlier state alliance with the Catholic Church and focuses on the Anglican Church alone) for over three centuries, and even in such colonies as Virginia and Massachusetts for approximately a century.[1] This pattern was decisively broken with the Constitution's ratification. For that reason alone, the American Constitution represented a bold and significant departure from previous political resolutions to the religious–political problem.

Yet opinions vary widely on the character of the precise solution to the political–religious problem adopted by the Founders. The range of disagreement is significant. Some commentators are persuaded that the Founders favored a Christian commonwealth in which church and state would be united in purpose (but not in form); others have argued that the Founders advocated a complete separation of church and state.[2] We believe that neither of these extreme views correctly captures the spirit, substance, and subtlety of the Founders' solution.

Any effort to define the new American direction in church–state relations is complicated by the fact that there were a number of prominent political leaders who offered their talents to the founding of the new nation, to the writing of the Constitution, and to instituting a new understanding of church–state relations. Furthermore, the author of some of the most influential writing on this subject was not technically an American Founder at all: Thomas Jefferson spoke clearly about the question of the proper relationship between politics and religion but did not participate in the 1787 Constitutional Convention. Thus, we will need to tolerate some imprecision and ambiguity inherent in the subject matter as we attempt to fathom the American answer to the historically vexing political–religious problem. However, even acknowledging the existence of such ambiguity does not preclude us from discovering several distinct and important elements of the Founders' solution that took root in colonial America.

THE COLONIAL EXPERIENCE

Often, we forget that before the Constitution was written, there existed a long and rich American history. This fact enabled that keen observer of early-day America, Alexis de Tocqueville, to remark that America was "the only country in which we can watch the natural quiet growth of society and where it is possible to be exact about the point of departure of the future of a state."[3] Notably, throughout that history, a redefined and evolving relationship between church and state had been emerging on a colony-by-colony basis.[4]

What struck Tocqueville was the startling idea that now seems unremarkable to Americans—namely, that the Anglo-American character had been shaped both by the spirit of religion and by the spirit of liberty.[5] In this respect, the American experience contrasted sharply with Europe's. There, monarchs ruled by divine right, which meant that their reign was legitimized specifically by their presumed special relationship to God.[6] Therefore, in Europe, the monarchical exercise of political power was necessarily grounded in theology. As a result, political disagreement was often indistinguishable from religious disagreement, and the line between sedition and heresy was often similarly indistinct. Against this political background, any movement in favor of greater liberty could easily be interpreted as a rejection of religion or, at least, a rejection of the monarch's religion.

But America was different. Tocqueville pointed out that in the colonies, the spirit of liberty and the spirit of religion reinforced each other. This relationship had developed gradually. Although many who first settled the colonies had fled religious intolerance, persecution, and warfare, they and their offspring had sometimes attempted to create political orders in which their religious views would dominate and reinforce their exercise of political power. Thus, a number of the colonial governments based their initial existence on a particular understanding of religious truth. Evidence of this trend continued through the Revolution until the Constitution's ratification. Although three states outlawed religious establishments during the Revolution (and one, Virginia, arguably during the 1780s), some form of multiple religious establishment persisted in six states as late as 1791. Heresy was still considered a violation of the criminal law in a number of states as late as the 1780s. Massachusetts' 1780 Constitution required that men exercise their public duty by worshipping God (although each could do so according to "the dictates of his own conscience..."). Baptists, a religious minority in Virginia, asserted as late as the 1780s that they had been victimized by religious intolerance and persecution at the hands of the state-established Anglican Church.

Specifics like these imperfectly reflect an old-world understanding of religion and politics, for an apprehension of religious truth both provided the foundation for the state's existence and gave it the derivative authority to punish those who believed differently. Yet by the final quarter of the eighteenth century in America, this view was becoming increasingly anachronistic.[7] What had happened was little short of amazing. Over time, an increasing emphasis upon liberty and equality accompanied the development of self-government within the colonies. Liberty coupled with the emerging idea of self-government had softened religious feeling and tended to promote toleration. This is not to deny that there existed a general opinion throughout the states that a widespread belief in a generalized Christianity was crucial to the perpetuation of a good and decent society. At the same time, the power of Christianity itself was weakening and continuing to fragment along doctrinal and liturgical lines.[8] Simultaneously, it was becoming increasingly clear that Christianity's advancement was not the proper province of government. Furthermore, Christianity's defenses were increasingly made in terms of its utility to general society (specifically because of its capacity to promote private virtue) and less on behalf of its truth.[9]

Replacing the idea that religious truth constituted the appropriate foundation for government was the growing belief that government needed to protect all citizens' individual rights. Ultimately, a state dedicated to the protection of citizens' rights was largely incompatible with a state established upon religious truth. Contributing to this gradual but profound change was the development of democratic political institutions and practices in the colonies and states prior to 1787. True, the evolution of self-government may seem modest by twentieth-century standards, but it was remarkable within the context of the time. The increasingly responsive political institutions created by and associated with this evolution yielded an increasingly egalitarian view of citizens (as opposed to the narrower view that there were certain privileged citizens whose special status was based on their affiliation with the official religion established by the government). Institutions or practices such as free political debate, trial by peers, extensive constitution writing, and regular elections all reinforced or anticipated the exercise of political liberty by equal citizens.[10] As the idea of citizens' equal freedom took root, it had important consequences for the political role of religion as it was then understood and practiced. For example, the very idea that citizens were entitled to equal freedom had devastating implications for the European theory of divine right. In the words of one astute commentator, a belief "in the natural equality of persons meant that government would not derive its just powers from the consent of the righteous."[11]

An important conclusion that follows from this insight is this: As free government developed in the colonies, a concomitant and necessary belief that emphasized citizens' equal right to liberty also developed. This belief affected religion, which (from the secular point of view) became individualized, privatized, and "tamed." Additionally, the public role of religion became profoundly altered. Religious truth faded as the true basis of civil society. Throughout the colonies, religion increasingly became identified with religious liberty, and religious liberty became just one important aspect of the more generalized idea of political liberty. Thus, the spirit of liberty and religion worked in harmony and reinforced each other in pre-constitutional America because the spirit of liberty overwhelmed the spirit of religion and transformed religious zealotry into religious toleration, increasingly championed in the name of religious freedom. In such circumstances, the spirit of religion did not vanish. As Tocqueville suggested, it remained within the human heart, providing that necessary moral instruction needed for the responsible exercise of liberty.[12]

What did this mean for the solution of the religious–political problem during the era in which the Constitution was written? It meant that by the 1780s, the defense of religion (when it was not couched in terms of its social utility) was increasingly made in terms of defending the individual's right of conscience. Government's obligation to safeguard individual freedom of religion and private conscience was quickly replacing any institutionalized religious sect's claim that divine truth provided the political basis of the state's involvement with religion.

This transformation could be seen most clearly in Virginia, in the years immediately before the Constitution's adoption. From that state's political dispute over religion emerged an answer to past problems of governmental persecution and religious conflict. The meaning of its successful resolution would be captured perfectly in President (and Virginian) George Washington's 1791 letter to the Newport Jewish congregation. He proclaimed to a people who had not been granted full citizenship anywhere for two thousand years that government viewed them as citizens with rights, not as heretics or atheists; Washington noted that "the government of the United States ... gives to bigotry no sanction, to persecution no assistance..." but "requires only that they who live under its protection should demean themselves as good citizens."[13]

ADVANCING RELIGIOUS LIBERTY:
THE STRUGGLE IN VIRGINIA

In Virginia, the Anglican Church had been established, first by the colony and then by the state. During the 1780s, a furious political battle erupted throughout the state over the question of whether government should be disassociated from the Anglican Church and prohibited from providing direct financial support to Christianity. Out of that controversy two famous documents emerged, each having since been cited by numerous judges because of its important and influential pronouncements regarding the relationship between government and religious freedom. The first document was Virginia's Statute for Religious Freedom, written by Thomas Jefferson. The second was James Madison's "Memorial and Remonstrance."

Originally drafted in late 1777, and initially debated in the Virginia House of Delegates in 1779, Jefferson's statute was not adopted until 1786. It sought to end the public advantages accorded to the Anglican Church. The proposed statute observed that "Almighty God hath created the mind free ... that all attempts to influence it by temporal punishment, or burdens, or by civil incapacitations, tend only to beget habits of hypocrisy and meanness, and are a departure from the plan of the holy author of our religion...."[14] Human reason, Jefferson suggested, was a divine gift. Thus, he argued that those who would employ the law and legal punishment in the attempt to enforce any particular belief about God violated not only human morality but God's will as well. Such rulers acted both sinfully and tyrannically. Furthermore, the individual exercise of conscience was not a proper concern of government. Governmental interference in this sensitive area ran contrary to the idea of natural rights, and enforced religious belief ultimately produced hypocrites and debased religion. Finally, Jefferson argued that political domination of religion ultimately destroyed religious freedom. Given these assertions, there is no doubt that for Jefferson, religious freedom, not state-supported religious orthodoxy, lay at the foundation of the just political state.

James Madison's "Memorial and Remonstrance" is similar in spirit to Jefferson's statute and contains, in clear, decisive language, a number of theoretical arguments for religious disestablishment. Madison's "Memorial" was written in 1784 to protest Patrick Henry's plan levying a tax supporting Christian teachers. Henry's own position was remarkably moderate, for he emphasized the societal benefit of such a tax, contending that "the general diffusion of Christian knowledge hath a natural tendency to correct the morals of men, restrain their vices, and preserve the peace of society."[15] Madison disagreed, contending that to have the state support Christianity for the sake of improving society's moral and general well-being constituted an impermissible means (state sponsorship of religion) to a legitimate and important state end (upholding morality). Against Henry's proposal, Madison presented fifteen different arguments. Among other points, he contended that religion was outside the jurisdiction of civil society; consequently, the individual's right to freedom of religion was beyond the power of the legislature, and even the smallest infringement of religious liberty had the potential to endanger society and weaken religion.

At the heart of Madison's "Remonstrance" was a denial that religious establishment was necessary for the support of civil government. The effect of ecclesiastical establishments upon civil society has sometimes been "to effect a spiritual tyranny on the ruins of civil authority; in many instances they have been seen upholding the thrones of political tyranny; in no instance have they been seen the guardians of the people."[16] Rather than championing such establishments, a just government "will be best supported by protecting every citizen in the enjoyment of his Religion with the same equal hand which protects his person and his property; by neither invading the equal rights of any Sect, nor suffering any Sect invade those of another."[17] Such statements help clarify James Madison's opinion about the relationship between religion and politics and between state religious establishment and the individual free exercise of religion (before the First Amendment's adoption). According to one authority, Madison believed that "establishment is detrimental to self-government; free exercise is essential for free government."[18] Madison's understanding, and the underlying difficulty, can be summarized as follows:

> Free exercise of religion will help shape citizens with a capacity for self-government. It will also foster private diverse groups or associations and thereby broaden the base of social and political consensus. The formation of such diverse groups will stand as a barrier to tyranny. Democracy, therefore, relies upon a particular irony; religion must remain politically impotent while furnishing the moral base for self-government.[19]

Through these writings by Jefferson and Madison, we see the outline of Tocqueville's emerging America fashioned in the compatible spirit of liberty and religion. But it is important to understand that behind this developing relationship lay a radical reformulation of the meaning of religion and the purpose of the secular state. The reformulation of religion was discussed in the previous chapter. Here we briefly note only that the effort launched by such philosophers as Thomas Hobbes, Benedict Spinoza, and John Locke to make Christianity (and all religion) reasonable was succeeding. Hoping to strip religion of the fanaticism responsible for past religious strife and persecution, these philosophers taught that it was not miracles or even revelation that constituted religion's essence or greatest importance; rather, it was rules of moral behavior. Understood in this way, religion became a promoter, as opposed to a destroyer, of peacefulness in society. In the United States, Thomas Jefferson was the most influential advocate of this point of view, both in his public writings and in his private correspondence. Jefferson's understanding of the relationship between government and religion was particularly indebted to John Locke's *Letter Concerning Toleration*.[20] To that end, Jefferson's

Bible provided the religious foundation for toleration while reflecting a significant reformulation of Scripture and providing a model of religion defined as ethical behavior. Jefferson's political views about religion take on additional significance when it is recalled that his opinions on the meaning of religious liberty in the United States remain the most quoted and cited by judges and historians alike.

The Virginia debates demonstrated that the idea of religion was being transformed, and they also revealed something similar regarding the purpose of the secular state. Not the divine right of kings, but the rejection of divine right, lay at the heart of the new political order. That much had already been made clear in 1776 by the fundamental American political document, the Declaration of Independence. Jefferson had drafted the Declaration (here again following Locke's lead, this time from his *Second Treatise of Civil Government*). The Declaration stated that all men were endowed by their Creator with unalienable rights, including the fundamental rights of life, liberty, and the pursuit of happiness. The Declaration went on to suggest that governments should be judged in part on their capacity to protect these rights. Finally, the Declaration announced that when governments destroyed those rights, then a people has a right to overthrow that government and found a new government that will rule according to the consent of the governed for the explicit purpose of protecting the rights that the previous government had destroyed.

What understanding of religion had the Declaration of Independence presented? God, referred to as nature's God, is identified as the author of natural rights. But note that in the Declaration, the legacy of God's beneficence was not miracles, or revelation, or faith, or piety: it was self-preservation and liberty. Furthermore, implicit in the natural right to liberty is the right to religious liberty—that is, the right to worship God (or not worship God) as one wishes. A belief in natural rights neither established nor acknowledged any single religious viewpoint. It sought only to secure the right of each individual to his or her own religious viewpoint.

Both God's will and what the Founders called the rights of man were discoverable by human reason, not by revelation or faith. This is one reason, but not the only reason, that authorities have sometimes concluded that the doctrine of natural rights is fundamentally at odds with traditional Christian theology.[21] Yet Jefferson and Madison constantly wrote and spoke in Virginia in such a way as to suggest that the two traditions were compatible (because they had been made compatible); they repeatedly argued that reason taught both that conflict and strife were destructive of natural rights and at odds with God's will. At the same time, in Virginia and throughout emerging America, the consensus developed that it was the obligation of government to protect the private right of individual conscience and religious liberty. As the idea of the state's obligation to protect individual liberty gained ascendancy, the belief that religion (or that a single religious truth or sect) might provide the moral foundation for any of the American states, or for the new American nation, rapidly lost favor.

THE CONSTITUTION AND RELIGION

The Declaration of Independence established the philosophical basis of the American nation, and Jefferson's Disestablishment Bill and Madison's "Memorial and Remonstrance" constituted powerful political statements in favor of the separation, privatization, and subordination of state-sponsored religion. The Constitution, the nation's fundamental legal document, continued this trend. It presumed the correctness of the natural rights doctrine and sought to effect a way that the doctrine could be safely and effectively realized. The Constitution's secular concern with protecting religious liberty, as opposed to founding and perpetuating a politics based upon God's revealed word, can be observed both by what the Constitution says and by what it leaves unsaid.

In fact, the formal Constitution says surprisingly little about religion. The Preamble lists as one of the ends of the newly founded government the securing of "the Blessings of Liberty to ourselves and our Posterity." Nowhere is the promotion of religion mentioned as an end of government. Indeed, if there is one conspicuous absence from the Constitution (other than its failure to mention slavery explicitly in its unamended version), it is the almost startling absence of any reference to God or support for religion. As Walter Berns has pointed out,

> One of the striking facts about the original, unamended Constitution, then is the absence of any statement invoking the name of God or providing for the public worship of God or according special privileges or places to churchmen or stating it to be the duty of Congress to promote Christian education as part of a design to promote good citizenship.[22]

In sum, had religion, rather than religious freedom, been the goal of good government, then one would have expected the Founders to say so in their nation's fundamental political document.

This point is further emphasized by the only part of the unamended Constitution that mentions religion: Article VI's prohibition of religious tests as a qualification for "any Office or public Trust under the United States." It is important to note that public officials are required to swear an oath, but it is an oath to uphold the Constitution. The implicit meaning seems obvious. It is not religious piety that the Constitution promotes, but rather the support of a document that endeavors to safeguard each citizen's rights to liberty.

Usually, what the Constitution says about religion is almost always reduced to an examination of the two religion clauses of the First Amendment. Essentially, Congress is prohibited from making any law respecting an establishment of religion or prohibiting religion's free exercise. Added by the first Congress after the Constitution's adoption, the amendments were originally and universally understood to impose restrictions only upon the new national government.

In Chapter Four, we will deal with the explicit problem of understanding the meaning of these two First Amendment clauses and the way the Supreme Court has interpreted their language. For the present, we will confine our observations only to their broadest, and least controversial, meaning.

At the most obvious level, the idea of rights against government (as in the Bill of Rights) hearkens back to the notion in the Declaration of Independence that there are natural rights that human beings possess. Thus, the new government created by the Constitution was to be limited because it was granted only certain (and not every possible) power and because the people maintained stipulated rights over which government could not, and should not, dominate. To that end, the Free Exercise Clause attempted to ensure that the Congress would not pass legislation that prohibited religious free exercise, which is to say a person's right to religious freedom. From the Constitution's point of view, it mattered hardly at all what a person's religious beliefs and practices were, or whether the beliefs and practices were widely shared. They are all protected, especially minority beliefs.[23] It mattered only that the national government refrain from enforcing religious beliefs upon citizens; the government is restricted from limiting an individual's religious free choice. Therefore, the purpose of government is not the advancement of any official religious orthodoxy, but only the creation and preservation of a secular nation composed of citizens who hold individualistic and differing religious beliefs.

The First Amendment's other religious provision, the Establishment Clause, has also been the source of great legal controversy. Yet almost every constitutional scholar agrees that, at a minimum, it was intended to prohibit the national government from founding a state church or showing favoritism to any one religious sect. What is wrong with founding a state church or with Congress showing favoritism toward a particular religious sect? The answer quickly becomes clear. In such a nation, there exists a high potential that religious minorities will be disadvantaged, discriminated against, and ultimately even persecuted. In other words, a government that passes laws respecting an establishment of religion will be a government that endangers religious liberty, and an endangered religious liberty is simply another away of saying that citizens' natural right to liberty has been imperiled.

Federalism

Another important constitutional factor that contributed to the way religious liberty in the United States was secured and understood was federalism. It is important to recall that the Bill of Rights, including the First Amendment's Establishment and Free Exercise Clauses, was originally championed as a restriction only against the national government. Not until the twentieth century did the Supreme Court, via the Fourteenth Amendment, apply the religion clauses to the states (see Chapter Four). Therefore, Federalism was important, not because it directly aided the development and protection of religious freedom, but rather because its existence had a material impact upon the adoption and original meaning of the First Amendment's Establishment and Free Exercise clauses. Concerns about the division of power between the new central government and the original states were combined with opinions regarding the role of religion and practical political considerations to motivate those who voted on the Bill of Rights.

Thus, the debate over the adoption of the Bill of Rights represented a dispute between Federalists who initially discounted the importance of a Bill of Rights (including the religion clauses) and Antifederalists, some of whom favored the idea of rights, others of whom feared the power of the newly created national government and embraced the Bill of Rights issue in an attempt to scuttle the new Constitution.[24] Later, those who supported the adoption of the First Amendment included a coalition of such representatives as James Madison, who favored restricting government's involvement with religion in principle, and more conservative representatives, who wished only to restrict the new national government, sometimes while preserving state religious establishments (a fact that certainly complicates any attempt to determine the original intent behind these amendments). Since efforts to extend Bill of Rights protection to the states were defeated by the first Congress, states were left free to follow their own inclinations regarding religion. At the time, six states maintained multiple religious establishments. Although the church–state relationship was changing within these states, some of those who championed broad restrictions on federal power did so intending to prohibit the new government from meddling in the religious affairs of the states. In this way, concerns about federalism had an impact on the way in which the religion clauses were understood, and they indeed had an impact on the entire Bill of Rights debate. Precisely for that reason, the political decision to adopt the Bill of Rights was, at its origins, never simply the outgrowth of a pure debate over the meaning of individual rights in the new American society.

James Madison's Multiplicity of Sects

The formal, unamended Constitution created a large, free, and (for its time) pluralistic nation. By so doing, it both reflected and advanced a political theory that proved extraordinarily important to the Constitution's passage. The purpose of this theory was to demonstrate how a large nation could guarantee its citizens liberty in general and, to a large extent, religious liberty in particular.[25] When the Constitution was crafted and then proposed to the states for ratification, the First Amendment did not exist. Yet James Madison, the Constitution's foremost author, believed that this document would ensure religious liberty. He based his optimism upon a new political theory that advanced the idea of a multiplicity of sects and factions. Did Madison's theory prove successful? Like the young student who, not knowing what prose meant, was startled to discover that he had spoken it all his life, so Madison's political theory has proven successful, yet has been similarly underappreciated in our age.

Prior to the Constitutional Convention, James Madison had taken time out of a busy public life to study politics and the history of free government. He came to an important conclusion. The chief problem that had destroyed previous republican governments was the "violence of faction." Different and conflicting economic classes, political parties, and (probably most importantly) religious sects had constantly destroyed the rights of minorities while undermining governments' political stability and tranquillity with violence and bloodshed. The question became (in Tocqueville's language) this: How could the spirit of liberty and the spirit of religion be combined without compromising either? The answer was through religious, economic, and political moderation. That was the goal of Madison's plan. Let us see how this plan would work.

As we have observed, European history provided good reason for the Founders' belief that religious conflict would endanger republican government and individual liberty. Madison's solution built upon the thought of Adam Smith, expressed in 1776 in his famous *Wealth of Nations*. Lamenting the dangers of religious fanaticism, Smith observed that "[t]imes of violent religious controversy have generally been times of equally violent political faction."[26] Yet answers were possible, and Smith pointed to the American colony of Pennsylvania as representing a political solution to this old and troubling political question. Pennsylvania displayed "philosophical good temper and moderation" in this matter. It had succeeded for two principal, interrelated reasons. First, the government showed no legal favoritism to any religion. Second, it had been the case that because

> those sects were sufficiently numerous, and each of them consequently too small to disturb the public tranquillity, the excessive zeal of each for its particular tenets could not well be productive of any very hurtful effects, but, on the contrary, of several good ones: and if the government was perfectly decided both to let them all alone, and to oblige them all to let alone one another, there is little danger that they would not of their own accord subdivide themselves fast enough, so as soon to become sufficiently numerous.[27]

Compare the observations of Adam Smith to the argument made by James Madison some eleven years later (and subsequently repeated in *The Federalist* and at the Virginia Constitutional Ratifying Convention). Madison's argument was straightforward: only a large nation, and specifically only a large republic the size of the one to be established by the Constitution, could produce a sufficiently large number of diverse religious sects (and economic interests):

> The lesson we are to draw from the whole is that where a majority are united by a common sentiment and have an opportunity, the rights of the minor party become insecure. In a Republican Govt. the Majority if united have always the opportunity. The only remedy is to enlarge the sphere, & thereby divide the community into so great a number of interests & parties, that in the 1st. place a majority will not be likely at the same moment to have a common interest separate from that of the whole or of the minority; and in the 2d place, that in case they shd. have such an interest, they may not be apt to unite in the pursuit of it. It was incumbent on us to try this remedy, and to frame a republican system on such a scale and in such a form as will control all the evils whc. have been experienced.[28]

Madison was so persuaded by the multiplicity argument that later, in the Virginia State Ratifying Convention, he referred to it as the best and only security for religious liberty in any political state.[29] Although fanatical religious minorities could be defeated by popular elections, Madison understood that the most formidable political danger was posed by a fanatical religious majority intent upon imposing its way upon an ill-protected minority. A nation encompassing a large geographical size, an increasing population, a basic human propensity to disagree about religious questions, and the political freedom that allows citizens to determine and pronounce divergent religious opinions could combine to help moderate any religious majority and help ensure a relatively harmonious society. Furthermore, this freedom of religion could be secured without limiting the activities of religious organizations or attempting to promote a single religious point of view. In other words, the problem of faction could be addressed without betraying the fundamental principles of popular government; Madison stated it this way: the multiplicity solution promised "a Republican remedy for the diseases most incident to Republican Government."[30] The growing religious diversity of contemporary America and its relative lack of religious persecution would seem to suggest that Madison's theoretical argument championing political and religious moderation has yielded good practical results.

Commerce

The argument about the multiplicity of sects and factions advanced by Adam Smith and James Madison could only be put into practice in a large and free nation; it also depended upon the existence of the right kind of economy, for a great number of interests could come about only "of necessity in civilized nations...."[31] For Madison, like Smith, a civilized nation was a commercial state whose economy created wealth, promoted cities and commercial interchange, encouraged trade and manufacturing, and promoted the specialization of labor and economic interdependence. Such a nation, by generating a great number of diverse interests and parties, had the practical effect of fragmenting economic and political power within the state. Economic and political diversity, if not outrightly encouraging religious pluralism, certainly made the favored and privileged support of a particular religion by government far more difficult. Indeed, Smith had observed that, historically, commerce had helped destroy the religious power of the church (as well as the aristocratic power of the feudal ruling class whose class privilege had been based solely upon birth). In Smith's words, "The gradual improvements of arts, manufacturing and commerce, the same causes which destroyed the power of the great barons, destroyed in the same manner, through the great part of Europe, the whole temporal power of the clergy."[32] Thus, one advantage of the commercial society was that it encouraged religious pluralism; another was that it had destroyed the authority of church–state unity. But there was a third advantage as well. The commercial state radically transformed the relationship among citizens and, by so doing, promoted peacefulness.

Thus, while much of Smith's economic theory emphasized competition among human beings, his *Wealth of Nations* also stressed how individual self-interest created human dependence and cooperation within society. "In civilized societies," wrote Smith, a human being "stands in all times in need of the co-operation and assistance of great multitudes, while his whole life is scarcely sufficient to gain the friendship of the whole people."[33] Similarly, Alexander Hamilton pointed out in *The Federalist* the vast interdependence among occupations and regions that existed within a large commercial nation, emphasizing that the Constitution promised to create a community of interdependent buyers and sellers.[34] But, it can fairly be asked, what does this concern with commerce have to do with religion? In a commercial society, people spend their time making money; there, Alexander Hamilton pointed out, "The assiduous merchant, the laborious husbandman, the active mechanic, and the industrious manufacturer, all orders of men look forward with eager expectation and growing alacrity to the pleasing reward of their toil."[35] Not only are citizens' private wants gratified, but individuals also become aware of how their success depends upon others. (In Smith's words, "without the assistance and co-operation of many thousands, the very meanest person in a civilized country could not be provided.") Thus, the commercial state focuses human attention on the affairs of this world, upon worldly success and the pursuit of peace, comfort, and wealth. Such a society is, by its nature, hostile to a destructive religious fanaticism and friendly to a harmonious religious toleration.

Thus, the commercial state made religious fanaticism unprofitable. Making money requires peacefulness, social harmony, and obedience to law. For that reason, the commercial state promised to replace the zealous proselytizing efforts of citizens undertaken in the name of eternal salvation with the more mundane effort to create wealth. The divisive and destructive passions unleashed by religion were to be superseded by a lower yet more socially useful desire for comfort and material acquisition. In a commercial state, economic interdependence replaced persecution, a prerequisite for acknowledging and protecting religious rights.

AN UNCERTAIN LEGACY: THE PROBLEM
OF RIGHTS AND COMMUNITY

So far, we have examined the specific elements of the Founders' solution to the uneasy relationship between government and religion. However, that solution, although remarkably successful, has proven to be imperfect. Specifically, the Founders' Constitution has given rise to its own specific tensions. In the next sections, we will examine two of these.

The first tension we examine is the tension between a large political nation dedicated to the protection of individual rights and the existence of a true political community. Today, at the end of the twentieth century, it seems that virtually every domestic political question in the United States is sooner or later framed in terms of rights. In the area of religion, this tendency has been fostered by the fact that the Supreme Court has become increasingly enmeshed in civil liberties questions involving individual rights stemming from Free Exercise and Establishment clause guarantees, reviewing such claims at every level of government. Thus, the limitation that originally confined the scope of the Bill of Rights has vanished as the Supreme Court in the twentieth century has applied its provisions against all levels of government. So prevalent has been the underlying litigation that we are inclined to forget the sense in which Hamilton believed that the Constitution itself (with its creation of multiplicity and perpetuation of commerce) was the true Bill of Rights.[36] Because of today's emphasis upon judicially enforced rights, it becomes particularly important to understand the theoretical idea that informs the concept of rights.

So what is entailed by the idea of rights? At the very least, judicially enforced legal rights are protections against government and/or against intemperate majorities who disapprove (and would curtail or punish) minorities because of their unpopular beliefs or practices. Rights are exceptions to majority rule; the idea of rights means that there are some matters that are beyond the rule of majorities. Furthermore, limitations on majority rule do not turn on the popularity of the right or the person claiming protection of the right. It is the very fact that a person or the religion he or she practices (or cause that is espoused) has few adherents or is unpopular that makes the right particularly important.

In what way does religion relate to this notion of rights? Such a relationship arises in two distinct and important ways. On the one hand, the need to protect religious minorities exists. In the Constitution, this issue is addressed most directly by the right to religious free exercise. Although the extent of this protection is open to interpretation, the importance of the right today is not. Earlier, we observed that such Founders as Madison saw zealous religious majorities as the greatest threat to religious liberty. Religious fanatics, as well as intemperate religious majorities, can threaten the right of individuals to exercise their religion. Thus, because religious practitioners can endanger legal rights, other religious practitioners can be the most deserving of this constitutional protection.

There is another, related way of understanding the meaning and importance of rights. A political society (like ours) that acknowledges the idea of rights by necessity presupposes an individualistic political order. An important champion of such an individualistic society was John Stuart Mill, whose thought has profoundly influenced our contemporary understanding of this matter. In his *On Liberty,* Mill would have allowed society to interfere with a citizen's freedom only when that citizen would cause harm to another (harm usually was understood as physical harm).[37] Applied to religion, such an approach would allow the maximum amount of freedom for religious beliefs and practices. Not only would government be required to permit and protect these beliefs and practices; it might also even be obligated to provide exemptions when laws unintentionally disadvantage such practices.

Although requiring government to act in a way that maximizes individual freedom and diversity, stressing individuality (especially in a large nation consisting of a multiplicity of sects and factions) is not without social costs. Interestingly, Mill himself recognized this and elsewhere pointed out the high social cost of individualism. Thus, Mill believed that every political community was bound together by a widespread belief among citizens and that within their constitution there existed "something which is settled, something permanent, and not be called into question, something which, by general agreement, has a right to be where it is, and to secure against disturbance, whatever else may change."[38] This feeling may attach to any of a number of objects— for example, God or gods, rulers, perhaps even to the very idea of individual rights and social equality. It is precisely such beliefs that enable communities to survive internal dissensions and disagreements. When these fundamental assumptions are seriously questioned for an extended period of time, what is undermined is "the habitual condition of the body politic, and when all the violent animosities are called forth which spring naturally from such a situation, the state is virtually in a position of civil war, and can never remain free from it in act and fact."[39]

According to this analysis, a community, any community, is bound together by certain shared fundamental beliefs. To the extent that certain important moral and ethical beliefs are rooted in the Judeo-Christian tradition, conservative observers sometimes argue that these beliefs, and the larger society, can be gradually eroded by too great an emphasis on protecting and even promoting eccentric minority religious practices and beliefs (or, conversely, by discouraging majority religious practices and beliefs). Furthermore, those who espouse such a critique argue that a political order disproportionately dedicated to the notion of rights discourages public spiritedness and a concern for the community's well-being while unleashing individualism and perhaps even selfishness.[40] The extent to which such a critique is accurate or true will be examined later.[41] Still, it is important to recognize that this is one of the most intriguing questions of political theory in contemporary American life.

The Uncertain Legacy Continued:
Private Religion and Public Morality

Maintaining community is one problem associated with the Founders' solution to the religious–political issue; concern for individual good character is a second, related problem. What exactly is the relationship between religion and character in the United States? So far, we have maintained that the United Sates was not founded on a single religious truth, but rather permitted and even encouraged many religious truths, all in the name of religious freedom and natural rights. In other words, the United States was founded as a secular state.[42] As a consequence, religious beliefs and practices increasingly became regarded as private concerns. This is the sense of Thomas Jefferson's famous observation that "it does me no injury for my neighbor to say that are twenty gods, or no God. It neither picks my pocket nor breaks my leg."[43] Jefferson's comment was written to indicate whom government could rightly punish: "The legitimate powers of government extend to such acts only as are injurious to others."[44] What citizens believed regarding religion caused no physical harm to others, and since physical harm constituted the only basis for punishment, each person could believe about God or gods what he or she wished. Clearly, a shared, publicly supported religion furnished no basis for inculcating habits of good character within and among citizens.

However, not only would the United States be founded in accordance with Jefferson's idea that there was no one religious truth; it would also be founded in accordance with the idea that the national government should exercise no direct power over the formation of citizen character. The Constitution was simply silent on this matter. Unlike the Greek *polis,* whose purpose Aristotle argued was to aid in the formation of virtuous character, or the medieval Christian political community, which presupposed and perpetuated a community of devout believers, the new government of the United States retained no such power. Said another way, the Founders did not believe that it was the state's purpose to pass laws securing human virtue and happiness; rather, as the Declaration of Independence asserted, the purpose of good government was merely to protect the much more individualistic right of a person to pursue his or her idea of happiness relatively unencumbered.

Although the purpose of government was not to pass laws in order to help form citizens' character, it is also safe to say that the Constitution, and the republican self-government it fashioned, already assumed the existence of a nation of citizens who possessed good character. Nonetheless, future challenges could not be discounted. Commerce and individualism (despite their advantages) promoted selfish tendencies that required constant vigilance. Furthermore, self-government, by its very definition, required citizens who were concerned about the public welfare as well as having some measure of personal integrity. The reason for this need was not hard to understand. In the words of Alexander Hamilton,

> All governments, even the most despotic, depend, in a great degree, on opinion. In free republics, it is most peculiarly the case: In these, the will of the people makes the essential principle of the government; and the laws which control the community, receive their tone and spirit from the public wishes.[45]

The Founders generally believed that religion had a necessary role to play in refining the tone and spirit of the public wishes and in combating individualism, selfishness, and materialism. Yet they understood that the practice of religion and the cultivation of good character were primarily private concerns. For that reason, it would be a mistake to say simply that the new American nation, or those who founded it, were hostile to religion. The Founders advocated religion, privately practiced, as a public good. Professor Berns states the matter well when he attributes to some of the most influential Founders the opinion that "whereas our institutions do not presuppose a Supreme Being, their preservation does."[46]

Thus, a widespread, private religion shorn of any vestige of zealotry was understood to provide a very important basis of public and private morality, especially important in a self-governing, commercial nation. It was for that reason that the Northwest Ordinance (passed by the last Congress under the Articles of Confederation in 1789 and repassed by the first Congress) not only declared that "no person, demeaning himself in a peaceable and orderly manner, shall ever be molested on account of his mode of worship, or religious sentiments, in said territory," but also pronounced that "[r]eligion, morality, and knowledge being necessary to good government and the happiness of mankind, schools and the means of education shall forever be encouraged."[47] It was also for this reason that George Washington, in his famous Farewell Address, declared that of "all the dispositions and habits which lead to political prosperity, religion and morality are indispensable supports," and further doubted that "morality can be supported without religion."[48] Finally, it was for this reason that Alexis de Tocqueville would come to fear a nation divorced from religion, observing that as soon as people "have lost the way of relying chiefly on distant hopes, they are naturally led to want to satisfy their least desires at once; and it would seem that as soon as they despair of living forever, they are inclined to act as if they could not live for more than a day."[49]

What Alexander Hamilton, the authors of the Northwest Ordinance, George Washington, and Alexis de Tocqueville had in common was a belief that religion was necessary for the perpetuation of republican self-government. Religion was valued because of its utility, not necessarily because of its truth. Western religion may or may not reflect the word of God, but its ethical teachings, combined with its hope and fear of the afterlife, could provide self-government with a foundation for morality and public virtue. On that basis, American statesman and political leaders would continue to speak favorably of religion or speak of their nation in religious terms for generations to come.[50]

Rendering religion private, protecting it as a right of citizenship, and viewing it as the private foundation of morality have proven to be a remarkably successful solution to the political problems of intolerance, violence, suppression, and persecution. Yet there are at least two contemporary problems that have come about because of the Founders' solution. We mention them here very briefly now, as a basis for provoking thought.

The first question we would pose is whether a privately based religion can, over a long period of time, endure in the face of an overwhelmingly influential secular culture. As we have seen, the Founders trusted it would (and Tocqueville hoped so as well), but is such an expectation realistic? For example, Christmas is among the most sacred of Christian holidays, celebrating the birth of a Savior whose love, compassion, humility, and asceticism instruct Christians to this day. But have not these traits embodied by Jesus been overwhelmed by the commercialism of American society, a society that often appears to emphasize the pleasures of materialism at the expense of the virtues of simplicity and sacrifice? In other words, has not contemporary secular American society at the very least altered the very religious spirit and significance of Christmas (and other Christian and non-Christian holidays and religious observances as well)?[51]

Another related concern about the enduring vitality of privatized religion is that the secular society can sometimes overwhelm private religious virtues and that modern technology, which blurs the very distinction between private and public, often exacerbates this tendency. This problem becomes apparent in the following illustration. The family is (literally) the home of the private while mass communications (for example, television and all interactive mass media) certainly constitute an example of a public medium that has a direct impact upon the home, and therefore upon the private realm. If one believes that the family is the molder and conveyer of both moral beliefs and behavior, can we also conclude that the popularity of a medium like television, with its immediate accessibility into the home, is not without some effect? Thus, while television is presenting a picture of societal reality, it also very likely helps shape individual attitudes, beliefs, and perhaps—over long periods of time—behavior.

Why does this matter? It matters because some thinkers believe that traditional religious virtues once nurtured by the family and media-portrayed behavior are in tension.[52] Consider the following: traditional Christian beliefs have held that sexual relations should be confined to marriage and that violence should be discouraged. Of course, not everyone's religious or secular beliefs coincide with these judgments. Certainly, television, as an entertainment medium, hardly avoids either issue. When it portrays sexual relations outside marriage (it is sometimes asserted that more than 90 percent of sexual activity portrayed on that medium is of this type) or gratuitous violence, it does so only to entertain or perhaps to "realistically" reflect what is happening in the larger society. Yet would it be too harsh a conclusion to think that heavy doses of television watching may also help fashion individual attitudes that are more receptive to active sexuality and gratuitous violence, thus undermining traditional religious beliefs?

Whatever conclusion one comes to regarding this example, a more general observation appears less controversial. It does seem that private life has found it virtually impossible to isolate itself from the conformist and arguably downward pressures of popular culture. For what better characterizes contemporary society if not technology's capacity to intrude on that which used to be private? Religion, once considered to be at the core of the private realm of the American family, now competes in an ever more mobile society against countervailing social forces that run the gamut from the chatter of talk radio, to the incessant violence of rented movies, to the "adult" entertainment of Playboy cable television programming. The problem of nurturing a politically harmless but morally efficacious religion continues; only the magnitude of the problem has changed, and it appears to be growing even more formidable in the last quarter of the twentieth century.

NOTES

1. See Edwin Scott Gaustad, "The Emergence of Religious Freedom in the Early Republic," *Religion and the State,* ed. James Woods (Waco, TX: Baylor Univ. Press, 1985), p. 25.

2. The Christian commonwealth position is most commonly associated with Jerry Falwell, but see Gary T. Amos, *Defending the Declaration: How the Bible and Christianity Influenced the Writing of the Declaration of Independence* (Brentwood, TN: Wolgemuth & Hyatt, 1989); and Russell Kirk, *The Roots of the American Order* (La Salle, IL.: Open Court, 1974). The strict separation view is most often closely associated with the voluminous writings of Leo Pfeffer, but also see Leonard W. Levy, *The Establishment Clause: Religion and the First Amendment* (New York: Macmillan, 1986), specifically and pp. 181–85.

3. Alexis de Tocqueville, *Democracy In America,* ed. J. P. Meyer, trans. George Lawrence (Garden City, New York: Doubleday & Co., 1966), vol. I, ch. 2, p. 32.

4. On this subject, see A. James Reichley, *Religion In American Life* (Washington, DC: Brookings Institute, 1985), pp. 53–96; Gaustad, pp. 25–41; and Thomas J. Curry, *The First Freedom: Church and State in America to the Passage of the First Amendment* (New York: Oxford Univ. Press, 1986).

5. Tocqueville, ch. 2, p. 47.

6. Thus, John Locke's seldom-read first treatise from his *Two Treatises of Civil Government* destroyed the idea of divine right as a prerequisite for the second treatise's treatment of liberty under law.

7. Even the six states that had multiple religious establishments at the time of the Constitution's ratification represented something of a diluted notion of religious establishment. In half of them, Christianity was the established religion; in the other half, Protestantism was. According to Leonard Levy, where Protestantism was established, "it was synonymous with religion, because there were either no Jews and Roman Catholics or too few of them to make a difference, and where Christianity was established, as in Maryland, which had many Catholics, Jews were scarcely known." The American notion of establishment differed significantly from the European practice, which established a single church at the explicit expense of other religions. Indeed, according to Levy, "Many different churches, or the religion held in common by all of them, that is, Christianity or Protestantism, were never simultaneously established by any European nation." See Leonard Levy, *The Establishment Clause: Religion and the First Amendment* (New York: Macmillan, 1986), p. 61.

8. William Lee Miller, *The First Liberty: Religion and the American Republic* (New York: Knopf, 1986), p. 249.

9. On this subject, Miller (p. 26) contrasts the establishment of religion that existed in Virginia in 1779 with Patrick Henry's proposal a mere five years later to subsidize Christian teachers, which was a far more moderate proposal and was written to counter the perceived decline in private moral virtue: "In 1779, the measure, as we have seen, had come complete with the specific establishment of Christianity and specific requirements of doctrine and worship. Now, in 1784, there were no such requirements—nothing about creed or worship. The short bill provided for a property tax, with the taxpayer determining the denomination to which his money would be given. It allowed for those who made no choice of denomination just to support the building of schools in their county.... Although the money otherwise thus raised was to be used to pay the clergy (in their role as "Christian teachers") and keep up church buildings, in the case of the Quakers and "Menonists," who had no clergy, the bill specifically provided that the money should go into the general fund 'to promote their particular mode of worship.'" On this subject (especially regarding Massachusetts), see Ralph Lerner, "Believers and the Founders' Constitution," *This World* 26 (Summer,1989), pp. 80–86.

10. As, of course, it was understood within the context of its time.

11. Jonathan K. Van Patten, "In the End is the Beginning: An Inquiry into the Meaning of the Religion Clauses," St. Louis *University Law Journal,* vol. 27, no. 1 (1983), p. 77.

12. Tocqueville, ch. 2, p. 47.

13. Washington to the Hebrew Congregation of Newport, R.I., August 17, 1790, in *The Writings of George Washington from the Original Manuscript Sources,* 1745–1799, ed. John C. Fitzpatrick (Washington, DC: Government Printing Office, 1931–44), vol. 1, p. 93.

14. *The Portable Thomas Jefferson,* ed. Merrill Peterson (New York: Penguin, 1985), p. 251. The spelling has been modernized. The citation is from Jefferson's original draft and not from the statute as later adopted.

15. Henry's Assessment Bill (Dec. 24, 1784) is reproduced in the supplemental appendix to Justice Rutledge's dissent in *Everson* v. *Board of Education,* 330 U. S. at 72. Also see footnote 8.

16. From the appendix to Justice Rutledge's dissent in *Everson* v. *Board of Education,* at 68.

17. *Everson* v. *Board of Education,* at 68.

18. Van Patten, p. 56.

19. Van Patten, pp. 56–57. For a brief elaboration of this "irony," see this chapter's last section, pp. 38–41.

20. S. Gerald Sandler, "Lockean Ideas in Thomas Jefferson's *Bill for Establishing Religious Freedom," Journal of History of Ideas* 21 (1960), pp. 110–116. Cf. Chapter 1, note 30.

21. A direct and spirited defense of this position is made in a letter written by Walter Berns in *This World,* no. 8 (Spring/Summer 1984), pp. 7–8. Berns's argument is developed at greater length in "Religion and the Founding Principle," in *The Moral Foundations of the American Republic,* ed. Robert Horwitz (Charlottesville, VA: Univ. of Virginia Press, 1987), 3rd ed., pp. 204–29 and in *Taking the Constitution Seriously* (New York: Simon & Schuster, 1887), pp. 147–80. Berns's analysis is very insightful, and we acknowledge our great indebtedness to it.

22. Berns, "Religion and the Founding Principle," p. 210.

23. That is, religious practices are protected at least insofar as they do not undermine the state.

24. Herbert Storing, "The Constitution and the Bill of Rights," *Taking the Constitution Seriously: Essays on the Constitution and Constitutional Law,* ed. Gary McDowell (Dubuque, IA: Kendall/Hunt, 1981), pp. 268–69.

25. Berns, "Religion and the Founding Principle," pp. 226-27.

26. Adam Smith, *The Wealth of Nations* (New York: Modern Library, 1937), p. 744. A similar argument is made by Paul Rahe, *Republics Ancient and Modern* (Chapel Hill: Univ. of North Carolina Press, 1990), pp. 594–95. Cf. Berns, p. 227.

27. Smith, p. 746.

28. *The Records of the 1787 Constitutional Convention,* ed. Max Farrand (New Haven, CT: Yale Univ. Press, 1966), vol. I, p. 136.

29. *The Debates in the Several State Conventions, on the Adoption of the Federal Constitution, as Recommended by the General Convention at Philadelphia, in 1787,* ed. J. Elliot (Philadelphia: Lippincott, 1859), vol. 3, p. 330.

30. Alexander Hamilton, John Jay, and James Madison, *The Federalist,* ed. Jacob Cooke (Middletown, CT: Wesleyan Univ. Press, 1961), no. 10, p. 65.

31. Cf. *The Federalist,* no. 10, p. 59, to Smith, p. 746.

32. Smith, p. 755.

33. Smith, p. 14.

34. *The Federalist,* no. 11, pp. 71–72.

35. *The Federalist,* no. 12, p. 74.

36. *The Federalist,* no. 84, p. 581.

37. An important difference between Mill and the Founders is that Mill did not base his free society on the basis of natural rights but rather on utility.

38. John Stuart Mill, *A System of Logic Ratiocinative and Deductive* (London: Longmans, Green, 1867), vol. 2, pp. 521–22. Emphasis ours.

39. Mill, pp. 521–22.

40. On this subject, see Tocqueville, vol. 2, pp. 506–08.

41. See the Afterword, p. 374.

42. Again, we are indebted to Berns, p. 215.

43. Jefferson, *Notes on the State of Virginia* (New York: Harper, 1964), p. 152.

44. Jefferson, p. 152.

45. Alexander Hamilton, "New York Ratifying Convention First Speech of June 21 (1788)" (Francis Child's Version) in *The Papers of Alexander Hamilton,* ed. Harold Syrett (New York: Columbia Univ. Press, 1962), vol. V, p. 37.

46. Berns, "Religion and the Founding Principle," p. 212.

47. Act of August 7, 1789, I *Statutes at Large,* p. 50.

48. "Washington's Farewell Address," in *Documents of American History,* ed. Henry Steele Commager (New York: Appleton-Century-Crofts, 1968), vol. I, p. 173.

49. Tocqueville, vol. 2, ch. 17, p. 548.

50. This has been called the doctrine of civil religion. A leading article on this subject is by Robert Bellah, "Civil Religion in America," in *The Religious Situation*—1968, ed. D. Cutler (Boston: Beacon 1968), pp. 159–88.

51. For example, the minor Jewish holiday of Chanukah has been elevated in importance (since it comes at Christmas time) and has similarly acquired a materialistic element. For a discussion of this problem, see Chapter 8, p.156.

52. Of course, this discussion does not even deal with another, related problem that presents even more reason for concern: the changing (and arguably) disintegrating character of the American family.

3

Religion in
Today's America

Religion is a major force in contemporary America. It is active, visible, and important. Public issues are in many ways defined by the concerns of American religious groups, and public policy is often greatly influenced by their efforts. Religion has always been a factor in American politics, but the strength and influence of religious groups have clearly grown since the early 1980s. This trend has disturbed some who believe that any involvement of religion in politics is a dangerous thing. As Kenneth Wald has pointed out, "at the heart of that concern lies the fear that religious controversy in politics will lead to extremism and polarization, infecting the body politic with unhealthy doses of fanaticism and ill will."[1] On the other hand, religious groups claim that they are actually serving popular government by giving a voice to people who are often overlooked by the dominant avenues of governmental representation.[2] We are led to ask a very important question: Is religious activism in our regime worrisome or healthy?

Broadly speaking, it appears that the American Founders succeeded in creating a regime that transformed the fanaticism that often characterized religion in earlier centuries into an acceptable, or civil, social force.[3] The activism of religion in our regime is a pale reflection of the force that religion had in European politics. In fact, the very term *activism* is significant; to say that religion is active in our regime is to acknowledge that it plays an important role yet does not dominate politics. Religious groups in America must compete for political influence with a multiplicity of interest groups, some religious and some secular.[4] Religious wars have been replaced by religious competition. To paraphrase Martin Diamond, the Founders transformed what was a divisive and potentially oppressive force into something that is safe and even energizing.[5] Our Founders created a regime in which religion could be important to politics without being the actual focus of politics.

This chapter will explore religious activism in America, and although this subject is far too broad to be dealt with in any kind of comprehensive manner here, an examination of the following three issues can help provide an introduction to the subject: (1) the tradition of religious activism in American politics, (2) religion and lobbying, and (3) religion in Congress.

THE TRADITION OF RELIGIOUS ACTIVISM IN AMERICA

Our Founders made a conscious effort to construct a new kind of political life in which religion could be active but not destructive. And, as Allen Hertzke has argued, the activism of American religion was also encouraged by unique historical circumstances: "faced with a new land and a seemingly endless frontier, religious leaders could not rely upon centuries-old social, political, and economic institutions to buttress the church. Churches had to be activist to survive, or at least to thrive."[6] In addition, religion in America was pluralistic by the standards of the day. A number of very different Christian denominations contended for power and made different claims of religious allegiance.[7] This sectarian diversity contributed to the new and milder forms of religious establishments that existed in the colonies (discussed in Chapter Two). And so, as Hertzke points out, "for the first time since Constantine, churches and religious leaders, in all their diversity, were reasonably independent of the state, and thus were in a unique political position to attack perceived evils of the day."[8] There are three important political movements that serve to illustrate both the vitality and the moderation of religious activism in America: the abolitionist movement, the prohibition movement, and the anti-abortion movement.

Abolition

The simple fact is that the antislavery movement began in America as a religious crusade. As Arthur Zilversmit has shown, "the history of the early abolitionist movement is essentially the record of Quaker antislavery activities."[9] Even though slavery was a part of Quaker life until shortly before the American Revolution, the Quakers struggled with the tension between their religious beliefs and the concept of ownership of human beings as early as 1688, as is documented in the Germantown protest.[10] As the founder of the Quakers, George Fox, had admonished his followers, "Christ died for all ... for the tawnies and for the blacks as well as for you that are called whites." By 1773, the New England Quakers agreed that their members should renounce their participation in slavery, and in 1783 they began to compensate their former slaves for the work they had done. And the very first antislavery organization in history was established in 1775 with Benjamin Franklin as its president and with a predominantly Quaker membership.[11] In 1832 William Lloyd Garrison established a journal called the *Public Liberator,* which advocated the abolition of slavery without compensation to the owners. "I will be as harsh as truth, and as uncompromising as justice," he proclaimed.[12] In 1832 he organized the American Antislavery Society, and by 1840 there were approximately 2,000 local chapters of the society in the North. Although the abolitionist crusaders did not succeed in bringing an end to slavery by religious persuasion of the Southern slaveholders, they did succeed in establishing a moral foundation for the movement.

Lincoln was not an abolitionist; he favored a more gradual approach to ending slavery that began with prohibiting the extension of slavery into the new states. But he was clear in condemning slavery as a wrong, and this position attracted to the Republican Party those with religious objections to slavery.[13] The Republican Party became the party of morality, attracting Protestants in large numbers.[14] This massive Protestant support for the Republican Party was at least partly responsible for Lincoln's election and for Republican presidential victories in eleven out of thirteen elections from 1860 to 1908.[15] Therefore, the power of religion led to a political movement and then to a political party with a specific antislavery program.

Prohibition

One of the most dramatic examples of the impact that religion can have on public affairs is that of Prohibition. Shortly before World War I, the whole world seemed to change, at least from the perspective of the Protestant majority in the United States. As Wald points out, rapid urbanization, the newly emerging authority of modern science, and the growth of non-Protestant communities as a result of massive immigration challenged the way of life that evangelical Protestants had thought would last forever. Some began to focus on liquor as either the cause of the evils they saw growing in the country or, if not the cause, at least the symbol of the spreading evils. As Rabkin has said,

> Enthusiasm for the "noble experiment" in national Prohibition was partly fed by fears that the virtues of nineteenth-century America were being overwhelmed by the loose morals and corruptions in the cities, with the non-Protestant majorities.[16]

The complaint against liquor was that it fostered ungodliness. Liquor was responsible for "dulling the conscience and obliterating [the] fear of God."[17] The argument was that liquor attacked self-control, and if self-control was lost, sin would triumph.[18]

The great revivalist movements of the nineteenth century had produced a strong emphasis on asceticism and had held up the standard of an austere private morality in which personal conversion was seen as the central religious experience.[19] This particular approach to Christianity was not shared by a majority of Catholics, Lutherans, and Episcopalians, and it was not shared at all by Jews. In 1914 the Central Conference of American Rabbis condemned the Prohibition movement as "born of fanaticism."[20] But evangelical Protestants continued to focus on liquor as a problem. Religious groups began to organize into political groups, and in 1893 the Anti-Saloon League was founded in Oberlin, Ohio. It was not the first American group to focus on the problem of drinking, but it was the first to concentrate entirely on prohibition.[21] By 1917, twenty-six states had passed Prohibition laws, and in 1919, the Eighteenth Amendment to the Constitution was passed.

There were nonreligious factors at work here as well. Businessmen often supported Prohibition because they felt that the productivity of their workers would increase if the men did not spend their evenings at the saloon.[22] But the main force behind Prohibition was moral argument derived from religious conviction. It is interesting to note that the fight against liquor came in the country at roughly the same time as the fight against Darwin in the public schools. (The famous Scopes Monkey Trial took place in 1925.) Religious groups were fighting a losing battle against change of all kinds. Prohibition gives us a clear example of a time when the Constitution itself was changed by religious activism. But the victory was short-lived. The repeal of Prohibition in 1933 is significant because it indicated that evangelical Protestantism was losing its hold on America. The evangelical movement had hoped that a general religious revival would redeem a changing country, but this did not happen.

Prohibition was successful only briefly, and this success—while it is impressive—is modest compared to the successes of religious establishments in the European tradition. In America, religion managed for a short while to make a beverage illegal. No one was forced to accept the religious doctrines behind the movement; no one was forced by law to attend a church against his or her will; no one was persecuted by a public power for opposing the evangelical movement.

Abortion

The religious opposition to abortion is one of the most important contemporary political issues (see Chapter Fifteen). Catholic groups traditionally opposed abortion, and they responded strongly to the increasing number of women who supported it in the 1960s and early 1970s. Two years before the Supreme Court's famous abortion decision, *Roe* v. *Wade,* the church had proclaimed that women getting abortions should be excommunicated.[23] The official position of the church is that life begins at conception; hence, abortion is the killing of a human being. The church found itself at odds with such groups as Planned Parenthood, and in order to oppose what came to be known as the "pro-choice" movement, the church was active in the attempt to get a constitutional amendment passed to prohibit abortion. By the mid-1970s, church leaders were actively coordinating grassroots lay organizations designed to support what they called "pro-life" candidates for political office and to unseat "pro-choice" candidates. Therefore, the Catholic church played and continues to play a significant role in the abortion debate. It did not succeed in changing the Constitution, but it succeeded in placing its own complaints and agenda into Congress and into the public consciousness.

Evangelical Protestants had turned away from an active political life after the repeal of Prohibition, but the turbulent period of the 1960s forced them to return. New challenges were made against the sanctity of the family and the remnants of public morality. The Vietnam War had left America more uncertain than ever of how to define itself. What did we stand for? This is the atmosphere that brought the New Christian Right into existence.[24] A number of issues helped to mobilize its efforts, including drug abuse, the feminist movement, pornography, and what was seen as the evils of popular music.[25] But the most serious was abortion, with protests beginning in earnest in 1973, after *Roe* v. *Wade* was decided. The response of the New Christian Right was disbelief and then defiance. Religious groups began to unseat legislators who supported abortion on demand, and hospitals and abortion clinics were picketed. Several groups, such as the Lambs of Christ and Operation Rescue, took protesters from town to town in order to support local groups seeking to close abortion clinics. These groups blocked entrances to the clinics by chaining themselves to fences and to each other. As Garry Wills has said, "The level of dedication seems as high as that of the civil rights and antiwar protesters, whom they have come increasingly to resemble."[26] But the tensions awakened by the abortion conflict also encouraged some violence. Although no anti-abortion group publicly condoned violence, several abortion clinics around the country were bombed, and two doctors who performed abortions were murdered in Florida by protesters in 1993 and 1994.[27] And in 1995, a gunman killed two receptionists and wounded several other people in abortion clinics in Massachusetts and Virginia.

In spite of the controversy, the abortion debate resembles any other secular debate in this country. People disagree, gather in groups to strengthen their positions, and make their opinions public. Some within the groups are moderate and some are extreme, but the existence of a small number of violent individuals does not mean for a moment that the abortion issue threatens public peace or the political process. The involvement of religious groups in this debate is natural and healthy.

These three political movements are representative of the role that religion has had in American politics; one might have chosen any number of other issues to explore (capital punishment, censorship of pornography, etc.). But one thing is clear: in a regime that allows its citizens significant freedom, religion will emerge as one of many political forces. As Madison said in *Federalist* 10, "liberty is to faction what air is to fire."[28] The only way to eliminate faction from political life is to abolish liberty, but doing so would make political life undesirable. Our history gives evidence of the vitality of religious activism, but it should also calm the fears of both those who fear religious involvement in politics and those who yearn for it. Religion has traditionally been a presence in American politics without being its defining characteristic.

RELIGION AND LOBBYING

Religious groups lobby more effectively today than at any time in the past. The number of major religious lobbying groups has also grown significantly, making their power much stronger.[29] Is this good or bad for American politics? Before we can answer this question, we have to explore what it is that religious lobbying groups do.

Hertzke points out that there are two major strategies of lobbying organizations: (1) home district pressure and (2) insider pressure.[30] Religious lobbying groups are fairly effective in generating home district pressure. That is, they are effective in encouraging their members to write or call their representatives in Washington to express their opinions about pending legislation. Both liberal and conservative religious groups maintain computer lists of "constituents" and can easily generate mass mailings to them. The Liberty Federation (which includes what was once called the Moral Majority) also has a sophisticated system to initiate computer-generated phone messages to its members, as does the Christian Coalition:

> The organization can make up to 100,000 phone calls per week, with tape messages targeted by issue orientation or religious orientation of the member. These tapes, "Call your Senator now," are even customized on the basis of preacher loyalty....[31]

These techniques can be used to produce a mass response. One religious group, Bread for the World, has used a technique called the "offering of letters." Members of churches that belong to the organization are asked from time to time to put letters to their representatives into the church collection plates instead of money.[32] The American Jewish Committee and the U.S. Catholic Conference use a different approach to generate home district pressure, one that they believe is more effective. They keep leading members of communities in every state well informed about their target issues; these members are doctors, lawyers, and businesspeople who have long-standing relationships with their congressional representatives. When an important issue arises, the American Jewish Committee or the U.S. Catholic Conference contacts these individuals to make personal appointments with their representatives on behalf of the lobbying organization. These contacts are very effective, perhaps even more effective than mass mailings by rank-and-file members of lobbying groups.[33]

Another approach to home district pressure taken by religious lobbying groups is direct electoral action. The most obvious example is Jesse Jackson's 1984 presidential campaign. According to Reichley,

> The black churches, mostly evangelical or mainline Protestant, continued to function as centers of black political activity. Many black ministers regularly endorsed favored candidates in Democratic primaries and urged support for the Democratic ticket in general elections. In order to protect their churches' tax exemptions, ministers usually designated these endorsements

as "personal." But most of them did not hesitate to put the moral prestige of their church behind their political recommendations.[34]

A number of religious lobbying groups issue "report cards" on candidates for office that include the candidates' positions on important issues and their voting records on these issues. These documents can be very influential in elections because they are written simply to expose the candidates' strengths or weaknesses in relationship to a particular religious perspective.[35]

However, most students of politics agree that the second lobbying strategy, insider pressure, is even more important in the political process. Washington politics is extremely complex, and a group cannot have an effect on the legislative process unless it really grasps the subtleties of the issues, the compromise needed to build coalitions, and the shifting power structures in a Congress that is desperately trying to survive without strong institutional leadership or clearly defined political parties.[36] Most religious groups are better at generating home district pressure than they are at producing real insider pressure, and Hertzke outlines a number of reasons for this situation. First, most religious groups have relatively small lobbying organizations. Second, they have a problem with focus: "Ethically minded, socially concerned religious leaders are tempted to take stands on a multitude of issues."[37] Finally, religious lobbying organizations often find it difficult on principled grounds to deal with issues on the level of detail necessary to effect change or to compromise on issues in order to achieve partial success in the process. This is true for both liberal and conservative religious lobbying groups. Many would rather announce their positions on what they perceive to be moral issues than engage in the nuts-and-bolts level of legislation. And compromise is often impossible. Hertzke refers to concerns that one congressional aide expressed over Lutheran lobbying efforts for a Civil Rights Restoration Act:

> Mainstream churches are strong in terms of consciousness-raising, but not nitty-gritty lobbying, i.e., how should it read? Congress searches for consensus policy. And the subtext [of legislation] is hard for them. We've had Lutheran groups come in and say on civil rights, "We want restoration." But the dispute over the bill was more technical: how to restore without opening up a can of unexpected worms.[38]

In other words, the Lutheran lobbying effort was hampered because it did not reach beyond a general moral position. The religious groups that are most effective are the ones who have moved beyond generalizations and learned to approach Congress on its own terms. These groups focus on legislative detail and tend to avoid overtly religious appeals to representatives—to present careful, narrow arguments for why they support or oppose legislation.

It follows from this discussion that religious lobbying is an effective way for a significant part of the American population to make its views known. Religious lobbying groups generate the kind of grassroots activity that can inform Congress about issues and perspectives that might otherwise go unnoticed. Religious concerns have been neglected in public life, and it is only appropriate in a democratic republic that they be included in political discourse. To some extent, then, these lobbying groups have an impact on the Congressional agenda and the tone of Congressional debate. But they do not control the legislative process. In addition, it seems that the legislative process itself moderates the impact of religious lobbying groups. Hertzke calls this the influence of "the congressional milieu," saying that the requirements of success in the legislative process also inform the agenda and tone of religious lobbying groups: "For those concerned that 'religious fanatics' are entering politics, the evidence should be reassuring. The norms and rules of the game appear to mold the message."[39] It is also important to understand that the tremendous variety of religious lobbying groups in Washington keeps any one group or any one perspective from having too powerful a voice. Liberal, conservative, and moderate groups of every religion compete for influence with one another, and they in turn must compete with secular groups. Hertzke concludes that "as a key American political institution," Congress is a "model of Madisonian wizardry, accommodating yet checking the various religious factions."[40]

RELIGION IN CONGRESS

We have examined briefly the attempts of religious lobbying groups to influence the legislative process. But how important is religion within Congress itself? There are three main questions that need to be addressed: How religious are our representatives in Congress? How influential is religion in Congressional voting? How representative is Congress of religion in America?

It is widely believed that Congress is dominated by people hostile to religion. This view is expressed emphatically by one critic:

> There can be no question that the humanists control our government, and have for many years.... Those 537 people [he includes the President and Vice-President] who control our national destiny represent sufficient humanistic philosophy or lack of true Christian consensus to have brought us to the threshold of fulfilling the humanist dreams of a secular, amoral society.[41]

The evidence actually suggests that "the majority of Congress is a believing Congress."[42] Almost all members of Congress (approximately 95%) say that they believe in God (or in an ultimate religious reality); a strong majority within Congress claims to believe that Scripture is more than myth and allegory, that heaven and hell exist, that God is involved in the course of history, and that there is a life after death where individuality is preserved. Critics of Congress like the one quoted above have assumed that secular legislation must come from secular representatives, but this is not the case. There are many reasons why a religious Congressman or Congresswoman might vote in a way that could be perceived as anti-religious. For example, one might believe (rightly or wrongly) that prayer in the public schools cheapens prayer; according to this view, a vote against school prayer would not necessarily reveal animosity toward religion. Or one might be opposed to abortion on religious grounds and still vote to allow abortion protesters certain First Amendment rights. It is especially important to remember that many Supreme Court decisions since 1947 have suggested that the Constitution requires separation of church and state. A deeply religious Congressman or Congresswoman might still believe that adhering to the Constitution demands voting on legislation in a way that scrupulously avoids strengthening religion.

Yet the problem seems to go deeper.[43] The suspicion that Congress has been hostile to religion cannot be dismissed by showing that members of Congress believe themselves to be religious. The real problem may be that people who think of themselves as religious may be confused or ignorant about their religion and what it may require of them. In other words, people who think they are religious may unintentionally undermine the dictates of their faith. Some of these issues will be addressed in the final section of this chapter.

However, even confused or ignorant views of religion may influence voting in Congress. Reichley points out that "religion can play a role in this [legislative] process by influencing the values of officeholders."[44] Legislators are chosen by popular election and tend to share the basic views of their communities. But even if legislators don't share the religion of the voters, "a dependence on public approval for reelection should motivate them to express the preferences of their constituents."[45] Studies that have focused on the church affiliation of legislators have not been especially helpful in determining the impact of religion on voting, but Benson and Williams looked beyond affiliation to the perceived beliefs of the legislators themselves. Using this broader approach, they found that religion does seem to be an important contributing factor to voting in Congress:

> Voting in the U.S. Congress is in all probability a behavior that is determined by a combination of forces, all working together in some kind of complicated formula. We are not ready to claim that religious beliefs and values are the most crucial part of the formula. But we think our findings are strong enough to suggest that religious belief should join some of the more commonly recognized factors, like party affiliation and constituent pressure, as forces that bear on political voting.[46]

Benson and Williams noted that religious beliefs that stress the individual correlate with support for the free enterprise system and military spending, but religious beliefs that stress the community correlate with support for foreign aid and the expansion of civil liberties.[47] However, no amount of study can ever determine with precision the importance of religion to voting. We know that it is a contributing factor, and that is all.

One of the most exciting things one can learn about Congress is that it is religiously diverse. One recent study revealed that 47% of the members of Congress were Protestants, 27% were Catholic, and 8% were Jewish.[48] This breakdown compares favorably with the general population, which is approximately 56% Protestant, 25% Catholic, and 2% Jewish (less than 1% of the population is

Muslim).[49] But if we look beyond the mere fact of affiliation, the diversity is even more significant. Benson and Williams found that six different types of religious belief were represented in Congress and that each religious group included from three to six of the different types of belief.[50]

Benson and Williams also compared their figures on belief in Congress with Gallup data on the American public and came up with some interesting results. They found that 95% of the members of Congress believe in God, compared to 94% of the American public. Also, 80% of our representatives believe that the Bible is the word of God, whereas 72% of the public holds this belief. And a striking 81% of Congressmen and Congresswomen believe in life after death, compared to 69% of the general population. In addition, our representatives are more likely to be members of churches of synagogues than we are (90% versus 67%). These figures lead to the conclusion that our Congress reflects the general religious character of the American people quite well. If anything, our representatives seem to be more involved with religion than is the American public.[51]

RELIGIOUS ACTIVITY TODAY

The American regime has, as we have seen, created a context for moderate religious activity. Religious groups have helped to free the slaves, change the Constitution, and lead social protest movements. They also work consistently to influence the legislative process. But has the character of religion and religious commitment changed in America?[52]

According to Gallup poll data, there seems to be a general decline in religious belief over the past forty years. Today, 58% of Americans say that religion is very important in their lives, but for those under thirty years of age, the figure is smaller: 46%. In the baby-boom age group (26–45 years old), only 39% of men say that religion is very important to them, although 58% of women in the same age group still maintain that it is very important. This represents a significant drop from 1952, when 75% of Americans said that religion was very important in their lives. In addition, 55% of Americans believe that the influence of religion is declining. So data of this kind show a decline in belief, especially among the young.[53]

On the other hand, polling data suggest that church attendance in America has remained constant during this same time period. Gallup figures show that in 1950, 39% of Americans had attended church within seven days of the poll. The 1991 figures put church attendance at 42%. As the Princeton report says, "while local pastors and church leaders may worry about declines in religious service attendance or exalt over bulging pews, attendance from a national perspective has been remarkably constant for the past several decades."[54] If the figures are broken down to reveal denominations, they show that 51% of Catholics attended church during the previous week as opposed to 46% of Protestants. So it seems from these figures that while religious belief is in decline, church attendance has actually remained constant.

However, the polling data produced by Gallup and other information-gathering organizations has recently come under fire. As one study has said, "If Americans are going to church at the rate they report, the churches would be full on Sunday mornings and denominations would be growing. Yet they are not."[55] Consider the contradictions explored in this study. If, for example, 2.5% of Americans are Episcopalian and if 35% of them attend church services regularly (as polling data suggests), then total attendance for one week should be more than two million. But as Hadaway, Marler, and Chaves point out, average weekly attendance was actually less than 900,000 in 1991. The actual attendance of Episcopalians was 16% rather than 35%.[56] In their study of Protestant attendance in one county in Ohio, Hadaway, Marler, and Chaves found that the Gallup figures for church attendance were 130% higher than the actual attendance.[57] Their research into actual church attendance reveals that "Protestant and Catholic church attendance is roughly one-half the levels reported by Gallup."[58] There are several possible reasons for the discrepancy, but the most likely is that people believe church attendance to be a desirable thing and therefore overreport it. So it seems possible that, contrary to the public opinion polls that show church attendance constant over the last forty years, attendance has actually declined significantly.

And what is the character of the religion that seems to be declining in America? New studies of religious commitment suggest that almost one-third of Americans are completely secular in outlook (in spite of claiming religious affiliation or church attendance) and only 19% of adult Americans regularly practice their religion.[59] There also seems to be great turmoil within both formal religious structures as well as in personal beliefs. Almost one-quarter of Americans have changed their faiths or denominations, and allegiance to religious institutions is weak.

In the midst of shaky institutional attachments, churches and synagogues have worked hard to attract members, going so far as to advertise on radio and television. According to Richard Ostling,

> Today, a quiet revolution is taking place that is changing not only the religious habits of millions of Americans but the way churches go about recruiting members to keep their doors open. Increasing numbers of baby boomers who left the fold years ago are turning to religion again, but many are traveling from church to church or faith to faith, sampling creeds, shopping for a custom-made God. A growing choir of critics contend that in doing whatever it takes to lure those fickle customers, churches are at risk of losing their heritage—and their souls.[60]

American individualism and commercialism are apparently taking their toll on religion. Most Americans believe that the church serves them, not the other way around.[61] There doesn't seem to be any doubt about the fact that religion meant far more to the Massachusetts colonist of 1760 (whose life centered around his or her faith) than it does to the contemporary practitioner of religion (although both might consider themselves "religious"). Consider the fact that, according to the Princeton study, 25% of those recently attending

Easter services did not know what Easter signified in the Christian faith.[62] Easter seems more likely to remind people of chocolate eggs or new hats than the resurrection of Jesus. And consider the following message displayed on an electronic sign in front of a private religious school: "HE IS RISEN YOUR WAY RIGHT AWAY BURGER KING." Another house of worship put the following message on its sign: "BINGO AIR CONDITIONING." Apparently, it was necessary to promise games and physical comfort to get people inside. And although 93% of Americans consider Christmas to be their favorite holiday, with 85% putting up Christmas trees and 78% sending Christmas cards, only 38% claim that Christmas is a strongly religious holiday. If these figures are inflated in the same way that church attendance figures apparently are, then it is possible that even a smaller number of Americans take Christmas seriously as a religious holiday. It seems that a significant number of Americans who attend church or who celebrate important holidays either do not understand them or consider them to be essentially secular or commercial.

Other forces have combined to weaken religious belief in contemporary America. Modern philosophy produced two powerful doctrines that have had an impact on American thought and therefore on the way in which religion is understood: positivism and historicism.[63] A full treatment of these doctrines is beyond the scope of this chapter, but a few points should be mentioned. Both doctrines deny the possibility of a transcendent divinity, divinely inspired truth, or our capacity to understand either. Positivism (in its contemporary form) is the view that science can verify only facts; values are completely subjective and hence arbitrary. Since religious belief falls in the realm of values rather than facts, it follows that religion itself can never be verified as true. Historicism (in its contemporary form) is the view that truth is a relative thing, determined by its relationship to particular historical periods. What seems to be true at one time will not be true for another. Hence, truth is transient. Both of these doctrines have been influential in American academia and have found their way (sometimes in slightly different forms) into popular consciousness. Gallup data indicate that seven out of ten adults believe that there are few (if any) moral absolutes and that "what is right or wrong usually varies from situation to situation." And only three people in ten believe that Scripture is the ultimate authority in matters of truth.[64]

The religious community has engaged in a great deal of soul-searching in its attempt to address the weakening of religion that has resulted from these strong forces. One recent book written by eight Christian theologians asks, "Just how far can modern Christianity depart from its scriptural and theological roots, or accommodate itself to religious pluralism, before Christian doctrine begins to look indistinguishable from the ethical credo of secular orthodoxy?"[65] Another book criticizes liberal Protestantism for being nothing more than a vague desire for a better society; it argues that this notion of Protestant Christianity has come to dominate the contemporary university. In other words, Christ has disappeared from Christianity: "A Christ whose gospel intends nothing more than what education, science, and legislation intend is an irrelevant Christ."[66] Similar concerns have been voiced by Jews. Irving Kristol recently argued that Judaism has also come to identify itself with contemporary liberalism. He offers a modest proposal: Jews ought to turn back to their religion as a foundation for their identity, but he is not overly optimistic about the chances for a true revival.[67] Christians and Jews alike are concerned that religion has somehow lost its real meaning.

We are left with a somber picture. Religion continues to be an active force in American politics, but it has been transformed by a regime that champions individualism and commercialism and by intellectual movements that question all religion. It is not at all clear that contemporary religion is still capable of nurturing the state and its citizens as our Founders hoped it would.

NOTES

1. Kenneth Wald, *Religion and Politics in the United States* (Washington, DC: Congressional Quarterly Press, 1992). Wald devotes one chapter of his book to making the cases for and against the active involvement of religion in politics.

2. Allen D. Hertzke, *Representing God in Washington* (Knoxville: Univ. of Tennessee Press, 1988), p. 199.

3. Some have gone so far as to trace the roots of modern terrorism to the early forms of religious fanaticism. For example, David Rappoport analyzes the activities of the Thugs, the Assassins, and the Zealots, who were (respectively) Hindu, Muslim, and Jewish radicals who used violence to achieve their goals. These groups, however, all attacked people they considered to be guilty; modern terrorists often attack those they know to be completely innocent. But whether or not modern terrorism does have its roots in religion, it is clear that the religious tradition includes groups capable of great violence. See David Rappoport, "Religion and Terror: Thugs, Assassins, and Zealots," in *International Terrorism: Characteristics, Causes, Controls,* ed. Charles Kegley, Jr. (New York: St. Martin, 1990), p. 146.

4. See the discussion of Madison's "multiplicity" argument in Chapter 2.

5. Martin Diamond, "The Federalist" in *American Political Thought,* ed. Morton

Frisch and Richard Stevens (Itasca, IL; Peacock, 1983), p. 69 See also Martin Diamond, *The Founding of the Democratic Republic* (Itasca, IL: Peacock, 1981), p. 77.

6. Allen D. Hertzke, *Representing God in Washington* (Knoxville: Univ. of Tennessee Press, 1988), p. 23. Much of the discussion in this section is indebted to Hertzke's excellent book.

7. Hertzke also points out (p. 21) that a small Jewish community arrived in New Amsterdam in 1654.

8. Hertzke, p. 25.

9. Arthur Zilversmit, *The First Emancipation: The Abolition of Slavery in the North* (Chicago: Univ. of Chicago Press, 1967), p. 55.

10. Zilversmit, p. 56.

11. A. James Reichley, *Religion in American Public Life* (Washington, DC: Brookings Institution, 1985), p. 190. See also John M. Blum et al., The National Experience (New York: Harcourt, 1968) p. 263.

12. Reichley, p. 191.

13. Here is an example of Lincoln's moral condemnation of slavery: "The Republican party think it [slavery] wrong—we think it is a moral, a social and a political wrong. We think it is a wrong not confining itself merely to the persons or the states where it exists, but that it is a wrong

in its tendency to say the least, that extends itself to the existence of the whole nation. Because we think it wrong, we propose a course of policy that shall deal with it as a wrong." See the Sixth Lincoln-Douglas Debate in Robert W. Johannsen, *The Lincoln-Douglas Debates of 1858* (New York: Oxford Univ. Press, 1965), p. 254.

14. Jews also turned to the Republican Party in the 1850s, but their numbers were not significant enough to have a major impact on politics. See Reichley, p. 230.

15. Reichley, p. 199.

16. Jeremy Ribkin, "Disestablished Religion in America" in *The Public Interest,* No. 86, pp. 57–69.

17. James Timberlake, *Prohibition and the Progressive Movement 1900–1920* (Cambridge, MA: Harvard Univ. Press, 1963), p. 4.

18. One famous revivalist preacher, Billy Sunday, was fond of pointing out that the whole country would be reborn once liquor was unavailable. In his "booze sermon," he said, "The slums will soon be a memory. We will turn our prisons into factories and our jails into storehouses and corncribs. Men will walk upright now, women will smile and children will laugh. Hell will be forever for rent." See Larry Engelmann, *Intemperance: The Lost War Against Liquor* (New York: Free Press, 1979), p. xi.

19. Timberlake, p. 5.

20. Timberlake, p. 32.

21. Reichley, p. 216.

22. See Charles Beard and Mary Beard, *The Rise of American Civilization* (New York: Macmillan, 1930), p. 733.

23. Wald, p. 232.

24. See Wald's discussion of the New Christian Right (pp. 228–37). This chapter draws heavily on Wald's fine treatment of the phenomenon.

25. Wald, p. 228.

26. Garry Wills, *Under God* (New York: Simon and Schuster, 1990), p. 328.

27. Dr. David Gunn was murdered in 1993, and an abortion protester murdered two people (including a doctor) in 1994. See *Newsweek,* Aug. 8, 1994, p. 22. For a more complete treatment of the abortion issue, see Chapter 15.

28. Hamilton, Madison, and Jay, *The Federalist* (New York: Modern Library, 1937), 10, p. 55.

29. As Hertzke points out, there were only sixteen major religious lobbies in Washington in 1950. By 1988 there were over eighty, and the number is still growing. See Allen Hertzke, *Representing God in Washington: The Role of Religious Lobbies in the American Polity* (Knoxville, Univ. of Tennessee Press, 1988), p. 5. This section of the chapter is heavily indebted to Hertzke for its argument and central examples.

30. Hertzke, p. 49.

31. Hertzke, p. 50.

32. Hertzke, p. 57.

33. Hertzke, p. 65.

34. Reichley, pp. 282–85. See also Hertzke, p. 65; he uses the term "direct electoral mobilization" to describe this approach to lobbying.

35. Hertzke, p. 67.

36. See Peter Woll, *Congress* (Boston: Little, Brown, 1985), p. 381. He says that "Lobbyists must understand the complex interconnections and subtleties of Washington politics to be successful. Congress is not always moved by electoral demands, which rarely exist in concrete form. Congress acts only when its entangled political machinery is put in gear, which can be accomplished only when intricate and diversified power interests among party leaders, committee chairmen, staff, and members themselves mesh."

37. Hertzke, p. 71.

38. Hertzke, p. 74. He also discusses several other problems that religious lobbying groups face in trying to exert insider pressure.

39. Hertzke, p. 88.

40. Hertzke, p. 200. See also Woll, p. 402. He argues that "pressure-group politics is a zero-sum game; that is, for every group that wins there is one that loses."

41. Tim LaHaye, *The Battle for the Mind* (Old Tappan, NJ: Fleming H. Revell, 1980), p. 17, quoted in Peter Benson and Dorothy Williams *Religion on Capitol Hill: Myths and Realities* (San Francisco: Harper, 1982), p. 58. This section of the chapter is deeply indebted to Benson and Williams's fine study of Congress. Unless otherwise noted, the evidence about congressional opinion is drawn from their book.

42. Benson and Williams, p. 59.

43. Richard Neuhaus, *The Naked Public Square* (Grand Rapids, MI: Eerdmans 1984). Also see our Afterword for a discussion of Neuhaus.

44. Reichley, p. 192.

45. Reichley, p. 192.

46. Benson and Williams, pp. 162, 164.

47. See Benson and Williams, pp. 160–63. Reichley discusses Benson and Williams's study on. pp. 195–96.

48. Norman Ornstein, Thomas Mann, Michael Malbin, *Vital Statistics on Congress, 1991–1992* (Washington, DC: Congressional Quarterly Press, 1992), p. 34.

49. Robert Bezilla, *Religion in America: 1992–1993* (Princeton, NJ: Princeton Religion Research Center, 1993), pp. 36-37.

50. Benson and Williams, pp. 137–39.

51. Benson and Williams, pp. 74–84.

52. For a more comprehensive treatment of this question, see the Afterword to this text.

53. The Gallup polling data is from Robert Bezilla, *Religion in America: 1992–1993*.

54. Bezilla, p. 42.

55. C. Kirk Hadaway, Penny Long Marler, and Mark Chaves, "What the Polls Don't Show: A Closer Look at U.S. Church Attendance," *American Sociological Review,* Vol. 58 (December 1993): 742.

56. Hadaway, Marler, and Chaves, p. 743.

57. Hadaway, Marler, and Chaves, p. 744.

58. Hadaway, Marler, and Chaves, p. 748.

59. See Kenneth Woodward, "The Rites of Americans," *Newsweek,* November 29, 1993, p. 82.

60. Richard Ostling, "The Generation That Forgot God," *Time,* April 5, 1993, p. 45.

61. Ostling, p. 45.

62. Bezilla, p. 48.

63. See Leo Strauss, *What Is Political Philosophy?* (Glencoe, IL: Free Press, 1959), pp. 18–27.

64. Bezilla, p. 23.

65. Julia Gatta, "Orthodoxy and the Renewal of Christian Identity," *Christian Century* (August 10–17, 1994), p. 751. This article reviews the book *Reclaiming Faith: Essays on Orthodoxy in the Episcopal Church and the Baltimore Declaration,* edited by Ephraim Radner and George Sumner.

66. See "Why Christ Was Expelled," *Christianity Today* (Aug. 15, 1994), p. 35. This essay is a commentary on *The Soul of the American University* by George Marsden.

67. Irving Kristol, "Why Religion Is Good for the Jews," *Commentary* (August, 1994), p. 21.

4

The Supreme Court
and the
First Amendment

The religion clauses of the First Amendment speak to us in straightforward language:

> Congress shall make no law respecting an establishment of religion, or prohibiting the free exercise thereof....

Sixteen words. It would seem simple enough. Yet perhaps half the words in these two clauses have been, and remain, controversial. Litigation invoking these two clauses seems unremitting. And the amount of space in legal periodicals and books (like this one) devoted to explaining and criticizing the resulting jurisprudence defies probability and maybe even common sense.

Why? There are a number of reasons that efforts to determine the meaning and the correct and consistent legal application of the religion clauses continue unabated. First, despite the seemingly simple, straightforward language (as we shall see), evidence regarding the precise meaning of the religion clauses is relatively sparse. A second reason that litigation and legal controversy endure is that so much rides upon how these clauses are interpreted. At stake is not only the ability of religious minorities to practice their religion unhampered by government, but billions of dollars of governmental programs that have both a positive and negative impact on religious beliefs and practices. The rise of the welfare state and the increasing size and responsibilities of local, state, and national governments, coupled with the proliferation of varying minority religious beliefs, ensure that conflicts have increased significantly. A third reason for the increase in litigation is that the Supreme Court in 1968 permitted certain types of taxpayer suits under the Establishment Clause, a rule it has extended to no other constitutional provision or amendment.[1]

A final reason that litigation and legal controversy continue unabated is the confusing (and many would say confused) opinions propounded by the Supreme Court over the last fifty years. Admittedly, while it has been a formidable task to make sense of the religion clauses within the context of a variety of specific cases, by now it is clear that nothing approaching legal clarity has ensued. Bitterly divided courts and spirited judicial arguments have often been the hallmark of religion clause jurisprudence. In this chapter, we will discuss the constitutional choices faced by the Supreme Court and gauge their results. We can do so only at the most general level. Nonetheless, it is our hope that examining the interpretive choices available and those acted upon by the Supreme Court will enable us to understand more fully the historical and contemporary legal relationship among law, religion, and politics in the United States.

INTERPRETING THE CONSTITUTION

Given the fact that the religion clauses are not self-interpreting, understanding these clauses is a necessary first step to evaluating the Supreme Court's efforts to interpret them. The rules about interpreting provisions of the Constitution are similar to those governing the interpretation of any other legal document. Justice Story (arguably the foremost interpreter of the Constitution) aptly observed over 150 years ago that "[t]he first and fundamental rule in the interpretation of all instruments is to construe them according to the sense of the terms and the intention of the parties."[2] Story cited Blackstone to the effect "that the intention of a law is to be gathered from the words, the context, the subject matter, and effects and consequence, or the reason and spirit of the law."[3] Before turning our attention to possible interpretations of the two religion clauses, it is useful to furnish some brief, general observations regarding the language, context, and history of these clauses.

Language[4] The religion clauses of the First Amendment contain two parallel provisions, each specifically directed at "religion." (In so doing, the Constitution does not differentiate religious institutions or organizations from individual religious beliefs or practices.) Regarding religion, the First Amendment declares that the government may not establish a religion; neither may it prohibit a religion. In this way (and at the most general level), the Constitution seems to address two equal and opposite dangers. The Establishment Clause appears (at a minimum) to prohibit any religious majority from founding a state-sponsored religion. The Free Exercise Clause appears to prevent a similar majority from substantially impeding the religious beliefs and practices of fellow citizens.

Context The religion clauses were part of the first ten amendments to the Constitution, passed by the first Congress and ratified by three-fourths of the states by the end of 1791. The Constitution quite literally constituted a new government intended to secure the rights to "life, liberty, and the pursuit of happiness" for citizens.[5] Religious liberty was one type of liberty that government was intended to secure, but religion (and religious zealotry) constituted the greatest danger to that same liberty. Story was probably correct when he explained that the purpose of the religion clauses was "to exclude all rivalry among Christian sects and to prevent any national ecclesiastical establishment which should give to a hierarchy the exclusive patronage of the national government," thus cutting off "the means of religious persecution (the vice of former ages), and the subversion of the rights of conscience in matters of religion, which had been trampled upon almost from the days of the Apostles to the present age."[6] Thus, the Constitution, including its amendments, was intended to protect life and liberty generally, and the religion clauses sought to safeguard religious liberty specifically, by helping to eliminate religious persecution at its source. To that end, the unamended Constitution had already banned religious tests or oaths as a prerequisite for holding office in government (Article VI, sec. 3).

Legally, both the Establishment Clause and the Free Exercise Clause invoked formal limitations upon government. They did not create governmental power, but rather limited power elsewhere described and apportioned in the Constitution. In that the Constitution created a new national government (which, consistent with the very idea of government, could directly exercise coercive power over individuals,[7]) and in that the relatively few Constitutional provisions that limited the *states* were clearly denoted as such (see Article I, section 10), a reasonable, contextual interpretation of the text suggests that the Bill of Rights in general, and the religion clauses specifically, originally limited only the new national government.[8]

History In the last, long days of the 1787 Philadelphia Constitutional Convention, George Mason proposed that a Bill of Rights be drafted, almost as an afterthought. Not a single state supported Mason's proposal. The Bill of Rights was later championed by Antifederalists, who generally feared that the new Constitution would create a tyrannical national government, endangering the rights of citizens and the powers of the states. Conversely, the Framers initially opposed the Bill of Rights, frequently agreeing with Madison that these amendments were largely unnecessary or with Hamilton that they might even be dangerous.[9] Eventually, it was Madison who endeavored to ensure the Constitution's passage by promising to favor a Bill of Rights, which he eventually did. Significantly, although the Bill of Rights specifically, and the religion clauses generally, are today often enshrined as the essential core of the American Constitution, they assumed their greatest importance in the twentieth century. Litigation under these two clauses has increased exponentially in the last fifty years.

It is now appropriate to examine the two religion clauses in greater detail. In each instance, we will discuss varying understandings of each clause (some compatible and others not). Additionally, we will comment upon both the extent to which the interpretation can be fairly supported by evidence regarding its original meaning and purpose. At the end of our discussion of each clause, we will briefly discuss the approaches and legal tests employed by the Supreme Court.

THE ESTABLISHMENT CLAUSE

Prevalent interpretations of the First Amendment's Establishment Clause include the following:

A. *The Establishment Clause prohibits the national government from founding and supporting a single church or religion.* This aim of the Establishment Clause, so far as we can tell, has been universally accepted as correct. In straightforward language, this clause explicitly prohibits the national government from founding, ratifying, or ordaining a state religion.[10] No part of the Constitution grants the newly created government power to undertake such a task, so this meaning of the Establishment Clause merely emphasizes what already existed constitutionally. Not surprisingly, no prominent Founder favored a union of a *national* church and the newly created state, and everyone who spoke on the subject condemned this European practice (especially as it had been undertaken in England).

Still, at the time of the Constitution's passage, six *states* maintained multiple establishments of religion. Unlike European religious establishments, which had actively favored a specific religious sect at the expense of other sects or religions (with associated prosecutions for heresy, apostasy, and even nonconformity), American state establishments at this time were far more benign (only favoring Christianity or, in the most homogeneous of states, Protestantism), and establishment was generally confined to "government aid and sponsorship of religion, principally by impartial tax support of the institutions of religion, the churches."[11]

B. *The Establishment Clause was adopted to restrain the national government from interfering with state religious establishments.* Here, again, there is no controversy. This formulation indicates an *additional* noncontroversial goal of the Establishment Clause and the Constitution. The Bill of Rights was championed by large number of people, many of whom had initially been Antifederalists. Many feared that an emboldened national government would swallow up the states, or at the very least, subvert state power. These individuals, a number of whom were prominent in the first Congress, were intent upon limiting national governmental power over religion. Thus, they feared that the newly established national government would disturb already existing church–government accommodations. (Prohibiting the national government from exercising power over the states could have had the opposite effect of prohibiting the national government from contracting state guarantees of religious liberty or requiring them to establish a state religion or religions.) Still, the fear of anti-religious intervention by the national government was the dominant political worry in 1789. That concern has been stated in several compatible ways. From the perspective of the national government, Justice Story, while indirectly reminding his readers of the Constitution's ban upon religious oaths, observed that

> the whole power over the subject of religion is left exclusive to the State governments, to be acted upon according to their own sense of justice and the State constitutions; and the Catholic and the Protestant, the Calvinist and the Arminian, the Jew and the Infidel, may sit down at the common table of the national councils without any inquisition into their faith or mode of worship.[12]

Regarding the perspective of ordinary Americans, a leading historian of religion in early America has observed that while the issues of church and state had been largely settled by the states, still Americans

> agreed that the federal government had no power in such matters, but some individuals and groups wanted that fact stated explicitly. Granted, not all the states would have concurred on a single definition of religious liberty; but since they were denying power to Congress rather than giving it, differences among them on that score did not bring them into contention.[13]

From the perspective of the Constitution, the Establishment Clause, like the Bill of Rights as a whole, reflected the important legal tenet of federalism:

> ...the Establishment Clause was enacted to prevent Congress from interfering with the church–state relationships that existed in 1791. Specifically, the Establishment Clause was intended to prevent Congress from interfering with the established state churches and with state efforts to accommodate religion. At the same time, the Clause disabled Congress from interfering with the states that had already disestablished their churches. In other words, the Establishment Clause was intended to embody a principle of federalism.[14]

C. *The Establishment Clause prohibits the national government from extending direct aid to or support for any or all religious sects or organizations.* The Establishment Clause simply reinforces the fact that no provision of the Constitution authorizes government to provide direct support for religion or religious organizations.[15] As we have just observed, it is commonly acknowledged that, as originally understood, such a restriction could only have limited the national government and not the states. The original understanding of the Constitution held that the states not only possessed the power to aid religion directly, but in fact legitimately had exercised such power. On the other hand, the new

Constitution did not grant the national government the power to aid religion directly, either in a discriminatory or nondiscriminatory manner.

Still, there are complications inherent in this commonly accepted interpretation that the Establishment Clause denied the newly founded national government any direct power to aid religion or religions. The problem is history. Shortly after the ratification of the First Amendment, Congress enacted legislation directly favoring religion. It passed a resolution authorizing a day of public Thanksgiving and prayer "for the many signal favors of Almighty." Money for a Congressional chaplain was allocated; subsequently, each session of Congress was opened with a prayer. Sometime later, in 1803, Congress appropriated money to support missionaries in converting Indians, including the authorization of the expenditure of $100 annually toward the support of a Catholic priest "who will engage to perform for the said tribe [of Indians] the duties of his office and also to instruct [the children of the tribe] in the rudiments of literature."[16] The problem is that the first two of these acts, and perhaps the third,[17] did not have any obvious constitutional authority. How did this happen? One prominent historian furnishes a convincing explanation:

> Customs like days of prayer and thanksgiving appeared not so much matters of religion as part of the common coin of civilized living. Sabbath laws enjoyed widespread support and were so little the subject of dissent that citizens never even felt challenged to think how those laws might impose a particular religious viewpoint....
>
> The vast majority of Americans assumed that theirs was a Christian, i.e. Protestant, country, and they automatically expected that government would uphold the commonly agreed on Protestant ethos and morality. In many instances, they had not come to grips with the implications their belief in the powerlessness of government in religious matters held for a society in which the values, customs, and forms of Protestant Christianity thoroughly permeated civil and political life. The contradiction between their theory and their practice became evident to Americans only later, with the advent of a more religiously pluralistic society, when it became the subject of a disputation that continues into the present.[18]

Thus, although the language of the Constitution afforded no explicit authority for the national government to favor religion or religions, such support was initially extended by Congress, no doubt in reference to prevailing social, cultural, and religious, beliefs.

D. *The Establishment Clause prohibits the national government from providing indirect aid or support that favors one or several religions or religiously affiliated organizations.* Alternately stated, the Establishment Clause does not bar the national government from indirectly providing aid to religion on a nondiscriminatory basis as part of a broader, secular governmental program. This interpretation of the Establishment Clause has been labeled an "accommodationist" interpretation of its language because it permits a certain latitude of governmental action that incidentally benefits religion or religious organizations. Again, regarding this interpretation of the Establishment Clause, it is the powers of the national government that are described. Yet, if this interpretation is accepted, note that the powers allowed to the national government over religion would, in the area of indirect aid or support for religion, duplicate those the state governments could also legitimately exercise (for it was assumed that the states clearly retained their power over religion, the Establishment Clause notwithstanding).

Here, the key Establishment Clause question is this: Did the Founders understand the national government to possess the power to pass nondiscriminatory acts affecting religion? One way of answering this question is to look at the historical record surrounding the adoption of the Bill of Rights and the Establishment Clause. But even the most passionate scholars admit that the historical record is sparse.[19] There are no records of the debates in the state legislatures that ratified the Bill of Rights, including the First Amendment's Establishment Clause. Regarding the first Congress, which wrote its provisions, the Senate then met in secret session, so there are no records of its debates (although there does exist a skimpy record of actions taken upon motions and bills). The House of Representatives produced a similar record, and a *Journal* as well, but the *Journal* was uneven and approximate. Nonetheless, careful examination of the *Journal* and the historical record has convinced a number of scholars[20] and influenced some Supreme Court Justices[21] to conclude that the Establishment Clause was consistent with nonpreferential, indirect aid to religion.

This understanding does not require interpreting the Establishment Clause as an empowering constitutional provision.[22] Rather, it merely holds that the Establishment Clause was not intended to prevent Congress from passing general legislation that also (in a nondiscriminatory fashion) benefits religion. This could happen in a number of specific ways, especially given the broad powers granted to Congress in Article I, Section 8 (and especially by the Necessary and Proper Clause). A noteworthy example of this method of constitutional interpretation can be discovered by examining the passage of the Northwest Ordinance of 1789. The Ordinance was passed under the authority of Article IV, Section 3, which stipulated that "[t]he Congress shall have power to dispose of and make all needful rules and regulations respecting the territory or other property belonging to the United States...." Congress here explained why it set aside federal lands for the eventual building of schools: "Religion, morality, and knowledge being necessary to good government and the happiness of mankind, schools and the means of learning shall forever be encouraged." Thus, although the Constitution gives the national government no direct or explicit power over religion, the legislation clearly implied (according to one scholar) "that the schools, which were to be built on federal lands with federal assistance, were expected to promote religion as well as morality." ("In fact," continued this expert, "most schools at this time were church-run sectarian schools.")[23]

Noting that the Constitution does provide a way for the national government to aid religion, advocates of this accommodationist interpretation of the Establishment Clause argue that it was intended merely to prevent the government from showing religious preference. By adopting this viewpoint, they differ dramatically from advocates of our next, and last, interpretive school.

E. *The Establishment Clause prohibits the national government from providing any indirect aid to or support for religion or religiously affiliated organizations.* This interpretation amounts to a separationist interpretation of the Establishment Clause, specifically championing the separation of church and state. This view of the Establishment Clause is so commonly referred to that people sometimes speak of the separation of church and state as if it were the Establishment Clause, not to mention the whole of the religion clauses. However, it is important to remember that even if this interpretation is correct and the Establishment Clause was intended to prevent government from extending any aid to religion, it was only the national government, not the states, that was originally targeted.

Perhaps much of the popularity of this separationist understanding of the Establishment Clause can be traced to Justice Black's influential 1947 *Everson* opinion,[24] in which the Supreme Court for the first time defined the Establishment Clause and did so in staunch separationist terms. Of course, the total separation of church and state is an ideal; as Black and virtually everyone else has acknowledged, not even the most fervent advocate of the separation implied in the Establishment Clause would deny houses of worship police and fire protection. Still, some Supreme Court justices have advocated the position that government can do virtually nothing to benefit religion, even indirectly, slightly, or symbolically. Most explicit was Justice Douglas's formulation, which prohibited all financial support for religion and drew the line at a single penny of financial support. Unconstitutional governmental assistance included all financial aids:

> There are many "aids" to religion in this country at all levels of government. To mention but a few at the federal level, one might begin by observing that the very First Congress which wrote the First Amendment provided for chaplains in both Houses in the armed forces. There is compulsory chapel at the service academies, and religious services are held in federal hospitals and prisons. The President issues religious proclamations. The Bible is used for the administration of oaths. N.Y.A. and W.P.A. funds were available to parochial schools during the depression. Veterans receiving money under the G.I. Bill of 1944 could attend denominational schools, to which payments were made directly by the government. During World War II, federal money was contributed to denominational schools for the training of nurses. The benefits of the National School Lunch Act ... are available to students in private as well as public schools. The Hospital Survey and Construction Act of 1946 ... specifically made money available to non-public hospitals. The slogan "In God We Trust" is used by the Treasury Department, and Congress recently added God to the pledge of allegiance. There is Bible-reading in the schools of the District of Columbia, and religious instruction is given in the District National Training School for Boys. Religious organizations are exempt from

the federal income tax and are granted postal privileges. Up to defined limits … contributions to religious organizations are deductible for federal income tax purposes. There are no limits to the deductibility of gifts and bequests for religious institutions made under the federal gift and estate laws. This list of federal "aids" could easily be expanded and of course there is a long list in each state.[25]

Like its opposing nonpreferentialist interpretation (C), the separationist interpretation of the Establishment Clause also turns on what the first Congress intended when it passed the First Amendment. Like accommodationists, who base their understanding upon the historical record, advocates of the separationist interpretation of the Establishment Clause have also often based their position upon the Founders' understanding of the Establishment Clause and particularly upon the historical record of the first Congress.[26] Thus, to a significant degree, a dispassionate observer's understanding of this clause may well turn upon how the historical record is read.

THE SUPREME COURT AND
THE ESTABLISHMENT CLAUSE

When the Supreme Court has spoken about the Establishment Clause, it has often done so in terms of legal tests.[27] In fact, the legal tests reflect the Establishment Clause understandings detailed in the previous section. In this section, we will confine our remarks to a few general comments about these tests, as well as their underlying assumptions.

Regarding those assumptions, the following points should be stressed. First, every modern Supreme Court Establishment Clause decision and test (recalling that the Court's litigation of this Clause began in earnest in 1947) has assumed that the national government was prohibited from creating a national religion (interpretation A). Every contemporary Establishment Clause decision has also assumed that the Establishment Clause prevented the national government from aiding religion and religious organizations directly (interpretation C). Finally, every Establishment Clause case decided by the modern Supreme Court has held that these two prohibitions applied both to the national government and to the states, violating the original understanding of the Establishment Clause (B), which prohibited only the national government from interfering with state religious establishments or from directly supporting religion. Nor did it matter that virtually every constitutional authority has held that preserving state autonomy over religion was one reason for its adoption (a point that will be discussed shortly).

The continuing Establishment Clause dispute in the Supreme Court has been between Justices who favor an accommodationist interpretation (D) and those who champion a separationist interpretation (E). To the end of supporting one or the other of these two interpretations, the Court has fashioned and employed the following tests regarding the Establishment Clause.[28] Significantly, no Supreme Court test has yielded clear, consistent results.

The *wall of separation* explanation of the Establishment Clause as initially expounded in the Supreme Court's landmark Everson case did seem to present an obvious instance of a separationist interpretation of the Establishment Clause. But applying this test proved surprisingly difficult; in *Everson,* the challenged legislation (funding bus rides to schools that included a Catholic parochial school) was upheld although this test seemed to preclude conferring such a governmental benefit. Therefore, both because the wall of separation test's language was more separationist than some Supreme Court Justices were willing to accept, and because its application to specific circumstances and disputes was uncertain, it was soon abandoned.

In time, the dominant Establishment Clause test became the *Lemon* test.[29] It remained the prevalent Establishment Clause test from 1971 for well over two decades, although it eventually became subject to increasing academic and judicial criticism, and by 1994 it no longer had the support of a clear majority of Supreme Court Justices. Basically, the *Lemon* test held that if a disputed legislation was to pass Establishment Clause muster, it must have a secular legislative purpose, have a primary effect that neither advanced nor inhibited religion, and must not have excessively entangled government with religion. Laws evaluated on the basis of the *Lemon* test almost uniformly were found to have a valid secular purpose; those laws the Supreme Court overturned inevitably failed either the primary effect or the excessive entanglement prong of the test. Yet it is important to recognize that each of these two prongs of the Lemon test was subject to the Court's interpretation and could be applied strictly or loosely. Thus, whether disputed legislation had the permissible primary effect of advancing a permitted secular or impermissible religious goal was clearly a matter of judicial interpretation. Similarly, the definition of entanglement[30] could be applied in different ways, depending upon what the Court regarded as excessive.

Thus, the meaning of the *Lemon* test was all in its interpretation and application. Loosely applied, the test merely required that the effect of governmental programs have a significant secular effect and that whatever interaction existed between government and religion be not "too much"—whatever "too much" meant. (This approach was sometimes described by Justices as promoting neutrality among believers and between believers and disbelievers, and was characterized as benevolent neutrality or wholesome neutrality, etc.) Interpreted or applied loosely, this application of Lemon represented an accommodationist approach to the Establishment Clause. On the other hand, a more rigid or unyielding application of the same test (which asked if the disputed legislation in any way markedly aided religion or religious institutions or if it required even modest church–state interaction or involvement) invalidated most contested legislation and therefore advanced a far more separationist understanding of the Establishment Clause. Naturally, any constitutional test that yielded such varying results tended to produce unstable law, and for this reason (among others) *Lemon* was widely criticized by legal authorities.

In the 1990s, as the *Lemon* test declined in influence, two alternate Establishment Clause tests were advocated by individual Justices as possible replacements (neither garnering the support of anything close to a clear majority of the Court, however). Justice O'Connor championed a nonendorsement test[31] that prohibited "direct government action endorsing religion or a particular religion's practice ... because it sends the message to nonadherents that they are outsiders, not full members of the political community, and an accompanying message to adherents that they are insiders, favored members of the political community."[32] The nonendorsement test permits indirect public aid to religion so long as government does not endorse it. This approach appears permissive regarding general governmental social welfare programs that include (but are not limited to) religious organizations; it appears restrictive when government institutes or allows religious symbolism or ritual (such as prayer in the public schools or holiday displays on public property). In this fashion, the nonendorsement test attempts to produce more predictable results than did the Lemon test. Because the law is less settled in the first area (involving generalized public funding that also aids religion) than it is in areas where government directly aids religion, it is probably true that O'Connor's formulation more often resolves the ambiguity inherent in the Lemon test in favor of an accommodationist, nondiscriminatory approach to the Establishment Clause (approach D).

By contrast, Justice Kennedy has championed a *noncoercion* test.[33] He has stated it by way of addressing "the fundamental limitations imposed by the Establishment Clause":

> It is beyond dispute that, at a minimum, the Constitution guarantees that government may not coerce anyone to support or participate in religion or its exercise, or otherwise act in a way which "establishes a [state] religion or religious faith, or tends to do so."[34]

By "coercion," Kennedy meant psychological coercion. For instance, in *Lee v. Weisman,* Kennedy successfully advocated overturning a nonsectarian invocation and benediction delivered by a rabbi at a middle school graduation ceremony because an objecting student was required to participate in a religious exercise. Especially disconcerting for Kennedy was that public and peer pressure required her to stand, or at the very least, maintain a respectful silence during the invocation and benediction. Thus, "psychological coercion existed," for "[r]esearch in psychology supports the common assumption that adolescents are often susceptible to pressure from their peers towards conformity, and that the influence is strongest in matters of social convention."[35] It made no legal difference for Kennedy that the student, Deborah Weisman, was not required to attend graduation. Kennedy argued that graduation was one of life's most significant occasions; therefore, to say that a teenage student has a real choice not to attend her graduation was "formalistic in the extreme."[36]

If adopted by the Court, Kennedy's psychological coercion test strikes a middle position between an accommodationist and separationist interpretation of the Establishment Clause. As applied, it was likely that Kennedy's test would produce sharply separationist effects (in the realm of prohibiting prayers in the public schools) while accommodating indirect financial aid to religion and perhaps public expressions of faith (Thanksgiving proclamations invoking God's name, religious holiday displays, etc.). Like O'Connor's nonendorsement test, Kennedy also intended to fashion an Establishment Clause standard that would yield predictable and consistent results. Also like O'Connor's test in light of outstanding issues facing the Court, Kennedy's approach was, on balance, probably more accommodationist in spirit than separationist. Still, it appears unlikely that Kennedy's coercion test will ever become a dominant Establishment Clause test. A large number of Justices have indicated their opposition, some because the test appears too friendly toward religion and others because it appears not friendly enough.[37] Furthermore, the test muddles the distinction between Establishment and Free Exercise Clause protections.[38] This is a particularly disconcerting problem, for, as we will see, the Free Exercise Clause, like the Establishment Clause, has been the source of varied and conflicting judicial interpretations. It, too, has provided the Supreme Court with formidable interpretive challenges.

THE FREE EXERCISE CLAUSE

Sparse as the evidence is regarding the Establishment Clause, the precise meaning of the Free Exercise Clause is, by almost everyone's admission, even more elusive. References to it in the 1789 Congressional debates surrounding its adoption were infrequent. Although a number of constitutional authorities have not always agreed with Michael Malbin's interpretation of the Free Exercise Clause's meaning, there is little controversy regarding his belief about the methodological complexity inherent in determining that meaning:

> The meaning of the free exercise clause is still unclear. After reading the congressional debates, we can guess that its purpose may have had something to do with the relationship between conscientious belief and its expression, but we are not given enough material to be more precise than that.[39]

Little wonder that scholars predominantly focus upon contemporary state practices in attempting to fix the Free Exercise Clause's original meaning. Commonly, it is acknowledged that individual religious belief (frequently referred to as a right to conscience) was protected from government interference and persecution, and religiously motivated actions often could be similarly protected. The essential dispute among scholars about the Free Exercise Clause has focused upon whether it provides an independent authority for the courts to enforce a right of religious exemption from the secular law. Yet inherent in the common dissection of state religious practices undertaken to resolve this dispute is something of an methodological–historical anomaly.

As with the Establishment Clause, the Free Exercise Clause was originally understood as a restriction only upon the national government and not upon the states. However, since there is so little evidence as to the precise meaning of the clause, the scrupulous examination of state practices to determine the scope of the clause's originally intended restrictions upon the national government may perhaps be necessary, but still seems curious.

Essentially, two fundamentally different interpretations of Free Exercise are maintained by constitutional scholars. Their main point of difference is whether the federal courts are sometimes obligated to extend exemptions to the civil law under the clause. Furthermore, it is worth noting that while Establishment Clause controversies frequently focus on the larger, mainstream religions (which usually are most often aided by broad-based secular legislation), Free Exercise cases generally, and the exemption question specifically, most often focus upon the (unanticipated) impact of government programs on minority religious practices. The two, contrasting understandings of the Free Exercise Clause are treated below.

A. *The Free Exercise Clause protects freedom of religious belief and some religious practices. Perhaps Congress (that is, the legislature) can exempt religious practitioners from the general law, but the Free Exercise Clause creates no right of exemption under the Free Exercise Clause that the courts are obligated to enforce.* This approach is what we will refer to as the *narrow* interpretation of the Free Exercise Clause. This understanding begins with the recognition that in the late eighteenth century, religious free exercise according to conscience was widely regarded as a personal matter. Religious beliefs and opinions were certainly protected under the Constitution; perhaps the Free Exercise Clause was intended to emphasize that freedom of religious speech, like political speech, was also explicitly entitled to constitutional protection.[40] Furthermore, a citizen cannot be punished for religious conduct solely because it is religious, or if it violates no secular law, the peace, and civic order. Thus, the Free Exercise Clause meant that the national government could not single out any religion or focus on any person because of his or her religious belief or conduct. According to this interpretation of religious free exercise, the government cannot treat religious practitioners differently from other citizens in terms of both their rights and obligations. According to this point of view, evidence does not support any intention by the Framers to provide a constitutional right of religious exemption under the Free Exercise Clause; rather, they favored equal civil rights. Religious liberty and free exercise are best secured by treating religious practitioners and those who believed and acted according to the dictates of their conscience no differently from any other citizen. The civil law required such an approach, and the Free Exercise Clause ensured that different legal standards could not be applied to different religious practitioners. Historically, this interpretation of the Free Exercise Clause makes sense, for "[i]n eighteenth-century America, where varied Christian sects bickered with one another and thrived, a constitutional right to have different civil obligations on account of religious differences was precisely what dissenters did not demand."[41]

B. *The Free Exercise Clause protects freedom of religious belief and some religious practices. The Court has the duty to exempt religious practitioners from the requirements of the secular law.* Again, advocates of this *broader* interpretation argue that religious beliefs are protected by the Free Exercise Clause. Generally, so are most religious practices that do not adversely affect society or violate the secular law. However, when (originally the national) government passes a law that inadvertently impacts religious conduct, under this interpretation, government has endangered a citizen's right under the Free Exercise Clause. In such circumstances, the courts are duty-bound to balance the government's interest against the individual's right of religious free exercise. On the Supreme Court, advocates of this judicial interpretation of the Free Exercise Clause often have argued for a fairly stringent standard of judicial review of government (that is, one tilted in favor of the individual), suggesting that when government hampers religious belief or practice, then it must demonstrate a compelling state interest in passing such a law (and sometimes also that no other less intrusive method of securing the same governmental objective was available).[42] In other words, according to this interpretation, religious free exercise is protected by singling out affected religious believers and practitioners for special religious protection under the Constitution.

Frequently, this interpretation of the Free Exercise Clause also relies upon historical inference. In recent years, the most influential advocate of this position has been Professor Michael McConnell.[43] McConnell has argued persistently that examining history leads to the conclusion that the Free Exercise Clause may well have been originally intended to exempt religious practitioners from civil laws that negatively affected religious practices. McConnell has not argued that this free exercise right was unlimited, only that peaceful religious practices that did not endanger important governmental interests were likely to be entitled to constitutional protection. Still, as we observe below, this interpretation of the Free Exercise Clause suggests a historical rationale for the Supreme Court's active subordination of the secular law, when practicable, to each person's individual judgment regarding the primacy of his or her religious obligations.

THE SUPREME COURT AND
THE FREE EXERCISE CLAUSE

Essentially, the Supreme Court has had to choose between the two interpretations of the Free Exercise Clause detailed above. Fortunately, the Court's interpretative approach can be described rather straightforwardly. Until 1963, the Supreme Court followed the first, narrower approach. Although it acknowledged the right of the Congress to exempt citizens from civic obligations (especially regarding exemption for conscientious objectors to the draft), it also never held that the Free Exercise Clause exempted citizens from government regulation. From 1963 until 1990, the Court often (but not always) employed the broader Free Exercise Clause test (B), which required the Court to balance the government's interest in maintaining and effectively administering its programs against the right of citizens whose religious practices were adversely affected. Supreme Court-ordered exemptions from the civil law sometimes resulted, particularly when unemployment compensation laws required, as a matter of law, that religious citizens work during religiously ordained days of rest.[44]

In 1990, with the Supreme Court's decision in the *Smith* case,[45] the bitterly divided Court indicated that it again favored a narrower interpretation of the Free Exercise Clause. It now viewed its previous decisions in the unemployment compensation cases as an aberration (arguing that only in these cases was the Free Exercise Clause alone the constitutional basis of denying a government benefit).[46] Amid significant controversy, the *Smith* majority contended that the Supreme Court had "never held that an individual's religious beliefs excuse him from compliance with an otherwise valid law prohibiting conduct that the State is free to regulate."[47] Allowing a limited scope for precedent, *Smith's* majority indicated its preference for Free Exercise interpretation A, which deferred religiously based exemptions to the legislature. *Smith* created a mountain of criticism in legal journals and led Congress to pass the Religious Freedom Restoration Act of 1993, which essentially overturned *Smith* and reestablished the broader interpretation of the Free Exercise Clause (B).

RECONCILING THE RELIGION CLAUSES

It is sometimes argued that the Establishment and Free Exercise clauses make up a single constitutional statement about the relationship between government and religion. There are two incentives for supporting this approach. First, some constitutional scholars believe that the two religion clauses were intended to serve a single purpose; therefore, a single statement of this purpose best captures its meaning. Second, other scholars have been motivated by an attempt to resolve a legal–logical problem that sometimes has arisen as a result of Supreme Court jurisprudence. When the Supreme Court adopted a broad free exercise interpretation, it inevitably favored a single religion or religious practitioner by granting to it a specific exemption from a government rule or law. But this interpretation of the Free Exercise Clause appears to conflict with virtually any interpretation of the Establishment Clause ever adopted by the Supreme Court (for all interpretations prohibit favoring any religion). Thus, there seems to exist a "seemingly irreconcilable conflict: on the one hand the Court has said that the Establishment Clause forbids government action whose purpose is to aid religion, but on the other hand the Court has held that the Free Exercise Clause may require government action to accommodate religion."[48] Although this dilemma has, from time to time, been commented upon by several Supreme Court Justices, reconciling the religion clauses has often proven to be something of a theoretical embarrassment that most Supreme Court Judges have avoided addressing.

Therefore, scholars have been the ones who have most frequently and persuasively addressed this problem. Not surprisingly, they have agreed upon the most general goals inherent in the Constitution, the First Amendment, and the religion clauses. Both government and religion were to be spared each other's domination. In a popular government (that is, a government beholden to majority rule) founded upon the precept that individuals possess natural rights to life, liberty, and the pursuit of happiness, it was particularly important that those rights be safeguarded from tyrannical majorities if government and religion were not to dominate each other. The successful accomplishment of this goal would secure political freedom by avoiding the religious strife and persecution that elsewhere had endangered those rights. That these are general goals of the religion clauses is well accepted by virtually every constitutional scholar and Supreme Court Justice.

At a general level, then, this understanding accommodated the generally acknowledged purpose of the two clauses. But how was specific constitutional language—language with the potential to produce contradictory results—to be translated into coherent constitutional doctrine? Here, its advocates contend, lies the true advantage of the single-meaning approach to the religion clauses. Yet even among scholars who advocate this approach to the religion clauses, unanimity does not exist. Interestingly, their reconciliations have tended to mirror the broad and narrow Free Exercise Clause interpretations described earlier. Therefore, some scholars believe that reconciling the two clauses is best accounted for by a broad *religion-conscious* pro-liberty interpretation that explicitly acknowledges that the clauses exist to protect religious liberty from government interference. Other scholars contend that the accepted goals and meaning of the religion clauses can best be maintained by a narrower constitutional understanding that does not take religion into account—in other words, by a *religion-blind* pro-neutrality constitutional interpretation that requires a governmental policy neutral to believers and between believers and nonbelievers. Although our brief discussion captures only the basics of two of the best-known attempts to reconcile the religion clauses, it should prove helpful in promoting an understanding of how the two clauses can be reconciled according to a single meaning.

A. *The Establishment Clause and the Free Exercise Clause were intended to protect religious liberty. Reconciling them requires that they be read together to have the single meaning of securing religious liberty from unwarranted governmental interference.* This reconciliation begins by recognizing what appears to be the primary truth of the First Amendment: namely, that its purpose and language are to protect liberty—of speech, of press, of assembly—but first of all, of religion. Once this truth is recognized, there will be no tension or conflict between the Establishment Clause and the Free Exercise Clause:

> There are not two religion clauses. There is but one religion clause. The stipulation is that "Congress shall make no law," and the rest of the clause consists of participial modifiers explaining what kind of law Congress shall not make....

The no–establishment part of the religion clause is entirely and without remainder in the service of free exercise. Free exercise is the end; no es-tablishment is a necessary means to that end. No establishment simply makes no sense on its own.[49]

Generally speaking, the pro–liberty reconciliation of the religion clauses generally champions a broad reading of the Free Exercise Clause and a narrow reading of the Establishment Clause, each of which proves quite friendly to-ward religion. Free exercise protection extends to all religions special protec-tion from unintended governmental intrusion and usually requires the courts to extend careful review to protect religious practitioners. Furthermore, a pro-liberty reconciliation of the two clauses would place no Establishment Clause bar on incidentally aiding religious institutions and organizations as part of a valid secular program.[50] Thus, the pro–liberty, religion-conscious reconcilia-tion of the two clauses favors religion by permitting both governmental pro-grams that can confer benefits upon religion while subjecting these and other governmental programs to review (and often to strict scrutiny) if they appear to hinder or oppress religious practice.

B. *The Establishment Clause and the Free Exercise Clause, taken together, create a powerful barrier prohibiting government from favoring or disfavoring religion or any reli-gions. The clauses require that the government be neutral regarding religion, and neu-trality can best be secured by requiring that government not explicitly single out religion for advantage or disadvantage.* Although this neutrality approach to resolving reli-gion clause tensions has been stated and applied in various ways, it usually as-sumes a religion-blind approach to those clauses. Government, when passing laws or dispensing benefits, cannot explicitly take account of religion. True religious freedom is best ensured when government cannot single out religion in any way.

Formulations of the neutrality principle vary from its simple proclamation to far more elaborate or elegant formulations. The best known of them has been that of Professor Philip Kurland, who contended that the religion clauses can be read together to mandate that "government cannot utilize religion as a standard for action or inaction because these clauses prohibit classification in terms of religion either to confer a benefit or to impose a burden."[51] Gener-ally, Kurland's neutrality standard can best be understood as combining an ac-commodationist interpretation of the Establishment Clause with a narrow interpretation of the Free Exercise Clause, with neither allowing government to aid religion in a nondiscriminatory fashion while at the same time prevent-ing government from exempting religion from the unintentional effects of secular legislation.[52] The neutrality standard sees religion clause goals (includ-ing religious freedom) being best actualized by prohibiting differentiated treat-ment of religion or any religion. However, it should be realized that adopting a neutrality interpretation of the two religion clauses does not automatically pro-duce obvious answers in concrete cases. Advocates of this school of constitu-tional interpretation still often differ in how they would apply this standard.[53]

MAKING SENSE OF
THE RELIGION CLAUSES

So far, our study of the religion clauses has yielded unclear results. The full meaning of the Establishment Clause and the Free Exercise Clause remains controversial, and the Supreme Court's interpretations of these two clauses have been unclear or conflicting. Furthermore, academic efforts to render a single meaning from the two clauses have not provided a straightforward resolution to their possible conflict. Little wonder, then, that making sense of the religion clauses proves no easy task.

Unfortunately, if anything, we are understating the difficulty of making sense of the Supreme Court's interpretation of the Constitution. Significant interpretive assumptions by the Supreme Court have rendered any coherent interpretation of the religion clauses virtually impossible. Specifically, we refer to important Supreme Court interpretive reevaluations of the meaning of federalism and religion. Also germane is the Supreme Court's understanding of its own role in the American political process. We will conclude this chapter by briefly examining each of these barriers to constitutional coherence.

Federalism

We have already observed that it is certain that the Bill of Rights generally, and the First Amendment specifically, was intended to restrict only the newly created national government. Furthermore, the Establishment Clause, by common consensus, was not only intended to prohibit the newly created government from founding a national church, but was enacted precisely because of the fear that such a church would overwhelm the church–state relationships then existing within the states. In other words, the religion clauses were intended to be something more than a charter of individual liberties, for they "reflect not only a philosophy of freedom but a theory of federalism." Indeed, "[w]e often forget that the framers were as much concerned with safeguarding the powers of the states as they were with protecting the immunities of the people."[54]

In light of this indisputable historical recognition, it is noteworthy that the Supreme Court has not only ignored the First Amendment's historical meaning but has actually reversed it. The vehicle of this historical reversal has been the doctrine of selective incorporation through the Fourteenth Amendment. The Fourteenth Amendment explicitly prohibits states from passing or enforcing any law that "shall abridge the privileges or immunities of citizens of the United States" or deprive "any person of life, liberty, or property, without due process of law, nor deny to any person within its jurisdiction the equal protection of the laws." In 1940 the Supreme Court selectively incorporated the First Amendment's Free Exercise Clause, arguing that the Fourteenth Amendment contained a guarantee of the free exercise of religion against state regulation.[55] In 1947 it explicitly did the same for the Establishment Clause,[56] performing something of a linguistic somersault.[57] In each instance, the

Supreme Court merely asserted that the Fourteenth Amendment made the Establishment Clause and Free Exercise Clause applicable to the states. No proof, no evidence, and no authority were provided to bolster the assertion.

For proving the assertion was impossible. Especially in the case of the Establishment Clause, the Supreme Court's legal assertion regarding the clause's scope, and the Court's utter disregard of the federalism aspect of that clause, did not simply have the effect of ignoring history; *it reversed it.* Originally, the Establishment Clause intended to keep the national government out of the affairs of the states, on the theory that American religious and civil liberty could best be secured by limiting only the national government. The Establishment Clause was no bar to the states' aiding religion. Now the Supreme Court held that this same Constitutional clause prohibited the very pro-religious action it previously allowed. The resulting logical problem is formidable and has not been lost on constitutional commentators:

> As originally understood, the Establishment Clause prevented the federal government from interfering with state authority over religion. However, incorporation achieves the opposite result—the elimination of such authority. Moreover, the incorporated Establishment Clause reflects only half of its original mission of neither forbidding nor requiring the states to have established churches. Although the states are not required to establish a religion, the Clause now *forbids* the states from establishing one. In short, not only is it impossible for the Establishment Clause to be incorporated while accurately reflecting its original federalist purpose, but is also cannot be incorporated without eviscerating its raison d'etre.[58]

The loss of the federalism inherent in the Bill of Rights not only renders discussion of what government can or cannot do according to the religion clauses unintelligible; it also makes state governmental cooperation with religion far more problematical than was intended. Nor is this the only reason that it is difficult to make sense of the law regarding the religion clauses.

The Meaning of Religion

Here (for better or for worse), the Supreme Court's understanding of this concept has also changed radically. As stated in the First Amendment, the idea of religion generally assumed (but was not necessarily strictly confined to) Christianity of one kind or another. The irreducible core of the eighteenth-century Western idea of religion was a belief in God. Noah Webster's first dictionary appropriately captured the traditional understanding:

> Religion, in its most comprehensive sense, includes a belief in the being and perfection of God, in the revelation of his will to man, in man's obligation to obey his commands, in a state of reward and punishment, and in man's accountableness to God; and also true godliness or piety of life, with the practice of all moral duties. It therefore comprehends theology, as a system of doctrines or principles, as well as practical piety; for the practice of moral duties without a belief in a divine lawgiver, and without reference to his will or commands, is not religion.[59]

This same understanding was accepted throughout the nineteenth century. The Supreme Court's most quoted pronouncement on the subject, formulated in 1890, observed that religion had "reference to one's views of his relations to his Creator, and to the obligations they impose of reverence for his being and character, and of obedience to his will."[60]

Beginning in 1947, this idea of religion has been significantly expanded to the point that it is presently questionable if religion has any distinct meaning at all. In 1947, in the *Everson* case, Justice Black, writing for the Court, listed Non-believers (capitalized in the case) along with Catholics, Lutherans, Mohammedans, Baptists, Jews, and Presbyterians as protected by the Free Exercise Clause from governmental discrimination in affording benefits. In 1961, in the case of *Torcaso* v. *Watkins,*[61] Justice Black, once again writing for the Court, counted among religions such well-established theologies as Taoism and Buddhism (which did not entail a belief in God) but also nonbelievers, Secular Humanists, and Ethical Culturalists, all of which explicitly denied such a belief. In *Torcaso,* as in *Everson,* Black did not reveal how religion might entail both the manifestation and the rejection of faith; for him, and for the Court, religion seemed to be *any* self-proclaimed disposition toward or away from God or godliness.

Justice Black has been unusually active in the Supreme Court's definitions of the meaning of religion. In a well-known 1970 conscientious objector case, Black, writing for the Court,[62] addressed the question of congressional intent and Supreme Court precedent in order to determine what "religious" beliefs qualified an individual for military combat exemption. In that opinion, Black explained his concept of the meaning of religion. He argued that ascertaining an individual's religious beliefs turned on determining whether that individual's ethical and/or moral beliefs played the same central role in that person's life that traditional religious beliefs had historically occupied in people's lives:

> If an individual deeply and sincerely holds beliefs which are purely ethical or moral in source and content but which nevertheless impose upon him a duty of conscience to refrain from participating in any war at any time, those beliefs certainly occupy in the life of that individual "a place parallel to that filled by ... God" in traditionally religious persons. Because his beliefs function as a religion in his life, such an individual is as much entitled to a "religious" conscientious objection exemption ... as is someone who derives his conscientious opposition to war from traditional religious tradition.[63]

For Black, and apparently for the Supreme Court, the key to religion was that it involved beliefs that had a moral content, that it occupied an important place in a person's life, and that it was sincerely believed. Black ruled out only beliefs not deeply held or based solely upon considerations of policy or expediency. Yet Black's argument that beliefs can be perceived as performing the function of religion is no definition of religion at all.[64] What matters is not the content of beliefs but the role those beliefs play in a person's life. In the end, Black and the Supreme Court furnished a psychological, not a substantive, understanding of religion. Perhaps this result is appropriate, given that religion itself is increasingly prone to be seen in psychological terms. Still, given the Supreme Court's relativistic and psychologized formulation of religious faith, it is hard to see how the Constitution's guarantee of religious free exercise means anything more than a general guarantee of personal freedom. Despite the Supreme Court's decisions and rulings that endlessly analyze the unique and continuing social and legal importance of religion and religious exercise in the United States, the Court's own decisions have rendered religion an indistinct and therefore virtually meaningless concept.

The Changing Nature of the Supreme Court

Coincident with the Court's outright reversal of the federalism component of the religion clauses, and with its obscuring of any clear meaning of religion, it is no wonder that the Court's religion clause jurisprudence makes little sense. Closely correlated with these doctrinal issues of interpretation is an important recognition: the Supreme Court today plays a far more active role in the affairs of the United States than was originally anticipated or historically practiced. It is not obvious whether the Justices' desire to increase the legal and political leverage of the Court is the cause and the shift in constitutional interpretation is the result, or vice versa; all that is indisputably obvious is that the two trends have occurred together.

In 1969, in a spirited dissenting opinion, Justice Black objected to a Supreme Court decision holding that public school students who wore black armbands protesting the Vietnam war were engaging in a form of (symbolically) protected free speech.[65] Near the end of his dissent, Black observed this: "I, for one, am not fully persuaded school pupils are wise enough, even with this Court's expert help from Washington, to run the 23,290 public school systems in our 50 States."[66] Obviously, Black doubted the wisdom of the Supreme Court's active intervention into the local school districts under the application of the First Amendment's free speech provision. Yet Black specifically, and the federal courts generally, has shown no hesitation whatsoever regarding the Supreme Court's active intervention under the authority of the religion clauses into virtually every aspect of American life, and especially into the schools. Rightly or wrongly, the Supreme Court has overturned a minute of silence in the public schools because a teacher had suggested prayer as one option and impermissible prayer had taken place; a federal court also ruled unconstitutional the practice of a kindergarten teacher who asked her class to recite the following:[67]

> We thank you for the flowers so sweet;
> We thank you for the food we eat;
> We thank you for the birds that sing;
> We thank you for everything.

Since the 1960s, the Supreme Court has most carefully examined many governmental practices that, in earlier days, would have escaped judicial scrutiny. The sheer number of cases reviewed by the federal courts has necessarily complicated the law and made its consistent interpretation and application even more complex. Still, advocates of the Supreme Court's growing activism have applauded the Court's enthusiastic concern for constitutional principles and civil liberties. Critics of the Court have doubted the validity of the constitutional doctrine under which it acted and asked if many of the issues it addressed were better handled at the local level through the ordinary political processes. Therefore, according to some observers, it is the role of the Court, as well as the law it applies and interprets, that has added to the complexity surrounding the relationship between church and state.

NOTES

1. See *Flast v. Cohen,* 392 U.S. 83 (1968). The Supreme Court declared a rule of standing that a taxpayer could sue under the Establishment Clause to enjoin federal expenditures paid to religiously supported schools.

2. Joseph Story, *Commentaries on the Constitution of the United States* (Boston: Little, Brown, 1891), vol. I, par. 400, p. 305.

3. Story, p. 305.

4. In several key respects, the discussion here closely follows and is indebted to Michael W. McConnell, "Accommodation of Religion: An Update and a Response to the Critics," *The George Washington Law Review,* vol. 60, no. 3 (March 1992), pp. 690–91.

5. On the issue of the Constitution and politically disadvantaged groups, see Robert Goldwin's lead essay in the book of the same title, *Why Blacks, Women, and Jews Are Not Mentioned in the Constitution,* and other unorthodox views (Washington, AEI Press, 1990), pp. 9–36.

6. Story, vol. II, par. 1877, p. 632.

7. Alexander Hamilton, James Madison, and John Jay, *The Federalist* (Middletown, CT: Wesleyan Univ. Press, 1961), ed. Jacob Cooke, no. 15, p. 93.

8. The matter was settled conclusively and uncontroversially by Chief Justice Marshall in *Barron v. Baltimore,* 7 Peters 243 (1833) at 247:

The constitution was ordained and established by the people of the United States for themselves, for their own government, and not for *the government of the individual states. Each state established a constitution for itself, and in that constitution provided such limitations and restrictions on the powers of its particular government as its judgment dictated. The people of the United States framed such a government for the United States as they supposed best adapted to their situation, and best calculated to promote their interests. The powers they conferred on this government were to be exercised by itself; and the limitations on power, if expressed in general terms, are naturally, and, we think, necessarily, applicable to the government created by that instrument. They are limitations of power granted in the instrument itself; not of distinct governments, framed by different persons and for different purposes.*

9. Regarding this last point, see Hamilton, Madison, and Jay, no. 84, p. 579.

10. The definition is from Noah Webster, *An American Dictionary of the English Language* (New York: Johnson Reprint, 1970), vol. I.

11. Leonard Levy, *The Establishment Clause: Religion and the First Amendment* (New York: Macmillan, 1986), p. 61. Also see Chapter 2, page 42, note 7.

12. Story, vol. II, par. 1880, p. 634.

13. Thomas J. Curry, *The First Freedoms: Church and State in America to the Passage of the First Amendment* (New York: Oxford Univ. Press, 1986), p. 194.

14. See "Rethinking the Incorporation of the Establishment Clause: A Federalist View," *Harvard Law Review,* vol. 105 (1992), p. 1703.

15. The direct/indirect distinction is not usually made by scholars, who generally focus their arguments on the more general question of whether the Establishment Clause permits or prohibits programs and policies that benefit religion. Nonetheless, the distinction is useful, for it reminds us of how far we have come from distinctions quite familiar to the Founders.

16. See Treaty between the United States and the Kaskaskia Tribe of Indians, August 13, 1803, 7 stat. 78, 79.

17. Actually, the issue of the government signing a treaty that it is entitled to enter into but that favors a particular religion (Roman Catholicism), hence violating the Constitution (here the Establishment Clause), raises, at the very least, a difficult and perhaps irresolvable constitutional conflict.

18. Curry, pp. 218, 219.

19. See Levy, p. 187.

20. For example, see James Antieau, Arthus Downey, and Edward Roberts, *Freedom from Federal Establishment: Formation and Early History of the First Amendment's Religion Clauses* (Milwaukee: Bruce, 1964); Robert Cord, *Separation of Church and State: Historical Fact and Current Fiction* (New York: Lambeth, 1982); and Michael Malbin, *Religion and Politics: The Intentions of the Authors of the First Amendment* (Washington, DC: American Enterprise, 1978).

21. For example, see Justice Rehnquist's dissent in *Wallace* v. *Jaffree,* 472 U.S. 38 (1985), and Justice Scalia's historical analysis in *Lee* v. *Weisman,* 112 U.S. 2649 (1992).

22. But see Levy, pp. 106, 116–17.

23. Malbin, pp. 14–15.

24. *Everson* v. *Board of Education,* 330 U.S. 1 (1947). The case is discussed in Chapter 13, p. 237.

25. 370 U.S. 421 (1962) at 436, n. 1. Douglas's footnote cites: "Fellman, *The Limits of Freedom* (1959), pp. 40–41." It is interesting to observe that Douglas earlier had advocated an accommodationist interpretation of the Establishment Clause; in *Zorach* v. *Clausen,* 343 U.S. 306 (1952), Douglas upheld a time-release asserting that "[w]e are a religious people whose institutions presuppose a Supreme Being"

(at 313) after contending (312–313) the following:

The First Amendment, however, does not say that in every and all respects there shall be a separation of Church and State.... Otherwise the state and religion would be aliens to each other—hostile, suspicious, and even unfriendly. Churches could not be required to pay even property taxes. Municipalities would not be permitted to render police or fire protection to their religious groups.... Prayers in our legislative halls; the appeals to the Almighty in the messages of the Chief Executive; the proclamations making Thanksgiving Day a holiday; "so help me God" in our courtroom oaths—these and all other references to the Almighty that run through our laws, our public rituals our ceremonies would be flouting the First Amendment. A fastidious atheist or agnostic could even object to the supplication with which the Court opens each session: "God save the United States and this Honorable Court."

26. Levy, pp. 63–119; also see Leo Pfeffer, *Church, State, and Freedom* (Boston: Beacon, 1967), rev. ed.

27. Sometimes, however, the Court has explicitly rejected the proposition that the Establishment Clause can be examined by a single test. See, for example, *Lynch* v. *Donnelly,* 465 U.S. 668 (1984) at 678–79.

28. This is not to say that all Establishment Clause cases have been decided by the Supreme Court according to a specific judicially formulated test. In fact, sometimes the Court's eschewing of a test speaks volumes (as when the Court in *Marsh* v. *Chambers,* 463 U.S. 783 [1983] avoided even mentioning the *Lemon* test, choosing to base its accommodationist decision (permitting state-supported chaplains in Nebraska's state legislature) upon supportive historical practices.

29. The origin of the test was *Lemon* v. *Kurtzman,* 403 U.S. 602 (1971). The case is discussed in Chapter 13, pp. 241–43.

30. Usually, entanglement dealt with the amount of administrative review and bureaucratic interaction government imposed upon religion; however, for a while excessive entanglement also referred to particular issues that were likely to give rise to political divisions along religious lines. When applied, this interpretation of

the excessive entanglement test tended to invalidate legislative programs. Still, there did not seem to be any defensible constitutional basis for applying this version of the excessive entanglement test, and it was eventually dropped.

31. Justice O'Connor first proposed this standard in *Lynch* v. *Donnelly,* 465 U.S. 668, at 591–93 (1984).

32. As stated in her concurring opinion in *Wallace* v. *Jaffree,* 472 U.S. 38 (1985) at 69.

33. See Justice Kennedy's opinions in *Allegheny* v. *ACLU,* 492 U.S. 573 (1989) at 659 and in *Lee* v. *Weisman.* It is significant of the Supreme Court's confusing jurisprudence in this area that it previously distinguished *the Free Exercise Clause* from the Establishment Clause because the Free Exercise Clause required a showing of coercion. See *Abbington School District* v. *Schempp,* 374 U.S. 203 (1963) at 223. ("Hence it is necessary in a free exercise case for one to show the coercive effect of the enactment as it operates against him in the practice of his religion. The distinction between the two clauses is apparent—a violation of the Free Exercise Clause is predicated on coercion while the Establishment Clause violation need not be so attended.")

34. *Ibid.* The cite is to *Lynch* v. *Donnelly,* 465 U.S. 668 (1984) at 678.

35. *Ibid.* Kennedy cited two psychological/ sociological scholarly articles to support his position.

36. *Ibid.*

37. Seven justices in *Lee* explicitly disavowed the test. Scalia's dismissal of the test as being wrong in principle is notable for its frank language:

The Court presumably would separate graduation invocations and benedictions from other instances of public preservation and transmission of religious beliefs on the ground that they involve "psychological coercion." I find it a sufficient embarrassment that our Establishment Clause jurisprudence regarding holiday displays … has come to "requir[e] scrutiny more commonly associated with interior decorators than with the judiciary." But interior decorating is a rock-hard science compared to psychology practiced by amateurs. A few citations of "[r]esearch in psychology" that have no particular bearing

upon the precise issue here, cannot disguise the fact that the Court has gone beyond the realm where judges know what they are doing. The Court's argument that state officials have "coerced" students to take part in the invocation and benediction at graduation ceremonies is, not to put too fine a point on it, incoherent. Ibid.

38. See note 31.

39. Malbin, p. 19.

40. Malbin, p. 37.

41. Philip Hamburger, "A Constitutional Right of Religious Exemption: An Historical Perspective," *The George Washington Law Review,* vol. 60, no. 4 (April 1992), p. 948.

42. See especially *Sherbert* v. *Verner,* 374 U.S. 398 (1963).

43. McConnell has written prolifically on this subject. Particularly informative are "The Origins and Historical Understanding of Free Exercise of Religion," *Harvard Law Review* 103 (1990), p. 1409; and "Accommodation of Religion: An Update and a Response to the Critics," *The George Washington Law Review* 60 (March, 1992), p. 685.

44. *Sherbert* v. *Verner,* 374 U.S. 398 (1963): *Thomas* v. *Review Board of Indiana Employment Security Division,* 450 U.S. 707 (1981): *Hobbie* v. *Unemployment Appeals Commission of Florida,* 480 U.S. 136 (1987). Also see *Frazee* v. *Illinois Department of Employment Security,* 489 U.S. 829 (1989).

45. *Employment Division, Department of Human Resources of Oregon* v. *Smith,* 494 U.S. 872 (1990).

46. "Alone" here includes the Fourteenth Amendment, which extended the Free Exercise Clause to the states.

47. Smith at 878–79.

48. Jesse Choper, "The Religion Clauses of the First Amendment: Reconciling the Conflict," *University of Pittsburgh Law Review,* vol. 41 (1980), p. 673. Another potential conflict rarely discussed asks if when the legislature furnishes exemptions, as for example in the case of conscientious objectors to military service, do such exemptions breach the Establishment Clause by favoring a particular religious understanding? The Court has never thought so, but this does present an interesting question.

49. Richard John Neuhaus, "A New Order of Religious Freedom," *First Things,* no. 20 (February 1992), p. 15.

50. We would go so far as to suggest that it is not obvious why, at least in theory, this interpretation would preclude direct aid to religion, or even direct, preferential aid to religion (although, in fairness, we would point out that such an interpretation has not been advocated).

51. Philip Kurland, "Of Church and State and the Supreme Court," *Selected Essays on Constitutional Law,* ed. Edward. Barrett, Jr. (St. Paul, MN: West, 1963), p. 779.

52. This is, admittedly, not a perfect characterization. For instance, Kurland's standard would seem to preclude some of the legal exemptions permitted by the Supreme Court under the Establishment Clause (especially in the area of the way religious organizations have to meet federal regulations regarding hiring, taxing, and so on).

53. See A. E. Dick Howard, "The Wall of Separation: The Supreme Court as Uncertain Stonemason," *Religion and the State,* ed. James Wood, Jr. (Waco, TX: Baylor Univ. Press, 1985), pp. 101–102 (regarding how different advocates of the neutrality test apply it differently).

54. Mark De Wolfe Howe, "Religion and the Free Society: The Constitutional Question," *Selected Essays on Constitutional Law,* ed. Edward Barrett, Jr. *et al.* (St. Paul: MN: West, 1963), pp. 731–32.

55. *Cantwell* v. *Connecticut,* 310 U.S. 296 (1940).

56. *Everson* v. *Board of Education,* 330 U.S. 1 (1947).

57. Edward Corwin argues that the Fourteenth Amendment's guarantee of liberty could not have intelligently encompassed the Establishment Clause, which was not a liberty in the way other Bill of Rights guarantees were. Edward Corwin, "The Supreme Court as National School Board," *Law and Contemporary Problems* 14 (Winter 1949), p. 19.

58. Note "Rethinking the Incorporation of the Establishment Clause: A Federalist View," *Harvard Law Review,* vol. 105 (1992), p. 1709.

59. Noah Webster, *An American Dictionary of the English Language* (Johnson Reprint, 1970), vol. II.

60. *Davis* v. *Beeson,* 133 U.S. 333 (1890) at 342.

61. 367 U.S. 468 (1961).

62. *Welsh* v. *United States,* 398 U.S. 333 (1970). Black's opinion was joined by three other Justices. There were one concurring and three dissenting opinions in this 5–3 decision.

63. Welsh at 340.

64. See Milton Konvitz, "The Problem of a Constitutional Definition of Religion," *Religion and the State,* (Waco, TX: Baylor Univ. Press, 1985), ed. James Wood, p. 156.

65. *Tinker* v. *Des Moines Independent School District,* 393 U.S. 503 (1969).

66. Tinker at 525–26.

67. See Chapter 11 generally. The first case is *Wallace* v. *Jaffree,* 472 U. S. 38 (1985); the second is *DeSpain* v. *DeKalb Country School District 428,* 348 F. 2d 836 (1967).

5

Religion and Elected Leaders

THE PROBLEM POSED

For years, sales representatives have been cautioned to avoid discussing religion and politics with customers. The reason for this long-standing advice is obvious; religion and politics both can inflame prejudices and passions, and inflamed passions are hardly good for sales. If religion and politics separately can be divisive, perhaps their combined effect might prove particularly inflammatory. Although most of this book will be concerned with examining their interaction by analyzing the effects of government upon religion, in this chapter we will concentrate upon the opposite situation, namely, the effect of religion upon politics. More specifically, we will observe the effect of religion upon elections, upon the selection and election of candidates for public office, and upon incumbents who have held those political offices.

In the United States, the extent to which religious belief does and ought to inform the convictions and political beliefs of individuals involved in public life remains a disputable question for many, although the specific focus of that question varies over time with changing circumstances. For instance, today the conservative Christian Coalition claims a million members nationwide. Politically, it aligns with the Republican Party and attempts to influence its political agenda. Religiously, it is loosely affiliated with Pat Robertson and the Pentecostal Church, and its members are religiously conservative Christians. Programmatically, it has focused much of its attention on grassroots efforts to elect its members to local school boards—where they have advocated that the schools emphasize patriotism (as opposed to multiculturism), increased acknowledgment of God, returning education to the basics, teaching abstinence in sex education classes (or doing away with sex education altogether), and restoring law and order to the schools.

What is most striking about the Christian Coalition—and about virtually all other contemporary examples of religiously motivated involvement in American public affairs and politics—is how remarkably calm the controversy has been. Such groups and individuals have been successfully integrated into politics-as-usual in the United States. Although religious group involvement may or may not be a good thing in democratic politics (depending on one's point of view), it poses no threat (as it does elsewhere in the world) to the stability of the political regime. One might speculate that this phenomenon is partially a result of the deliberate decision of the Founders to establish the United States upon secular political principles and partially due to the declining influence of religion in American life.[1] In the cases examined here, we will discover that the law of the Constitution usually proves to be remarkably clear. Somewhat more complex are the political and religious attitudes of the electorate, whose opinions and judgments frequently form the basis of American political life.

EXAMPLE 1

Otero v. *State Election Board of Oklahoma,* 975 F.2d 738 (10th Cir. 1992)

Facts: Mr. Otero, an atheist and candidate for mayor, was required to vote in a church. He challenged this practice, arguing (in part) that the First Amendment's Establishment and Free Exercise clauses were violated by using churches as polling places in Oklahoma state and municipal elections.

Result: An atheist's assertion that entering a church in order to vote oppressed his beliefs does not constitute a violation of either the First Amendment's Establishment or the Free Exercise Clause as applied to the states.

Argument of the Case: Logan, Justice. Plaintiff's argument appears to contend that requiring him to vote in a church atmosphere "disadvantages a candidate like [the] plaintiff, who is an atheist, by increasing the influence of the religious affiliation of the candidates beyond that which would be the case if voting were held in a nonchurch place." Otero also contends that his atheistic views do not permit him to enter a church. Yet this latter contention is frivolous. Even if atheists are equally protected from government action, still Otero does not show that not entering a church is truly rooted in his religious (that is, atheistic) belief. The Establishment Clause does not prevail, for the *Lemon* test is not breached; using churches as voting places has a clear secular purpose (providing a place to vote), it has a primary effect that neither advances nor inhibits religion, and church–state entanglement is not excessive. Furthermore, voting in a church building does not require Otero "to attest to the nature of his religious beliefs," so the burden on free exercise is very slight.

Discussion

The federal circuit court was not very impressed with either the form or substance of Mr. Otero's argument. The form of his argument was less than persuasive; in the court's words, Otero's "forty-five page complaint makes a profusion of contentions that are difficult to follow."[2] Nor was the Court persuaded by Otero's formal constitutional assertions. It reasoned that the government possessed a clear public interest that prompted the city and state to select the churches as voting sites. Voting locations needed to be conveniently located (especially in residential areas). This was the consideration that resulted in a variety of churches being selected. Thus, nine out of twenty-nine polling places in Miami, Oklahoma, were churches of varying denominations (for example, Catholic, Baptist, Presbyterian, Episcopal, Assembly of God, and Christian); this religious diversity was pointed out by the state, which argued that its true concern was to identify convenient location, not to advance religious indoctrination.

Acknowledging the government's strong secular interest in securing convenient polling locations, the circuit court balanced the government's interest against Otero's two separate First Amendment religion clause claims. In each instance, the state won hands down. The court suggested that the Establishment Clause would be violated only if Otero could demonstrate that excessive church–state entanglement had occurred (the other prongs of the *Lemon* test having been satisfied). Yet the court implied that Otero's entanglement argument was hypothetical and speculative. Thus, the court reluctantly conceded that Otero "is perhaps correct in his argument that voting in a church might remind voters of religion, which might make some think of the religious affiliation of a candidate on a ballot or remind them of the candidate's stands on issues on which the voter's church also has taken a stand."[3] Still, the court simply could not believe that these slender reeds constituted an excessive church–state entanglement that outweighed government's secular interest. Similarly, Otero's free exercise argument failed. Although he was an acknowledged atheist, it was not evident how by merely entering and voting in an Episcopal Church he had violated his "religious" views. But even if his religious opinions had been compromised, and having to vote in a church raised a legitimate free exercise concern, it still did not outweigh the state's legitimate interest in identifying convenient polling places. For these reasons, the court was unpersuaded and rejected Otero's analogy comparing his reluctance to enter a church to asking Christians to vote "in a house of demonic worship containing pervasive symbols of Satan."[4]

In order to reach its decision, the court did not have to evaluate whether (or the extent to which) Otero's atheistic opinions were protected by the First

Amendment's religion clauses (although there was good reason to believe that they were).[5] Although the courts have widely accepted the proposition that individual religious or religious-like belief or lack of belief is none of the government's business, the government cannot guarantee, nor does the Constitution require, that all of its valid, secular decisions and laws will be inoffensive. Otero demonstrates that a government providing for the efficient functioning of elections in a religiously neutral fashion proves to be no exception to this rule. But actually limiting religiously ordained citizens' participation in the election process is quite another matter, as the Supreme Court's opinion in our next case amply demonstrates.

EXAMPLE 2

McDaniel v. *Paty,* 435 U.S. 618 (1978)

Facts: The first Tennessee Constitution of 1796 and Article IX, section 1 of the current Tennessee Constitution contain the following language: "Whereas ministers of the gospel are, by their profession, dedicated to God and the care of Souls, and ought not to be diverted from the great duties of their functions; therefore, no ministers of the gospel, or priests of any denomination whatever, shall be eligible to a seat in either House of the legislature." In 1977 the state legislature passed a law based upon the authority of this constitutional clause with the intention of affecting its 1977 limited constitutional convention. The law declared that any "citizen of the state who can qualify for membership in the House of Representatives of the General Assembly may become a candidate for delegate to the convention...." McDaniel, an ordained Baptist minister, filed as a candidate for the constitutional convention and was elected. His election was challenged by one of his opponents.

Result: The Tennessee law that prohibits McDaniel from serving as a delegate to Tennessee's constitutional convention violates his free exercise rights under the First Amendment as applied to the states.

Argument of the Case: Burger, Chief Justice:[6] Seven of the thirteen original states and six other states historically excluded clergy from holding some political offices (Massachusetts being the last to do so in 1833). For the most part, these laws were subsequently abandoned. Nonetheless, early American history and advocates such as the influential philosopher John Locke and the political leader Thomas Jefferson demonstrate that "at least during the early segment of our national life, those provisions enjoyed the support of responsible American statesmen and were accepted as having a rational basis." However, the Free Exercise Clause (which now applies to the states) certainly encompasses the right of a minister to preach and perform religious functions. Tennessee acknowledges the right of adult citizens to seek and hold political office. Yet "under the clergy disqualification provision, McDaniel can not exercise both rights simultaneously because the State has conditioned the exercise of one on the surrender of the other." Penalizing McDaniel's status as minister violates his Free Exercise rights.

Blackmun does not participate in the deciding of this case.

Brennan concurs.[7] The law, to the extent that it incorporates the Tennessee Constitution's prohibition of clergy from serving in the legislature, violates both the Establishment Clause and the Free Exercise Clause of the First Amendment as applied to the states. The law establishes a religious classification regarding eligibility for public office; such a classification burdens religious belief and violates the Free Exercise Clause. Furthermore, the law appears to manifest patent hostility toward religion, having the primary effect of inhibiting religion by influencing a minister or priest "to abandon his ministry as the price of public office...."

Stewart concurs. The First Amendment prohibits a state from barring from office individuals whose choice of vocation is dictated by religious belief.

White concurs. Tennessee's disqualifying of clergy from serving as delegates to the state's constitutional convention violates the Equal Protection Clause of the Fourteenth Amendment.

Discussion

McDaniel settled an extremely interesting political controversy that, as Burger's plurality opinion pointed out, had existed since the beginnings of the republic. Even before the Constitution was written, Thomas Jefferson had proposed in his draft of the Virginia Constitution that clergy be barred from holding political office. Jefferson's wall of separation between church and state was steep and impenetrable. It was not simply that he thought religion and government should be separated for their own good; he actually distrusted revealed religion and its official representatives, believing each inadequately appreciated human reason. Occasionally, Jefferson dismissed religion and religious officials as promoters of superstition, describing religion's harmful effects of warfare and persecution. In his famous "Notes on the State of Virginia" Jefferson observed that "millions of innocent men, women, and children, since the introduction of Christianity, have been burnt, tortured, fined, imprisoned; yet we have not advanced one inch toward uniformity [of opinion]."[8] Given such an judgment, it was hardly surprising that Jefferson wished to free government from every vestige of religious control. Yet it was Madison's objection to Jefferson's constitutional provision, and not Jefferson's proposal or argument, that Burger cited approvingly in *McDaniel*. In Burger's opinion, Madison's response to Jefferson's proposed ban on clergy correctly anticipated and reflected "the spirit and purpose of the Religion Clauses of the First Amendment." Madison had focused upon the harm imposed upon citizens by a prohibition upon clergy holding office. He contended that such a restriction would strip clergy of their civil liberties; thus, Madison asked, does "not the exclusion of Ministers of the Gospel as such violate a fundamental principle of liberty by punishing a religious profession with the privation of a civil right?"[9]

As good as Madison's response was, it hardly ended the dispute. In 1947 (some 31 years before *McDaniel*), in the very important case of *Everson* v. *Board of Education*,[10] the extent of clergy's involvement in politics arose again. Although the *Everson* case was cited approvingly in Justice Brennan's concurring *McDaniel* opinion, *Everson*'s dicta regarding the matter of clergy involvement in government was ignored by all Justices. In *Everson*, Justice Black's majority opinion declared that "[n]either the state nor the Federal Government can, openly or secretly, participate in the affairs of any religion organizations or groups or *vice versa*."[11] Thus, in the only case where the Supreme Court had previously considered the question of clergy involvement in government, the Supreme Court had sided with Jefferson, a fact conveniently ignored by every Justice in the *McDaniel* case.

Tennessee, too, had sided with Jefferson, arguing that the Establishment Clause and the idea of church–state separation supported its banning clergy from holding public office. Yet, if the Supreme Court in *McDaniel* was a little less than fully forthcoming in acknowledging *Everson*'s embarrassing language regarding clergy participation in politics, it was united in its implicit rejection of this specific language's import. The Supreme Court clearly held that clergy, simply because they were clergy, could not be excluded from participating in the political process. That is the clear lesson of *McDaniel*.

No Justice dissented from this opinion, but perhaps not surprisingly, there were differences among the Justices' rationales—even among the seven (of the eight) who saw this issue as controlled by the Constitution's religion clauses. Burger's constitutional ground for the Court's decision was straightforward enough—this was a free exercise question, pure and simple, and the Free Exercise Clause prevented excluding McDaniel from holding a political position simply because he was a minister. By contrast, Brennan and Stewart argued that the constitutional problem was that the state had impermissibly required the profession of a particular religious belief as a precondition for holding office. Brennan additionally thought that Tennessee had violated the Establishment Clause by displaying outright hostility toward religion.[12]

Although *McDaniel* conclusively settled the law of the Constitution regarding the right of all American citizens—including clergy—to involve themselves in politics and government, a theoretical question has lingered in American politics. The question becomes this: Does a religiously related profession adequately or poorly qualify an individual for elected office, and specifically for high public office? Perhaps it makes little or no difference. After *McDaniel*, this is a political and not a legal question.

Yet the issue has arisen in recent times in American politics. Both in 1984 and in 1988, Jesse Jackson sought the nomination of the Democratic Party. In 1988 Pat Robertson pursued the Republican nomination for President. Jackson and Robertson had little in common. Jackson was African American;

Robertson was white. Jackson was a liberal Democrat; Robertson was a conservative Republican. Politically, they agreed on virtually nothing. Yet they shared one important characteristic besides the fact that they each wished to be President and that each had never held elected office. Both Jesse Jackson and Pat Robertson were ordained Christian ministers.

Pat Robertson had come to the forefront because of his "televangelism" efforts; he was an ordained Southern Baptist minister who built the Christian Broadcasting Network into a major media force. His greatest point notoriety was the "700 Club," a sort of religious–political television talk show. Robertson advocated a conservative political agenda generally associated with the evangelical right. He championed a strong defense policy, a pro "family values" political agenda, prayer in public schools, anti-abortion legislation, limiting recognition of homosexual rights, and so on. Significantly, much of Robertson's campaign and financial support initially grew out of a religious network with roots in the Pentecostal Church. Thus, a combination of modern media and churches was indispensable for helping launch and maintain Robertson's political candidacy.

Similarly, Jesse Jackson's 1984 and 1988 campaigns for President also reflected the fact that he was a Baptist minister. His political agenda, and the language Jackson employed to advocate it, reflected his religious indoctrination. In the words of one authority, Jackson's "entire platform rested on a belief in the kinship of humankind through its common link to God; in this view, poverty, racism and sexism are not merely social problems but sins against the divine spark in all people." Furthermore, Jackson "portrayed political action in messianic terms, constantly invoking biblical metaphors…" and espoused a platform that "bore strong traces of both the Social Gospel and liberation theology."[13] But even more important was the fact that Jackson garnered much of his political support from African American churches. His was, in the words of a *Time* magazine article, "the first major presidential candidacy in U.S. history to be built largely on church support."[14] Jackson was quoted in that same article to say that "[w]e must translate pulpit power into political power." To that end, African American churches provided him with not only a forum, but also volunteers and money.[15]

Regarding the political efforts of Robertson and Jackson, three points should be emphasized. First, the candidacy of prominent clerics with little or no political experience grows out of important structural features that the American political system is currently experiencing. Second, while the political emergence of powerful clerics may appear new, the existence of powerful religious contingencies has strong historical precedents. Wald integrates these first two themes well:

> In an age of weak political parties and generally low rates of political participation, the support of religious groups is usually seen as a valuable asset in a political campaign. Through several mechanisms, religiously involved people can supply resources to help favored candidates or, conversely, to defeat candidates they find unacceptable. Simply providing the candidate a

forum from which to address the membership gives free publicity and the opportunity to spread a message among attentive audiences. As organizations possessing membership lists and other resources, the churches may even be pressed into action as the core of a candidate's campaign effort. In bidding for presidential nomination in 1988, both Jesse Jackson and Pat Robertson, ordained ministers, relied heavily on sympathetic churches for leadership, funding, platforms, and various types of support services. Though major political parties in the United States attempt to draw support from different religious groups, several minor parties have been built almost exclusively on specific religious constituencies. That was true of the antislavery and prohibitionist parties in an earlier age.[16]

The third point grows out of the first two: despite the religious affiliations of Robertson and Jackson, and despite their widespread religious support, public concern and criticism of this aspect of their campaign were relatively muted.[17] The long-established political and legal tradition of secular politics in the United States proved effective; the union of church and state so feared by the Founders appears, in the arena of everyday politics, to be more a distant memory than an imminent threat.

So far in this chapter we have analyzed two distinct aspects of the effects of religion on American elections. *Otero* raises the question of to what extent the balloting process must be free from any vestige of religion or religious symbolism while *McDaniel* focuses upon whether a religious occupation can disqualify a citizen from taking part in the political process. But after the voters have voted and the candidates have been elected or defeated, what about assuming office? What about a state official's religious or nonreligious beliefs (having nothing to do with clergy status)? More specifically, what happens when a state mandates that public officials swear an oath that they believe in God? That question is examined in detail in our next example.

EXAMPLE 3

Torcaso v. *Watkins*, 367 U.S. 488 (1961)

Facts: Article 37 of the Declaration of Rights in the Maryland Constitution stipulates that "no religious test ought ever to be required as a qualification for any office of profit or trust in this State, other than a declaration of belief in the existence of God...." Torasco was appointed to the office of Notary Public by Maryland's governor. He was refused a commission to serve because he would not declare a belief in God. Torasco brought suit so that he might retain his office.

Result: When government insists upon any sort of religious oath as a prerequisite for holding office, it violates the First Amendment's Establishment Clause as applied to the states by the Fourteenth Amendment.

Argument of the Case: Black, Justice:[18] There is no doubt that Maryland has enacted a religious oath. *Everson* provides good guidance; it suggests that the First Amendment prevents government from forcing a person to profess a belief or disbelief in any religion. It is an inadequate excuse to suggest that no person is compelled to hold public office; whether or not there exists a right to public employment, still "the Maryland religious test for public office unconstitutionally invades the appellant's freedom of belief and religion and therefore cannot be enforced against him."

Discussion

The challenged Maryland constitutional provision that legally required candidates to take a religious oath before assuming office was unanimously invalidated by the Supreme Court some seventeen years before the *McDaniel* decision. The message of the case was clear: the Constitution permits states to impose no formal law pertaining to the religious beliefs of individuals holding state offices. Later in this section, we will examine the extent to which informal voter influences regarding candidates' religious beliefs have affected elections and political candidates. In that regard, we will pay special attention to the 1960 Presidential election.

Before examining this issue, however, it is important to point out that the constitutional provision challenged in the *Torasco* case had a revealing and instructive history. Maryland's first Constitution in 1776 had guaranteed a right to hold office to all who would subscribe to a "declaration of belief in the Christian religion." This provision was more restrictive than it seemed. For instance, Jews were prohibited not merely from holding political office, but even from becoming attorneys, because lawyers were held to be officers of the court and were therefore presumed to hold state office. In 1826 a bill was passed exempting Jews from the clause's operation. Just over forty years later, in 1864, the Maryland Constitution was revised again to require either "a declaration of belief in the Christian religion" or the belief "in the existence of God, and in a future state of rewards and punishments." Three years later, the 1867 Constitution passed, retaining only the provision that an officeholder declare "a declaration of belief in the existence of God." It was this provision of the Maryland Constitution that *Torasco* subsequently challenged.

This brief historical recounting makes clear that Maryland's religious oath requirement had been constantly liberalized over the years. Even so, Maryland was one of the minority of states that had retained such oaths in the twentieth century and one of the very few that had ever enforced them. The Constitution was clear regarding the legal restrictions upon the national government regarding this issue. Article VI explicitly required "that no religious Test shall ever be required as a Qualification to any Office or public Trust under the United States." In other words, Maryland's law could not have passed constitutional muster as a federal requirement.

However, the Court chose not to consider whether Article VI's prohibition against religious oaths should be applied against the states (much in the way that the two religion clauses have been applied against the states, in that case via the Fourteenth Amendment). Rather, it saw the legal controversy in *Torcaso* most appropriately resolved by the application of the religion clauses generally and by the Establishment Clause specifically.[19] Black's main point was that the State could not prescribe or proscribe any religious belief or nonreligious belief as a condition of holding office. In the process of making this point, Black defined religion broadly, including within his definition religions that do not advance a belief in the existence of God, including Buddhism and Taoism, and belief systems that have not always or even usually been understood to be religions, especially Ethical Culture and Secular Humanism.

Although invalidating Maryland's religious oath law created virtually no controversy on the Supreme Court, the same lack of controversy has not always attended the informal religious "requirement" that sometimes seems in place for American public office, particularly for the office of the Presidency. Of course, there is no formal religious requirement for President, yet it is difficult to deny that Americans have maintained informal expectations about candidates. Americans expect their President to be religious (and not atheist or agnostic); all major candidates for the Presidency explicitly proclaim a religious faith. Furthermore, these religious beliefs have tended to be Protestant. There have been no Jewish, Mormon, or non-Christian major-party candidates for the Presidency. In 1928, in a campaign marked by pronounced bigotry and prejudice, the first Roman Catholic candidate for President, Democrat Al Smith, lost the Presidency partially because of his religion. For this reason, the Presidential race of 1960 and the resulting election of John F. Kennedy represented something of a political and religious landmark—the election of the nation's first Roman Catholic President. The 1960 election not only rolled back the informal religious "restrictions" that had prevailed in American politics since the nation's inception, but it also probably helped cause a steep decline of religious prejudice in the United States. Because it is useful to contrast the effortless way that the 1961 Supreme Court invalidated a formal, state-imposed religious bar to holding public office with the formidable—yet informal—religious parameters that Americans have traditionally imposed upon Presidential candidates, in the remainder of this section we will briefly examine the political–religious aspect of John F. Kennedy's quest for the Presidency.

As it became clear that Kennedy would receive his party's Presidential nomination, pragmatic political considerations dominated. How feasible was the candidacy of a Roman Catholic? Would Kennedy suffer the same fate as had Al Smith? At least one columnist pointed out that Catholics in 1959 constituted 23.6% of the nation's vote compared to only 10% in 1928.[20] Furthermore, it was highly probable that anti-Catholic prejudice had declined in the United States. The critical calculus of votes, put forth by the reigning political pundits, was frequently advanced in such quantitative terms; analysts asked whether the "Catholic vote" was sufficient to outweigh the ballots of those voters who did not wish to see a Roman Catholic elected President.

This discussion often presumed a debatable proposition—that there existed a cohesive "Catholic vote" at all, that is, that the religious association between voter and candidate significantly outweighed any other. Some political observers doubted that it existed at all; others believed that just as anti-Catholic prejudice had diminished, so the strength of that vote (assuming it had existed in great numbers) had also diminished. As the Democratic convention approached, commentators feared that either Kennedy's nomination, or his lack thereof, might be explained in divisive religious tones. Kennedy's response to this political commentary was predictable and effective. He repeatedly asserted that he was running as a political candidate and not as a religious representative. He wanted no votes cast on account of his religion; he did not even "want anyone to support my candidacy merely to prove that this nation is not bigoted—and that a Catholic can be elected President."[21] Kennedy repeatedly blamed the media for raising the religious issue: "I spoke in Wisconsin ... on farm legislation, foreign policy, defense, civil rights and several dozen other issues." Kennedy further complained that he rarely found these subjects covered in the press—"except when they were occasionally sandwiched in between descriptions of my hand-shaking, my theme-song, family, haircut, and, inevitably, my religion."[22] Later, Kennedy complained that one magazine article "supposedly summing the primary up in advance, mentioned the word Catholic twenty times in fifteen paragraphs—not mentioning even once dairy farms, disarmament, labor legislation or any other issue."[23]

Kennedy also played down the whole issue of whether there was a Catholic vote, again emphasizing the secular aspects of his candidacy. Thus, he admitted (in response to a press question) that, in the Wisconsin primary, he had run well in cities and, yes, there were great numbers of Catholic voters in those cities, but there were, according to Kennedy, also substantial numbers of "union members and older voters and veterans and chess fans and basswood lovers."[24] Ridiculing analyses of the Wisconsin vote that discussed his voter appeal primarily in religious terms, Kennedy observed that he had run "strongest in those areas where the average temperature in January was 20 degrees or higher, and poorest in those areas where average temperature in January was 20 degrees or lower—and that I ran well in the beech tree and basswood counties and not so well among the hemlock and pine." Summing up his tongue-in-cheek analysis, Kennedy implied that trees and where they were grown held the key to his election and therefore noted that it had been "suggested that to offset my apparent political handicaps I may have to pick a running-mate from Maine, or, preferably, Alaska."[25]

In addition to the persistent questions of how many votes might be gained or lost to the Democrats if they nominated a Catholic candidate, there was a different, specific question that hounded Kennedy. That question asked the proper relationship between religion and politics and specifically took the form of questioning the extent to which a Catholic President would be influenced, not merely by his specific religious beliefs, but more significantly by the Catholic religious hierarchy. This was the infamous "dual-citizenship" accusation, which was more whispered than explicitly stated. Kennedy responded to the fear that the Catholic Church might exercise some sort of unwelcome influence over his possible Presidency with three distinct arguments. First, he emphasized that his policy opinions did not necessarily coincide with certain policies favored by most Catholics or by the Catholic Church. For instance, Kennedy both opposed governmental aid to parochial schools as well as sending an American ambassador to the Vatican. Second, he argued that there was no justification for applying a religious test exclusively to one office, the Presidency. Kennedy complained that the religious question was not raised when he sought election to the Senate or the House, or when he was appointed as a naval officer. Furthermore, other world leaders were Catholic without even a hint, much yet a threat, of religious interference. Finally, Kennedy constantly emphasized his understanding of the relationship between religion and politics. He believed in a strict separation of church and state. His understanding of the Constitution (which, by oath, he was bound to uphold) prohibited religious leaders from interfering with the secular political process.

Kennedy's remarks helped convince a number of Americans to vote for a Roman Catholic for President. But his efforts proved not completely successful. Thus, thirteen thousand Southern Baptists, meeting in convention and speaking as the second largest Protestant denomination, expressed fears about electing a Roman Catholic President on the ground that one who was committed to the Catholic Church would not be able to separate himself from doctrines "in open conflict with our American pattern" of religious liberty and church–state separation.[26] Some three weeks before, the National Association of Evangelicals, representing thirty-five religiously and politically conservative Protestant denominations, passed a resolution expressing doubt that a Roman Catholic President "could or would resist fully the pressures of the ecclesiastical hierarchy."[27] Nor was concern limited to conservative Protestants. A few Catholic publications took issue with Kennedy's political–religious pronouncements. Responding to Kennedy's comment that irrespective of his private religious beliefs, his oath to uphold the Constitution took precedence over other considerations, *The Ave Maria* (a national weekly published at the University of Notre Dame), asserted that Kennedy's statement reflected an attitude "not only unrealistic but dangerous as well: for something does indeed take precedence over the obligation to uphold the Constitution—namely conscience."[28]

Ultimately, Kennedy's Catholic beliefs proved no barrier to his election. After he assumed office, the religious issue never reemerged with any intensity. But certainly it is possible (perhaps even probable) that an elected official can face a conflict regarding public duty and religious obligation. After election to public office, what is and should be the effect of an individual's religious beliefs on his or her public acts? That question is examined in our next "case." Unlike our earlier examples, it comes from a well-known speech, rather than a Supreme Court case.

EXAMPLE 4

Facts: On September 13, 1984, New York Governor Mario M. Cuomo delivered a oft-cited speech titled "Religious Belief and Public Morality: A Catholic Governor's Perspective" at the University of Notre Dame. The speech dealt with the dilemma of being a Catholic governor who must publicly pronounce on the subject of abortion, a subject about which he maintains his own religious/personal opinions. It was divided into four parts.[29] First, Cuomo stated the issues he wished to address. Second, he stated the reason he held the opinions that he did on abortion. In the third section, he attempted to reconcile his political and religious understanding. Finally, at the conclusion of his speech, he urged his audience to emulate Jesus' example and show love and compassion to the poor, the weak, and the dispossessed.

Discussion

Our discussion of Governor Cuomo's speech will follow the approximate outline summarized in the "facts" above. Cuomo began by pointing out that he spoke both as a politician and as a Catholic, "a lay person baptized and raised in the pre-Vatican schools, attached to the Church first by birth, then by choice, now by love."[30] Cuomo acknowledged that to be a Catholic means to believe in certain religious dogmas that distinguish the faith. These dogmas are not merely to be believed, but are to be translated into action. This is particularly difficult in contemporary America, which is "a consumer society, filled with endless distractions, where faith is more often dismissed than challenged, where the ethnic and other loyalties that once fastened us to our religion seem to be weakening."[31]

At the same time, a Catholic who holds public office does so in a pluralistic society, elected to serve "Jews and Moslems, atheists and Protestants, as well as Catholics...."[32] Such an officeholder helps create conditions where all citizens can live in dignity and freedom, including citizens who hold different and even contradictory beliefs. In this context, Cuomo mentioned opinions and laws that protect people's right to divorce, use birth control, and even choose abortion. Yet a Catholic public official cheerfully takes an oath to protect these citizens' freedom, understanding full well that by defending the opinion of those with whom he or she disagrees, the public official protects his or her own freedom. The religious freedom of Catholics, like the religious freedom of others, is rooted in the very idea of freedom. In other words, Cuomo contended that it was the idea of equal freedom, not religious truth, that provided the theoretical basis of the United States as well as furnished the political safeguard for unhindered individual religious practice.[33]

Cuomo then applied this framework to the everyday world of politics. Favoring a nuclear freeze or opposing the funding of contraceptives can be advanced because such a policy benefits the whole community. Similarly, "I can, if so inclined, demand some kind of law against abortion not because my bishops say it is wrong but because I think that the whole community, regardless of its religious beliefs, should agree on the importance of protecting life—including life in the womb, which is at the very least potentially human and should not be extinguished casually."[34] Cuomo acknowledged that he is free to make this and similar arguments and that the Constitution affords him the right to do so. The question is, should he?

Before answering this key question, Cuomo drew some important distinctions regarding the question of whether religious values were to be admitted into American public affairs. Some were. The fact that certain broadly held moral values are rooted in religion does not necessarily mean that they cannot be accepted in the public arena. However, what is far more problematical is when religious values are used to support positions that would impose restrictions upon people that they find unacceptable. And, in any case, simple answers should be avoided. It will not do to simply favor a Christian nation. Whose understanding of Christianity? asked Cuomo. He asserted that it would be wrong to speak for God and suggest that God favors only some of the American people or a single political party: "The 'Christian nation' argument should concern—even frighten—two groups: non-Christians and thinking Christians."[35]

In the second part of his speech, Cuomo clarified his own opinion regarding "issues of life and death that raise questions of public morality," particularly abortion.[36] As a Catholic, in his private life, Cuomo has adopted the Catholic teachings regarding these issues, including abortion. Catholic teaching governs private behavior; regarding political behavior, it generally accepts the civil law (for example, it does not contest the law that permits divorce and birth control). Abortion has been an exception for the Church, perhaps because it is a matter of life and death. Yet even with abortion, the Church's position is not prescriptive regarding the public positions an elected representative need promote. Thus, "while we always give our bishops' words respectful and attention and careful consideration, the question whether to engage the political system in a struggle to adopt certain articles of our belief as part of public morality is not a matter of doctrine; it is a matter of prudential political judgment."[37]

In politics, opinions regarding abortion are divided. Many advocates of social justice, representing different religions, have worked with Catholics on other issues but disagree with Cuomo and the Catholic position regarding abortion. Although Catholics should not alter their moral beliefs to conform to public opinion, public opinion does affect the capacity to translate Catholic beliefs regarding morality into civil law. Here, moral truths must be balanced against political reality (that is, prudence must prevail). While the Church's teachings are clear, the application of those teachings into practice admits flexibility:

> With regard to abortion, the American bishops have had to weigh Catholic moral teaching against the fact of a pluralistic country where our view is in the minority, acknowledging that what is ideally desirable isn't always

feasible, that there can be different political approaches to abortion besides
unyielding adherence to an absolute prohibition. This is the American-
Catholic tradition of political realism. In supporting or opposing specific
legislation in this country, the Church has never retreated into a moral
fundamentalism that will settle for nothing less than total acceptance of its
views.[38]

Noting that individual Catholics had earlier disagreed whether the bishops
had gone too far in endorsing a constitutional amendment allowing the states
to prohibit abortions, Cuomo added that "Catholics are allowed to disagree
on these technical political questions without having to confess."[39]

Applying this "realistic" pragmatic approach to the abortion question,
Cuomo opposed a ban on abortions and a proposed constitutional amendment allowing the states to prohibit them. He also opposed the political attempt to preclude Medicaid funding for abortions. Health and medical needs
ought to predominate, not an officeholder's personal views of morality. Furthermore, Catholics are divided on the question of abortion, tending to support it in the same proportion as the rest of the population, raising a painful
question: "Are we asking government to make criminal what we believe to be
sinful because we ourselves can't stop committing the sin?"[40] Catholics should
first heal themselves. Cuomo advocated that Catholics "educate ourselves better to the value to the values that define—and can ennoble—our lives" and
work to find ways to avoid abortions. Hence, he suggested working politically
to provide funds and opportunities that would allow women to bring their
child to term and better teach young men their responsibilities in creating and
caring for human life. Also, medical care, which would lower infant mortality
rates, can and should be improved.

Having indicated that despite private opposition to abortion, he nonetheless supported it and its public funding, Cuomo attempted in the third part of
his speech to minimize his departure from Catholic teaching caused by his
public support of abortion. Cuomo contended that "[a]bortion has a unique
significance but not a preemptive significance."[41] Presumably, this meant that
while abortion was singularly important, abortion did not require a political
approach that differed radically from other life-and-death issues such as nuclear weapons, hunger, and joblessness, all of which required applying Christian responsibility to secular political life. Therefore, candidates for political
office (and, presumably, holders of political office) should be judged on a wide
range of issues.

In the fourth section of his speech addressed to fellow Catholics, Cuomo
expressed hope that his address would spur dialogue on this issue. But he also
desired that this dialogue not be long or divisive. Catholics must live in this
world; they must also maintain their own faith and not become increasingly
assimilated into "a larger, blander culture." Despite this challenge, a person
can still be both a Catholic and a politician.

Governor Cuomo later remarked that when he gave this speech at Notre
Dame, he felt like he was going to biology class—not as the teacher, but as the

frog.[42] There was no doubt that the task before him was difficult. What was the proper public position of a Catholic who opposed abortion in his or her own life? Perhaps it should be noted that Cuomo's political position was not one in which he was obligated to enforce a civil law irreconcilably at odds with his private religious beliefs. Rather, on policy grounds he favored a political policy permitting abortion, even though he made clear that, as a Catholic, it was not a practice he would have supported in his private life. Was this position sensible, or even logically possible? Cuomo's rationale provides one way to reconcile these two positions. Although there was a sharp division of opinion about how successfully Cuomo had completed his task, his attempt merits serious study.

When analyzing the tension between private religious belief and public responsibility, it is important to separate the example of abortion from its specific context. This tension must be understood as an important problem irrespective of one's opinion regarding abortion. Although in this case, the Catholic Church's anti-abortion teaching was conservative and the political programs and pro-abortion political policy advocated by Governor Cuomo were liberal, this scenario can easily be reversed. It is quite possible that an individual officeholder may be conservative and encounter a liberal church or religious doctrine or interpretation. For example, the Bishop's Pastoral Letter on the "The Challenge of Peace" was a liberal document that minimized nuclear deterrence and balance-of-power politics; it also could have placed a politician with more conservative leanings in a dilemma similar to that in which Governor Cuomo found himself (although, admittedly, abortion is more of a core Catholic issue).

Since Governor Cuomo's address, the tension between privatized religious belief and public responsibility about the matter of abortion has become more intense. In March 1995 Pope John Paul II's papal encyclical "Evangelium Vitae" (The Gospel of Life) condemned abortion, as well as a number of other procedures, including euthanasia and related practices. The Pope asserted that statutes sanctioning these practices were immoral because they attacked human life in its most vulnerable forms (the unborn and the elderly). Concluding that "[t]he most direct and voluntary killing of an innocent human being is always gravely immoral," the Pope contended that elected officials could not justify enforcing pro-abortion laws on the ground that they had no right to impose their private (anti-abortion) values on others. Nor did it matter that abortion has widespread popular support. In fact, the encyclical asserted that there did not even exist an obligation to obey the secular law involving abortion because it contradicted the moral law—i.e., God's law. It was the religious duty of all Catholics, including elected officials, to oppose laws permitting abortions although "where it is not possible to overturn" a law permitting abortion, a legislator who opposes abortion can in good conscience "support proposals aimed at limiting the harm done by such a law and at lessening its negative consequences...."

The Pope's encyclical allows democratic legislators some latitude on the abortion question, in that they can easily take public positions consistent with their core religious beliefs and can, if they desire, advocate and support compromises, if made in the name of diminishing the scope of abortion. But a harder case confronts state governors. If their oath of office requires them to enforce the law and the Constitution (many abortions being a matter of legal and constitutional right), and if the encyclical condemning this law is (as the Pope asserts) binding upon all Catholics, there would seem to be an irresolvable conflict. For that reason, the encyclical renders Governor Cuomo's speech problematical. Cuomo had contended that the Church's position was not prescriptive regarding an elected official's public position. Yet the Pope, some eleven years later, made clear that he regarded all law sanctioning abortion as immoral and would prohibit Catholics from participating in its enforcement. Because in Catholicism it is the Pope, as head of the Roman Catholic Church, and not the individual Catholic who determines the individual's religious status, the Pope's opposition to abortion is crucial to the very definition of who is a Catholic in good standing within the Catholic Church. Thus, the Catholic governor who performs his or her constitutional duty to enforce the law must, by definition, ignore important portions of the Pope's encyclical and thereby jeopardize his or her religious status in the eyes of the Church.

Ultimately, what is most important is the answer to this question: What happens when an officeholder is required or chooses to carry out policies or laws at odds with the fundamental religious teachings of his or her faith? Whether Cuomo had successfully reconciled his private religious beliefs and secular political opinions and responsibilities is, on the one hand, a matter for theologians and philosophers to muse about and, on the other hand, a matter for voters to decide. Yet Governor Cuomo, like President Kennedy before him, had made one point indisputably clear. Under the Constitution, even a devout political leader's first obligation is to the secular realm and the citizens who elected him or her. Political arguments supporting or opposing specific policies and programs must be presented in public terms and defended in secular language. If this is not possible, it may be difficult for a devout Catholic to hold public office. Still, this is what the Constitution envisioned, and this is the way American politics has always been understood. It remains so to this day.

SUMMARY

American political life has been conducted primarily in secular terms. This is even more true in recent times. Slight and incidental interaction between government and religion, such as voting in churches, has been allowed, but only because the influence, entanglement, and effect on each have been minimal.

The religious beliefs of candidates and elected officials, or their nonreligious beliefs, are constitutionally irrelevant. Clergy cannot be barred from holding political offices; neither can the state require any oath that stipulates religious belief as a condition of holding office. What about the privately held religious beliefs of candidates and elected officials? When do they possess significant political importance? Both John F. Kennedy and Mario Cuomo have argued strenuously that the two should not be confused. Private religious belief may form the basis of private conduct; it does not necessarily require the advocacy of particular public policies, and it should never interfere with the required enforcement of the law. Elected officials of every religion have a secular responsibility to enforce the law. This maxim has become a firmly ingrained principle of American public life.

NOTES

1. For a discussion of those secular principles, see Chapter 2. For a brief consideration of the declining public influence of religion in America, see Chapter 4, p. 78 and the Afterword.

2. *Otero* v. *State Election Board of Oklahoma,* 975 F.2d. 738 (10th Cir. 1992) at 739.

3. *Otero* at 740. Emphasis ours.

4. *Otero* at 739.

5. See *Everson* v. *Board of Education,* 330 U.S. 1 (1947) at 16.

6. This opinion is joined by Justices Powell, Rehnquist, and Stevens.

7. This opinion is joined by Justice Marshall.

8. Thomas Jefferson, "Notes on the State of Virginia," *The Portable Thomas Jefferson,* ed. Merrill Peterson (Marmondsworth, Middlesex, England: Penguin, 1986), p. 212.

9. 435 U.S. 618 (1978) at 625.

10. 330 U.S. 1 (1947). This case is discussed in Chapter 13.

11. *Everson* at 16.

12. The core of the disagreement between Chief Justice Burger, on the one hand, and Justices Brennan and Stewart, on the other, centers on the question of whether *Torasco* v. *Watkins,* 367 U.S. 488 (1961), was controlling. Burger denied that it was; Brennan and Stewart believed that it was. The dispute over *Torasco* was largely a debate over *Everson* and its "wall of separation" language. *Torasco* is the next case to be analyzed.

13. Kenneth D. Wald, *Religion and Politics in the United States* (Washington, DC: C.Q. Press, 1992), 2nd ed., pp. 319–20.

14. "Jesse Takes Up the Collection," *Time* (Feb. 6, 1984), p. 57.

15. "Jesse," p. 57.

16. Wald, pp. 180–81.

17. *Time* did wonder if candidate speeches, followed by the passing of the collection plate for political contributions, violated the Internal Revenue Code granting churches tax exemption only if they do not take part in any political campaign on behalf of any candidate for public office. "Jesse Takes Up the Collection," p. 16.

18. Justices Frankfurter and Harlan, without separate opinions, concurred in the result.

19. As in *Everson,* there was some lack of clarity about the precise boundaries of the Establishment Clause and the Free Exercise Clause. See Chapter 13, p. 237.

20. See the editorial by Leo Eagan, *New York Times,* Apr. 17, 1960 (sec. 4, p. 4).

21. "Text of Speech by Kennedy before the American Society of Newspaper Editors," *New York Times,* Apr. 22, 1960, p. 16.

22. "Text of Speech by Kennedy," p. 16.

23. "Text of Speech by Kennedy," p. 16.

24. "Text of Speech by Kennedy," p. 16.

25. "Text of Speech by Kennedy," p. 16.

26. "Baptists Question Vote for Catholic," *New York Times* (May 21, 1960), p. 12.

27. "Catholic President Stirs Evangelicals," *New York Times* (Apr. 30, 1960), p. 47.

28. "Catholic Magazine Critical of Kennedy," *New York Times* (Feb. 24, 1959), p. 43.

29. Our analysis, both in the summary and the larger discussion, follows in form the summary and analysis of Charles M. Wheelen, "Religious Belief and Public Morality," *America* (Sept. 19, 1984), pp. 159–63.

30. Mario M. Cuomo, "Religious Belief and Public Morality," *New York Review of Books* (Oct. 25, 1984), p. 32.

31. Cuomo, p. 32.

32. Cuomo, p. 32.

33. This theme is developed at length in Chapter 2.

34. Cuomo, p. 32.

35. Cuomo, p. 33.

36. Cuomo mentions the right to die, artificial insemination, embryos in vitro, birth control, and nuclear war, in addition to abortion. Cuomo, p. 33.

37. Cuomo, p. 33.

38. Cuomo, p. 34.

39. Cuomo, p. 35.

40. Cuomo, p. 35.

41. Cuomo, p. 36.

42. Wheelen, p. 160.

PART II

General Issues

6

Can the Government Escape Regulating and Defining Religion?

THE PROBLEM POSED

As we have already observed, the American relationship between church and state has often been defined in terms of separation.[1] In fact, in everyday discussion, Americans frequently speak of the separation of church and state as if this phrase actually defined the First Amendment's religion clauses. Yet it should be recognized that important assumptions underlie this somewhat controversial formulation. For example, it is widely believed that just as government is best preserved when freed from religious control, so religion is most often kept vigorous when freed from governmental domination. Thus, the separation doctrine suggests, at minimum, that government ought not to define or regulate religion or religious faith in any way, and that any involvement of religion in politics is potentially dangerous. For this reason, freedom of religion in the United States is frequently thought to mean freedom from government and is sometimes even thought to mean complete freedom from all governmental regulation. However, in this chapter we will observe that while some people still cling to the idea of complete separation of church and state as a goal, as a practical matter it is impossible. Try as it might, the government simply cannot completely avoid regulating and occasionally even defining religion, although it can effectively minimize the impact of this action.

It is not difficult to understand why complete separation of church and state is impossible. Consider: government routinely confers a vast number of benefits and important services, requires mandatory reporting obligations, and imposes significant penalties for violations of its laws and rules. Furthermore, in many respects religious organizations act like their secular counterparts; for instance, they hire people, own property, and sometimes express political, economic, or social opinions. In these instances, the following question inevitably arises for religious organizations (and, in some circumstances, for religious individuals): How are they to be treated—the same as nonreligious organizations and citizens, or differently?

More specifically, we need to know precisely what governmental action or inaction is required by the separation of church and state (or by any other constitutional doctrine). Consider the fact that in municipalities throughout the United States, local taxes are raised to provide police and fire protection. Should church–state separation exempt religious organizations from paying property taxes to support such services?[2] What about the services themselves? Does anyone really believe that separation of church and state requires (for instance) that a burning church should be ignored by state-supported fire departments?[3] Or, to take another example, when government imposes a civic or legal obligation, should religious organizations and believers be exempted? And if they are even partially excused (as, for instance, conscientious objectors have been from combat requirements[4]), how should those who are eligible for exemption be identified? Given the fact that there always will be citizens who, wishing to avoid the unpleasantness, hardship, and the risk to life or limb that occur in war, might not some individuals falsely claim conscientious believer status? In such instances, in order to acknowledge the religiously rooted conscience of believers and exempt true conscientious objectors from military duty, the government cannot avoid evaluating the religious claims and convictions of all those who would claim exemption. Thus, in order to promote church–state separation, government must become somewhat involved with religion, at least long enough to evaluate its claims.[5]

On rare occasions, the extent to which government becomes involved in religion appears both justified and surprising. For instance, in November of 1991 many newspapers carried an Associated Press account of District Court Judge Robert Cashen's court-ordered settlement of a heated dispute that had rocked the New Morning Star Missionary Baptist Church in Peoria, Illinois. Controversy over Pastor Thomas had divided the 900-member congregation. The pastor had staunch supporters, yet opponents criticized him for being aloof, for applying too strict an interpretation of the Bible, and for being a failed charismatic preacher. So unhappy were his critics that they began to hold separate services, took up different collection plates, and formed a church within the church. Tensions increased. Church and members actually scuffled during worship services, requiring police visits to restore order! Pastor Thomas then padlocked the church, but opponents cut through the chains. Meanwhile, police imposed a curfew.

Judge Cashen's settlement thrust the state directly into the religious affairs of the New Morning Star Missionary Baptist Church. The court order required a church election, it mandated that everyone who voted sign a covenant promising both to accept the election results and to refrain from behaving in any way that discredited the process, it barred separate collections and separate services, and it stipulated that Pastor Thomas resign within seven days should he lose the election (but, should this happen, he would be allowed to give a farewell sermon). This level of intervention by the courts in the affairs of religious institutions was extreme and hardly typical. Yet intervention by the state becomes inevitable when fundamentally important secular interests are at stake. In this instance, the peace and tranquillity of society and the physical safety of citizens were jeopardized. As we shall see, while courts are generally reluctant to interfere in internal ecclesiastical matters, there are still a variety of religiously related problems that government simply cannot ignore.

EXAMPLE 1

Presbyterian Church in the United States v. *Mary Elizabeth Blue Hull Memorial Presbyterian Church*, 393 U.S. 440 (1969)

Facts: In Savannah, Georgia, two Presbyterian churches withdrew from their national church organization and formed independent Presbyterian churches. Their members had been upset by pronouncements of the national Presbyterian church organization, including those allowing the ordination of women, urging the removal of prayer and Bible reading from the schools, and advocating various liberal social and political positions. The Presbyterian Church of the United States eventually acknowledged the split and proceeded to confiscate the local church's property until new local leadership could be appointed. The local churches sued, claiming trespassing. Under Georgia law, the right to property previously used by local churches turns on a civil court jury's determination of whether the central church abandoned or departed from the tenets of faith and practice it held at the time the local churches affiliated with it (the so-called departure from doctrine standard). The legal question of the case asked if the Georgia law violated the First Amendment's protection of religious liberty.

Result: The Georgia law requiring a civil jury to determine if the central church has abandoned its original doctrine is an unconstitutional interference with religion in violation of the First Amendment.

Argument of the Case: Brennan, Justice. The state does have a legitimate and general interest in resolving property disputes, and a civil court is the proper forum for such a resolution. But the problem here exists because the state passes judgment over church doctrine and practice. Precedent decrees that the First Amendment prohibits the courts from passing judgment upon ecclesiastical questions, although precedent also reveals that there may be some very narrow exceptions. Courts may intervene when there is evidence of "fraud, collusion or arbitrariness" in purely ecclesiastical matters,[6] or courts may decide church property disputes that do not involve questions of doctrine by means of the ordinary principles of the secular law (the so-called neutral principles doctrine). Neither of these exceptions apply in this case, however. Furthermore, by requiring juries to determine (1) whether "the challenged actions of the general church depart substantially from prior doctrine," and (2), if they have, "whether the issue on which the general church has departed holds a place of such importance in the traditional theology as to require that the trust be terminated," Georgia's law requires civil courts to assess "the relative significance of the [religious] tenets from which departure was found." This state law is unconstitutional because "[p]lainly, the First Amendment forbids civil courts from playing such a role."

Discussion

This case poses a clear example of the limited extent to which government will interfere with ecclesiastical self-governance. Thus, by overturning the Georgia law, the Supreme Court left it to the embattled religious organizations to settle their own dispute, or (if that was not possible) it required Georgia to resolve such conflicts according to the same neutral rules it would apply in other, secular cases (that is, by examining titles, deeds, church charters, and so on).[7] Certainly, the Supreme Court had no intention of involving itself (or the government in general) in any doctrinal disputes.

Still, it is important to recognize that the government cannot completely separate itself from religious concerns, broadly defined. As the Court admitted at the very beginning of its opinion, the state (through its court system) involves itself by performing a legitimate and important role in settling property disputes. Actually, the principle according to which the state will intervene in ecclesiastical matters is narrow and can be stated as follows: government will intervene *only* when the religious organization, institution, auxiliary, or any of its officials or members (acting on its behalf) claims rights under the secular law, and the religious organization is incapable of resolving the matter internally. At that point, religious organizations will be governed by the same legal rules and obligations as all nonreligious organizations and officials. In other words, the protection afforded by the First Amendment's religion clauses affords religious organizations a broad latitude to settle doctrinal disputes and their related conflicts internally.

In Chapter Two, we noted that the United States was not founded upon the idea of a religious truth.[8] Religious liberty, not religious truth, was at the foundation of the new American nation. It is now appropriate to observe that just as the Constitution reflected no official view of God or religion, so government can endorse no one view (or any view) of God, or make any official endorsement of religion or of any religion. *Presbyterian Church* clearly reinforces the proposition that the Constitution does not permit government to involve itself in matters of theological controversy. However, it might be noted that even this mild action by the Supreme Court (as part of the government) reveals that church and state cannot be completely separated; the Court is involved in a kind of limited intrusion even when it attempts to limit the extent of the intrusion.

The government's need to keep a safe distance from religious organizations' internal theological disputes seems clear enough (as are its infrequent exceptions, when the ownership of property is disputed or the public peace is endangered). But a more difficult problem arises when the organization in question has both religious and secular characteristics. In the next case, we will observe that the Deseret Gymnasium was owned and run by corporations owned by the Mormon Church.[9] Yet this nonprofit health club was open to the public for the purpose of promoting exercise and health. Certainly, this does not seem to be a religious mission (although the gymnasium had been dedicated more than 75 years earlier in the hope that "all who assemble here, and who come for the benefit of the health, and for physical blessings, [may] feel that they are in a house dedicated to the Lord").[10] The legal questions raised by such an organization are numerous. We will concentrate upon the following: To what extent can such quasireligious organizations be regulated? To what extent can they be governed, or should they be governed? Finally, is their religious character (and legal definition) so evident that they can discriminate against employees of a different religion who perform purely nonreligious jobs?

EXAMPLE 2

Corporation of the Presiding Bishop of the Church of Jesus Christ of Latter-Day Saints et al. v. *Amos et al.,* 483 U.S. 327 (1987)

Facts: The Deseret Gymnasium was classified as a nonprofit facility and open to the public, although run by entities associated with the Mormon Church. The appellant, a man named Mayson, had worked as a building engineer in the gymnasium for sixteen years. However, when he could not produce a certificate that he was a member of the LDS (Mormon) Church and hence eligible to attend its temples, he was discharged. Mayson (and others) filed a class-action suit, alleging discrimination under section Title VII, section 703 of the 1964 Civil Rights Act, which prohibited religious discrimination in employment. The Mormon Church countered by citing section 702 of the same law, asserting that (as amended) it exempted religious organizations from the law's prohibition against employment discrimination on the basis of religion. The legal question posed by the case was if this exemption to the 1964 Civil Rights Act violated the Establishment Clause—in other words, were religious employers allowed to discriminate on religious grounds in the hiring (and firing) of employees holding nonreligious jobs (that is, jobs related to the secular activities of religious organizations)?

Result: Section 702 of the 1964 Civil Rights Act, which exempts religious organizations from the obligation not to discriminate on religious grounds in the hiring and firing of certain employees, does not violate the Establishment Clause or the "benevolent neutrality" that it seeks to promote.

Argument of the Case: White, Justice. Determining the constitutionality of the Civil Rights Act of 1964's exemption allowing Deseret Gymnasium to discriminate in religious employment requires applying the three-part *Lemon* test.[11] The purpose of the *Lemon* test was to promote government neutrality (that is, government cannot promote religion or any particular religious point of view). First, the exemption here serves the permissible legislative purpose of alleviating "significant governmental interference with the ability of religious organizations to define and carry out their religious missions." Second, the exemption does not have the principal or primary effect of advancing (or harming) religion. This is because a "law is not unconstitutional simply because it allows churches to advance religion, which is their very purpose." Rather, for "a law to have forbidden 'effects' … government itself [must have] advanced religion through its own activities and influence." Such an advancement has not occurred in this case. Finally, because the exemption effects a more complete separation between church and state, it can hardly be said to excessively entangle the two. In addition to passing the *Lemon* test, the exemption does not violate Mayson's equal protection rights. Even though employees of religious employers are less protected than employees of secular employees, still the government does not discriminate among religions (all religions being afforded this exemption). For that reason, the exemption constitutes a rational (and therefore acceptable) means to the end of minimizing governmental interference in religion. Although Mayson's freedom of choice in religious matters is impinged upon, it is critical that the law neither directly requires Mayson to qualify for temple eligibility nor requires his dismissal.

Brennan concurs.[12] Authorizing religious discrimination with respect to nonreligious activities surpasses reasonable church–state accommodation and would seem to constitute an impermissible supporting of religion in violation of the Establishment Clause. What makes this conclusion difficult to implement is that the religious–secular distinction is not easy to apply in practice. This problem suggests a case-by-case determination of whether an activity is secular or religious, yet this approach unconstitutionally entangles religion and government and chills the activities of religious organizations. Furthermore, this case raises important tensions between the right of a religious organization to autonomy in the ordering of its internal affairs and an individual's right to practice his or her religion without suffering employment discrimination. The best available solution requires confining the categorical exemption from religious discrimination to nonprofit activities of religious organizations. These activities are fundamentally religious and often fulfill the religious purpose of providing important community services (and not simply engaging in commerce). Such an exemption confines the religious organization's ability to discriminate in nonprofit activities while still permitting the religious organization sufficient leeway so that its religious activities are not chilled.

Blackmun concurs. Although the case is correctly decided and the exemption for nonprofit (religiously sponsored) organizations is constitutional, the Court's (White's) rationale is not limited to exempting such organizations. Agreeing with O'Connor (see below), Blackmun emphasizes that the Court has not determined that the constitutionality of the exemption applies to for-profit activities undertaken by religious organizations.

O'Connor concurs. The Court is wrong to rely upon *Lemon* as an appropriate Establishment Clause test. Abstractly, that test poses contradictory, unacceptable alternatives between the Establishment Clause and the Free Exercise Clause. Thus, a strict interpretation of Lemon invalidates exempting religious practitioners from generally applicable government obligations (because such an exemption would have a principal or primary effect of advancing religion). This interpretation of the Establishment Clause inhibits religious organizations' right to practice their religion freely and thus impedes the free exercise of religion. However, in a laxer interpretation of *Lemon*, where the courts defer to the legislature, "all legislation that purports to facilitate the free exercise of religion would completely vitiate the Establishment Clause." The Court attempts to solve this dilemma by asserting that the Establishment Clause is not violated when the government allows religious organizations to advance religion in contrast to the government directly advancing religion. But this distinction is too obscure, for "[a]lmost any government benefit to religion could be recharacterized as simply 'allowing' a religion to advance itself, unless perhaps it involved actual proselytizing by government agents." In this case, the distinction between the government advancing religion and religion advancing itself does not withstand scrutiny because the "Church had the power to put Mayson to a choice of qualifying for a temple recommend[13] or losing his job [only] because the Government had lifted from religious organizations the general regulatory burden imposed by section 702." A better (that is, more honest) approach would be (1) to recognize that the government exempting a religion from regulation does advance religion and (2) to "separate those benefits to religion that constitutionally accommodate the free exercise of religion from those that provide unjustifiable awards of assistance to religious organizations." Since the contested exemption, as applied to nonprofit activities of religious organizations, constitutes a permissible government accommodation of religion and conveys no message of endorsement ("as perceived by an objective observer acquainted with the text, legislative history, and implementation of the statute"), the exemption is constitutional. Since it is likely that a for-profit activity conducted by religious organizations will not be as "directly involved in the religious mission of the organization," the constitutionality of exempting such activities is not decided.

Discussion

How can the firing of a gymnasium employee raise so many difficult and complex constitutional problems? The beginning of an answer emerges from understanding the great extent to which the government in modern times cannot escape classifying and defining religion while carrying out its duly constituted functions. The 1964 Civil Rights Act was enacted under Congress's power to regulate interstate commerce. It outlawed (among other things) discrimination in public accommodations (hotels, public transportation, amusement parks, and so on) as well as discrimination in employment. The aim of the law was motivated by Congress's intention to end all vestiges of segregation and racial discrimination, but other forms of discrimination, including religious and gender discrimination, were also banned. The government's wide authority to eradicate these practices, sustained by the courts, made clear that the distinction between the public sector (the government) and the private sector (business) was little distinction at all.[14] Thus, the 1964 Civil Rights Law allowed the government to prohibit religious discrimination, exempting only the religious activities of religious employers from this requirement. Later (in 1972), this exemption was broadened to exempt all activities of religious organizations (the question in this case examined the employment practices of the gymnasium, focusing only upon the secular, nonprofit activities of a religious organization). For our purposes, the broad, salient point is this: Congress's desire to eliminate discrimination throughout society necessarily involves it and government generally in the regulation (or nonregulation) of religion and religious practices. Here, the government, originally through the Congress, and later (in this case) through the courts, determined the extent of permissible intrusion into the realm of church and state separation (itself something of a technical violation of strict separation).

In this case, the Supreme Court approved Congress's self-imposed exemption from its previously passed law as it applied to the Deseret Gymnasium. In order to exempt the organization from governmental regulation, the Court first had to determine the extent to which (1) the Deseret Gymnasium could be classified as religious and therefore deserving of exemption and (2) whether Congress violated the Constitution (and specifically the First Amendment's Establishment Clause) by granting to this gymnasium an exemption from the law. These two questions formed core issues in the case, and, interestingly, they did not lead to great disagreement among the Supreme Court Justices. Regarding the first question, although the gymnasium was generally open to the public, the fact that it was owned and operated by religious entities associated with the Mormon Church proved sufficient to classify it as a religious organization. Its distinctive character and very reason for being gave it the authority to employ only those who shared its faith.

What about the constitutionality of the employment exemption, as applied to the gymnasium? Critical for several of the Justices was the fact that the gymnasium was a nonprofit religious organization (a distinction not mentioned in the original congressional exemption). For Brennan, the gymnasium's

nonprofit status meant that the Court did not have to become excessively entangled with religion or chill (threaten) the religious organization's activities
or autonomy by reviewing every religiously sponsored activity on a case-by-
case basis. Brennan believed religiously sponsored, nonprofit organizations undertook activities that promoted community services, as opposed to mere
commerce, and reinvested their earnings to finance the publicly valuable activities they offered (as opposed to distributing any surplus to the sponsoring
religious organization). Both these characteristics minimized the Establishment Clause concern that the government had unconstitutionally promoted
religion by exempting nonprofit religious organizations from government regulation. Similarly, Justice O'Connor favored the profit/nonprofit distinction
but for quite a different reason: she believed it likely that nonprofit activity was
more likely to be directly involved with the religious mission of the larger organization and therefore (more than for a for-profit activity) was entitled to exemption.[15] Despite their differences in emphasis, both Brennan and O'Connor
(along with Marshall and Blackmun) indicated that exemptions for for-profit
religiously affiliated organizations posed potentially more difficult constitutional considerations (perhaps implying that Congress may have surpassed the
Constitution's proper bounds in providing restrictions relating to for-profit religiously sponsored organizations). Regarding the central issue of this case,
they joined the Court and, answering our second question, found that the
challenged congressional exemption, as applied to the Deseret Gymnasium,
did not violate the Constitution's Establishment Clause.

Thus, the contested constitutional question posed by this case was easily
settled, even if there was significant disagreement regarding the appropriate
constitutional test to be employed and over the proper scope of Congress's religious exemption prohibiting nondiscrimination in hiring and firing. Also
complicating the case was that the profit/not-for-profit distinction directly
raised the difficult question of precisely how a religious organization ought to
be defined (that is, directly as a religious organization, different from all other
nonreligious organizations, or as one of a variety of nonprofit organizations).
Nor was the issue of religion, and government's obligation not to jeopardize
its practice, confined to the employment practices of the Deseret Gymnasium.
Mayson's right not to suffer religious discrimination was also at stake. Although the free exercise issue was in the background of this case, it could not
be doubted that Mayson's religious beliefs were burdened by the congressional
exemption. Justice Brennan puts it most clearly: "An exemption says that a
person may be put to the choice of either conforming to certain religious
tenets or losing a job opportunity, a promotion, as in these cases, employment
itself." Simply put, when Congress exempted religious organizations from the
anti-religious discrimination provisions of the Civil Rights Law, it favored the
autonomy of religious organizations at the expense of the free exercise right of
individuals.

Identifying the most important religious claim in this case involves a true
complicating factor; closely related is the inherent tension within the Constitution (which was discussed in Chapter Four). Applied to this case, the tension is as follows: the more the Supreme Court frees religious organizations

from governmental interference (either by upholding broad-based exemptions from regulation or by expansively defining what defines religious organizations), the broader is the Establishment Clause protection upholding the autonomy of religious organizations. And the more the Court protects the autonomy of religious organizations under the Establishment Clause, the more narrowly interpreted are the religious free exercise rights of individuals. (Conversely, the more narrowly the Establishment Clause is interpreted, the greater will be the protection afforded individuals under the Free Exercise Clause.) What is intriguing about the *Amos* case is that it provides a practical example of both a religious organization's claim of religious autonomy under the Establishment Clause and the individual assertion of freedom of conscience and belief under the Free Exercise Clause, making clear how the two clauses can be in tension with each other.

There are many other subtleties and points for discussion raised by the *Amos* case. One is that the Establishment Clause, according to White (and to the Court's majority), intended to establish (through the *Lemon* test) a relationship of benevolent neutrality between government and religion; for Justice O'Connor the Establishment Clause required only that the Constitution did not convey a message of endorsing religion. However, no matter who was correct, still not a single Justice in the *Amos* case contended that the government could remain completely separated from religion, nor did any believe that the government could refrain completely from determining the extent to which religion ought to be regulated. Nor did any Justice think that the government could escape determining the extent to which religious interests deserving of protection should be defined.

In *Amos,* an important question raised was how a religious organization was to be defined. A related question presented asked how an individual's religious belief should be determined. Because of the vast amount of regulation inherent in the modern state and because of the significant number of benefits and regulations allocated by government, religion becomes a way that individuals can claim special exemptions from some of the rules and regulations imposed by government. Because being religious permits individuals to claim secular advantage, the government must constantly wrestle with the extent to which it allows those who hold religious beliefs special status, and must occasionally deal with the matter of whether such beliefs are legitimate or sincerely held. Although such a task may be difficult (and to some Justices repugnant), it cannot be avoided, as the following example suggests.

EXAMPLE 3

United States v. Ballard, 322 U.S. 78 (1944)

Facts: Guy Ballard and members of his family headed the "I Am" movement. Mr. Ballard (whose former aliases included Jesus and George Washington) claimed to be the divine messenger of Saint Germain on earth (not to mention having claimed to have shaken hands with Jesus). He asserted that he had been selected to convey the good saint's teachings and had been given the power to heal people afflicted with illnesses and injuries. According to the government (which cited eighteen alleged misrepresentations in twelve indictments), Ballard and his family had used the U.S. mails to defraud individuals of their money by misrepresenting who they were and their special relationship to the divine, and by falsely claiming to have cured individuals of their afflictions. Ballard contended that the government indictment attacked his religious beliefs in violation of the Free Exercise Clause of the First Amendment. The precise point of legal conflict focused upon the trial judge's instruction to the jury that prohibited it from evaluating the truth of the Ballards' religious beliefs. The judge's instructions permitted the jury to consider only whether the Ballards really believed what they said (the assumption being that if they did not sincerely hold their religious beliefs, then they were, *ipso facto*, guilty of fraud). The jury found their religious beliefs insincere. The government defended the trial judge's distinction. The Ballards argued that their indictment and subsequent conviction should have been set aside, for the Free Exercise Clause required that the truth of the Ballards' religious beliefs (which the Circuit Court of Appeals had ruled could be submitted to a jury) and the sincerity with which the Ballards held those beliefs were both beyond the purview of the state and therefore should have been withheld from consideration by the jury.

Result: The trial judge's instructions (and the Ballards' conviction) were upheld; the Ballards' free exercise rights under the First Amendment were not violated by allowing the jury to consider the sincerity of the Ballards' beliefs in determining whether they had used the U.S. mails for fraud. But the Circuit Court of Appeals erred in concluding that the truth of the religious beliefs could be submitted to a jury.

Argument of the Case: Douglas, Justice. The First Amendment precludes submitting to the jury the truth of the respondents' religious doctrines or beliefs. In a previous case, the Supreme Court had noted that "the law knows no heresy, and is committed to the support of no dogma, the establishment of no sect."[16] A previous Supreme Court also had observed that, regarding religious free exercise, the First Amendment protects freedom of thought absolutely and (to a much more limited extent) freedom to act.[17] Freedom to believe is implied by freedom of thought and is of no concern to the state. That a religious belief may seem to others to be strange, unusual, or even preposterous is therefore of no consequence. Often, people believe what they cannot prove. Even those who take their gospel from the New Testament would not have supposed that they could be tried before a jury charged with determining if teachings such as "the miracles of the New Testament, the Divinity of Christ, life after death, the power of prayer" contained false representations. The Founders, aware "of the varied and extreme views of religious sects, of the violence of disagreement among them, and of the lack of any one religious creed on which all men would agree," fashioned "a charter of government which envisaged the widest possible toleration of conflicting views." Their Constitution is violated when juries (as triers of facts) pass on the truth or falsity of religious beliefs.

Stone dissents.[18] The Court is correct that the sincerity of the Ballards' religious views can be submitted to the jury; the Court is also correct that the Ballards' conviction should be upheld. However, the majority is likely mistaken in its belief that the Constitution protects all alleged religious beliefs. Thus, freedom of thought and worship does not include the Ballards fraudulently procuring money by false statements regarding their religious experiences. The jury can determine whether the Ballards honestly believed that the alleged religious experiences occurred. Furthermore, the truth of alleged religious beliefs may well be susceptible to proof regarding factual particulars. Thus, "if it were shown that a defendant in this case had asserted as part of the alleged fraudulent scheme, that he had physically shaken hands with St. Germain in San Francisco on a day named, or ... by the exertion of his spiritual power he 'had in fact cured ... hundreds of persons afflicted with diseases and ailments,' I should not doubt that it would be open to the Government to submit to the jury proof that he had never been in San Francisco and that no such cures had ever been effected."

Jackson dissents. The Court is wrong; the conviction should be reversed. Although the Ballard family's religious teachings are nothing but "humbug," still they cannot be prosecuted successfully without compromising traditional religious freedom under the First Amendment. Neither the question of the truth nor the sincerity of the Ballards' religious beliefs should be submitted to the jury; in Jackson's words, "I do not see how we can separate an issue as to what is believed from considerations as to what is believable." Thus, "[h]ow can the Government prove those persons know something to be false which it cannot prove to be false?" William James has pointed out that the vitality of religion is experiences that include "conversations with the unseen, voices and visions, responses to prayer, changes of heart, deliverance from fear, inflowings of help, assurances of support," and so on. How can government ascertain the truth or sincerity of such experiences? If the Ballards can be prosecuted for their religious opinions, isn't there realistic fear of wholesale religious persecution? Jackson would "dismiss the indictment and have done with this business of judicially examining other people's faith."

Discussion

The *Ballard* case directly raises the specter of religious hucksterism. All the judges were suspicious of the Ballards. The Ballards' "religious" beliefs were nothing if not curious, although as Justices Douglas and Jackson pointed out, many mainstream, more familiar, religious beliefs also seem (to the unpersuaded observer) to be curious, unprovable, and even irrational. But, even more important, all the Judges except Stone agreed that the Free Exercise

Clause of the First Amendment precluded the government from passing any judgment upon the content, or truth, of a religious belief.

Of course, the district court trial jury originally had concluded that the Ballards did not believe the religious claims they had made. Yet their religious beliefs became an issue only because the Ballards had used them to garner contributions by claiming the power to heal people. Although the Ballards' self-proclaimed special relationship to God was unlikely (but could not be proven false), their claim to have cured individuals, as Chief Justice Stone pointed out, could be verified, and whether they honestly believed the religious claims they made to others could properly be determined by a jury. This was the rationale by which eight Justices on the Court upheld the Ballards' conviction; the jury, in order to determine whether fraud truly had existed, had a right to consider whether the Ballards had knowingly communicated false information to the public. For instance, the government's indictment accused the Ballards of knowingly and falsely claiming that they could cure incurable illnesses. Evaluating such a claim did not enable the Court to pass judgment upon the truth of the Ballards' overall religious beliefs, but only to gauge the sincerity of specific promises that they had made to others. Although only Justice Jackson would have allowed *no* inquiry by the jury into *any* aspect of the Ballards' religiously related claims or promises, his opinion does raise some of the case's most interesting issues and therefore merits examination.

Jackson argued that the core of all religious belief was supernatural and based upon miracles and revelation. Within any religion, there is a great diversity of interpretation. For example, among those who believe in Scriptures, some read the Bible literally, and others read it as an allegory or a metaphor. Thus, it is quite difficult to determine "in matters so mystical to say how literally one is bound to believe the doctrine he teaches and even more difficult to say how far it is reliance upon a teacher's literal belief which induces followers to give him money."

Jackson believed that the chief wrong perpetrated by false prophets was not financial, but rather was "mental and spiritual." But it was precisely this realm that was beyond the scope of the government and that constituted the price of religious freedom in the United States. In other words, the ongoing price of religious freedom was (and is) the toleration of some "rubbish."

Let us, for a moment, expand upon and examine Jackson's point. Sinclair Lewis, the famous twentieth-century American novelist, wrote the novel *Elmer Gantry* about a hypocrite who stumbled into the religion "business." Although Gantry preached against drink and casual sex, he engaged in both. Gantry sold religion as a vehicle for hope in an everlasting life with great enthusiasm and even greater financial success. The revival tents filled (at least for a time) with enthusiastic followers who generously filled collection plates. Gantry reasoned that he had committed no crime (or sin), for he had provided the people with comfort and hope. Had he had not made their lives happier? And if these folks were gullible and if they believed what was not true, must the government be in the business of preventing stupidity?

That the Constitution does not prohibit stupidity or outlaw gullibility is clear. Yet when the law is violated and when money is taken from individuals under factually false circumstances, or when a specific provision of the federal tax law is violated, then the courts usually have disallowed religious belief as a defense. Such religious claims usually prove to be an inadequate justification against cheating people out of their worldly possessions. Although Elmer Gantry may have been a fictional character, there have been analogous, larger-scale, real-life cases, including the tax-evading schemes of Jim Bakker, the television evangelist who misrepresented his financial dealings to the Internal Revenue Service and who sold and repeatedly resold the same time shares at the hotel of his religious theme park.

The approach of the Court in *Ballard* has governed almost all such cases. Thus, when considering individual or organizational religious claims, the federal courts usually have avoided passing judgment on the veracity or even the sensibility of unusual religious beliefs (even when presented with new interpretations of mainline religions or with unorthodox religions that are sometimes labeled "cults," such as the Founding Church of Scientology, the Worldwide Church of God, and the International Society for Krishna Consciousness and the Unification Church).[19] Although some interaction between religion and government has been unavoidable, the courts have attempted to decide such cases on nonreligious grounds. Thus, *Ballard* reveals one specific way this can be accomplished, where juries attempt to gauge the sincerity of a religious belief, punishing its practitioners for illegal acts if the promises made in the name of religion can be shown to be either factually false or insincerely held.

Enhancing the attractiveness of the *Ballard* approach has been the Supreme Court's notable hesitancy and difficulty in defining religion.[20] This reluctance has contributed to the discrediting of a diametrically opposed method of combating religious fraud—namely, defining religion and then disallowing religious claims that do not conform to the definition. In 1890 the Supreme Court was more confident than it is now and defined religion with some specificity, noting that it "has reference to one's views of his relations to his Creator, and to the obligations they impose of reverence for his being and character, and of obedience to his will."[21] Neither in that case nor in subsequent cases has a definition of religion become the routine basis for excluding religious claims. Furthermore, in more contemporary times, any definition of religion employed by the Supreme Court has become so watered down as to be virtually unhelpful. Thus, in two opinions written by Justice Black, atheists as well as Secular Humanists and Ethical Culturalists were defined as religious practitioners.[22] Furthermore, when it comes to interpreting the meaning of religion or religious beliefs as these terms are affected by the statutory law, the Supreme Court has been equally vague, concluding in the military draft cases that religious belief is defined by its role in a person's overall belief structure, not by its content. Religious beliefs are simply those that a person perceives as performing the function of religion in that individual's life; as long as these beliefs occupy something like a moral, ethical, or religious core belief and as long as they are sincerely held, they are classified as "religious" beliefs.[23] This approach amounts to little more than an effort to define religion by avoiding its definition.[24]

The attraction of the *Ballard* approach was that it not only spared the government from the necessity of inquiring into the truth or falsity of religion, but it also absolved it from attempting to define religion. Instead, *Ballard* directed the conflict between government and religious hucksters to the purely secular area of the law. One important battleground for such conflicts occurred from the late 1960s through the 1980s, when certain individuals claimed to have founded a church or become church ministers in order to take advantage of provisions of the tax code (which declared certain organizations tax-free and which declared individuals employed or certified by such organizations entitled to certain important income tax benefits).[25] The best known of these organizations was the Universal Life Church. The primary activity of this church was to ordain ministers (which it did by providing honorary doctor of divinity degrees by mail) and to issue church charters. From 1963 to 1980, it ordained some 10 million ministers and issued fifty thousand church charters.[26] In order to become a minister, all that was requested (but not demanded) was a contribution of $20. Doctrinally, the Church maintained the broadest and most inoffensive creed imaginable, proclaiming that it believed in that which is right, while championing the idea that each person should maintain and express his or her own conviction about that which is right.

Little wonder the Internal Revenue Service conclude that this and a number of other mail-order ministries were not truly religious at all, but simple tax-avoidance schemes. The Universal Life Church raised the same sort of question highlighted in the *Ballard* case—namely, to what extent were individuals or groups knowingly disseminating false or fraudulent religious beliefs for the purpose of gaining monetary advantage? In the instance of the Universal Life Church, those who were potentially defrauded were the American taxpayers.

How did the government react to the sort of transparent religious claim made by the Universal Life Church? At the most immediate level, the IRS made an initial examination of the religious doctrine and practices of this "religious" order, sufficient to conclude (in its opinion) that the church was not essentially religious. However, its attempt to deny tax benefits to the church was overturned in the federal courts. (The United States District Court announced that "[n]either this Court, nor any branch of this government, will consider the merits or fallacies of a religion.... Nor will the Court praise or condemn a religion, however excellent or fanatical or preposterous it may seem."[27]) But the IRS did not give up its belief that the Universal Life Church was conducting a tax scam. It has continued to prosecute individuals who benefited inordinately from its activities (under an IRS rule that specifies that an organization is not operated for a religious purpose if it serves a private rather than a public interest, or if its revenues benefit private individuals).[28] As in *Ballard,* conformity to the precepts of the secular law, not the truth or falsity or the reasonableness or lack of reasonableness of the questioned religious beliefs, constituted the basis for the government's actions.

In cases involving fraud and deception, the courts, following *Ballard*, have generally attempted to find independent, secular legal standards which demonstrate that the claimed "religious" advantage was illicitly pursued for individual gain. On occasion, however, when faced with a claim for exemption or advantage because of religion, the courts may invalidate the claim by simply granting the sincerity of a person's self-proclaimed religious belief but then finding that the claim of religious free exercise is insufficient to allow the disputed action in the face of the contested governmental law or regulation. Thus, when drug advocate and former Harvard psychology professor Dr. Timothy Leary was indicted for (among other things) smuggling marijuana into the country, there was probably good reason to doubt both the substance and the sincerity of his defense that the use of marijuana was essential to the free exercise of his religion.[29] Leary asserted that in Mexico he had undergone "the most intense religious experience of his life" after ingesting several "sacred mushrooms." He then converted to Hinduism, set up a shrine in his house, and since had engaged in the religious and scientific use of psychedelic drugs. The United States Appeals Court had some trouble believing Leary's explanation, pointing out that there was no evidence that the use of marijuana is a formal requisite to the practice of Hinduism. Nonetheless, what mattered to the court was the fact that the Congress considered marijuana dangerous and sought to outlaw it. In other words, religion or no religion, sincere or insincere belief, what really mattered was the secular harm that Congress had chosen to prohibit. Like the *Ballard* approach, this method of weighing a religious claim by balancing it against a governmental interest also permits courts to avoid inquiring into the truth of a person's religious belief.

SUMMARY

The controversies and cases examined in this chapter provide important help in answering the question of whether the government can remain entirely separated from religious organizations (and organizations that claim to be religious). The short answer is that it cannot. Government is constantly faced with evaluating the importance, sincerity, or even authenticity of claims made by organizations or individuals claiming to be religious. This task cannot be avoided. The courts are frequently put into the position of reviewing these claims and (as a part of the government) evaluating decisions made by other branches of the government. In such instances, the courts must apply their understanding of the First Amendment's Establishment Clause or Free Exercise Clause. When making these decisions, government cannot avoid affecting religion and those individuals who profess religious beliefs, but it generally attempts to avoid passing judgment on the truth of religious claims. Only rarely does it intrude itself into the affairs of religious organizations. Thus, it might fairly be said that while government cannot avoid some evaluation and regulation of religion, especially given the nature of the modern, complex nation–state, hardly ever is it required to define religion, and if it must, it generally undertakes interactions that are justified solely upon secular grounds and that are minimally invasive.

NOTES

1. For a discussion on this point, especially see Chapter 4, p. 67. Also see chapters 2 and 3, pp. 31 and 45.

2. See Chapter 19 for a general discussion of this issue.

3. No, according to the Supreme Court. See *Everson* v. *Board of Education,* 330 U.S. 1 (1947), 17–18.

4. They are required to perform alternate service. See Chapter 20. For a discussion regarding questions of conscience and civil disobedience, see Chapter 10, p. 183.

5. For this reason, under the oft-employed *Lemon* test (used by Justice White in the *Amos* case discussed below), the courts have held that the Establishment Clause prohibits only *impermissible* entanglement between government and religion.

6. A limited exemption was pronounced in 1929 when Justice Brandeis observed for the Supreme Court in *Gonzales* v. *Archbishop,* 280 U.S. 1 (1929), that the courts might afford "marginal" review to decisions rendered by church authorities if there had been fraud, collusion, or arbitrariness. On the limited extent of this exemption, see *Serbian Eastern Orthodox Diocese for the United States and Canada* v. *Milivojevich,* 426 U.S. 696 (1976).

7. For a full discussion of this approach, see *Jones* v. *Wolf,* 443 U.S. 595 (1979).

8. See p. 26.

9. The church is properly called the Church of Jesus Christ of Latter-Day Saints.

10. 483 U.S. at 327.

11. The test is discussed in fuller detail in Chapter 4, p. 69.

12. Justice Marshall joins this opinion.

13. This is a certificate that he is a member of the Church and eligible to attend its temples. Temple recommends are given to persons who observe church teachings in such matters as regular church attendance, tithing, and abstinence from coffee, tea, alcohol, and tobacco.

14. This helps explain why the law was passed under the Commerce Clause of Article 1, section VIII of the Constitution, as opposed to section V of the Fourteenth Amendment, which had previously been narrowly interpreted in *the Civil Rights Cases,* 109 U.S. 3 (1883). In those cases, the Court had interpreted Congress's power under the Fourteenth Amendment to require only state governments, not private businesses, to extend to all citizens the equal protection of the law.

15. O'Connor believed that exempting from the provisions of law the religious activities of a religious organization was a constitutionally permissible accommodation to the exercise of religion rather than an unconstitutional endorsement of religion.

16. The case was *Watson* v. *Jones,* 13 Wallace 679, 728 (1872).

17. *Reynolds* v. *United States,* 98 U.S. 145, 164 (1878).

18. Justices Roberts and Frankfurter join this opinion.

19. Leo Pfeffer, *Religion, State and the Supreme Court* (New York: Prometheus, 1984), Ch. 7.

20. This issue is examined in Chapter 4.

21. *Davis* v. *Beeson,* 133 U.S. 333 (1890), at 342.

22. *Everson* v. *Board of Education of Ewing Township,* 320 U.S. 1, 15–16; and *Torasco* v. *Watkins,* 367 U.S. 488, 495 (1961).

23. See Chapter 19.

24. Milton R. Konvitz, "The Problem of a Constitutional Definition of Religion," *Religion and the State,* ed. James E. Wood, Jr. (Waco, TX: Baylor Univ. Press, 1985), p. 154.

25. Schemes varied but assumed two general forms. Each was a charade. One variation called upon the individual to become an ordained minister, to found an organization that passed itself off as a church, and then contribute up to 50% of taxable income to the church (the contribution being tax-deductible), in return for which the church provided the individual with a residence and certain living expenses. A second variation called for the individual to take a "vow of poverty" and assign earned income to a church or religious organization (thus evading taxation). The earned income was then used as the individual's necessary "living expenses." There is reason to believe that one motivation of some individuals associated with the Universalist Life Church was to force the federal government to end tax exemptions to all churches. See "Student Notes and Comments," *Tax Lawyer,* vol. 33, no. 3, p. 962.

26. Richard B. Flowers, "Tax Exemption and the Clergy: On Vows of Poverty and Parsonage Allowances," in Wood, Jr., p. 362.

27. *Universal Life Church, Inc.* v. *United States,* 372 F.supp. 770, 776 (1974).

28. Section 501(c)(3) requires that a group must both be organized and operated exclusively for a religious purpose if it is to qualify for tax-exempt status. The requirement that a religious organization be exclusively organized for a religious purpose runs into significant free exercise problems when litigated, especially in light of the need for (and the absence of) a clear definition of religion. Therefore, the IRS acted under this operational rubric when moving against the Universalist Life Church.

29. *Leary* v. *United States,* 383 F.2d. 851 (1967).

7

❖

What Happens When Individual Religious Beliefs and Practices Are Unintentionally Hampered by Government?

THE PROBLEM POSED

It seems obvious that religious freedom effectively promotes religious diversity. However, in the *Federalist Papers* (especially *Federalist* 10), James Madison argued that the reverse was also true, that religious diversity, secured by numerous religious sects, effectively promotes religious freedom. It would seem that religious liberty and religious diversity can be mutually reinforcing. The ongoing religious freedom and the increase of religious diversity in the United States provide modest support for this proposition. Indeed, James Madison would be pleased; it is estimated that in the United States today there are hundreds, perhaps even thousands, of religious sects.

However, the large number of religious sects pales in comparison to the vast number of laws passed, or on the books, at all levels of the United States. Why compare the number of religious sects with the number of laws? What does one have to do with the other? The relationship between the two is important in the following sense: when government passes its many laws, it must (according to the Supreme Court's interpretation of the Constitution) do so for a secular and not a religious reason. But when these laws are enacted, what happens if government *unintentionally* harms religion, especially individual religious beliefs and practices? Note that such unintentional harm can easily happen, given government's many laws and the American people's vast array of religious beliefs and practices. There seems to be little controversy that the legislature can, when it passes a law (and should it detect probable political–religious conflicts), exempt individual religious practitioners from the effect of secular laws. The disputed question is what the Constitution *requires* the courts to do. In a few cases, the radical constitutional question is whether the Free Exercise Clause invalidates legislation that unintentionally hampers minority religious practitioners. However, this is not usually the kind of constitutional challenge made in suits seeking to overturn laws that have an unintentional impact on religious minorities. Far more often, such suits assert only that the Constitution requires that religious practitioners be exempted from the secular law.

In examining whether exemptions from the secular law should be granted to religious practitioners, several issues emerge. They include the following: (1) As a philosophical and legal matter, should Americans with diverse religious beliefs who are unintentionally harmed by secular laws be treated any differently by those laws? In other words, does true religious freedom require treating all citizens similarly, or some citizens differently? (2) If religious practitioners are to be granted exemptions, to what extent, and by what standard, should the Supreme Court require (as opposed to allow) government(s) to extend such exemptions?[1] This is partially a question of how assertive a role the Court should play in the American political system; it raises the issue of judicial activism and restraint. (3) If religious practitioners are to be granted exemptions, how should the exemptions be reconciled with the Establishment Clause, which requires government to be neutral between religion and nonreligion? This is a problem of constitutional consistency (or inconsistency). With these three questions in mind, we turn our attention to some important, and interesting, cases.

EXAMPLE 1

Sherbert v. *Verner,* 374 U.S. 398 (1963)

Facts: Sherbert was a Seventh Day Adventist. Saturday was her Sabbath, and working on that day violated her religious beliefs. She was fired for not working Saturdays, and, because of her refusal to work Saturdays, she could not obtain new employment. Additionally, she was denied unemployment insurance. According to South Carolina law, a person must be available for work. Sherbert, by refusing to work Saturdays, was not, so she was ruled ineligible for unemployment insurance.

Result: Denying Sherbert unemployment insurance attempts to regulate, and hence violates, her religious beliefs, infringing upon the Free Exercise Clause as applied to the states.

Argument of the Case: Brennan, Justice. Government cannot compel a citizen to profess a repugnant religious belief, nor can it penalize or discriminate against those who profess such views. Although acts that follow from religious belief can be regulated by government (particularly when they pose a threat to public safety), that regulation must be justified by a compelling state interest. Government would also have to demonstrate that no less restrictive alternative form of constitutional regulation was possible. Here, Sherbert's religious free exercise has been burdened by government. She must choose between her religion and receiving unemployment benefits. The state interest in safeguarding state funds by discouraging fraudulent claims of those pretending to hold religious beliefs that preclude Saturday work is not compelling.

Douglas concurs. It is easy for government to trod upon unusual minority religious beliefs under the guise of health or police regulation. Here, its regulation violates religious free exercise.

Stewart concurs. The result is correct, but the Court's opinion is flawed. The Constitution (that is, each religion clause) requires government to create an atmosphere of hospitality to religious freedom. In the past, the Supreme Court has impermissibly expanded the Establishment Clause while remaining insensitive to Free Exercise infractions, thus creating a severe tension between the two. The Court's decision (despite its disclaimers) is at odds with these precedents.

Harlan dissents.[2] Sherbert was not denied benefits because of her religion; she was denied benefits because she was unavailable for work. The state law compensates people for involuntary unemployment, but Sherbert is voluntarily unemployed. Furthermore, the case violates Free Exercise Clause precedents. Although the state may choose to create an exemption for religion, the Constitution does not compel it to do so. Seldom does the Constitution require religion to be treated differently. In this case, Sherbert is not the object of governmental compulsion; the law's effect upon religious free exercise is remote while the direct financial assistance provided religion by the Court's decision is considerable.

Discussion

Justice Brennan's opinion for the Court did not merely uphold Sherbert's Free Exercise claim; it cut a wide swath of free exercise protection. According to his opinion, the government could not defend a policy or law inhibiting an individual's religious free exercise by demonstrating a reasonable or usual interest but only by showing a *compelling* state interest—that is, an interest essential for government's continued functioning where there existed no less-restrictive constitutional way of achieving the same policy objective. Brennan's test decisively tilted the balance of proof against the government. Under such a test, governmental programs, or their application, that endangered religious free exercise were presumed to be impermissible. The burden of proof was left to the government to demonstrate that the challenged program (as applied) was constitutional.

Several Justices, who did not join Brennan's opinion, disagreed among themselves regarding *Sherbert's* consistency in two key respects. The first was precedent. Justices Douglas, Stewart, Harlan, and White (who disagreed on some legal issues but not on this point) all agreed that the Court's decision was at odds with its previous Sunday closing decisions, particularly *Braunfield* v. *Brown*.[3] In *Braunfield,* the Court had ruled the states could declare Sunday a day of rest and were not obligated to exempt religious practitioners who celebrated their Sabbath on Saturday from its provisions (it being of no constitutional consequence that such individuals were required to choose between following their religious beliefs by not working on Saturdays and suffering economically by not working on two days, or violating their religious beliefs by working on Saturdays). Brennan distinguished *Braunfield* on the grounds of stronger secular interest and weaker governmental infringement upon individual religious liberty. But Justice Harlan directly challenged Brennan's opinion. He thought the law upheld in *Braunfield* had a weaker secular purpose (Harlan thought providing a uniform day of rest was less important than protecting the state from fraud) while imposing a higher price upon religious practitioners who both obeyed the law and followed their religious convictions. Brennan had also argued that the designation of Sunday as the mandated day of rest posed no constitutional problem, for there was simply no other reasonable secular alternative available for achieving this objective.[4] Yet while it was important for the Court to distinguish *Braunfield* (for the sake of consistency), it was not obvious that Brennan had done so successfully. Thus, Harlan believed that *Sherbert* had effectively overturned *Braunfield,* and three other Justices detected, at the very least, significant inconsistencies between the two cases.

The other problem pointed to by dissenting Justices was a perceived inconsistency between the Establishment Clause and the Free Exercise Clause. Both Justices Stewart and Harlan (with White) were particularly concerned about this difficulty, although they expressed their concern in different ways. Each pointed out that in *Sherbert,* the Court had explicitly favored actions growing out of religious beliefs. Stewart pointed out that had Sherbert refused to work Saturdays because she was lazy (perhaps because she wished to watch Saturday television), or alternately because she was unable to obtain child care, she would not have been granted an exemption.[5] Thus, the Court in *Sherbert* had accommodated religion and championed religious liberty.[6] Unfortunately, such an advocacy of religious liberty was at odds with what Stewart took to be wrongly decided Supreme Court Establishment Clause decisions that forbade the government from supporting any one religion, or from providing any support for religion (the Court had so held in decisions outlawing prayer and Bible reading in the public schools). Hence, *Sherbert* triggered a conflict between constitutional interpretations advocated by the Supreme Court in establishment and free exercise cases.

For Justice Harlan, the problem was somewhat different. He believed that neutrality between religion and nonreligion was the chief value advanced by the religion clauses; although neutrality in *Sherbert* did not require the government to make special exemptions for religious practitioners, it did allow for these exemptions. Harlan believed that the Court's opinion had ignored reconciling the law decided under the Establishment and Free Exercise clauses. This concern, raised by Justices Stewart and Harlan, had been laconically dismissed by the Court, which had asserted only that the Sherbert decision generally advanced religious neutrality.

Having observed that Brennan's opinion for the Court carved out a very large area protecting religious belief and practice unintentionally and adversely impacted by law, we would be negligent if we did not also add that the standard itself would eventually be revised. A more restrictive standard of religious free exercise would be imposed more than twenty-five years later, when the Court would adopt a more confining test of that clause. Although *Employment Division, Department of Human Resources* v. *Smith*[7] also involved a denial of welfare benefits and although the Court's majority attempted to minimize its departure from *Sherbert,* the Supreme Court did advocate a significant departure (although the *Sherbert* standard later was restored at the expense of the *Smith* case when Congress passed the Religious Freedom Act of 1993). However, it is also noteworthy that even when the broad *Sherbert* test garnered a clear majority of the Court's Justices, religiously motivated acts did not always prevail over the state's interest.[8] In the following case, the unique nature of the government's interest makes clear at least one reason that this was so.

EXAMPLE 2

Goldman v. *Weinberger,* 475 U.S. 503 (1986)

Facts: S. Simcha Goldman was accepted into the Armed Forces Health Professions Scholarship Program and placed on inactive reserve status while he pursued his doctoral studies in psychology. The program provided him stipends for tuition, books, and fees for three years. After obtaining his degree, Goldman was inducted into active service in the Air Force as a commissioned officer. He was required to serve three years (one for each year of subsidized education he had received). He served as a clinical psychologist at a mental health clinic on base. As an Orthodox Jew and an ordained rabbi, he wore a yarmulke (a religious skullcap). Air Force regulations prohibit the wearing of headgear indoors.

Result: The Air Force regulation does not violate the First Amendment's Free Exercise Clause as applied to Goldman. The Air Force's interest in uniformity is high, for it is by necessity a specialized society with its own rules.

Argument of the Case: Rehnquist, Justice. Civil liberties are far more constricted in the military than they are in the general society, and the Supreme Court accords it far more deference. The military requires the subordination of the individual and does so by prohibiting visible religious apparel. It is the professional judgment of the Air Force that "the traditional outfitting of personnel in standardized uniforms encourages the subordination of personal preferences and identities in favor of the overall group mission."

Stevens concurs.[9] Although *Goldman* presents an attractive case for an exemption, if his petition for exemption is granted, then other requests for exemptions (including turbans, saffron robes, and dreadlocks) will also have to be respected.

Brennan dissents.[10] Goldman's free exercise claim is sincere and serious. The Court simply defers to the military, yet there is no evidence that Goldman's yarmulke is disruptive or that Air Force discipline or uniformity is compromised. Wearing a yarmulke no more promotes individuality than does wearing up to three rings (which is permitted). Yarmulkes no more identify individuals than does attending religious services. Although other religious, obtrusive clothing may raise future problems, such disputes are presently hypothetical; the government can insist upon reasonable standards.

Blackmun dissents: "The Air Force simply has not shown any reason to fear that a significant number of enlisted personnel and officers would request religious exemptions that could not be denied on neutral grounds such as safety, let alone that granting these requests would noticeably impair the overall image of the service." In such circumstances, judicial deference to the military seems unwarranted.

O'Connor dissents.[11] The Court decides this case without even enunciating a free exercise standard. In those "rare instances where the military has not consistently or plausibly justified its asserted need for rigidity of enforcement, and where the individual seeking the exemption established that the assertion by the military of a threat to discipline or esprit de corps is in his or her case completely unfounded, I would hold that the Government's policy of uniformity must yield to the individual's assertion of the right of free exercise of religion."

Discussion

Initially, one cannot help being sympathetically disposed toward Goldman. His religious motivation was universally acknowledged to be sincere. Furthermore, a yarmulke is a well-established religious symbol. As worn, it was hardly noticeable and posed no real threat of disruption. Goldman had avoided controversy, in the words of the Court, "by remaining close to his duty station in the health clinic and by wearing his service cap over the yarmulke when out of doors." Furthermore, it appeared that the enforcement of the military rule against Goldman may well have been retaliatory. For a time, he had not been prevented from wearing his yarmulke. Pressure that he conform to the rule occurred only after he testified as a defense witness in a court-martial proceeding.

Additionally, there was the constitutional standard that the Court had applied in *Sherbert* v. *Verner*. *Sherbert* had established a legal test imposing a heavy burden upon government; in order to deny an individual a religiously motivated exemption under the Free Exercise Clause, the government had to demonstrate that it had a compelling interest in disallowing a religion-based claim and that it had no alternate way of securing its objectives. Clearly, the *Sherbert* test would have invalidated the Air Force regulation outlawing the wearing of headgear indoors, as applied to Goldman. However, for the majority, the *Sherbert* test was not appropriately extended to the military. Nor did the Court even require that the regulation be defended as rational. Brennan complained that the Court had adopted a "subrational" standard—one that accorded unlimited deference to the armed services. Justice O'Connor agreed (and also objected):

> The Court rejects Captain Goldman's claim without even the slightest attempt to weigh his asserted right to the free exercise of his religion against the interest of the Air Force in uniformity of dress within the military hospital. No test for Free Exercise claims in the military context is even articulated, much less applied. It is entirely sufficient for the Court if the military perceives a need for uniformity.[12]

Justices Brennan and O'Connor's complaint was largely irrefutable. The Court admitted that it had accorded the military great deference, suggesting that its rules and regulations were ultimately the responsibility of the President and Congress. Rehnquist also asserted that the Court was ill-equipped to determine the impact upon discipline of any particular rule or regulation. The Air Force's minute rules of dress had their own intrinsic logic:

> The considered professional judgment of the Air Force is that the traditional outfitting of personnel in standardized uniforms encourages the subordination of personal preferences and identities in favor of the overall mission. Uniforms encourage a sense of hierarchical unity by tending to eliminate outward individual distinctions except for those of rank. The Air Force considers them as vital during peacetime as during war because its personnel must be ready to provide an effective defense on a moment's notice; the necessary habits of discipline and unity must be developed in advance of trouble. We have acknowledged that "[t]he inescapable demands of military procedures and orders must be virtually reflex with no time for debate or reflection."[13]

In other words, the Court accepted the need for a uniform military and also accepted the military's explanation of the manner by which this goal should be advanced.

There are a few areas (military life being one, prison life being another[14]) where First Amendment religion clause claims simply have a very limited scope. Goldman had contended that the First Amendment required the military to make an exception for his dress, that it was unobtrusive, that it provoked no danger, and that it provided no threat to discipline. The Court's answer made clear that the First Amendment required no such exemption, as long as all service personnel were treated equally:

> The desirability of dress regulations in the military is decided by the appropriate military officials, and they are under no constitutional mandate

to abandon their considered professional judgment. Quite obviously, to the extent the regulations do not permit the wearing of religious apparel such as a yarmulke, a practice described by petitioner as silent devotion akin to prayer, military life may be more objectionable for petitioner and probably others. But the First Amendment does not require the military to accommodate such practices in the face of its view that they would detract from the uniformity sought by the dress regulations. The Air Force has drawn the line essentially between religious apparel which is visible and that which is not, and we hold that those portions of the regulations challenged here reasonably and even-handedly regulate dress in the interest of the military's perceived need for uniformity.[15]

Significantly, Rehnquist spoke only for himself and for Justice Powell; he depended upon three concurring Justices (Stevens, joined by White and Powell) in order to form a majority upholding the disputed military regulation. The concurring Justices' positions were thought-provoking. They agreed with Goldman that his religious dress was unobtrusive and that, because it was worn primarily in his counseling practice, it was also minimally disruptive. However, they still voted to support the military. Their difficulty was that they could not see on what principled basis they could permit Goldman's religious headgear while ruling out more conspicuous apparel, given the military's interest in uniformity ("which," in the Court's words, "we must recognize as legitimate and rational even though personal experience or admiration for the performance of the 'rag-tag band of soldiers' that won us our freedom in the revolutionary war might persuade us that the Government has exaggerated the importance of that interest".)[16] Uniformity had another dimension; it precluded the military from having to distinguish mainstream "acceptable" religious dress from that which might be regarded as more extreme or unusual. According to the Stevens opinion, such a selection would inevitably favor some religions over others, primarily based upon their appearance. To the government's contention that "while a yarmulke might not seem obtrusive to a Jew, neither does a turban to a Sikh, a saffron robe to a Satchidananda Ashram-Integral Yogi, nor do dreadlocks to a Rastafarian," Stevens observed that the difference among all these religious symbols was not merely how they looked but what they represented. Religious appearance and wardrobe stood for profound religious differences that the government was constitutionally obligated to treat identically. Blackmun (dissenting) suggested one way the Court might distinguish among differing religious apparel and appearance without extending favoritism: "In general, I see no constitutional difficulty in distinguishing between religious practices based on how difficult it would be to accommodate them...."[17]

The Court declined Blackmun's proposed test, perhaps struck by the difficulty of determining, on a case-by-case basis, the danger that individually motivated religious apparel and appearance posed to such legitimate military concerns as safety. When one analyzes the various judicial opinions in *Goldman*, it is clear that there was no question that civil liberties in general, and free religious exercise in particular, were constricted within the military. The central questions in dispute asked how constricted they were and how much justification the Court would require from the military to justify their limited scope (keep in mind that Congress was always free to establish and alter military regulations[18]). It would seem that the military posed a special exemption to *Sherbert's* broadly crafted protection for religion. But how special was it?

EXAMPLE 3

Bowen **v.** *Roy,* 476 U.S. 693 (1986)

Facts: Steven Roy and Karen Miller are parents of two-year-old Little Bird of the Snow, and all are descended from the Albenaki Indian tribe. They applied for and received benefits under the Aid to Dependent Children and Food Stamp programs. However, the Pennsylvania Department of Public Welfare required, as a precondition for participation in these programs, that Roy obtain a Social Security card and number for their daughter. Roy objected to Congress's requirement that Social Security cards be used in distributing social welfare benefits; he also contended that obtaining and furnishing to the government a Social Security number would violate his and his family's Native American religious beliefs.

Result: The Free Exercise Clause does not prevent state welfare agencies from using such account numbers in the administration of welfare programs.

Argument of the Case: Burger, Chief Justice.[19] (A) Congress's requirement that state agencies shall use Social Security numbers in the administration of the Aid to Dependent Children plan is constitutionally appropriate. The Free Exercise Clause is a right possessed by individuals against government action; it has never been understood to require the government to act in a way that suits with the religious beliefs of individual citizens. Neither is Congress's 1978 Joint Resolution concerning American Indian religious freedom (which makes it the policy "of the United States to protect and preserve for American Indians their inherent right of freedom to believe, express and exercise the tradition of the American religions of the American Indians") violated, for "the Federal Government's use of a Social Security number for Little Bird of the Snow does not itself in any degree impair Roy's 'freedom to believe, express, and exercise his religion.'" (B) The government can additionally require all individuals to furnish a Social Security number to it as a condition of participating in a welfare program. Religious convictions "do not automatically entitle a person to fix unilaterally the conditions and terms of dealing with the government"; thus, "[n]ot all burdens on religion are unconstitutional." The requirement that a Social Security number be furnished is religiously neutral; seeking to prevent fraud does not invidiously discriminate against any religion. Regarding the government's action, "We conclude then that government regulation that indirectly and incidentally calls for a choice between securing a governmental benefit and adherence to religious beliefs is wholly different from governmental action or legislation that criminalizes religiously inspired activity or inescapably compels conduct that some find objectionable for religious reasons." *Sherbert* does not apply; in that case government would have shown hostility toward religion had it not extended an exemption. Here, the constitutional standard is different: "Absent proof of an intent to discriminate against particular religious beliefs or against religion in general, the Government meets its burden when it demonstrates that a challenged requirement for governmental benefits, neutral and uniform in its application, is a reasonable means of promoting a legitimate public interest."

Blackmun concurs, in part. The Court is correct that the Free Exercise Clause cannot be stretched to prohibit the government from using already assigned Social Security numbers. The record is far from clear regarding the facts surrounding Roy's objection to providing a Social Security number, and it is not obvious that the Court need decide this question. If it needed to be decided, the *Sherbert* standard would govern. Little Bird of the Snow cannot be denied aid "solely because her parents' religious convictions prevent them from supplying the Government with a Social Security number for their daughter."

Stevens concurs, in part. The Court correctly decides that the government can use Social Security numbers, for the Free Exercise Clause does not permit individuals to dictate to the government how it must keep records. The case's record regarding whether Roy must provide a Social Security card for his daughter is unclear, and because it is based upon the confusing record, is either not ripe for decision or moot.

O'Connor concurs, in part, and dissents, in part.[20] The Free Exercise Clause does not bar the government from using information already in its possession. However, the government's requirement that a Social Security number be furnished cannot be sustained. The government's interest in avoiding welfare fraud can be satisfied in other ways (for example, cross-matching without Social Security numbers). While such an approach might place an inconvenience upon government, the Free Exercise Clause imposes a higher standard upon government for denying benefits.

White dissents. *Sherbert v. Verner* and other subsequent cases dictate invalidating the government's position.

Discussion

Bowen v. *Roy* is a complicated case. Legally, it is complex because there were different distinct yet interrelated questions facing the Court. Essentially, the Court decided, by a decisive majority, that the Free Exercise Clause did not bar the government from *using* Social Security numbers for the purpose of administering governmental welfare programs in an efficient, nonfraudulent manner. However, regarding the second question it faced—whether the Free Exercise Clause prohibited government from requiring individuals to *furnish* it Social Security numbers in violation of their religious beliefs—confusion reigned. While the lower court order was vacated and the case remanded, the Court simply offered a mere outline of an answer to this question.

Part of the Court's fragmentation could be attributed to the confusion inherent in the facts of this case. Originally, at the state administrative hearing, the state contended that it denied public assistance benefits because Roy would not apply for a Social Security number for his daughter. Roy testified that he had recently developed a religious objection simply to obtaining the card. He further testified that this religious objection extended to simply having to obtain a Social Security *number*. Finally, Roy testified that neither using the phonetics of his daughter's name to derive a Social Security number nor the listing of his daughter's full tribal name would overcome his religious objections. Why not? Roy's Native American religious belief held that control over one's life was essential to spiritual purity. His discussions with a Abenaki chief led him to conclude that technology was robbing the human spirit, that his daughter's spiritual power required that he (Roy) was required to keep his daughter's spirit unique, and "that the uniqueness of the Social Security number as an identifier, coupled with the other uses of the number over which she has no control, will serve to 'rob the spirit' of his daughter and prevent her from attaining greater spiritual power."[21]

Initially, according to the undisputed facts of the case, both sides had stipulated that Little Bird of the Snow did not have a Social Security number. On the last day of the trial, however, a federal official inquired, during a court recess, if this were true. He discovered that such a number had been assigned at birth (a practice the government sometimes employed for those it thought might be unwilling to obtain a number of their own). According to Justice Stevens's recounting of the case, this discovery had a "dramatic impact" on the litigation! The government suggested the case had become moot (in that Roy's complaint had become meaningless because Little Bird of the Snow's spirit had already been robbed). However, Roy simply changed his request for relief and asked for the cancellation of the existing number. Given this complex array of facts, it was hardly surprising that the Court had some difficulty agreeing upon how (or if) to apply the law of the Constitution to these facts of the case, specifically to Roy's legal assertion that the Free Exercise Clause protected him from having to obtain a Social Security number.

Further confusing this ambiguous factual record was another complication. Justices Rehnquist and Powell, joining Chief Justice Burger, sought to answer this legal question by overturning, or at the very least restricting, the scope of the *Sherbert* test. *Sherbert* may have supported Roy's claim that he was excused from obtaining a Social Security number for his daughter, but in Burger's words, "This is far removed from the historical instances of religious persecution and intolerance that gave concern to those who drafted the Free

Exercise Clause of the First Amendment."[22] No doubt, Burger believed that *Sherbert* gave too much scope to multitudinous and illegitimate free exercise claims, unnecessarily enfeebling government. As will be recalled, when government unintentionally hampered religious free exercise, *Sherbert* required that the government show a compelling interest why exemptions from the disputed legislation should not be granted. In order to do so, the government had to demonstrate that the application of the law to the religious practitioner was essential and/or no less-restrictive alternative existed.

The government could, in rare instances, win under such a test. For instance, in *United States* v. *Lee,*[23] the Supreme Court denied Amish citizens' religiously rooted objection to forced payment of Social Security taxes, contending that, in principle, such a withholding could not be distinguished from religious reservations regarding the payment of income taxes, and further asserting that "the government's interest in assuring mandatory continuous participation in and contribution to the Social Security system is very high."[24] The precise comparison between a "compelling" and a "very high" state interest was neither crystal clear nor explained in *Lee,* but that case did provide an example of the sort of essential governmental program that the Supreme Court was prepared to affirm as essential and for which it was unwilling to make individual exemptions.

The other, related aspect of the *Sherbert* test—whether there existed a less-restrictive governmental alternative to the challenged governmental practice—was rather heatedly debated in *Bowen* v. *Roy.* Justice O'Connor (also speaking for Justices Brennan and Marshall) lauded the merits of "cross-matching" as a governmental substitute for requiring Social Security numbers. In this procedure, various computerized lists are compared with the welfare rolls to detect various fraudulent practices. O'Connor admitted that under such a system the government's burden would be more difficult, but argued the Constitution's recognition of free religious exercise required such individualized accommodation. Not surprisingly, Chief Justice Burger disagreed, citing a number of factors. He noted the welfare programs being discussed were of "truly staggering magnitude," involving many millions of families and billions of dollars. They posed formidable administrative challenges, especially when it came to guarding against waste. In Burger's opinion, Social Security numbers and computers in combination formed the best check against fraud and abuse. Even if the increased risk of fraud because of cross-matching was slight, the government was still not obligated to endure it and appellants "may not use the Free Exercise Clause to demand government benefits, but only on their own terms particularly where that insistence works a demonstrable disadvantage to the Government in the administration of the program."[25] In other words, for Burger, administrative inconvenience was a sufficient reason for rejecting free exercise claims demanding individualized exemptions from governmental regulations.

To that end, Burger sought to change a *Sherbert* test that tilted the balance in favor of such religion-based exemptions. Concerned not only about the effect of requiring specific exemptions in this case, but also anticipating the enormous number of unpredicted (and unpredictable) religion-based objections to general governmental programs, Burger proposed a different constitutional standard. His free exercise test would have placed far fewer requirements upon government: "Absent proof of an intent to discriminate against particular religious beliefs or against religion in general, the Government meets its burden when it demonstrates that a challenged requirement for governmental benefits, neutral and uniform in its application, is a reasonable means of promoting a legitimate public interest."[26]

What about the *Sherbert* case and test? Burger sought to confine each to narrow boundaries. He pointed out that in that case (and in *Thomas* v. *Review Board* as well), the challenged unemployment laws had declared a person was ineligible for unemployment compensation benefits if, "without good cause," he or she had quit work or had refused available work. In those laws, however, "good cause" did not include religious conflicts. Burger contended that where such language created the means for individualized religious exemptions and then refused to extend them, it exhibited hostility, not neutrality, toward religion. Under such circumstances (and presumably only under such circumstances), a compelling reason for denying the exemption was warranted. Thus, only in instances where government permits generalized exemptions for eligibility to a governmental benefit program, and then refuses to recognize religion-based objections, must a compelling governmental interest be shown.

Yet a majority of the Court refused to accept Burger's revised Free Exercise Clause test as well as his attempt to confine *Sherbert,* at least insofar as it applied to the question of whether government had to provide an individualized exemption to the requirement that Roy apply for a Social Security number.[27] In Justice O'Connor's words,

> The Court's opinions have never turned on so slender a reed as whether the challenged requirement is merely a "reasonable means of promoting a legitimate public interest." The CHIEF JUSTICE appears to believe that the added inconvenience to the State of administering a selective exemption overbalances any burden on individual religious exercise. But this Court has held that administrative inconvenience is not alone sufficient to justify a burden of free exercise unless it creates problems of substantial magnitude. See *Sherbert* v. *Verner.*[28]

Bowen v. *Roy* continued the battle over the vitality and applicability of the *Sherbert* test; it did not resolve that controversy. The case is instructive, however, for it reflects the kind and variety of unintended harm that seemingly benign governmental regulations can cause to religious free exercise. Here, intelligent and reasonable judges disagreed about (among other things) how the respective balance between governmental authority and individual free exercise should be tipped in the numerous cases before them. What is constantly surprising is the great variety of legal claims resulting from the unexpected impacts of secular governmental programs, a point reemphasized by our next case.

EXAMPLE 4

Lyng v. *Northwest Indian Cemetery Protective Association,* 485 U.S. 439 (1988)

Facts: The United States Forest Service intended to complete a 75-mile road between two California towns by constructing a 6-mile road within a national forest. Historically, this area had been used by members of three Indian tribes for religious rituals. Essential to these rituals were privacy, silence, and an undisturbed natural setting, all of which would be significantly compromised by the road. After conducting a study of the road's effect upon Native American religious sites (which recommended against its construction), the Forest Service announced its intention to proceed with construction. Archaeological sites were avoided, and the road was as far as possible removed from the sites used by the Indians for spiritual activities. The Forest Service also adopted a plan allowing for the harvesting of timber in the area, with one-half-mile protective zones around the specific religious sites.

Result: Neither the plan to build the road nor the plan to harvest the timber violates the Free Exercise Clause of the Constitution.

Argument of the Case: O'Connor, Justice: "It is undisputed that the Indian individuals and organizations who bring suit have sincere religious beliefs and that the proposed road will adversely affect their ability to practice their religion. Like *Roy* v. *Bowen*, where the Court sustained the government's power to use Social Security numbers in the face of a Free Exercise challenge, here, too, respondents impermissibly ask government to conduct its own internal affairs in ways that comport with their religious beliefs. The Free Exercise Clause provides individual protection from certain forms of governmental compulsion; it does not permit individuals to dictate the conduct of the government's individual procedures. The building of a road or the harvesting of timber on publicly owned land cannot meaningfully be distinguished from the government's use of a social security number. Although in each case, the government's action would interfere significantly with individuals' ability to pursue spiritual fulfillment; nonetheless, in neither case would these individuals be coerced by the government into violating their religious beliefs nor would the government's action penalize religious activity by denying any person an equal share of the rights, benefits, and privileges enjoyed by other citizens."

Brennan dissents.[29] The Court concludes that federal land-use decisions rendering the practice of a given religion impossible do not burden that religion in violation of the Free Exercise Clause because governmental policy neither coerces conduct that violates religious beliefs nor penalizes religious activity. Yet the Free Exercise Clause does not make such fine distinctions. The Court refuses to even acknowledge the legal injury suffered and provides Native Americans with "absolutely no constitutional protection against perhaps the gravest threat to their religious practices...." Past precedents do not support the Court's interpretation of the Free Exercise Clause.

Discussion

Here, again, we have a complex case fraught with subtleties. Yet, as they say, it is important not to miss the forest for the trees. In addition to posing many matters of detail, *Lyng* raises the central question posed by this chapter in an important, straightforward way. What happens when individual religious beliefs and practices are unintentionally hampered by government? For that reason, it is both an interesting and instructive case.

Let us begin our analysis by examining both the government's and the Native Americans' interest. The federal government owned the land on which it intended to build a six-mile segment of paved road between two northern California towns, Gasquet and Orleans. Having a road between these two towns fulfilled several purposes. It completed a road that otherwise would have dead-ended in the forest, it provided a route for hauling the timber that government intended to cut, it enhanced public access to the forest and to natural landmarks, and it aided in fire control. In order to ameliorate the effects of its decision, the government undertook a variety of measures, including not disturbing ritual sites and taking steps to reduce the visual and auditory impacts of the road upon the surrounding countryside. Yet to the Native American organizations and individuals affected, these measures were insufficient. As Justice Brennan explained at length (and as the Court seemed to acknowledge), building the road and harvesting the timber could virtually destroy their ability to practice their religion. To Native Americans, the land itself was sacred.

This Native American religiously based objection to governmental policy proved quite troubling to the Court's majority. While the Court's opinion carefully considered the facts of the case, it also focused upon the general theoretical problem that such a case posed. O'Connor stated it in specific terms as follows: "However much we might wish that it were otherwise, government simply could not operate if it were required to satisfy every citizen's need and desires." Indeed, while a "broad range of government activities—from social welfare programs to foreign aid to conservation projects—will always be considered essential to the spiritual well-being of some citizens, often on the basis of sincerely held religious beliefs," others "will find the very same activities deeply offensive, and perhaps incompatible with their own search for spiritual fulfillment and with the tenets of their religion."[30] Even in the confined context of the case before it, the potential for political conflict and religiously motivated litigation seemed virtually unlimited. Given the many millions of acres of publicly owned lands, there certainly existed, as Justice Brennan acknowledged, "the specter of future suits in which Native Americans seek to exclude all human activity from such areas."[31]

O'Connor's solution to the potential nightmare of endless religiously motivated litigation began with an argument that it was not solely the Supreme
Court's responsibility to address and solve this problem. Citing *Federalist* 10
(which had argued that disputes and competition among various religious sects
are best resolved through competition within the legislative branch), she observed that the "Constitution does not, and courts cannot, offer to reconcile
the various competing demands on government, many of them rooted in sincere religious beliefs, that inevitably arise in so diverse a society as ours." Who
is responsible for the solution? "That task, to the extent that it is feasible, is for
the legislatures and other institutions," declared O'Connor.[32]

To her mind, free exercise protection did not extend to the Native Americans in this case. The Supreme Court could not invalidate the government's
program case and in any clear, logical manner distinguish its results from many
other potential free exercise suits. As we have seen, O'Connor feared that
many such successful suits would debilitate government, essentially grinding it
to a halt. Even Brennan, in dissent, was willing to admit the problem's existence, although he focused on the immediate facts of the situation. Brennan
proposed to meet future constitutional claims that federal lands be undisturbed
by having the courts determine if the claim was central or indispensable to the
practice of Native American religions. (Yet Brennan also acknowledged that
the centrality test had no clear meaning to Native American culture.[33]) O'-
Connor was more straightforward, simply siding with the government. Individuals, whatever their religious claim, could be afforded some protection
from the application of governmental programs; however, the Constitution
did not give individuals the right to dictate the conduct of the government's
internal procedures.

Therefore, the essential free exercise interpretation advanced by O'Connor was that individual, religiously rooted exemptions to constitutional governmental programs or policies could be upheld, while religiously rooted
claims that required their cessation or overturning would be rejected. This
standard did not primarily turn upon the effect of the disputed governmental
practice upon individual religious belief or practice. This was the key to understanding the majority's use of precedent. Thus, *Sherbert* was interpreted to
have held that where the incidental effect of legitimate governmental programs had the effect of coercing individuals (that is, requiring them to choose
between their religious beliefs and a government benefit), government was required to demonstrate a compelling state interest for denying an exemption.[34]
Roy was interpreted to have upheld the right of the government to administer
its programs efficiently, even though its actions may offend individual religious
beliefs or practices. In each case, the Court stressed that individual coercion
was the key to understanding the Free Exercise Clause. Where a constitutional
governmental program worked a differentiated individual hardship that could
be accommodated by government without invalidating the overall program,
then it was up to government to justify why it could not grant an exemption.
But surely Brennan was right to point out that in *Lyng* and elsewhere, such an

approach was utterly indifferent to the strength of the individual's religious claim. In *Lyng,*

> the proposed logging and construction activities will virtually destroy respondents' religion, and will therefore necessarily force them into abandoning those practices altogether. Indeed, the Government's activities will restrain religious practice to a far greater degree here than in any of the cases cited by the Court today. None of the religious adherents in … Sherbert, for example, claimed or could have claimed that the denial of unemployment benefits rendered the practice of their religions impossible; at most, the challenged made those practices more expensive. Here in stark contrast, respondents have claimed—and proved—that the desecration of the high country will prevent religious leaders from attaining the religious power or medicine indispensable to the success of virtually all their rituals and ceremonies.[35]

On the one hand, *Lyng* presents a Native American legal challenge that, if successful, would have invalidated a governmental program; on the other hand, it also presents a government program capable of destroying a people's religion. In this area of constitutional law, apparently there are no happy answers, only agonizing problems.

SUMMARY

When everything was said and done in *Lyng,* the general outlines of the Supreme Court's constitutional approach had, at last, become clear. On the one hand, the Free Exercise Clause provides the basis for limited forms of individual exemptions from general governmental programs. On the other hand, the clause generally does not furnish the basis for invalidating those programs.

Motivating the Supreme Court's approach has been the recognition that, given the enormous variety of religious beliefs that exists in the United States, there are an almost infinite number of unintended, religiously related effects that follow from otherwise perfectly constitutional secular legislation. Therefore, the major portion of the Supreme Court's attention has focused upon determining the context and extent to which the Constitution requires individual exemptions. As we observed in *Goldman,* the Court has determined that, in some environments (in this case, the military), the Free Exercise Clause has a significantly reduced capacity to mandate individualized exemptions to general rules. In more routine contexts, both *Sherbert* and *Roy* reflect the fact that Supreme Court Justices most often disputed the constitutional standard by which exemptions were extended to individuals. *Sherbert* (whose constitutional authority subsequently would be widely disputed) argued that where governmental programs required individuals to choose between governmental programs and important religious beliefs and practices, government must show a compelling interest (and the existence of no less-intrusive method of managing its program) in order for exemptions to be denied. In cases like *Roy* (and in other, later cases), the *Sherbert* standard was challenged on a variety of grounds. These included the recognition that while religious exemptions were laudable, they were not constitutionally required; that they were properly extended by the legislature as opposed to the Court; that they unduly hampered the functioning of government; and that their direct favoring of religious belief conflicted with the Supreme Court's persistent interpretation of the Establishment Clause's requiring governmental neutrality between the religious and secular realms. As we have observed, these areas of dispute continue today, within the context of various new free exercise cases.

NOTES

1. In constitutional law, this is more of a pressing question regarding laws of states and localities, as opposed to Congress, to which the Supreme Court has traditionally accorded greater deference.

2. This opinion is joined by Justice White.

3. 366 U.S. 599 (1961). For a discussion of *Braunfield* and related cases, see Chapter 17, p. 309.

4. But note Douglas's objection previously raised in his dissent in *Braunfield* and in a companion case, *McGowan* v. *Maryland*, 366 U.S. 420, 576 (1961):

The State can, of course, require one day of rest a week: one day when every shop or factory is closed. Quite a few States make that requirement. Then the "day of rest" becomes purely and simply a health measure. But the Sunday laws operate differently. They force minorities to obey the majority's religious feeling of what is due and proper for a Christian community; they provide a coercive spur to the "weaker brethren," to those who are indifferent to the claims of a Sabbath through apathy or scruple. Can there be any doubt that Christians, now aligned vigorously in favor of these laws, would be as strongly opposed if they were prosecuted under a Moslem law that forbade them from engaging in secular activities on days that violated Moslem scruples?

5. 374 U.S., 415–416.

6. Although Stewart's phrasing was curious: "And I think that the guarantee of religious liberty embodied in the Free Exercise Clause affirmatively requires government to create an atmosphere of hospitality and accommodation to individual belief *or disbelief*. In short, I think our Constitution commands the positive protection by government of religious freedom—and only for a minority, however small—not only for the majority, however large—but for each of us." See *Sherbert* at 415–16. Emphasis ours.

7. 494 U.S. 872 (1990). The case is discussed in Chapter 9.

8. However, until *Smith*, important cases were decided according to *Sherbert*'s precepts. An arguable application took place in *Wisconsin* v. *Yoder*, 406 U.S. 205 (1972), while the clearest application could be found in *Thomas* v. *Review Board of the Indiana Employment Security Division*, 450 U.S. 707 (1981). These cases are discussed in Chapters 14 and 17, respectively.

9. Justices White and Powell join this opinion.

10. Justice Marshall joins this opinion.

11. Justice Marshall also joins this opinion.

12. *Goldman* v. *Weinberger* at 528.

13. *Goldman* v. *Weinberger* at 508.

14. In *O'Lone* v. *Estate of Shavazz*, 482 U.S. 342 (1987), the Supreme Court upheld a prison policy, justified by a concern for security, which prohibited prisoners with outside work assignments from returning to prison except in emergencies, even though the policy had the unintended effect of preventing Muslim prisoners from attending Jumu'ah, a weekly service held on early Friday afternoons.

The Court noted that while "convicted prisoners do not forfeit all constitutional protection by reason of their conviction and confinement in prison," nevertheless, "[l]awful incarceration brings about the necessary withdrawal or limitation of many privileges and rights, a retraction justified by the considerations underlying our penal system." 482 U.S. 348. The Court found the regulation reasonably related to the state's legitimate penological interests.

15. *Goldman* v. *Weinberger* at 509-10.

16. *Goldman* v. *Weinberger* at 512.

17. *Goldman* v. *Weinberger* at 527.

18. And in 1988, Congress did essentially overrule *Goldman* by amending the relevant law to permit members of the armed forces to wear religious apparel while on duty. Of course, this was done as a matter of law, not of right.

19. The Burger opinion speaks only for Justices Powell and Rehnquist regarding the question of whether requiring a Social Security number violated the Free Exercise Clause (point B).

20. This opinion is joined by Justices Brennan and Marshall.

21. *Bowen* v. *Roy* at 696.

22. *Bowen* v. *Roy* at 703.

23. 455 U.S. 252 (1982).

24. *U.S.* v. *Lee* at 258.

25. *Bowen* v. *Roy* at 711–12.

26. *Bowen* v. *Roy* at 707–08.

27. Regarding the other question posed by the case, whether government could be prohibited from using Social Security numbers, the Court neither applied nor rejected a *Sherbert* approach. As has been observed, it simply declared that individuals could not require the government generally to act in ways it believed appropriate; therefore, it declared that this did not create a claim supported by the Free Exercise Clause.

28. *Bowen* v. *Roy* at 730–31.

29. This opinion is joined by Justices Marshall and Blackmun.

30. 485 U.S. at 452.

31. *Lyng* v. *Northwest Indian Cemetery* at 473.

32. *Lyng* v. *Northwest Indian Cemetery* at 453.

33. "Although this requirement limits the potential number of free exercise claims that might be brought to federal land management decisions, and thus forestalls the possibility that the Government will find itself ensnared in a host of lilliputian lawsuits, it has been criticized as inherently ethnocentric, for it incorrectly assumes that Native American belief systems ascribe religious significance to land in a traditionally western hierarchical manner.... It is frequently the case in constitutional litigation, however, that courts are called upon to balance interests that are not readily translated into rough equivalents. At their most absolute, the competing claims that both the Government and Native Americans assert in federal land are fundamentally incompatible, and unless they are tempered by compromise, mutual accommodation will remain impossible." *Lyng* v. *Northwest Indian Cemetery* at 474.

34. *Lyng* v. *Northwest Indian Cemetery* at 450–51.

35. *Lyng* v. *Northwest Indian Cemetery* at 467.

8

When Are Religious Beliefs and Practices So Fundamental That They Require Secular Expression?

THE PROBLEM POSED

Although the United States was not founded upon any single religious truth and the Constitution does not refer to God, the influence of religion and public references to God endure. One obvious explanation for this phenomenon is that most Americans understand themselves to be religious. Furthermore, since our nation's inception, religion has been understood and championed as the foundation of a shared national morality.[1] Therefore, it is quite understandable that numerous public displays of, and public references to, America's religious legacy and contemporary practices endure. The question posed by this chapter is this: Are public expressions of religion compatible with our present-day understanding of the Constitution, especially the Establishment Clause? In this chapter we will find that this question has not been easily or consistently answered by the Supreme Court.

One difficulty in classifying even the brief references to God or religion in public prayers, religious symbols, or public displays is that they share a dual nature. Such communication often conveys both a sectarian and secular meaning. Therefore, in our nation, religiously inspired references to God are often justified by their capacity to enhance a national community, advance society's core moral values, or both. In a historical, worldwide context, it is worth noting that almost all civilized societies have shared similar moral precepts, despite the fact that these precepts can be based on quite divergent religious understandings and traditions. This proposition is argued most forcefully by

C. S. Lewis in his book *The Abolition of Man*.[2] It is possible to see varying religious traditions and different societies and civilizations as alternate (and more or less successful) ways of achieving similar patterns of moral behavior (for example, honoring parents, practicing magnanimity, and achieving justice).[3]

American issues of church–state conflict invariably involve a shared Jewish-Christian perspective (and in a very few instances, simply a Christian perspective). No other single example reflects the interrelationship between the mutually reinforcing goals of strengthening specific religious teaching and promoting desirable moral behavior as does the case that follows.

EXAMPLE 1

Stone v. *Graham,* 449 U.S. 39 (1980)

Facts: A Kentucky law requires that a copy of the Ten Commandments be posted on the wall of each public school classroom. The law stipulates that the posted copies must be purchased with private funds.

Result: The Kentucky statute requiring the posting of privately funded (16-by-20 inch) copies of the Ten Commandments in public school rooms has no secular purpose and therefore violates the Establishment Clause of the First Amendment.

Argument of the Case—Per Curiam: In order to determine if the Establishment Clause has been breached, the *Lemon* test must be applied. The first part of that test asks if the contested statute serves a secular purpose. Kentucky's argument fails (it being that the law's secular purpose was evidenced by the legislature's requirement that the Commandments contain, in small print at the bottom of each display, the notation that "[t]he secular application of the Ten Commandments is clearly seen in its adoption as the fundamental legal code of Western Civilization and the Common Law of the United States"). The legislature's avowed reason for posting the Commandments conflicts with the act's preeminent purpose, which is religious in nature, evidenced by the fact that the Commandments are a sacred Jewish and Christian text. The first part of the Commandments concerns the religious duties of believers, including the commandment that God alone be worshipped. Nor are the Commandments integrated into the curriculum; they are not used to study about religion (which would be constitutionally permissible). It also does not matter that the Bible verses were only posted (and not read aloud); minor as well as major encroachments on the First Amendment are constitutionally prohibited. Finally, it is the posting and not the funding of the Ten Commandments that violates the Constitution; therefore, it does not matter that their printing was privately funded.

Burger and Blackmun dissent, without opinion.[4]

Stewart dissents, without opinion.[5]

Rehnquist dissents. The Court's opinion that posting the Ten Commandments has *no* legislative purpose but has a preeminent religious purpose impermissibly rejects the Kentucky legislature's stated secular purpose in enacting the law. The Constitution does not require, nor is it either possible or desirable, to secularize all knowledge completely (for example, the development of art and music cannot be understood apart from their religious roots).

Discussion

The Ten Commandments can be viewed from two somewhat different perspectives. It is both a statement of moral rules and a proclamation of divine authority. Even from the perspective of revealed religion, this distinction is not always clearly delineated. For instance, the Ten Commandments constitute a small number of the 613 specific commandments issued by God that are delineated in the Bible. (The Hebrew term for commandment is *mitzvah,* the singular being a *mizvot.*) But a mizvot also denotes the idea of a good deed, so the term is often understood to be a good deed commanded by God.[6] For the traditionally religious person, the connection is clear; certain moral actions are good because they are willed by God (or sometimes, more loosely, because they are consistent with God's Commandments). It follows from this point of view that individual morality is measured by one's ability to conform his or her attitudes, beliefs, and behaviors according to God's will.

But one need not be Jewish, Christian, or religious at all to affirm the wisdom of many of the Commandments, especially those that prohibit murder, theft, adultery, and so forth. Although an atheist would not agree that these rules are good because God willed them (not believing in God at all), such a person might well think that these precepts are morally right and necessary if a political society is to survive and prosper. Such an individual may care little about a Commandment's origin: she or he would be much more concerned about its content and its individual and societal effect.

The question is this: Can the secular be separated from the religious in the Ten Commandments? The Supreme Court's majority in *Stone* tended to argue that it couldn't.[7] The Court's point can best be understood as an attempt to view the Ten Commandments from two interrelated perspectives. First, in order to conclude that posting the Commandments had a predominantly religious and not a secular purpose, the Court viewed the Commandments as a whole, interrelated document. In the Court's words, the Commandments "do not confine themselves to arguably secular matters...." They are not simply confined to declaring secularly important prohibitions against murder, adultery, stealing, covetousness, and lying (as well as advancing the positive injunction to honor one's parents). Rather, the "first part of the Commandments concerns the religious duties of believers; worshipping the Lord God alone, avoiding idolatry, not using the Lord's name in vain, and observing the sabbath day."[8]

The second perspective from which the Court viewed the contested Kentucky law was that of the established law. It cited clearly stated legal precedent regarding prayer and Bible reading in the public schools. In 1963, in *Abington School District* v. *Schempp,*[9] the Supreme Court had ruled against the reading of Bible verses and the Lord's Prayer in the public schools. Although the public schools had justified posting the Ten Commandments on secular grounds (specifically that these practices helped promote moral values), prayer and Bible reading had also been defended on secular grounds, and in each instance the Supreme Court found the contested practice to be blatantly religious, in violation of the First Amendment's Establishment Clause. Although *Schempp* did permit teachers to lecture about different religious traditions in the curriculum, they were prohibited from engaging in or promoting religion. Therefore, the Court's argument in *Stone* built upon *Schempp* (although not always as explicitly as one might expect). Like reading Bible verses, posting the Ten Commandments involved the schools, and therefore the state, in advocating a sacred text that contained a religious message. In the Court's opinion, this was an action that the Constitution's Establishment Clause was designed to prohibit.

Reformulating the Supreme Court's language somewhat, its argument roughly assumed the following form:

1. The state impermissibly promotes religion when it *in any way* advances or endorses Scripture (especially Scripture that imposes a religious duty to God) or any form of prayer.

2. Either reciting or reading Scriptural language as a lesson to be followed (as opposed to simply teaching about religion) means that the state is impermissibly advancing or promoting religion.

3. The Ten Commandments constitute Scripture.

4. Posting the Ten Commandments in order that it might be read constitutes the promotion of Scripture and hence constitutes the promotion of religion.

5. Posting the Ten Commandment is therefore constitutionally impermissible.

Once one grants the first premise, that the state (for example, any level of local, state, or national government) can *in no way* promote Scripture or prayer, then the rest of the argument follows logically. Justice Rehnquist attempted to counter the Court's argument (and its first premise) by suggesting that the legislature's stated purpose was secular and that its stated secular intention should prevail. Additionally, he cited the inscription that the legislature required to be placed at the bottom of the posted Commandments, which emphasized their secular importance. He also noted that simply posting the Commandments did not compel anyone to read or follow them. What about the fact that the Commandments had a clearly defined religious component? Rehnquist countered by contending that the fact that the Commandments reflected the religious nature of an ancient era was not sufficient reason to remove them, given their secular importance. And the Commandments were important, for they "have had a significant impact on the development of secular legal codes of the western world." Rehnquist also asserted that "for good or for ill, nearly everything in our culture worth transmitting, everything which gives meaning to life, is saturated with religious influences...." Therefore, it was impossible and undesirable to remove the pervasive religious influences that are part and parcel of the larger culture, including art (cathedrals), (sacred) music, and basic moral precepts. As opposed to that of the Court, Rehnquist's argument therefore looked something like this:

1. The state does not impermissibly promote religion when it advances or endorses Scriptures, just as long as the motivating purpose behind its action is secular and the Scripture's content has secular value.
2. The legislature's motivation regarding the posting of the Ten Commandments was secular, and the Ten Commandments do possess secular value.
3. Posting the Ten Commandments in public school classrooms is therefore constitutional.

Again, we would emphasize the essential difference in first premises between the Court's majority and Justice Rehnquist's formulations of the Establishment Clause issue. We would also note that while neither the Court's opinion nor Justice Rehnquist's opinion is precisely argued (and each can be criticized on a number of counts), Rehnquist's dissent is particularly problematical in one specific respect: the attempt to discount the religious content of the Commandments. As was noted, he attributed their divine injunctions regarding religious obligations to the fact that they "reflect the religious nature of ancient era."[10] Yet his approach denigrates both the importance and truth of religious revelation. It also helps perpetuate a fundamental confusion— namely, confounding the teaching of religion with teaching about religion. Hence, Rehnquist justified posting the Ten Commandments because the elected representatives of Kentucky recognized that the Commandments have had significant impact on the development of secular legal codes of the western world. Later, Rehnquist selectively cited fragments from prior court cases to reach the following conclusion:

> This Court has recognized that "religion has been closely identified with our history and government," *Abington School District* and that "[t]he history of man is inseparable from the history of religion," *Engel v. Vitale.* Kentucky has decided to make students aware of this fact by demonstrating the secular impact of the Ten Commandments.[11]

But how did posting the Ten Commandments in schools teach *about* the history of religion, or the development of legal codes in the western world? Other than the brief inscription under the Commandments, which simply asserted their historical and secular importance, it was by no means obvious that any systematic curricular effort had been made to explain the Commandments' importance historically or comparatively. Although *Schempp* clearly allowed schools to teach about religion (as opposed to teaching religion), there simply was no evidence that this is what had happened in the Kentucky case. Furthermore, if Rehnquist was asserting that the secular historical impact and importance of an arguably religious activity or document was sufficient to transform it from religious to secular, then is it not conceivable that virtually any religious activity could be so legitimized?

One possible explanation for these tensions within Rehnquist's opinion was that while he found *Schempp* misguided, he was nonetheless reluctant to say so directly in this case. Rather than arguing that *Schempp* should be overruled, Rehnquist attempted to squeeze his *Stone* dissent into the framework of previous separationist cases like *Schempp* (where it did not fit well at all) by arguing that posting the Ten Commandments helped familiarize students with their history, culture, and law. At bottom, Rehnquist was simply unwilling to disallow the posting of the Ten Commandments in school classrooms because they had a religious component. He did not understand the Establishment Clause to effect such a barrier against religion. *Schempp,* which laid the foundation for the *Lemon* test, posited neutrality between government and religion as the core Establishment Clause value. Yet Rehnquist did not believe that the Establishment Clause required this kind of neutrality, a point he would be far more explicit about five years later when he wrote that "nothing in the Establishment Clause requires government to be strictly neutral between religion and irreligion, nor does that Clause prohibit Congress or the States from pursuing legitimate secular ends through nondiscriminatory sectarian means."[12]

Of course, a substantial number of ordinary citizens agreed with Rehnquist that it was somehow "wrong" not to allow the posting of the Ten Commandments in school classrooms. Although not expert in constitutional law, many wondered why so many references to God or to religion endured in public life while being so uniformly forbidden to students in the schools. Three years later they would discover that even Supreme Court Judges, who are presumed to be experts in constitutional law, had difficulty with a very similar problem.

EXAMPLE 2

Marsh v. *Chambers,* 463 U.S. 783 (1983)

Facts: Ernest Chambers, a member of the Nebraska legislature and a taxpayer of the state, objected to the State's practice of beginning each of its session with a prayer offered by a chaplain. The chaplain is chosen biennially by the Executive Board of the Legislative Council and is paid out of public funds. The chaplain, who had served for sixteen years at the time of the suit, was a Presbyterian minister.

Result: The practice of employing a member of the clergy to invoke an opening prayer for Nebraska's legislature does not violate the Establishment Clause of the First Amendment.

Argument of the Case: Burger, Chief Justice. Opening legislative sessions (as well as other deliberative bodies, including the Supreme Court) with a prayer is deeply embedded in the history and traditions of the United States. This 200-year history is not overcome by the fact that a chaplain of only one denomination—Presbyterian—had been selected for sixteen years. There is no proof that a chaplain of one faith advances the beliefs of a particular church. To the contrary, this individual was selected because he was acceptable to the body appointing him. Nor does payment with public funds invalidate this practice. The Continental Congress, Congress, and many state legislatures (including Nebraska for well over a century) have paid their chaplains out of public funds. Finally, the fact that the prayers are in the Judeo-Christian tradition has posed, and continues to pose, no real threat to the establishment of religion, for there is no evidence that the prayer has been used to proselytize for or disparage any religious faith.

Marshall and Brennan dissent. Had the Supreme Court applied the usual Establishment Clause standards, then the contested practice would have been disallowed. Its purpose is preeminently religious, its primary effect is clearly religious, and entanglement can result either from the necessary government supervision or from the resulting political divisiveness. Core Establishment Clause values of separation and neutrality are endangered by the Court's opinion.

Stevens dissents. In a democratically elected legislature, the religious beliefs of chaplains reflect the faith of the majority in the legislature. Minority religious views tend not to be represented. Thus, a chaplain who serves for sixteen years implies the preference of one faith over others in violation of the Establishment Clause.

Discussion

Surprise! The same Court that required the removal of the Ten Commandments from public school classrooms three years before now allowed Nebraska to begin its legislative sessions with a prayer, paid for by public revenues. In fact, there was not even a single mention of *Stone* v. *Graham* in the body of the Supreme Court's opinion in *Marsh* v. *Chambers*. Furthermore, the traditional Establishment Clause test by which *Stone* had been decided, the tripartite *Lemon* test, was not even mentioned in *Marsh*. Finally, while the *Stone* majority had cited precedent demonstrating that it was "no defense to urge that the religious practices here may be relatively minor encroachments on the First Amendment,"[13] in *Marsh* v. *Chambers* the Court cited a different opinion to the effect that it was "of course true that great consequences can grow from small beginnings, but the measure of constitutional adjudication is the ability and willingness to distinguish between real threat and mere shadow."[14]

The two cases seem plainly contradictory. There are possible ways of reconciling their arguments and results, but they do not prove persuasive. True enough, Chief Justice Burger dissented in *Stone* and wrote the majority opinion for the Court in *Marsh* (proving, perhaps that he, if not the Court, was consistent). Additionally, the Court noted in *Marsh* that "the individual claiming injury by the practice is an adult, presumably not readily susceptible to 'religious indoctrination' or peer pressure." In other words, while there might exist some capacity to indoctrinate schoolchildren by religious instruction (in a case like *Stone*), adults, such as state legislators, were far more immune to such risks.[15] Yet these distinctions ultimately would prove small solace indeed for one who prizes consistency in the law. After all, state-sponsored prayers seemed much more of a religious exercise than the mere posting of the Ten Commandments. Justice Brennan, dissenting, put a positive if somewhat controversial construction upon the matter, noting that the Court's "narrow" opinion was governed by a "limited rationale" and, because of its "unique history," constituted an exemption from the First Amendment's Establishment Clause.

Despite Brennan's construction, Chief Justice Burger's opinion for the Court in *Marsh* did not argue that state-funded legislative prayers amounted to an exception to the First Amendment Establishment Clause. Rather, Burger contended that the fact that such prayer had been historically permitted gave insight into the very meaning of that clause:

> Standing alone, historical patterns cannot justify contemporary violations of constitutional guarantees, but there is far more here than simply historical patterns. In this context, historical evidence sheds light not only on what the draftsmen intended the Establishment Clause to mean, but also on how they thought that Clause applied to the practice authorized by the First Congress—their actions reveal their intent. "An act" passed by the first Congress assembled under the Constitution, many of whose members had taken part in framing the instrument ... is contemporaneous and weighty evidence of its true meaning." *Wisconsin* v. *Pelican Ins. Co.*[16]

At bottom, the problem facing the Court in the *Marsh* case was that its historical account of the Establishment Clause's meaning (which helped explain many of the traditional references to God common in everyday public life) was at odds with the prevailing constitutional interpretations formulated in previous Supreme Court decisions. Thus, the then dominant *Lemon* test, ignored by the Supreme Court's majority in the *Stone* case, required government to be neutral regarding religion and not to become excessively (translated, *much*) involved in its practice or precepts. In theory, a straightforward application of *Lemon* would have dictated outlawing both the posting of the Ten Commandments *and* chaplain-led public prayers. Nonetheless, references to God in public life, in prayers before legislative and Supreme Court sessions, in "The Star Spangled Banner," and in the Pledge of Allegiance, are routine and well-established. A reasonable consistency would seem to dictate that the Supreme Court should be willing to outlaw such practices in the name of its understanding of the Establishment Clause or alter its formulation of the Establishment Clause's meaning. Yet the Court chose neither course to the exclusion of the other. In fact, it is safe to say that the Court has been unable to reconcile these two conflicting forces and fashion a coherent doctrine able to resolve the underlying, nagging legal problem.[17]

Sometimes, the Supreme Court has adopted rather "interesting" approaches to the problem of determining the constitutionality of public religious expression. The approach used in the following case has become increasingly popular although it, too, is not without its difficulties.

EXAMPLE 3

Lynch v. *Donnelly,* 465 U.S. 668 (1984)

Facts: Each year, the city of Pawtucket, Rhode Island, in cooperation with its downtown merchants, erects a Christmas display. The display is constructed in a park owned by a nonprofit organization in the heart of the shopping district. The display contains a Santa Claus house, reindeer pulling Santa's sleigh, a Christmas tree, an elephant and a teddy bear, hundreds of colored lights, and a large banner that reads "SEASONS GREETINGS." The display also contains a creche, or nativity scene. The city expends nominal money on lighting and maintaining the creche.[18] Pawtucket residents and individual members of the Rhode Island affiliate of the American Civil Liberties Union challenged the inclusion of the creche in the annual Christmas display.

Result: Notwithstanding the religious significance of the creche, Pawtucket has not violated the Establishment Clause or any part of the tripartite *Lemon* test: the city has had an adequate secular purpose, it has not impermissibly advanced religion, and including the creche does not create an excessive entanglement between religion and government.

Argument of the Case: Burger, Chief Justice. The Constitution and the Establishment Clause do not require a complete separation of church and state. History, and many official acknowledgements of God in American public life, requires that this clause not be constructed according to a literal, rigid, absolutist view. The creche must be viewed in the context of the Christmas holiday season and the display as a whole. There is a secular purpose for the creche, which is celebrating and depicting the origins of Christmas, a national holiday. Although one effect of Pawtucket's action is to advance religion incidentally and indirectly (which is constitutionally permissible), the advancement of religion is hardly the primary effect of the city's action. Furthermore, no serious church–state entanglement exists. The creche is part of a display that encourages a "friendly community spirit of good will in keeping with the season."

O'Connor concurs. It is not clear how the *Lemon* test relates to the principles enshrined in the Establishment Clause. The real question is this: Has the government endorsed (or disapproved of) religion (that is, Christianity) by its display of the creche? No, the "evident purpose of including the creche in the large display was not promotion of the religious content of the creche but celebration of the public holiday through its traditional symbols," since celebrating "public holidays, which have cultural significance even if they also have religious aspects, is a legitimate secular purpose." The overall holiday setting negates any message of endorsement. Celebrating a holiday does not endorse its religious content. Indeed, the creche "is a traditional symbol of the holiday that is very commonly displayed along with purely secular symbols, as it was in Pawtucket."

Brennan, with Marshall, Blackmun, and Stevens, dissents. This case appears hard because the Christmas holiday seems so familiar and agreeable. Nonetheless, it is important to recognize that a creche is a distinctively sectarian symbol. Thus, inclusion of the creche in the display does not reflect a clearly secular purpose and fails the other prongs of the *Lemon* test as well.

Blackmun, with Stevens, dissents. *Lemon* requires disallowing the presence of the creche in a municipally sponsored display. Furthermore, the Court does injustice to the creche and the message it promulgates; it is a sacred symbol that exists for some other purpose than engendering "a friendly community spirit of good will in keeping with the season." The majority opinion relegates the creche "to the role of neutral harbinger of the holiday season, useful for commercial purposes, but devoid of any inherent meaning and incapable of enhancing the religious tenor of a display which it is an integral part."

Discussion

The dispute here involves a clear example of a religious symbol, a nativity scene sponsored by a city government. In addition, the challenged practice was traditional; nativity scenes have been commonly displayed during the Christmas season for decades. Nonetheless (unlike in *Marsh* v. *Chambers*), Chief Justice Burger thought it appropriate to apply the *Lemon* test in order to determine if the Establishment Clause had been violated.[19] So did virtually everyone else, with only Justice O'Connor expressing explicit reservations regarding the efficacy of this test. Thus, it was generally the application of the *Lemon* Establishment Clause test, and not its selection, that defined the range of legal disagreement that emerged within the Supreme Court.

In order to emphasize that the Constitution permits accommodation between government and religion, Chief Justice Burger pointed to a number of frequently cited examples. He contended that there was "an unbroken history of official acknowledgement by all three branches of government of the role of religion in American life from at least 1789."[20] Thus, the same week the Congress approved the Constitution's Establishment Clause (as part of the Bill of Rights), it enacted legislation to provide for paid chaplains in the Senate and House of Representatives. Other examples of accommodation cited by Burger included a day of Thanksgiving, which was proclaimed by President Washington and his successors to be a religious holiday thanking God; Christmas, also declared to be a national religious holiday by Presidents and Congresses (note that federal employees receive paid days off during its celebration); the national motto "In God We Trust," which Congress and the President mandated to be on American currency; the statement "One nation under God," which is part of the Pledge of Allegiance (repeated by school-children throughout the nation); publicly funded art galleries that exhibit religiously inspired art or art that conveys religious messages; a National Day of Prayer, with Congress directing the President to proclaim a national day "on which the people of the United States may turn to God in prayer and meditation at churches, in groups, and as individuals"; and various Presidential proclamations that have also have been issued, including those commemorating Jewish Heritage Week and the Jewish High Holy Days.

Burger hoped this historical recounting would "help explain why the Court consistently has declined to take a rigid, absolutist view of the Establishment Clause."[21] Actually, the conclusion Burger derived from the evidence was, if anything, modest. A stronger conclusion could have been deduced from the evidence cited—namely, that the Establishment Clause of the First Amendment was not intended or traditionally understood to prohibit accommodation, cooperation, and perhaps even delineated forms of governmental support of religion. The trouble was that such a forceful, theoretical approach would have required overruling clear precedent (dating back to 1947)[22] that required significant separation of church and state and (later) emphasized that the proper role of government toward religion was one of neutrality. Undoubtedly, Burger could never have gained a majority for such an opinion (as it was, his opinion gained only the support of three other Justices and maintained a majority only because of Justice O'Connor's concurring opinion). Thus, Burger employed evidence of state support of certain, limited religious practices to support an accommodationist interpretation of the *Lemon* test, which (among other things) had been originally constructed to show that neutrality was a core Establishment Clause principle.

In order to make the *Lemon* test work, Burger had to demonstrate that government was not *really* supporting religion. He did this by arguing that the *context* of the creche rendered it essentially nonreligious. Actually, there were two somewhat interrelated contexts pointed to by Burger, each designed to demonstrate that "Pawtucket's display of its creche ... does not communicate a message that the government intends to endorse the Christian beliefs represented by the creche."

The first important context was the general holiday season, which Burger painted in broad, secular strokes. It was a "public holiday" with a "very strong secular component and traditions," so the nativity display did not constitute an endorsement of religion. Furthermore, Burger argued that the government's recognition and celebration of Christmas have never been understood to mean governmental endorsement of a religious message. The Supreme Court's approach here was similar to that invoked by the circuit court majority in the Sioux Falls Christmas carol case discussed in Chapter Eleven.[23] Against the objection that "Silent Night" constituted a sectarian exercise whose words conveyed an explicit religious message, the circuit court emphasized the general, public, nonreligious nature of Christmas. Additionally, the court made reference to the context in which Christmas carols could be constitutionally permitted under newly adopted school guidelines. The carols were surrounded by secular songs of the season. In a sense, "Frosty the Snowman" and "Rudolph the Rednosed Reindeer" saved the constitutionality of "Silent Night" and rendered it contextually nonreligious.

This second, programmatic context also could be seen in the Pawtucket case. It was pointed out by Justice Brennan that the creche was situated within the display near Santa's House and the talking wishing well. Chief Justice Burger put the matter a bit more delicately, and more generally as well, when he observed that the display "engenders a friendly community spirit of good will in keeping with the season." In addition to pointing to its secular effect, Burger presented an analogy. In a typical museum setting, a religiously motivated painting retains its religious meaning. The fact that the painting is hung in a museum, where many other works of art are displayed, mitigates any possible message that the museum endorses the painting's content. Similarly, in this case, the creche retained its religious meaning, but the fact that it was situated within a substantially larger holiday display containing numerous secular symbols nullified the impression that the government had endorsed the religious message of the creche.

In addition, the fact that the creche existed within a larger seasonal and physical context allowed Burger to distinguish this case from the Supreme Court's previous decision in *Stone* v. *Graham*. According to Burger, there was no larger context in *Stone*. The Ten Commandments served an exclusive religious purpose; it was not integrated into the school curriculum and was not part of the study of history, ethics, or comparative religion. (On the other hand, Burger avoided pointing out that the Ten Commandments amounted to less of an exclusive representation of religiosity than did the creche.) What mattered to Burger was whether the contested practice or symbol could be placed in a larger, secular context. This approach would receive additional support in the 1989 case of *County of Allegheny* v. *American Civil Liberties Union*.[24] There, the Supreme Court invalidated a creche (displayed by itself) constructed on public property (the Grand Staircase of the Allegheny County Courthouse). What was important was its context (or more precisely its lack of context):

> Under the Court's holding in *Lynch,* the effect of the creche display turns upon its setting. Here, unlike *Lynch,* nothing in the context of the display detracts from the creche's religious message.... Here, in contrast, the creche stands alone: it is the single element of the display on the Grand Staircase.[25]

What saved the constitutionality of the creche in the Pawtucket case was the fact that it existed within the context of a larger secular display. Thus, a religious symbol or exercise can pass the *Lemon* neutrality test only by minimizing its religious significance. Justice Blackmun (along with Stevens) commented upon the irony of the situation. He suggested in *Lynch* that the "creche has been relegated to the role of a neutral harbinger of the holiday season, useful for commercial purposes, but devoid of any inherent meaning and incapable of enhancing the religious tenor of a display of which it is an integral part."[26] Thus, Blackmun argued that while Pawtucket had won a victory, it was only a Pyrrhic one. A holy religious symbol was now regarded by the Supreme Court simply as another sign of seasonal good will.

Underlying this point was something of an unstated assumption. The exhibit was not only arguably tasteless or garish; it also was aimed at something more than the mere promotion of Christmas good cheer. Blackmun cited expert testimony at the district court trial to the effect that the Pawtucket display invited people "to participate in the Christmas spirit, brotherhood, peace, and let loose with their money." In other words, the purpose of the display was blatantly commercial. This perspective raised not so much a constitutional question, but a more basic societal question: Was there not something crass and even sacrilegious about turning a sacred symbol of the birth of He who taught the insufficiency of the things of this world into a celebration of acquisitiveness and commerce? In the end, the Pawtucket display represented not only the complexities and ironies of American constitutional law, but also the inherent tensions buried deep within contemporary American society.

SUMMARY

There are fundamental religious expressions and practices that today endure as integral parts of American culture and society. Almost always, they are rooted in historical practice and precedent. However, they often, but not always, have run afoul of First Amendment Establishment Clause tests. Given this continuing tension between historical practice and constitutional interpretation, perhaps it is not surprising that the Supreme Court adjudication has not always produced consistent results, or even predictable ones.

If we examine the cases discussed in this chapter, no clear pattern emerges. Briefly, posting the Ten Commandments in public schools was disallowed, praying before the start of legislative sessions was allowed, and creches were allowed (but only if they were surrounded by nonreligious symbols). The problem of ensuring a necessary consistency and predictability in the law is complicated by the recognition that the least exclusively religious symbol of the three was arguably the Ten Commandments, which contain secular injunctions that are quite capable of standing alone, irrespective of their religious origin.

In order to determine the validity of contested religious practices and symbols, a variety of Establishment Clause tests have been employed. By far, the most common was the *Lemon* test, whose application remained ever controversial among the Justices.[27] By contrast, Justice O'Connor preferred a variation of the *Lemon* test, interpreting it to preclude state endorsement of religion. These tests generally aimed at ensuring an attitude of neutrality between government and religion. That approach was rejected at least temporarily by Chief Justice Burger in *Marsh* v. *Chambers,* arguing that practices with long and established histories dating back to the Constitution's origins were constitutional. Burger's approach, which seemed limited to a defined number of well-recognized practices, was phrased in terms of avoiding hostility between church and state, but actually assumed a rather benign, accommodating, and supportive, if somewhat limited, relationship between them.

The continuing inconsistencies of results and the incessant judicial squabbling regarding the application and applicability of different Constitutional tests reflect continuing constitutional disagreement on the Supreme Court. At the level of law, the disagreement is over the Establishment Clause's meaning at the end of the twentieth century. At a theoretical or philosophical level, the dispute asks to what extent ought references to God be permitted or even encouraged as means of solemnizing public occasions or promulgating or emphasizing civic responsibilities and obligations. Today, this issue endures as a question that tugs at the emotions of believer and nonbeliever alike.

NOTES

1. This point is made in Chapter 2. See p. 40.

2. C. S. Lewis, *The Abolition of Man* (New York: Macmillan, 1947).

3. However, it is by no means clear that Lewis accepts the idea of different civilizations. (See pp. 95–96.) Also, it should be emphasized that neither Lewis nor the authors wish to argue that all political regimes embody moral principles; rather, the argument is that universal moral principles are embodied within a wide variety of religious and social traditions.

4. Theirs was a technical point. They disagreed with their colleagues on the Court who had decided the case without having heard oral arguments.

5. Stewart simply asserted that the Kentucky courts whose judgment was reversed by the Supreme Court appeared to have applied correct constitutional criteria in reaching their decisions.

6. Actually, the linguistic origins and translations of *mizvot* are complicated by its Yiddish usage, which has more secular importance. See Moshe Waldoks, "Mizveh," in *Contemporary Jewish Religious Thought: Original Essays on Critical Concepts, Movements, and Beliefs,* ed. Arthur A. Cohen and Paul Mendes-Flohr (New York: The Free Press, 1987), pp. 627–28.

7. Paul R. Rodriguez has posited a "secular" Ten Commandments. Rodriguez compares specific Texas secular laws that parallel each of the Commandments, pointing out that they could be constitutionally posted. He argues that

these "secular commandments" mirror the Ten Commandments, with one major exception:

they do not take their authority from a supreme being, but, rather from the secular state. Yet it is obvious that these statutes reflect the Judaeo-Christian roots of our society, roots in which the majority of Americans still believe.

See Paul M. Rodriguez, "God is Dead: Killed by Fifty Years of Establishment Clause Jurisprudence," *St. Mary's Law Journal,* vol. 23: 1155 (1992), pp. 1156–58.

8. 449 U.S. at 39, 42.

9. 374 U.S. 203 (1963). For a discussion of this case, see Chapter 11.

10. Rehnquist cited *Anderson* v. *Salt Lake City Corp,* 475 F.2d 29, 33 (A10 1973), to this effect. The case upheld the construction on public land of a monument inscribed with the Ten Commandments because it had "substantial secular attributes."

11. 449 U.S. at 46.

12. See Justice Rehnquist's dissenting opinion in *Wallace* v. *Jaffree,* 472 U.S. 38 at 113.

13. 449 U.S. at 42. *Abington School District* v. *Schempp* was the precedent cited.

14. 463 U.S. 783 at 795. The citation was to Justice Goldberg's concurring opinion in *Abington School District* v. *Schempp.*

15. A similar distinction has provided the basis for the Supreme Court's more lenient view toward governmental aid to religiously affiliated colleges, as opposed to religiously sponsored elementary and secondary schools. See, for instance, *Tilton* v. *Richardson,* 403 U.S. 672 (1972). Also see Chapter 13.

16. 463 U.S. at 790.

17. The reason that this is the case turns upon the way the Supreme Court has abrogated the federalism aspect of the original Constitution. See Chapter 4, p. 77.

18. According to the Court:, "In 1973, when the present creche was acquired, it cost the City $1365; it now is valued at $200. The erection and dismantling of the creche cost the City about $20 per year; nominal expenses are incurred in lighting the creche. No money has been expended on its maintenance for the past 10 years."

19. However he did assert that the Court had never been confined by any one Establishment Clause test. 465 U.S. at 679.

20. 465 U.S. at 674.

21. 465 U.S. at 678.

22. See *Everson* v. Board *of Education,* 330 U.S. 1 (1947).

23. *Florey* v. *Sioux Falls District 49–5,* 619 F. 2d 1311 (1980).

24. 492 U.S. 573 (1989).

25. 492 U.S. 573 at 598. Interestingly, the Court did, in this same case, affirm the constitutionality of a Pittsburgh display that included a menorah, a Christmas tree, and a sign celebrating liberty.

26. 465 U.S. at 727 (1984).

27. See Justice Kennedy's opinion in *Allegheny* v. *American Civil Liberties Union,* 492 U.S. at 655 (1989). Kennedy fashions an accommodationist *Lemon* test.

9

When Are Religious Practices So Disagreeable or Harmful That the Government Should Prohibit Them?

THE PROBLEM POSED

Many religious people are extremely fond of the rituals and ceremonies traditionally associated with their worship. Often, when they attend a church or synagogue service away from home and find services just a little different, they wish that the music, the prayers, or even the order of the service would duplicate more familiar rituals. Certainly, part of the attraction of religion is the emotional and spiritual feeling associated with the customary ceremonies practiced in the service. Yet what is familiar, meaningful, and even sacred to some may seem unusual to others who do not share their beliefs and convictions. For example, sacraments such as communion and baptism may be among the most meaningful religious ceremonies to many believers. On the other hand, some outside this religious tradition (and particularly those completely unfamiliar with these rituals) could well find these practices puzzling and even strange.

That a religious practice or ritual may seem illogical or even strange to others—or even to a majority within a particular community—does not give government the authority to interfere with it. Religious free exercise and the underlying idea of religious liberty preclude such an action. However, it is also important to recognize that while the freedom accorded religious practices is significant, it is not absolute. The government can regulate religious practices, especially when it believes them to be harmful. Of course, *harmful* has more than one meaning (in fact, we can easily identify at least six distinct meanings). Precisely for that reason, it is important to recognize and reflect upon these differing meanings so that we can make dispassionate judgments about whether interventionist efforts by government are truly warranted (that is, because the actions it seeks to prohibit are sufficiently dangerous). Thus, we first recognize that *harmful* can mean capable of causing physical injury or death. (Thus, ritual murder would never be legally permitted on religious grounds.) Second, *harmful* might indicate that the practice in question violates some provision of the Constitution or the criminal law. Third, *harmful* can reflect that the disputed religious practices are perceived as unjust or morally wrong in principle. Fourth, a harmful act might specify an action that unduly disadvantages other people or even society at large.[1] Fifth, a harmful action might connote a religious or religiously motivated practice whose very existence is regarded as undermining or endangering the moral consensus that exists within any community. Finally, harmful rituals can mean that the public (as opposed to the private) practice of certain religious acts may greatly offend a substantial number of citizens within a community.[2] Of course, the idea of harm can encompass some combination of these definitions.

If the disputed religious practice is thought to be harmful, then its alleged harm to others and to society must be balanced against the defendant's free exercise rights to practice religion freely. Throughout most of American history, this determination has been regarded as a task for the legislature. However, most state legislatures (and the Congress as well) have been reluctant to exempt perceived harmful or disagreeable practices, and are content to pass laws that apply equally to all citizens (the states generally enacting such laws under their police powers—that is, their general authority to govern over the health, welfare, and morality of their citizens). Later, beginning in the early 1960s, the courts more often assumed responsibility for balancing religious liberties against societal harm. During this time, the Supreme Court acted in a more activist, liberal manner. An activist Court was more inclined to review and decide such cases. A more liberal Court constructed balancing tests that restricted government's power to curtail offensive or harmful religious rituals and practices or that required government to exempt "harmful" religious practices from the law. Even more recently, however (with the opinion in the 1990 *Employment Division, Department of Human Resources of Oregon* v. *Smith*), the Supreme Court signaled its desire to return to the older practice of routinely upholding the constitutional validity of legislatively passed laws that equally obligated all citizens.

Having pointed out the elusive and different meanings of *harm,* as well as noting differing historical approaches by the Supreme Court to the conflict between individual religious practice and societal harm, we are now in a position to see how courts have balanced religious liberty against societal harm in respect to disagreeable or harmful religious practices. We begin with a classic Supreme Court case, one that represents the restraintist approach that the Supreme Court has advanced throughout most of its history.

EXAMPLE 1

Reynolds v. *United States,* 98 U.S. 145 (1879)

Facts: In 1862, under immense public pressure, the United States Congress passed the Morrill Act, which punished the practice of polygamy in the territories. Specifically, the law punished bigamy, defined as any person with a living spouse who marries another. George Reynolds, private secretary to Mormon leader Brigham Young, was convicted of having violated this statute. Reynolds asserted that polygamy was an important duty of his church and faith, that it had been divinely commanded, and that failure to follow this religious tenet would cause him to be eternally damned. Reynolds contended that his religious liberty, guaranteed by the First Amendment's Free Exercise Clause, was violated by his arrest.

Result: Precisely because polygamy undermines the civic order, the Supreme Court held that its practice was not protected by the Free Exercise Clause of the First Amendment.

Argument of the Case: Waite, Chief Justice. Congress has the general power to pass laws for its territories, although it has no power to abridge an individual's free exercise of religion. Therefore, the "precise point of the inquiry is, what is the religious freedom which has been guaranteed?" The Court cited history and Thomas Jefferson's letter to the Danbury Baptists ("…religion is a matter which lies solely between man and that he owes account to none other for his faith or his worship; *that the legislative powers of Government reach actions only, and not opinions,* I contemplate with sovereign reverence [the Establishment and Free Exercise Clauses], thus building a wall of separation between Church and State … Adhering to this expression of the Supreme will of the Nation in behalf of the rights of conscience, I shall see … the progress of those sentiments which tend to restore man to all his natural rights, *convinced he has no natural right in opposition to his social duties*"[3]). Thus, according to Jefferson's understanding of the First Amendment, Congress was deprived of all legislative power over mere opinion, but was free to prohibit actions that violated social duties or were subversive of good order. Like human sacrifices or a wife throwing herself upon her dead husband's burning funeral pyre, polygamy undermines the civil order. Therefore, it is not protected by the Free Exercise Clause of the Constitution.

Discussion

Reynolds is one of the most important early cases in which the Supreme Court discussed and defined the meaning of the First Amendment's Free Exercise Clause. In it, the Court deferred to the legislature. It simply reaffirmed Congress's power to prohibit polygamy, finding no judicial obligation under the Free Exercise Clause to protect this religiously motivated practice.

This delimited interpretation of the Free Exercise Clause was not justified by any extensive discussion of the proper relationship between the courts and the legislature in a democracy. Rather, it was the harm of polygamy that dominated the Supreme Court's opinion. The Court argued that polygamy was so harmful that no constitutional protection for its practice could be legitimately fashioned. Despite the fact that polygamy did not directly raise the specter of immediate physical harm, the Supreme Court (in this case and others[4]) condemned the practice in antagonistic language seldom seen in Court opinions. It found polygamy harmful because it was offensive, and because polygamy had been offensive from the earliest history of England until the day this case was decided, it was clear to the Court that polygamy could never have been intended to have constitutional protection. In fact, the Court could not hide its disdain (or its prejudice), declaring that "polygamy has always been odious among the Northern and Western nations of Europe and, until the establishment of the Mormon Church, was almost exclusively a feature of the life of Asiatic and African people." Furthermore, the Court argued that "it may safely be said there never has been a time in any State of the Union when polygamy has not been an offence against society, cognizable by the civil courts and punishable with more or less severity."[5]

The Supreme Court was not content to define polygamy's harm in terms of offensiveness. This practice also was morally wrong, and it had the effect of undermining the social fabric of society. Marriage, the Court proclaimed, presumed monogamy, and monogamy and polygamy were simply incompatible. Furthermore, the Court also seemed to imply that polygamy would not be peacefully endured by the larger, monogamous society.

Thus, the Supreme Court believed that polygamy was harmful because it violated the criminal law, because it undermined the moral consensus that existed within the American community, and because it was offensive to citizens within that community. The Court did not mention (and probably could not legitimately have mentioned) that the criminal law, the endangered moral consensus, and the offensiveness that defined American society's relationship with polygamy was, to a large extent, rooted in Christianity and Christianity's concept of marriage. Rather than directly acknowledging this fact, the Supreme Court chose to couch its opinion in language that asserted that polygamy was a morally backward and primitive practice.

Yet it is worth remembering that none other than the famous nineteenth-century British philosopher John Stuart Mill thought an enlightened, progressive society would permit polygamy.[6] Mill admitted that polygamy "seems to excite unquenchable animosity" when practiced by English-speaking, self-professed Christians. Furthermore, Mill expressed his personal disapproval of the practice on the ground that it demeaned women. He thought that the origin of the practice taught "women to think marriage the one thing needful," a belief that makes "it intelligible that many a woman should prefer being one of several wives, to not being a wife at all."[7] Still, Mill reminded his readers that polygamy was voluntary; women, presumably, chose to enter such a relationship. Given his core belief that "the sole end for which mankind are warranted, individually or collectively, interfering with the liberty of action of any of their number is self-protection,"[8] Mill could come to no other conclusion than that polygamy, however distasteful, should be allowed. For Mill, it would not have been sufficient that the Mormon practice was morally offensive or was perceived as weakening the moral bonds that united society. Mill's society of autonomous individuals, living within a wide circle of liberty, offers a different evaluation of societal requirements than that presented by the Supreme Court in the *Reynolds* case.

Polygamy, even though religiously motivated, was nonetheless deemed by the Supreme Court to be sufficiently harmful to be denied constitutional protection. Some time later, various state courts were called upon to rule on the constitutionality of another controversial practice. Like polygamy, snake handling is a ritual exercised by religiously motivated individuals. Unlike polygamy, however, the potential harm associated with snake handling is hardly abstract. Yet this religiously motivated practice is hardly free from the philosophic questions that have so often characterized secular–religious issues in the United States.

EXAMPLE 2

Lawson, et al. **v.** *Commonwealth,* 291 Ky. 437, 164 S.W. 2d 972 (1942)

Facts: Tom Lawson and several others were convicted of displaying and handling snakes during a religious meeting. They believed that snake handling was a test of their religious faith, so this activity was deserving of constitutional protection. For that reason, Lawson and others maintained that the Kentucky statute prohibiting the handling of snakes in connection with any kind of religious service was unconstitutional.

Result: The Kentucky Court of Appeals found the law did not violate the United States Constitution and its passage and enforcement fell within the legitimate powers of the state.

Argument of the Case: Tilford, Judge. The court began by asserting the appropriateness of the statute's language.[9] Many snakes are poisonous, but "only [the] zoologist, herpetologist, or experienced woodsman is able to distinguish those which are not." Kentucky's legitimate legislative power (to enact laws to protect the health, welfare, and morals of the state's citizens) is not invalidated because only some of the prohibited snakes are poisonous, because only an expert can tell them apart. For that reason, "the Legislature had the right, unless forbidden by the State or Federal Constitution from so doing, to prohibit the practice altogether." Regarding Lawson's claim that prohibiting the handling of snakes, as a test of faith, violates freedom of religion (and hence the Free Exercise Clause), the court cited precedent. It noted that religious liberty in the First Amendment is safeguarded by (a) forestalling governmental legal compulsion that would require the acceptance of any creed, religious practice, or form of worship that would curtail freedom of conscience, while (b) safeguarding an individual's free exercise of religion. Thus, a person has the right to believe and the freedom to act according to those beliefs. Freedom to believe is absolute, but freedom to act cannot be absolute.[10] Freedom of religious action is limited by "the power of the state to regulate the times, places, and manner of its exercise when such regulation is necessary for the safeguarding of the health, good order, and comfort of the community." Indeed, citing another legal authority,[11] laws "enacted for the purpose of restraining and punishing acts which have a tendency to disturb the public peace or to corrupt the public morals are not repugnant to the constitutional guaranties of religious liberty and freedom of conscience, although such acts may have been done pursuant to, and in conformity with, what was believed at the time to be a religious duty."

Discussion

What is initially striking about the Kentucky Court of Appeals decision in this case (as well as other court decisions in similar cases[12]) is the easy manner in which it settled the issue. The court did not question the sincerity or importance of Lawson's religious beliefs. (Generally, the belief in snake handling is biblically rooted: "They shall take up serpents; and if they drink any deadly thing it shall not harm them; they shall lay hands on the sick and they shall recover," Mark 16:17–18, *King James* ed.). Nor did the court analyze or even consider the issue of to whom the snakes were dangerous: it made no difference if the snakes endangered only those participating in the service, or if they posed an additional danger to those observing the service, or even if they endangered the larger community. The court did discuss the distinction between poisonous and nonpoisonous snakes, but only long enough to point out that the law that prohibited the display and handling of both to be eminently reasonable in light of the fact that snakes are difficult to tell apart and those who shared Lawson's beliefs made "no pretense that the snakes handled or exhibited by the appellants were nonpoisonous, since the very purpose sought to be accomplished by their handling was to demonstrate appellants' immunity, through faith, to the fatal consequences which would ensure to those who possessed it not."[13]

The court cited history and precedent to support its conclusion. It paid special attention to Thomas Jefferson, who, in the words of the court, championed the right of conscience but "had no thought of depriving the legislature of its inherent power to legislate for the welfare and safety of its citizens." Beneath the court's decision rested both a factual assumption and a philosophical understanding. Factually, the court assumed as self-evident that handling poisonous snakes was dangerous and that it endangered the life, health, and welfare of the state's citizens. It was precisely the existence of such an obvious harm that bolstered the state's case for prohibiting snake handling (although, we should note, there are a few who doubt the fact that handling poisonous snakes is particularly harmful[14]).

Philosophically, a more disputable issue lies at the heart of these kinds of cases, one that the courts generally do not consider. In Chapter Sixteen, we will analyze a case that raised a similar kind of concern, namely the case in which a woman refused a lifesaving blood transfusion because of her religious beliefs.[15] What made this a very difficult case was the tension that existed between society's desire to protect her life (and life in general) and respect for her freedom of choice, particularly her freedom of religious choice. *Lawson* raises similar concerns. Insofar as snake handlers are adults, do not directly endanger nonparticipants, and freely choose to test their faith by handling poisonous snakes, the cases appear to be analogous. The two cases certainly are alike to the extent that in each instance an individual is willing to put her or his life in jeopardy for the sake of a deeply held religious belief. It is true that snake handlers such as Lawson voluntarily choose to enter a situation where their lives are in jeopardy, whereas the woman in the hospital did not (in the sense that she did not choose to become ill and she did not know that she would require a blood transfusion when she entered the hospital). Still, there are sufficient similarities between the two examples to raise the question of whether testing one's faith by handling snakes—a repulsive and dangerous activity—is nonetheless the sort of decision that is best left to individuals and whether governmental intervention designed to uphold human life and well-being grows out of a wise concern for the welfare of citizens or out of an objectionable governmental paternalism.

It turns out that government not only limits "harmful" activities of individuals, but also of organizations. In that respect, the following case is intriguing, for it presents government's imposition of law upon a private organization and also presents quite a different understanding of the idea of harm.

EXAMPLE 3

Bob Jones University **v.** *United States,* 461 U.S. 574 (1983)

Facts: Bob Jones University is a Christian fundamentalist college. Blacks were completely excluded from the college until 1971. From 1971 to 1975, unmarried blacks were not accepted for admission. After 1975, the college admitted all blacks except those who were intermarried. The rules of the college prohibited advocating or practicing interracial dating. The University cited the Bible as the source of its racial views. In 1970 the Internal Revenue Service altered its policy of granting tax-exempt status to private schools without regard to their racial policies. It also altered its policy of granting charitable deductions to individuals contributing to such schools. Bob Jones University contended that depriving it and potential contributors of tax advantages contradicted the Free Exercise Clause of the First Amendment.

Result: The Supreme Court did not sustain Bob Jones University's religiously based objection to the IRS revised policy, arguing that its admissions policies contradicted established public policy of nondiscrimination.

Argument of the Case: Burger, Chief Justice. For an institution to qualify as a charity (and thus meet the IRS standard for tax deductibility), it must conform to the definition of a charity under law and its activity must conform to settled public policy. While Bob Jones University is "organized and operated exclusively for religious, charitable … or educational purposes," taken as a whole the law also reveals Congress's intent that each organization "must serve a public purpose and not be contrary to established public policy." This latter requirement has historical precedent. American public policy favors the eradication of racial discrimination. The IRS did not exceed its authority in insisting that Bob Jones University acted contrary to public policy and was not, for that reason, entitled to be classified as a charitable institution. Although the Free Exercise Clause "provides substantial protection for lawful conduct grounded in religious belief," still the "governmental stake here is compelling."

Powell concurs.[16] The Court is correct to deny Bob Jones University's free exercise claim and is therefore correct in denying it charitable status. However, it is not obvious that Bob Jones University does not benefit the public (through its curricula and degrees). Also, it seems that the Court's claim that charitable organizations must serve the public interest encourages a dangerous conformity (not pluralism) and does "suggest that the primary function of a tax exempt organization is to act on behalf of the Government in carrying out governmentally approved policies." Finally, it is for Congress, not the IRS, to balance interests and make policies like that contested in this case.

Rehnquist dissents. The disputed interpretation is properly a congressional, not an IRS, decision. Furthermore, nowhere in the law is there any explicit reference to a public purpose requirement. Until Congress acts, the IRS interpretation exceeds its proper authority.

Discussion

This complicated case raises a number of legal issues whose consideration is somewhat beside the purposes of our book. The point we would emphasize is that the Supreme Court went to some lengths to withdraw tax advantages to Bob Jones University. In coming to this conclusion it made several judgments, some controversial, others not. First, it rejected the university's contention that it did not discriminate against blacks. The Court observed that the university emphasized "that it now allows all races to enroll, subject only to its restrictions on the conduct of all students, including its prohibitions of association between men and women of different races, and of interracial marriage." The Court did not even choose to argue against this proposition, dismissing it with the statement that although "a ban on inter-marriage or interracial dating applies to all races, decision of the Court firmly establishes that discrimination on the basis of racial affiliation and association is a form of racial discrimination." Given the history of racial discrimination practiced by Bob Jones admissions policy, the tenets of legal precedent (that is, *Brown* v. *Board of Education*'s declaration that "separate but equal is inherently unequal"), and salient American social and legal history, there seemed good reason for the Court's belief that Bob Jones University practiced racial discrimination against blacks. Nor did it matter that Bob Jones was a private institution intent upon interpreting the Bible in a way it believed best advanced its religion mission. Educational and religious pluralism, and the autonomy of private institutions to pursue their private mission as they wished, were no doubt important goals, but in this case Bob Jones University's private ownership afforded it no legal protection from governmental intervention.[17]

The odious harm of racial discrimination overcame these considerations. Even though the IRS regulations said nothing explicit about racial discrimination, or even about prohibiting organizations that act contrary to established public policy, the Court still found it possible to invalidate Bob Jones University's tax-exempt status. The Court argued that Congress had extended tax exemptions on the belief that the government was compensated for its loss of revenue by private contributions to charity that benefited the public. Naturally, racial discrimination did not benefit the public. Thus, the government's compelling interest was paramount, concerned with "eradicating racial discrimination in education—discrimination that prevailed, with official approval, for the first 165 years of this Nation's history."[18] Furthermore, there existed no less-restrictive means of achieving the government's interest.

The ill effects of racial discrimination were so obvious that the Court did not specify its specific harms. Yet most of our earlier definitions of *harm* would seem to apply in this case: racial discrimination is unjust, capable of undermining the moral consensus within American society in favor of equality; it is offensive and repugnant; and in many circumstances, it also violates the criminal law. In this case, the Court assumed the obvious nature of all these harms as it pursued the controversial course of eradicating a form of public financial support for racially discriminatory practices.

Bob Jones proved controversial, partially because of the pronounced tension between the private ownership and presumed autonomy of the university, and the generalized notion of harmful public policy, both of which motivated and authorized the government to act. Equally controversial was the Supreme Court's ruling in the following case, which also assumed important legal significance.

EXAMPLE 4

Employment Division, Department of Human Resources of Oregon v. *Smith,* 494 U.S. 872 (1990)

Facts: Alfred Smith and Galen Black worked for a private drug-rehabilitation organization. They were also members of the Native American Church, which used peyote (a hallucinogenic drug) as a ritual of worship.

Smith and Black were fired from their jobs because they ingested peyote for sacramental purposes at a religious ceremony, in violation of Oregon's law that prohibits the knowing or planned possession of a controlled substance, including peyote. Subsequently, Smith and Black were denied unemployment compensation because they had been discharged for work-related misconduct.

Result: The Free Exercise Clause of the First Amendment does not require Oregon to extend unemployment benefits to individuals who violate the criminal law because of their religious convictions.

Argument of the Case: Scalia, Justice. This case is unlike previous unemployment cases in which the Supreme Court required government to demonstrate a compelling state interest before refusing unemployment compensation to individuals whose joblessness is attributable to their religious convictions or practices. In those cases (and in those cases only), free exercise rights triumphed over the state's interests, but those cases presented no violation of the criminal law.[19] Here the criminal law was violated. Although a person has an unlimited right to believe, religious beliefs do not excuse that individual from behaving in conformity with an otherwise valid law. Given the variety of religions that exist, virtually every law can be challenged, and many important regulations will not be able to be justified by a compelling interest. For that reason (among others), exemptions for peyote use should be accommodated through the political process in the Oregon legislature.

O'Connor concurs.[20] The Court is mistaken; both religious practices and beliefs enjoy broad protections under the Free Exercise Clause of the Constitution. The Court is also mistaken when it contends that the government does not have to demonstrate a compelling state interest when it curtails religiously motivated practices. Furthermore, the Court's approach unfairly disadvantages minor religions. But disallowing unemployment benefits is still permissible because there does exist a compelling state interest in this case. That interest is in preventing the possession and use of peyote, which is harmful and dangerous.

Blackmun dissents.[21] The Court is misguided; case law interpreting the First Amendment's Free Exercise Clause requires that religious exemption must be granted unless there is a compelling state interest that cannot be served by a less restrictive means. Since peyote's harm is disputable and unproven, the state cannot have such a compelling interest in prohibiting it, so Smith and Black's unemployment claim should be upheld.

Discussion

The *Smith* case has proven to be important and controversial, because it appeared to most observers that it reversed the compelling-state-interest balancing test that, for over twenty-five years, had been more or less employed by the Supreme Court in interpreting the Free Exercise Clause.[22] Justice Scalia's analysis was consistent with the free exercise approach found in cases such as

Lawson and *Reynolds,* examined earlier in this chapter. Compared to the compelling-state-interest test, it was more restraintist in that Scalia placed the responsibility with the state legislature or Congress to balance the interests of society against the religious free exercise of minority religious practitioners (and to fashion or not fashion individualized exemptions from the law accordingly). Scalia's approach was also more conservative in that the result of his analysis upheld government's power to pass generally valid laws as opposed to exempting, as a matter of right, the religious practices of those who were unintentionally disadvantaged by the passage of such laws. There is little wonder that advocates of judicial restraint and political conservatives mostly praised Scalia's opinion, while judicial activists and civil libertarians roundly denounced it. In 1993 the Congress passed the Religious Freedom Restoration Act, essentially setting aside *Smith's* interpretation of the Free Exercise Clause and restoring *Sherbert* v. *Verner's* compelling-state-interest requirement.

The Religious Restoration Act notwithstanding, *Smith* is an interesting and important case and merits examination. Particularly interesting in *Smith* was the fluid notion of harm that pervaded the Supreme Court's varying opinions. Unlike other cases examined in this chapter, the Justices disagreed among themselves exactly how the harm should be applied to Smith and Black's actions. In Scalia's opinion for the Court, the idea of harm was assumed by the fact that Smith and Black had violated the criminal law (the fact that their criminality was religiously motivated provided insufficient reason for them successfully to claim Free Exercise Clause protection). Furthermore, Scalia argued that granting exemption from the criminal law contained an additional harm for society. Scalia's argument on this point was straightforward. Government had the right to pass laws for the health, welfare, morality, and general welfare of its citizens. However, given the wide variety and almost unlimited number of religious claims that individuals could espouse, society would be endangered by being forced to grant exemptions to numerous legitimate and even spurious religious claims. Exempting them all would have the effect of undermining every conceivable civic obligation expected of citizens, from paying taxes to obeying traffic laws. ("Any society adopting such a system would be courting anarchy, but that danger increases in direct proportion to the society's diversity of religious beliefs, and its determination to coerce or suppress none of them...."[23])

There was some evidence for Scalia's position. As it was, courts have had to wrestle with the problem of numerous objections to every conceivable secular law on a continuing basis. To cite but one (amusing) example: in July 1992 the Associated Press reported that two Amish farmers had been fined $108 for failing to obtain outhouse permits. Why had they refused? The representatives of this religious sect that favors both simple dress and living saw the law as infringing upon their religion. "I feel like we're losing more religious freedoms by going along and getting permits,"[24] said one of the two defendants.

Even in the realm of illegal drug use there has been no escape from numerous legal attacks advanced in the name of religious free exercise. In a well-known case, drug advocate Timothy Leary was arrested for smuggling marijuana into the United States, and he contended that its use was part of the expanded consciousness that facilitated his religious practice of Hinduism; a skeptical United States Appeals Court refused to set aside his conviction.[25] Of course, cases like *Leary* can be and have been decided, yet they were (pardon the pun) trying. They took time and expense, and often required the courts to examine the sincerity of the defendant's religious beliefs. Cases of this nature also invited justices to try to determine the centrality of the contested practice (illegal drug use) to a person's overall religious convictions or examine the plausibility of that individual's religious claim, yet these were precisely the judgments that many justices, including all the Supreme Court Justices in the *Smith* case, explicitly disdained and thought inappropriate.

In contrast to Scalia, both O'Connor (concurring) and Blackmun (dissenting) emphasized not the harm of violating the law, but the harm of the defendants' act (ingesting peyote). This difference existed because both O'Connor and Blackmun emphasized the independent power of the Free Exercise Clause and urged that the Court (as opposed to the legislature) reconcile the conflicting claims of society and individual free exercise of religion. However, O'Connor proved more restraintist (and, in terms of result, more conservative) than Blackmun, because while she perceived a judicial responsibility to balance governmental powers against individual First Amendment free exercise claims, she seemed quite content to accept the legislature's determination of the harm that would result from peyote use. That is, believing the prohibition of peyote use to be of compelling importance, she unquestionably accepted the Oregon's legislature's determination that it was dangerous.

Not so the dissenters, who did not emphasize the general harm posed by unrestricted peyote use, but the far more limited harm posed by the restricted use by religiously motivated users. The dissenters pointed to the fact that numerous states and the federal government had granted exemptions for religiously motivated peyote use and contended that this indicated support for the conclusion that there was "no evidence that the religious use of peyote has ever harmed anyone."[26] Unlike the "irresponsible and unrestricted recreational use of unlawful drugs," the Native American Church's "internal restrictions on, and supervision of, its members' use of peyote substantially obviate the State's health and safety concerns...."[27] The dissenters thus reviewed not simply the constitutional authority of the Oregon legislature's decision against granting individualized exemption for religiously motivated peyote use, but the soundness of its apparent policy belief that society and individuals would be harmed by such use.

The *Smith* case reversed the well-known 1964 California Supreme Court case of *People* v. *Woody*,[28] which had been decided in a way largely compatible with Blackmun's dissent in *Smith*. *Woody* was interesting because there a court advanced the argument that a peyote use was so important religiously, and so lacking in danger, that the government should not be able to prohibit it (and when the government did prohibit it, it acted harmfully!). In *Woody*, a group of Navajo Indians had met in a hogan near Needles, California, to perform a religious ceremony that included the use of peyote. Police officers arrested several of the participants, who were later convicted of violating the State Health and Safety Code, which prohibited the unauthorized use of peyote. The California Supreme Court, in overturning the convictions, carefully examined not simply the state rationale for passing the law (and whether prohibiting peyote amounted to a compelling state requirement), but if refusing to grant a specific exemption to the Navajos could be justified by a compelling state interest in preventing the harm of peyote use. After pointing out the centrality of peyote to the Navajo's worship (it served as a sacrament, as do bread and wine in some Christian ceremonies; as an object of worship to whom prayers are directed, such as the Holy Ghost; and as a teacher and protector), the Court dismissed the state's argument that because religiously motivated peyote use was dangerous, an exemption for its use would also be dangerous. California had offered two rationales for enforcing the law against the Navajos. First, the drug had unfortunate effects upon the Indian community. Specifically, the state contended that the Navajos tended to use this drug rather than receiving proper medical care, that its use had adversely affected small children, and that there was a correlation between peyote use and the use of more harmful drugs. Second, allowing the Navajos to use peyote placed a great burden "upon the enforcement of the narcotic laws because of the difficulty of detecting fraudulent claims of an asserted religious use of peyote."[29]

The California Supreme Court rejected the state's rationales, finding them not compelling, and challenged most of them as being factually untrue. It did not believe that the Navajos used peyote instead of receiving proper medical care. Neither did it believe that Navajo children were indoctrinated, citing the infrequent use of the drug among Native American children and teenagers. Finally, it did not believe that there was hard evidence that peyote use correlated with the ingestion of other, more dangerous drugs. In fact, according to the Court, it was the opinion of scientists and other experts that peyote "works no permanent deleterious injury to the Indians." Regarding the state's fear that many fraudulent requests for peyote or drug use might arise in the name of free religious exercise, the Court observed that "the state produced no evidence that spurious claims of religious immunity would in fact preclude effective administration of the law or that other 'forms of regulation' would not accomplish the state's objectives."[30]

Cases like *Smith* and *Woody* are complex partially because the idea of harm underlying them is so elusive and partially because there are so many philosophical and theoretical questions raised by their consideration. Drug use can be considered harmful because it violates the criminal law or because it can physiologically and/or psychologically damage the individual and simultaneously harm society. Yet the actual degree of harm associated with any particular drug can be controversial, as can be the extent to which that harm is diminished by its more limited use in ritual religious ceremonies. Furthermore, even conceding that peyote is dangerous, ought government dedicated to the protection of religious freedom be required to give special consideration to those religiously motivated individuals who assume responsibility for their own actions (as opposed to those who would use drugs only for recreational purposes)? Compounding this problem are others: If it is generally agreed that peyote is dangerous, harmful, or disagreeable, will the government be able to successfully distinguish religiously motivated users from fraudulent recreational users? Finally, if such a judgment is difficult for government to make consistently and competently, does this fact pose any sort of problem for the larger society?

In one factual instance, however, there has been little disagreement on the Supreme Court. Where government targets a specific religion for regulation, then the Free Exercise Clause protects the ritual practices of practitioners, even if they seem very unusual (and assuming they are not immediately dangerous). Our next, and last, case reflects this principle.

EXAMPLE 5

Church of Lakumi Babalu v. *Hialeah,* 111 S. Ct. 2217

Facts: Members of the Santeria Church—a religious sect that had moved to Florida by way of Africa and Cuba and that combined elements of native African religion with Roman Catholicism—practiced animal sacrifice as part of their religious devotion. When residents of Hialeah, Florida, discovered that a Santeria Church was about to open, they pressured their city council, which passed a series of laws prohibiting such practices under its authority to protect the community's health and to prohibit cruelty to animals.

Result: Hialeah's laws that restrict the sacrifice of animals, by being either overly broad or underinclusive, fail the strict scrutiny required when religious practices are targeted by government.

Argument of the Case: Kennedy, Justice.[31] The ordinances were written in such a way to suppress the practice of the Santeria religion. The secular killing of animals is allowed (for example, hunting and fishing, extermination of pests, euthanasia of unwanted animals); only most all of the religious killing and disposal of animals is disallowed, making the statute underinclusive. Furthermore, the laws were written in such a way as to prohibit more religious conduct than is necessary to fulfill the purposes of the public and anti-cruelty purposes of the ordinances, making the statutes also underinclusive. Because they are not neutral, generally applicable statutes, strict scrutiny must be applied. In order to be deemed constitutional, they must be narrowly tailored, which they are not. The Constitution commits government to religious tolerance and does not allow persecution of any religious sect.

Scalia concurs.[32] Unlike Justice Kennedy (who discovered in the legislative record bias against the Santerians), the subjective motivation of lawmakers cannot be determined; attention should be focused exclusively on the object of the laws.

Souter concurs.[33] The case is decided but does nothing to resolve the free exercise tensions inherent in *Smith*.

Blackmun concurs.[34] Free exercise protection extends beyond those rare occasions when government targets religion.

Discussion

This intriguing case reflects a number of disagreements as well as a bedrock area of agreement among the Justices. The legal status and wisdom of *Smith* remained in dispute, with Justice Souter in particular desiring to reargue the merits of that decision. Another area of judicial disagreement focused on how one determines whether anti-religious legislative bias exists. Justice Scalia, disagreeing with Justice Kennedy, doubted that the courts should review the legislative record in search of legislative meaning and intent; he preferred to confine the Supreme Court to the language of the statute.

But all the Justices, whatever their view of precedent and procedure and whatever constitutional test they would employ, thought that Hialeah had drafted a series of laws intended only to affect one religious group—practitioners of the Santeria religion. Nor was there any evidence that the ritual animal killings of Santeria posed any immediate physical harm to the general public. Ritual slaughter may have been repugnant to many of the community's citizens, but this case reflects the principle that generalized community repugnance to a sect's religious practices amounts to a harm insufficient to justify the abrogation of a constitutionally protected right of religious free exercise. No matter what precedent or constitutional test is employed by the Supreme Court, this case makes clear that the contemporary Court stands ready to defend the religious practices of small, unusual minorities against the legal power of the majority.

SUMMARY

Polygamy, snake handling, racial discrimination, illegal drug use, and ritual animal sacrifice all constitute public harms that are widely recognized. The question becomes this: What happens when a person, or a group of people, or a private organization is motivated by religious convictions to undertake such practices? That is, what happens when harmful practices are defined not simply as a secular wrong, but as a religious ritual or as a religious commandment?

We are now prepared to furnish several tentative answers to these questions. Traditionally (before 1960), when a religiously motivated practice seemed particularly disagreeable or harmful, federal courts were reluctant to insist that the Free Exercise Clause of the First Amendment required them to provide a tailored exemption to valid laws serving important state purposes. This approach was both restraintist and conservative. Those advocating this approach frequently defended it because it spared the courts the burden of hearing and deciding thousands of potential cases, all challenging secularly valid laws on the often fraudulent or trivial ground that the law endangered the practice of their religion. On the other hand, those opposed to this approach (including the majority of the Supreme Court Justices who decided the *Sherbert* case) question whether the courts have abdicated their responsibility to protect minority religious practices, leaving their protection to legislatures that, all too often, have been insensitive to the rights of unrepresented, or sparsely represented, minorities.

An intriguing question is to what extent the Court has been influenced by the very repugnance of the acts described in this chapter. For instance, were snake handling, polygamy, racial discrimination, or illegal drug use so repulsive to Justices and judges that they were inclined to side with the state at the expense of minority religious practitioners who sought protection? At bottom, this question probably cannot be answered with certainty. Some might observe that in the first four cases considered in this chapter, the courts upheld judgments or ruled against those who claimed constitutional protection for a practice that the larger society regarded as disagreeable or harmful. But it should also be noted that the Supreme Court in *Lakumi Babalu* recently and unanimously upheld what to most people was the repugnant practice of animal sacrifice, as practiced by an obscure and unpopular religious sect.

NOTES

1. An excellent discussion of the distinction between categorically wrong acts, and contingently wrong acts (a distinction that treats acts that are harmful in principle and acts that are harmful in a utilitarian sense) is found in Hadley Arkes, *First Things: An Inquiry into the First Principles of Morals and Justice* (Princeton, NJ: Princeton Univ. Press, 1986), pp. 85–115.

2. This distinction is pointed to by H. L. A. Hart, *Law, Liberty,* and *Morality* (New York: Books, 1963), pp. 43–48. Acts that are not immoral and may be regarded as praiseworthy or sanctified when conducted in private may be offensive when conducted in public—for example, sex between married partners.

3. Emphasis ours. Interestingly, it is Jefferson's language regarding the separation of church and state that has endured, not the portions of Jefferson's letter that the Supreme Court in *Reynolds* explicitly relied upon in rejecting Reynold's constitutional argument.

4. Eleven years after *Reynolds*, in *Davis* v. *Beason* (133 U.S. 333, 341–42 1890), Justice Field wrote for the Court:

Bigamy and polygamy are crimes by the laws of the civilized and Christian countries. They are crimes by the laws of the United States and they are crimes by the laws of Idaho. They tend to destroy the purity of the marriage relation, to disturb the peace of families, to degrade woman and to debase men. Few crimes are more pernicious to the best interests of society and receive more general or more deserved punishment. To extend exemption from punishment for such crimes would be to shock the moral judgment of the community. To call their advocacy a tenet of religion is to offend the common sense of mankind.

5. 98 U.S. 145 (1879) at 164.

6. John Stuart Mill, *On Liberty* (Chicago: Henry Regnery, 1955), pp. 134–37.

7. Mill, p. 135.

8. Mill, p. 13.

9. Thus, the Court revealed that it would disfavor any challenge to the Kentucky law on the ground that it prohibited the handling of *all* snakes in connection with any religious service, and thus was overbroad.

10. Although this distinction was initially raised in *Reynolds* v. *United States*, the Kentucky Court cited it as deriving from *Cantwell* v. *Connecticut*, 310 U.S. 296 (1940).

11. According to the Court, "Other cases of similar, import may be found in the footnotes to Sections 206a and 206b, 'Constitutional Law' 16 Corpus Juris Secundum, pages 599 to 603, from which we quote the following excerpt...." 164 S.W .2d at 976.

12. Generally, court decisions in other snake-handling cases have been consistent with *Lawson* and have been decided with relatively little controversy: See, for instance: *State* v. *Massey*, 229 N.C. 734 51 S.E. 2d 179 (1949); *Hill* v. *State*, 38 Ala. App. 404, 88 So. 2d 880 (1956); *State ex rel. Swann* v. *Pack*, 103 Tenn. (1975); 527 S.W. 2d 99 *cert. denied*, 424 U.S. 954 (1976).

13. 291 Ky. 437, 164 S.W. 2d 972 (1942) at 973.

14. See "Comment: Snakehandling and Freedom of Religion," *Washington University Law Quarterly*, vol. 353 (1976), pp. 353, 363, 365–66.

15. See p. 293.

16. Powell concurred partially with the Court's opinion (as indicated) and with its judgment.

17. Not surprisingly, the extent to which this case posed a threat to the autonomy of private institutions has been much debated since *Jones*.

18. 461 U.S. 574 (1983) at 604.

19. That is, Scalia contended that the Supreme Court had never invalidated any government action solely under the Free Exercise Clause except those that involved the denial of unemployment compensa-tion (and in no case did this denial involve a violation of the criminal law).

20. O'Connor concurs in the Court's judgment. Justices Brennan, Marshall, and Blackmun dissent regarding her (and the Court's) judgment; they also join her criticism of the majority's opinion, specifically her argument that the Free Exercise Clause protects both religious beliefs and religiously motivated actions, and that in order for these actions to be prohibited, government must demonstrate a compelling interest.

21. Blackmun's dissent is joined by Justices Brennan and Marshall.

22. The key case establishing this test was *Sherbert* v. *Verner* , 374 U.S. 398 (1963). The case is discussed in Chapter 7, pp.127–29.

23. 494 U.S. 872 (1990) at 888.

24. *Argus Leader* (Sioux Falls, South Dakota), July 9, 1992, p. 4c.

25. 383 F.2d 851 (1967). The conviction was later reversed on technical grounds. See *Leary* v.*United States*, 395 U.S. 6 (1969).

26. 494 U.S. 872 (1990) at 911–12.

27. 494 U.S. 872 at 913.

28. 61 Cal. 2d 716, 394 Cal. 2d 813, 40 Cal. Rptr. 69 (1964).

29. 394 Cal. 2d 813 (1964) at 818.

30. *People* v. *Woody* at 819.

31. We summarize here only that portion of Kennedy's opinion in which he speaks for the Court. Although all the Justices would overturn the law, seven of the remaining Justices concur with only a portion of Kennedy's larger opinion.

32. Scalia concurs in the judgment and with part of Kennedy's opinion. He is joined by Chief Justice Rehnquist.

33. Souter concurs in part with Kennedy's opinion and with the Court's judgment.

34. Blackmun concurs in the Court's judgment and is joined by Justice O'Connor.

PART III

✥

Religion and Education

10

When Is the Secular Law So Disagreeable That It Should Be Disobeyed?

THE PROBLEM POSED

Many years ago, the famous Walt Disney character Jiminy Cricket (featured in an equally famous Disney animated film, *Pinocchio*) offered a simple solution for life's many difficult and perplexing problems. They can be solved, he counseled his young audience, if only you "let your conscience be your guide." Jiminy Cricket's seemingly simple advice retains considerable attractiveness in an age beset with serious and persistent social, political, economic, and moral challenges. Wouldn't it be good, and—more to the point—wouldn't it be right, if we all acted in a way that enabled our consciences to be our guide?

Of course, before adopting or even accepting Jiminy Cricket's moral maxim, we would need to know more about the idea of conscience. Such knowledge is particularly important in light of the central question posed by this chapter. Here we will consider what happens when the secular law is so disagreeable that it should be disobeyed. Note: to ask this question is directly to raise the issue of the propriety, morality, and necessity of civil disobedience. Frequently, Jiminy Cricket's answer applies in this area of citizen conduct—it holds that when a law appears morally repugnant, then disobedience becomes a necessary consequence of making conscience be our guide.

If civil disobedience is rooted in the idea of conscience, then we need to examine and understand exactly what the idea of conscience entails. As we analyze civil disobedience, there are at least three important questions regarding conscience to keep in mind:

1. What exactly is meant by conscience? Certainly it is not the same as opinion or feeling, although it is often used in such a trivial sense. For example, political scientists frequently remark that American elected representatives either vote their constituents' interests and opinions or vote "their [own] consciences." But surely such a characterization diminishes the significance of this term.

2. Is conscience a reliable guide for human conduct? If so, does this imply that all human beings are endowed with consciences? Additionally, what do we make of some people (for example, sociopaths) who do not seem to have a conscience, while other people, some historically important (Hitler, Stalin) not only act cruelly but embrace evil and derive pleasure from violating commonly accepted dictates of conscience?

3. If conscience is universal or at least prevalent among human beings, does it lead in a single direction? If not, what are the social and political implications of violating the law because of the dictates of conscience?

One final point should be emphasized. It was made poignantly by a foremost champion of civil disobedience, Martin Luther King, Jr. In October 1960, from a jail cell in Reidsville State Prison in Tattnall County, Georgia, King observed that imprisonment was "the cross that we must bear for the freedom of our people."[1] Such allegorical language reminds us that the root of civil disobedience has, for some time, frequently been traced to conscience rooted in religion and religious belief. Little wonder that the relationship between individual conscience and societal rules and laws bears essential scrutiny in a book examining law, religion, and politics.

What Is Civil Disobedience?

During the nineteenth and twentieth centuries, many famous people have addressed the subject of civil disobedience (the best-known being American essayist David Henry Thoreau, Russian novelist Leo Tolstoy, Indian political leader Mohandas Gandhi, and American Martin Luther King, Jr.). Civil disobedience has played an especially important role in contemporary American history, where it was practiced with great effect by King and his followers in their effort to end segregation. Later in the United States, Vietnam war dissenters and abortion law critics each claimed they were practicing civil disobedience. Still, it is civil disobedience's close association with the struggle for equal rights within the United States that helps explain much of its favorable reaction as well as its enduring legacy.

Irrespective of how Americans have felt or feel about such controversial political questions and the appropriateness of practicing civil disobedience to express these opinions, it is important to evaluate the legal and moral appropriateness of civil disobedience *in principle*. We begin with a candid confession: there has hardly been universal agreement regarding the essential meaning of civil disobedience.[2] Yet it seems to us that any definition of civil disobedience has at its core the recognition that civil disobedience constitutes a deliberate violation of the law undertaken for the sake of a moral principle. Inherent in this understanding is both an action (breaking of a law) and a motivation (a sincere belief that the challenged law, or some law fundamentally related to it, is significantly or profoundly immoral or unjust).[3] Underlying the whole discussion of civil disobedience is a generally agreed-upon assumption—namely, that citizens are generally obligated to obey laws, insofar as they are not grossly immoral and have been fairly enacted and enforced.[4] Thus, the justification for civil disobedience is inevitably rooted in an understanding of justice or morality (an understanding that *may* have a religious origin). Of course, not all laws have a moral content. Thus, there is a qualitative difference between a law with no moral content such as those prohibiting motorists from driving on the left (or right) side of the road, and laws with a moral content, such as those punishing theft, prohibiting (or perhaps, in evil political regimes, requiring) murder, laws enforcing contracts, or laws requiring or prohibiting legally enforced racial separation. Civil disobedience is generally directed only at overturning laws that have a moral component.[5] Its practitioners and advocates reject the notion that such laws embody the highest standard of moral behavior (much less an acceptable standard of behavior). By so doing, they spurn the idea that *legal* and *moral* are necessarily identical (and emphatically reject the idea that might makes right or, more vulgarly, in the words of an old German proverb, the notion that God is with the stronger army). Thus, civil disobedience theorists all share a common capacity to speak of unjust or immoral laws because all share an idea that there are standards of right and wrong that transcend the laws of nations.

The Ethical Basis of Civil Disobedience

But from where does this idea of right and wrong come? On what basis should a law be resisted? In other words, how does a person conclude that a law is wrong and ought to be disobeyed? Historically, different answers to this question have been given. A *theistic* approach usually (but not always) grows out of the biblical distinction between God and Caesar, and the related notion that while citizens are obligated to obey each, in case of conflict the duties toward God are the highest, and the importance of the next life transcends the fleeting concerns of this existence. (This theory was more fully developed by medieval Christian thinkers.) By contrast, a *classical* consideration of this problem was put forward by several political philosophers as divergent as Socrates and Cicero, who, while not furnishing a comprehensive theory of the problem of when to disobey the law, nonetheless presented a way that one could distinguish among particular laws, rulers, and regimes and a universal sense of justice discovered by reason. Finally, beginning in the seventeenth century, political thinkers increasingly emphasized the priority of the individual to the state, eventually producing an *individualistic* approach to the discovery of right or wrong that grew out of an inevitable tension between the rights of individuals to live autonomous and meaningful lives and the dangerous and coercive power of the state exercised through its laws.[6] Increasingly, advocates of individualistic civil disobedience relied upon an understanding of conscience that spoke less about God's law or natural right or justice, and more about individual reason and feelings; for them, the thought or feeling of the individual was key, not the existence or violation of an external standard.

Thus, the practice of what is today called civil disobedience is actually quite old. Its earliest recorded instance presents an example of theistically motivated breaking of the law and can be found in the Book of Exodus in the Hebrew Bible. The Egyptian ruler Pharaoh, fearing the growing number and potential power of the people he had enslaved, ordered the deaths of all male Hebrew babies. Many Hebrew midwifes deliberately disobeyed, refusing to carry out Pharaoh's order. According to scripture, they disobeyed because they feared God.[7] Thus, God's commandments furnished a basis of citizen defiance of Pharaoh's commandment.

A somewhat similar conclusion is reached in Sophocles' famous play *Antigone*. It provides a second example of theistic civil disobedience. In the play, Antigone is appalled that Creon, ruler of Thebes, has refused a proper burial for her brother. Creon's position is influenced by the fact that Antigone's brother had been an enemy of the city who was killed attacking Thebes. On the other hand, Antigone asserts that she is motivated by familial obligation; she claims piety and cites the unwritten laws of the gods in her behalf.[8] So motivated, she defies Creon's order and buries her brother. Sentenced to death for her deed, she kills herself (her fiancé, who is Creon's son, and Creon's wife also commit suicide) before Creon is able to revoke the punishment. Creon, grieving, alone, and disgraced, is left to ponder the consequences of his decisions.

But God is not the only source of a higher obligation that has justified civil disobedience. As we have noted, certain Greek thinkers had long recognized that the traditions and laws of particular political communities varied significantly from one another as well as from the dictates of justice; these philosophers distinguished between convention (that which existed because of agreement) and nature (that which was simply true).[9] Although this distinction did not lead to a theory of individual political action such as civil disobedience (the closest, a distant cousin, being that of tyrannicide[10]), this classical account of right and wrong (founded in the distinction between convention and nature) was itself rooted in reason's potential to discern a larger truth. Reason's capacity to discover moral distinctions, and act upon them, was developed early by such Roman stoics as Cicero and particularly Gratian and remains an important influence to this day.[11]

Occasionally, writers in the great religious traditions attempted to make revelation and reason compatible as the source of moral insight.[12] For instance, St. Thomas Aquinas argued that reason enables human beings to discover good and evil, and by making this effort, reflects within us the divine by enabling us to discover God's law (and may limit our obedience to secular rulers when they violate God's justice).[13] Thus, for Aquinas, human reason is a reflection of God's will.

This effort did not ultimately prevail. By the seventeenth century a new, secular, individualistic understanding of political obligation emerged in Europe. For the most part, references to God or abstract justice were largely absent; government was to be obeyed or disobeyed to the extent that it promoted or endangered human survival, well-being, or rights individually determined. Nor was civil disobedience the key to individual disagreement or defiance; frequently, other political action was more natural (such as rebellion or revolution). In each case, however, the emphasis had shifted from some trans-human standard of right and wrong to that which was human-based. Thus, some Enlightenment thinkers (most notably Immanuel Kant and followers such as Hermann Cohen) would suggest that God was essentially the reflection of pure reason, whose dictates could be formed within us.[14] Of course, not all thinkers in modern times have emphasized reason as the sufficient source of human action in this way, although virtually all civil disobedience thinkers, like Thoreau in his famous "Essay on Civil Disobedience," have pictured the acts of civil disobedience as an individually determined right perpetrated against the injustices of governmental power. For Adam Smith, emotion was also important. In his famous 1759 work *The Theory of Moral Sentiments,* he emphasized sympathetic emotion by postulating within human beings the existence of an "impartial spectator"—a natural source of sympathy for others that arose naturally by our imagining "what we ourselves *should* feel in the like situation."[15]

The Idea of Conscience

It is this notion of something like a disinterested inner voice—differently expressed, but nurtured, directed, and perpetuated by the family, or the law, or the community and inevitably grounded in reason or revelation and even feeling (or some combination thereof)—that makes up the essence of contemporary understanding of conscience. It is in the name of conscience that civil disobedience has been increasingly advocated in the twentieth century. Significantly, the very idea of conscience has undergone important changes in meaning over time.[16] For Aquinas (the first significant thinker to discuss the matter in these terms), conscience was an activity or habit of the soul that relies upon *external* first principles. These axioms of practical reason informed the reasoning part of the soul regarding matters of practical (that is, moral and political) knowledge. In other words, Aquinas understood conscience as the natural starting place for prudence (practical wisdom).[17] From this it followed that when a person acted according to conscience in the face of the doubts and opposition of many others, he or she was obligated to reexamine the underlying conscience and practical reasoning that led to the disputed beliefs. For Aquinas acknowledged that individual conscience, as well as the secular law, could err.

Two great historical figures who exercised civil disobedience in the name of conscience were Socrates and Thomas More. Since their actions were at variance with our contemporary understanding of civil disobedience, their actions and explanations can help us understand more clearly the origin, meaning, and limits of conscience. In the *Apology,* Socrates recounts instances when a sort of demonic voice restrained him from taking part in the improper arrest of someone the ruling oligarchy wished to execute. Additionally, it had led him to decline presiding over the collective trial of ten generals who had offended the prevailing religious sentiments of family members and citizens by not burying the dead after an important battle. Socrates believed that such a trial was contrary to law and justice. Another aspect of what is commonly understood to be an act of conscience occurred at his trial. Declaring his innocence regarding the charge of not believing in the gods of the city and corrupting the youth of Athens, Socrates also communicated his intention to continue philosophizing. Obviously, Socrates was unwilling to bow to the law regarding this one matter. Nonetheless, he did accept the guilty verdict of the Athenian jury, refusing to flee and escape punishment. Despite a strong personal conviction that impelled him to philosophize, Socrates also respected the laws of the regime that had protected, sustained, and educated him. In exchange for their benefits, he made clear his obligation to accept the punishment.

Thomas More's dilemma was rooted in religion, not philosophy. He refused to recognize King Henry VIII's divorce, which violated Catholic Church law. Asserting that he had not committed treason, More nonetheless refused to proclaim in public that King Henry was the head of the church in England. Although he privately thought that Parliament's act was contrary to the law of God and the King could never be supreme within the church (opinions uttered explicitly only after he was condemned to death), More also believed that the secular law should have protected his silence and therefore should have safeguarded his act of conscience. After his sentence was announced, More neither denied nor resisted the authority of the state to punish him, maintaining only at the time of his death, in 1535, that he had been "the King's good servant, but God's first."

Socrates and More's idea of conscience (and hence their practice of what we commonly call civil disobedience) share certain important characteristics:

> As in the case of Socrates, the actions from conscience of More are inactions. More's conscience restrained him; it did not urge him on. As in the case of Socrates, More was guided by what he understood to be the law. That is, in neither case is it a matter of idiosyncratic moral sense. In both cases, knowledge is involved and knowledge is shared. Neither was acting from what we should today call subjective understandings. Finally, More, as Socrates, resolutely, quietly and one might even say magnanimously faced death as an alternative easily preferable to abandonment of conscience.[18]

In our time, it is worth noting that the notion of conscience has changed significantly.[19] Today, conscience, the most usually cited source of civil disobedience, frequently impels people to action as opposed to simply restraining them from action. Furthermore, conscience is commonly understood to be a justification for violating the law, rather than a reason to uphold it.[20] Also, conscience today is usually regarded as something profoundly personal (and therefore subjective), so, by definition, it is not generally thought to be open to outside scrutiny.[21] Moreover, acts of conscience are not always accompanied by the clear recognition of the citizen's obligation to follow the law and an unequivocal acceptance of the political regime's right to punish illegal behavior. Finally, perhaps it is also worth noting that Socrates and More each faced death with a courage that denied even the appearance of self-interest or cowardice; this is not necessarily the case today.

Varieties of Civil Disobedience

The differences between the types of civil disobedience practiced by Socrates and Thomas More, and the way civil disobedience is commonly understood today, require us to distinguish more precisely among different kinds of civil disobedience. Before probing these differences, however, we should consider what all civil disobedience practitioners have in common. Faced with a law that is morally intolerable, such a person has two fundamental choices. One can choose to comply with the law or choose to disobey it. Naturally, practitioners of civil disobedience select the second alternative.

Yet among the people who choose the practice of civil disobedience, there are significant differences in perception, motivation, and judgment regarding the extent of their citizenly obligations and their personal motives as these relate to the resistance to immoral laws. Furthermore, as we noted in the previous section, our understanding of conscience has changed significantly over time. Therefore, it may be useful to distinguish three types of individuals who practice civil disobedience. First, there are people who practice civil disobedience for the purpose of attempting to influence political policy, hoping to effect the repeal of a particular law or cluster of laws. Such actions constitute the practice of *political* civil disobedience. Second, some individuals find a law morally repugnant, refuse to obey it, but have no desire to persuade others to follow their course of action. These people undertake acts of *private* civil disobedience. Finally, a third group of persons may refuse to obey a law or laws because they do not wish to cooperate with, or wish actively to oppose, a particularly heinous or illegitimate political regime. (In the case of violent anarchists, law-breaking may indicate opposition to *any* regime.) These individuals are practitioners of *revolutionary* civil disobedience.

The most recognizable form of civil disobedience is that which we have labeled political. This public display of law-breaking, motivated and justified in the name of a higher moral principle, can assume different forms. For instance, student demonstrators may circle an college's administration building, simultaneously protesting and violating an administration edict that prohibits student demonstrations that interfere with the rights or obligations of other students. Or they may undertake such a demonstration and violate the same college edict as well as state trespass laws in order to protest another law altogether (for example, a draft law essential to the fighting of a controversial war).[22] In each instance, the demonstrators' protest violates the law.[23] In each case, civil disobedience exists to the extent that the students were motivated by a belief that the law they protested contradicted some fundamental moral principle. In each case, the protestors were moved not only by a belief that the law should be disobeyed, but also by a desire to influence public opinion to repeal the law.

Thus, those "pro-life" protestors who circle abortion clinics in violation of anti-loitering statutes, or anti-war protestors who similarly surround military recruiting centers, to the extent that they wish to influence changes in the law (and if they intentionally violate the law for the sake of a moral principle) practice political civil disobedience. In contemporary times, the most famous practitioner of political civil disobedience was Martin Luther King, Jr. King believed that the segregation laws he violated and protested were morally wrong, not only as applied to black citizens, but for everyone. They corrupted and debased the whole political system. Thus, when King and his followers refused to obey a particular law (or an interrelated group of laws), they sought to change the law through word and deed by calling attention to the perceived injustice. Underlying this approach was a belief that while segregation laws imposed immoral obligations upon citizens, the entire system of laws that emanated from and made up the political system should be retained and respected. Thus, while King proclaimed his disdain for Jim Crow laws and sought their eradication, he simultaneously proclaimed his belief in the American ideal of justice and asked the American nation to live up to its long-declared political ideal of equal rights and racial justice. In this manner, King sought important political changes that would reform, rather than overthrow, the political system.

The public nature of political civil disobedience stands in sharp contrast to the actions of individuals whose act of civil disobedience is fundamentally private. Like Thomas More, modern-day Amish in the United States, or an anti-war protestor who deliberately and silently chooses to disobey the law because he or she believes it to be morally wrong but does not publicize the act, such individuals simply refuse to comply with laws that they regard as profoundly offensive (or refuse to obey a law fundamentally related to a related government action or policy that they regard to be profoundly offensive). Although such people are usually recognized by what they *refuse* to do, it is important to recognize the limits of their action. They judge the law they refuse to obey wrong, but they make no concerted effort to convince others that obeying the contested law is wrong for everyone. Additionally, practitioners of private civil disobedience generally exhibit a respect for the law of the state and usually acknowledge its right to punish them. Finally, these individuals do not aim at affecting or reforming the political system, but merely intend to exempt themselves from certain morally offensive laws. It is important to recognize that even acts of private civil disobedience (despite the person's intention) can have an effect upon the body politic, especially if the person is well-known. Furthermore, should an individual publicize law-breaking activities in an attempt to influence others (as did Henry David Thoreau when he wrote about his refusal to pay taxes as a means of objecting to the fugitive slave laws and the Mexican War), private civil disobedience can become transformed into political civil disobedience (or even revolutionary civil disobedience, as we see below).

In contrast to political or private civil disobedience, a person's refusal to obey a law and accept the right of government to punish its violation sometimes grows out of a belief that the law is so vile that it undermines the moral authority of the entire regime, or a conviction that the statute is merely one of many laws of a regime that is so fundamentally reprehensible or illegitimate that obedience to any of its rules indicates acquiescence in evil (or, in the case of a revolutionary anarchist, a belief that laws passed by *any* regime should be opposed).[24] Choosing to disobey a law (or perhaps many such laws) for this reason, at a minimum, is an act of citizen noncooperation and often assumes the form of an act of active renunciation or opposition. As defined here, revolutionary civil disobedience is revolutionary in the sense that it intends to create a radical break between citizen and regime. It establishes a moral distance between the two and, in its most extreme stage, seeks the actual overthrow of the government. This kind of revolutionary civil disobedience is exhibited in various individual acts, including active opposition to the ruling political regime (for example, joining the underground in order to oppose a repressive government) or in wide-scale public protests (admittedly somewhat unusual, but consider the case of Gandhi's public demonstrations in India, which intended to replace colonialism with self-determination by overthrowing British rule). However, even if the individual does nothing other than disobey the law out of a belief that the regime is lacking in moral authority and is therefore illegitimate (perhaps fearing to convey his or her opposition to anyone), such an act of civil disobedience has not lost its revolutionary character.

Practitioners of both political and private civil disobedience support the political system as a whole. Theirs is true *civil* disobedience, for they undertake actions appropriate to *citizens* who feel obliged to support the systems of law in the regime. By contrast, practitioners of revolutionary civil disobedience wish or seek its destruction. Admittedly, discerning the difference between a citizen who profoundly objects to a law or a number of interrelated laws and an individual who despises the government as a whole and regards it as illegitimate turns upon the accurate assessment of the motivation or judgment of the person choosing to disobey the law. This can sometimes be a slippery distinction. An individual may not even know his or her own mind well enough to know whether it is a single law or a number of related laws, or the government as a whole, that ought to be opposed or even overthrown. Yet the fact that the distinction exists and can be clearly discerned in many cases, even if it is not clear in every case, is ample reason for recognizing its existence.

Political Civil Disobedience: Self-Imposed Limitations

Political civil disobedience occupies our primary attention in this book, since it has had the greatest effect on the political life of our democracy. Additionally, when Americans argue about the propriety of civil disobedience, it is almost always political civil disobedience to which they refer.

Practitioners of political civil disobedience have often been perceived as enemies or opponents of society, or of society's best interests. This problem has three dimensions. The first complexity regarding the way practitioners of civil disobedience are perceived assumes the following form: by breaking the law, these people are, by definition, lawbreakers. Yet practitioners of political civil disobedience do not regard themselves as ordinary criminals. Almost always, ordinary criminals are motivated by some combination of self-aggrandizement, greed, arrogance, selfishness, and general antisocial sentiments. By contrast, those who practice political civil disobedience regard their actions as the product of moral principle; even though their acts are illegal, their motive and character differ qualitatively from those acts of ordinary criminals.

A second, related problem is that when political civil disobedience is practiced, the practitioner may not so much appear to be an ordinary criminal as a revolutionary zealot. As we have noted, the line between revolutionary and nonrevolutionary civil disobedience is not always clear. Amid the heated controversy that can sometimes characterize democratic politics, it is not shocking that those who practice political civil disobedience may be accused of inciting revolution. Since revolutionaries can be the most despised of political activists, those who practice political civil disobedience inevitably attempt to demonstrate that they are innocent of such charges.

A third problem encountered by civil disobedience practitioners who claim to be motivated by sincerely held moral principle is that they are not always believed. (For human beings frequently act in a way to maximize their narrow self-interest, and even when they do not, still it is extraordinarily difficult to ascertain anyone's true motivation.) Thus, Jones may oppose the draft out of a sincere and deeply held moral belief that all war is wrong; his conscience dictates that military registration and draft laws should be violated because they help promote war, but since Jones is eighteen years old and (in our scenario) can be drafted, he is open to the charge of acting out of self-interest or even cowardice (as opposed to true moral principle). Therefore, the accusation of crass self-interest, as well as the charges of common criminality or outright subversion, can sometimes confront the practitioner of political civil disobedience.

In order to distinguish themselves from criminals, revolutionaries, and crassly self-interested individuals, many practitioners of political civil disobedience have adopted several maxims regarding its practice. These prudential maxims (described below) have the effect (and, as well, may have been originally fashioned) to present the person practicing civil disobedience in the best possible public light so that the public influence of any law breaking act might be maximized. We would stress that none of these maxims is absolutely necessary to the practice of civil disobedience. That is, although they may be commonly employed and widely praised, these maxims serve to reemphasize the fundamental fact that civil disobedience means that an individual breaks the law because it violates a meaningful moral sensibility. Additionally, we would emphasize that, in some cases, the maxims listed below often are not mere prudential rules, but can constitute ethical principles strongly and sincerely held by their advocates. (This holds especially true for the principle of nonviolence.) Finally, we should mention that most of the maxims discussed below are closely associated with Martin Luther King, Jr., whose words as well as deeds continue to prove influential in the area of civil disobedience theory.[25] The five most well-known maxims commonly associated with the practice of political civil disobedience are as follows:

1. *The law should be violated only as a last resort.* Simply stated, no method short of civil disobedience is capable of providing any avenue of relief from the perceived injustice. As a way of calling attention to, and attempting to remedy, that injustice, civil disobedience represents the least radical and most responsible approach.

2. *The violation of the law should be done openly, even lovingly.* What this means is that the violation of the law done in the name of civil disobedience must take place in plain sight, out of respect for the law. There is no effort to undertake clandestine behavior or any effort to hide the crime or evade detection. Such a maxim has both a tactical and ethical dimension. Tactically, it publicizes the violation of the law. This is an essential component of political civil disobedience, because a major reason for violating the law is to stir the conscience of the nation in the hope of overturning or repealing morally offensive laws. Ethically, violating the law in an open fashion makes clear that the purpose of law-breaking is not personal gain or crass self-interest but rather an attempt to promote justice.

3. *The person who violates the law should be willing to accept a penalty, if it is necessary.* This maxim serves roughly the same purpose as (1) above. Thus, the practitioner of political civil disobedience is seen as not simply an ordinary criminal or as a crassly self-interested person, but rather as a sincere and serious person acting from conscience for the sake of a moral principle. A willingness to accept punishment for violating the law is an uneasy compromise of sorts between outright ordinary criminality on the one hand and morally laudatory behavior on the other (behavior where the sincerity of the individual may be praised even while the act undertaken is condemned). Essentially, the civil disobedience practitioner says to the government, "You tell me I have an obligation to obey the law. I, on the other hand, cannot obey the law in good conscience. Although we both accept the binding character of the law, there does exist a difference regarding its moral status. Therefore, I propose and will act in the following manner: since I believe that I cannot ethically obey the law, I must disobey it. Yet I will also accept the punishment for violating the law.[26] Although accepting the punishment does not necessarily excuse my act, it will accomplish two important objectives. First, it will highlight my opposition to the contested law, allowing the conscience and convictions of public opinion an opportunity to reconsider and perhaps repeal it (thus achieving my original objective). Second, freely accepting the punishment for my illegal act will allow me to make clear my support for the law."

Regarding this last point, there is some theoretical unclarity.[27] The formulation was Martin Luther King, Jr.'s, who argued that accepting the law's punishment reflected a respect for it and seemed to suggest that this approach would apply in any political regime.[28] But surely respect for "the law" implies respect for a lawful regime, a regime in which the right of conscience has some possibility of success. Willingness to accept the penalty may make sense when one is defying racist laws in the United States (as did King) or British rule in India (as did Gandhi[29]). Openly accepting punishment makes less far less sense in a repressive or totalitarian regime (such as Nazi Germany, where virtually every vestige of conscience had been stamped out by state repression).

4. *The act of civil disobedience ought to be nonviolent.* Many of those who have practiced civil disobedience have advocated nonviolence as a matter of moral principle (Gandhi and King being the most famous). Additionally, nonviolence serves a number of utilitarian purposes. Coupled with civil disobedience, nonviolence emphasizes the moral high ground. It stresses that the practitioner of civil disobedience wishes no harm to those who may be affected by the breaking of laws. Sometimes, it places the practitioner of civil disobedience in a position where he or she may be the passive victim of violence, a position that in an age of mass media can shock a nation into recognizing the injustice inherent in the contested laws.[30] Finally, nonviolence effectively emphasizes the way in which the civilly disobedient person differs from ordinary criminals, who often will resort to any number of antisocial methods to obtain their illegal ends.

5. *Acts of civil disobedience should be confined, substantial, and clear violations of justice or right.*[31] In other words, civil disobedience ought to be confined to first moral principles and perhaps to fundamental matters of equal liberty.[32] Confining acts of civil disobedience in this way recognizes the harm that persistent law-breaking can inflict upon a social order. Such an approach simultaneously recognizes the value of the social order while emphasizing the particular importance of the individual act of civil disobedience. Finally, self-imposed restraint also serves to emphasize the moral integrity of the perpetrator, separating him or her from both criminals and revolutionaries.

The five maxims help to establish the moral sincerity of those who practice political civil disobedience. But important questions remain. Perhaps the most noteworthy is a practical matter. For despite the self-imposed restraints frequently adopted by practitioners of civil disobedience, still it is not obvious how the political state ought to deal with them. Therefore, we must now directly confront the question of whether, in our democracy, conscience can ever afford a politically acceptable guide to action. (That is, should acts of conscience that defy the law ever be ignored or rewarded by the political state?) At bottom, this question assumes another, even more fundamental question: How does one *know* when a seeming injustice really is a fundamental wrong that ought to be opposed by illegal action? These prove to be difficult questions to answer, as the following three case studies reveal.

EXAMPLE 1

Rosa Parks's Civil Disobedience

Facts: The lives of Martin Luther King, Jr., and Mrs. Rosa Parks were, for a key moment in time, intertwined by her act of civil disobedience. Mrs. Parks had worked hard on this December 1 day in 1955.[33] Her job as a tailor's assistant in a Montgomery, Alabama, department store had left her tired and sore. Furthermore, the bus she took home was especially crowded. Only one row of seats—the row immediately behind the first ten seats that were always reserved for whites—had vacancies. She took an aisle seat, sitting next to or across from three other black passengers. As more white passengers boarded the bus, the driver asked (as was the practice) these blacks to move and stand so that the whites could be seated. Although the other three passengers moved, Mrs. Parks refused. Neither frightened nor angry, Mrs. Parks recalled later that "I was thinking that the only way to let them know I felt I was being mistreated was to do just what I did—resist the order.... I had not thought about it and had taken no previous resolution until it happened, and then I simply decided that I would not get up. I was tired, but I was usually tired at the end of the day, and I was not feeling well, but then there had been many days when I had not felt well. I had felt for a long time, that if I was ever told to get up so a white person could sit, that I would refuse to do so." She was arrested by two police officers. Initially charged with violating Montgomery's segregation ordinance, Mrs. Parks was prosecuted under a state statute that mandated segregation and gave bus drivers unlimited enforcement powers. In a five-minute proceeding, she was found guilty and fined $10.

Discussion

Rosa Parks's simple act of courage led to the famous Montgomery Bus Boycott of 1955–56 and the beginnings of Martin Luther King's efforts to combat legal white supremacy throughout the South. The Supreme Court's famous decision in *Brown* v. *Board of Education*[34] had been rendered just over six months before her arrest, so Parks's act helped galvanize the civil rights movement. Yet in the first days after Rosa Parks's arrest, organized opposition to Montgomery's practice supporting white racial superiority was initially tentative. At first, the twenty-six-year-old King hesitated to join efforts made on behalf of the fledgling boycott (citing family and church responsibilities) while the protest movement itself initially argued (unsuccessfully) only for a more courteous form of segregation rather than pressing for the abolition of segregation laws.[35]

Rosa Parks could only have reasonably anticipated her arrest, not the long-term historical importance of her action. Given the near certainty of punishment, what had moved her to act as she did? Made-in-Hollywood movies sometimes picture such moral decisions as agonizing, requiring sleepless nights of moral torment. In Parks's case, one is struck by how straightforward her action was. Admittedly, she had thought about disobeying the bus segregation rules in advance (and had *acted* in such a way before, having been physically thrown off a bus some ten years earlier when, after paying her fare, she had refused to exit the bus and reenter it via the back door). Yet when the time came to act, when she faced circumstances not of her making, Rosa Parks simply responded in a straightforward, almost reflexive manner.

By contrast, Martin Luther King's decision to involve himself in the protest seemed more dramatic. Thrust in the leadership of the fledgling civil rights movement, his life threatened repeatedly, feeling alone, King thought about how his comfortable life had been transformed by a "lady by the name of Rosa Parks [who had] decided that she wasn't going to take it any longer.... It was the beginning of a movement ... and the people of Montgomery asked me to serve them as a spokesman, and as the president of the new organization ... that came into being to lead the boycott. I couldn't say no." Fearing he was weak, he faced a personal crisis of confidence. Then and later, King said he derived courage from an experience that he saw as a moving account of conscience informed by revelation. One midnight, after a threatening phone call,

> ...it seemed at that moment that I could hear an inner voice saying to me, "Martin Luther, stand up for righteousness. Stand up for justice. Stand up for truth. And lo I will be with you, even until the end of the world...." I heard the voice of Jesus saying still to fight on. He promised never to leave me, never to leave me alone. No never alone. No never alone. He promised never to leave me, never to leave me alone.[36]

Thus, King followed Thomas Jefferson's belief that "the rights of conscience we have never submitted, we could not submit" for "[w]e are answerable to them to our God."[37] But King (also like Jefferson) was aware that an individual's claim to conscience would extend to actions as well as beliefs, and he knew that such claims could not be effortlessly confined to claims advanced by a Rosa Parks (or a Martin Luther King). Thus, a little over seven years later, from a Birmingham jail, King both recognized the importance of conscience and civil disobedience as he tried to specify the conditions under which illegal action could be regarded as morally legitimate by the larger society. He wrote that an unjust law, a law that could rightly be challenged by people of conscience, was one that distorted and damaged the human personality, or one that had been passed by a majority group with the intention of binding a minority group but that neither permitted that group a voice in enacting the statute and/or that only enforced the statute against the minority group and not against itself.[38]

Later, we will examine if King's efforts to distinguish laudable from impermissible civil disobedience were successful. For the time being, let us see why it was necessary.

EXAMPLE 2

Southern Governors' Civil Disobedience

Facts: The civil rights movement encountered severe resistance, especially from Southern governors exercising state power. Some of the most notable examples: protesting *Brown,* Arkansas Governor Orville Faubus had closed the public schools in Little Rock. This caused President Eisenhower in September 1957 to federalize Arkansas National Guard units and enforce *Brown* v. *Board's* desegregation order. Five years later, Governor Ross Barnett of Mississippi led efforts that four times successfully prevented James Meredith from integrating the University of Mississippi. The fifth time Meredith proved successful, but only with the armed support of federalized Mississippi Army and National Guard units and federal marshals and after an extensive riot that led to two deaths as well as the injury of at least 160 marshals. Approximately six months later, Governor George Wallace stood in the door of the University of Alabama's Administration Building and defied a federal court order by preventing two black students (who were accompanied by the Attorney General of the United States) from enrolling. Later in the day, after President Kennedy federalized Alabama's National Guard units, Governor Wallace stood aside when the commanding general returned with the students at day's end. These Southern governors accompanied their acts of symbolic defiance with words, inevitably arguing that court-ordered integration violated state law, the national Constitution, moral law, and their right of personal conscience. Governor Barnett went so far as to suggest that such integration was so wrong that he was prepared to go to jail for the sake of his beliefs.[39]

Discussion

The symbolic resistance of Southern governors during the decade after the Supreme Court's *Brown* decision was certainly racist and therefore appears repugnant. Yet, despite this evaluation, an important question remains: Insofar as the position of Governors Faubus, Barnett, and Wallace rests on an appeal to conscience, or upon their private belief regarding what the good society should be like, to what extent can their actions be distinguished *in principle* from those more laudable acts of civil disobedience undertaken by Rosa Parks and Martin Luther King, Jr.? Frequently, scholars caution against attempting to evaluate acts of civil disobedience in terms of good or bad, or on the basis or our agreement with the position being advocated.[40] The sense of this position is as follows: civil disobedience on behalf of a political position that seems to us to be morally right inclines us to sympathize with the protestors. Yet such a position still can be dangerous from the perspective of society, for it leads to the notion that society can and ought to accept violations of its own rules and laws, despite the fact that "[o]rderly social living would be impossible if people only obeyed the laws they happened to like."[41] Nor can we distinguish the civil disobedience practiced by Martin Luther King from that practiced by Southern governors on the basis that King and the pro-civil rights protestors in good faith believed the laws they disobeyed violated the Constitution, whereas Southern governors defied clear federal court directives.[42] Although the federal courts and the Supreme Court render legally binding interpretations of the Constitution, and violating the law is required in order to test its constitutional validity, the moral dignity of civil disobedience still does not turn upon the illegality of the law contested but rather upon its alleged injustice or immorality.[43]

What about the standards of evaluation provided by Martin Luther King as a means for distinguishing, in a principled fashion, permissible from impermissible acts of civil disobedience? Recall: King presented two criteria for making such a judgment. First, he argued that if a law distorts the human personality, then it justifies civil disobedience. Will this criterion withstand critical scrutiny? Certainly, segregation laws demeaned the dignity of black citizens; in that sense, one might fairly conclude that their personality was distorted. Yet it should not come as a great surprise that King's standard is not easy to interpret and is somewhat loose. For that reason, it is very likely over-inclusive and therefore too permissive; it simply sanctions far too many illegal actions. Furthermore, not only are enormous numbers of laws open to the potential charge that they demean one's personality; King's standard also leaves it open to each individual to determine whether a particular law distorts his or her personality.

King's second criterion—that an unjust law is one that is passed with the participation of only a majority, with the intention of enforcing it only against the excluded minority group—fares better. This procedural criterion would seem to present a good example of an unfair process likely to result in an unjust law (although one can conceive of exceptions, especially regarding groups that are defined by their acts and not by any inherent or unchangeable characteristics[44]). Significantly, King's second criterion does adequately provide a standard of justice that distinguishes his position from the Southern governors who opposed him. King's standard points to the conclusion that Faubus, Barnett, and Wallace were bound by the Supreme Court's interpretation of the law of the land because it was equally applied to all citizens by a process to which they (as governors and citizens) had acquiesced. In this sense, they were differently situated from blacks in the South, who had been excluded from a political process that had propagated the segregation laws which singularly had disadvantaged them. Thus, King's second criterion for distinguishing justified from unjustified civil disobedience has true theoretical utility.

Nonetheless, this formulation by King will not suffice as a general theory of determining unjust laws. King's political inclusion standard assumes that the basis of human justice is equality; those who would reject such a standard would also object to his formulation.[45] A less extreme reservation holds that King's standard works well for certain racially defined groups adversely affected by racially discriminatory laws but does not cover a whole host of government actions that may be morally offensive and wrong for everyone yet are nonetheless duly enacted and equally applied. Thus, King's standard works well for race-related issues, but what does it have to say to those who would practice civil disobedience in order to overturn existing abortion laws, for example? Furthermore, it is possible to conceive of an unjust law passed by democratic means that works an equal hardship against all manner of citizen (for instance, a blatantly popular war of aggression supported by a legally instituted draft). Therefore, King's second principle for defining injustice cannot provide a comprehensive definition of an unjust law; precisely for that reason it is underinclusive.

Our next example speaks somewhat to this matter. So far, we have emphasized political acts of civil disobedience centrally related to the key American political question of promoting equal rights for all citizens under law. The public importance of this issue is obvious. But what happens when questions of conscience (from the perspective of the political order) are far more mundane and when the act of civil disobedience grows out of an individual assessment that the government is misacting (according to a judgment simply irrelevant to Martin Luther King's criteria)? Usually, such an act of disobedience would remain personal. But such an act may sometimes have a public dimension and can therefore become particularly noteworthy. In this regard, the federal circuit court's opinion in the case of FBI Agent John C. Ryan proves instructive.

EXAMPLE 3

Ryan v. United States Department of Justice, 950 F.2d 458 (7 Cir. 1991)

Facts: John C. Ryan was an FBI agent in charge of domestic security and terrorism investigation at the FBI office in Peoria, Illinois. At the time of his firing he had been an agent with twenty-one years of exemplary service (and was nine months short of his fiftieth birthday, when he would have been eligible to retire with an immediate pension). Ryan's firing came about because he declined to investigate vandalism at military recruiting stations because it was linked to nonviolent peace organizations. As a Roman Catholic, Ryan believed that the 1983 U.S. Bishops Pastoral Letter on War and Peace prohibited him from investigating nonviolent anti-military activity. Ryan was fired because his act of disobedience defied a direct order. The FBI maintained that permitting agents to pick and choose among direct orders would hinder the bureau's efficient operation.

Result: The FBI's decision to fire Ryan did not violate his Free Exercise rights under the First Amendment, nor was he religiously discriminated against under the 1964 Civil Rights Act.

Argument of the Case: Esterbrook, Judge. Although "sympathy for a dedicated agent trapped between his career and his faith comes easily," nonetheless the Constitution was not violated. The Free Exercise Clause permits the state to be neutral regarding religiously motivated acts.[46] The FBI treated Ryan no more severely than it treated other agents who sought to choose among their assignments. Title VII of the 1964 Civil Rights Act, by forbidding religious discrimination (that is, by prohibiting an employer's religion as the basis of employment decisions), places greater restrictions on the FBI than does the Constitution. Employers may defend employment decisions by demonstrating that they are unable reasonably to accommodate an employee's religious practices without undue hardship to their business. The FBI defense prevails because Ryan had refused to trade assignments with a fellow FBI agent, because Ryan had proposed no other means of accommodation except discontinuing the investigation, and because obedience is particularly important characteristic in a law enforcement agency. Thus, "[c]ompelled, as it is by Title VII, to have one rule for all of the diverse religious beliefs and practices in the United States, the FBI may choose to be stingy with exceptions lest the demand for them overwhelm it."

Discussion

Agent Ryan's act of civil disobedience was somewhat unorthodox. True, he acted for moral reasons; in that sense his action was quite ordinary. But he disobeyed a directive issued by a superior at the FBI, not technically a law of the United States. The directive was issued in pursuance to the law, which directs the FBI to investigate crimes against federal property. Furthermore, while Agent Ryan's act was an act of private civil disobedience (for he did not desire to persuade anyone of the rightness of his cause, as is often the case with such acts), his action did affect the body politic. Precisely because he was an agent of the FBI, charged with protecting federal property, his personal act of disobedience was not without public consequences.

The federal courts have encouraged accommodation in the workplace without holding that it is required by the Constitution. It is significant in this case that Agent Ryan refused to pursue any kind of accommodation; for example, he rejected trading work assignments with a fellow agent. When such informal accommodations have proven unsuccessful, the courts have emphasized the necessity of obedience to law and the notion that actions based upon conscience do not exempt individuals from punishment. We may well respect the sincerity that informs a civil disobedience practitioner's vision of justice, as we may value the courage of those who feel compelled to practice civil disobedience. But—at least so far as the courts are concerned—not their sincerity, nor their vision, nor even their courage exempts their *actions* from punishment.

SUMMARY

Acts of civil disobedience pose a number of problems for the legal theorist. As we have seen, the act of civil disobedience is not easily defined. Furthermore, while those who practice civil disobedience violate the law because they believe it unjust or immoral, often they differ among themselves regarding their motives and their attitude toward the political state (that is, they can be practitioners of private, political, or revolutionary civil disobedience). Thus, some may favor individual action or inaction; others champion large-scale political change; still others would prefer to overthrow the political order.

With narrow exceptions, few people doubt the propriety or necessity of nation states enforcing their own laws. Law-breaking may appear to be morally justified, or perhaps even morally compelled, to the individual who undertakes acts of civil disobedience. Nonetheless, even the notion that when a law appears to be unjust there exists a responsibility or perhaps a right to break it is by no means obvious. (Some thinkers have even argued that law-breaking is difficult or impossible to justify.[47]) Still, given the fact that such acts will occur, the question persists regarding the state's proper response. Unfortunately, there is no simple resolution to this tension. Both the individual and the state are compelled to act in predictable ways. Just as the practitioner of civil disobedience may well believe that he or she is morally compelled to act, so the political state cannot afford be indifferent to law-breaking whether its motive be private, political, or revolutionary.[48] Ultimately, a liberal democracy that respects individual rights and human dignity may display an attitude of uneasy compromise, recognizing that practitioners of civil disobedience are generally not governed by selfish or cowardly motives (especially in the case of political civil disobedience), but at the same time emphasizing that it can never let citizens *individually* determine which laws they are to obey. For an ultimate resolution of the issue, one cannot do much better than cite the political philosopher whose ideas so profoundly influenced the American regime, John Locke. Writing in 1667, Locke posed the problem of civil disobedience problem directly—and suggested an unequivocal answer. We would conclude this chapter by noting that his view has lately come to be shared by federal courts throughout the United States:

> But some may ask, What if the magistrate should enjoin anything by his authority that appears unlawful to the conscience of a private person?... I say that such a private person is to abstain from the action that he judges unlawful, and he is to undergo the punishment which it is not unlawful for him to bear. For the private judgment of any person, concerning a law enacted in political matters, for the public good, does not take away the obligation of that law, nor deserve a dispensation.[49]

NOTES

1. Cited in David J. Garrow, *Bearing the Cross. Martin Luther King, Jr., and the Southern Christian Leadership Conference: A Personal Portrait* (New York: William Morrow, 1986), p. 5.

2. Many of the difficult aspects of defining civil disobedience are defined by Burton M. Leiser in *Liberty, Justice, and Morals* (New York: Macmillan, 1979), pp. 342– 75. Although we do not agree with all aspects of Leiser's discussion, we acknowledge our indebtedness to his work and acknowledge as well that aspects of this chapter build upon certain important distinctions made in Leiser's book.

3. Thus, one can directly refuse to obey a law that one believes to be morally objectionable, one can directly disobey a law perceived to be fundamentally related to an morally objectionable law (for example, a person may refuse to pay taxes should he or she believe that they are used in a morally offensive way), or one may disobey any law of a fundamentally unjust regime, believing that the regime possesses no moral authority to pass *any* law.

4. As noted above (note 3), it is commonly acknowledged that there exists no general obligation to obey the law when the government is perceived to be illegitimate or grossly immoral.

5. Again, in the case of an illegitimate or fundamentally unjust regime, all laws may seem immoral, so citizens may choose to disobey any law. Also, anarchists may choose to disobey any law because they believe all laws of all regimes to be illegitimate.

6. This is in opposition to classical thinkers (and some American Founders such as Alexander Hamilton), who pictured government as a necessary means to guarantee liberty.

7. Exodus 1:15.

8. Whether this is her true or dominant motivation (as compared to, for example, pride) is a difficult question we simply raise but do not undertake to answer. Creon's motives are also complicated. He sees himself as the protector of the city's Temples and hence religion; his motives also could be said to be partly religious.

9. See Leo Strauss, *Natural Right and History* (Chicago: Univ. of Chicago Press, 1965), pp. 91–164.

10. For a discussion of tyrannicide see Franz Neumann, *The Democratic and the Authoritarian State* (Glencoe, IL: The Free Press, 1957), pp. 149–52.

11. See Leiser, pp. 346–47.

12. Note especially Maimonides (1135–1204) in the Jewish tradition and Alfarabi (?–950), the great Islamic thinker.

13. Thomas Aquinas, *Summa Theologica*, 1a 2ae, quae. 91, art. 2 and 1a 2ae, quae. 95 and 104, 6.

14. This is opposed to Aquinas's belief that human reason, although critically important, represents an incomplete understanding and manifestation of God's wisdom. Regarding Kant, see Copleston's general discussion and note his observation (with accompanying proofs) that, for Kant, "[the categorical imperative is for us the voice of God, and God is manifested in the consciousness of moral obligation, through the natural law. See Frederick Copleston, *A History of Philosophy* (Garden City,: Image Books, 1974), vol. 6, part II, p. 113. Regarding Cohen, see *Religion of Reason: Out of the Sources of Judaism* (New York: Frederick Unger, 1972).

15. Adam Smith, *The Theory of Moral Sentiments*, ed. by D. D. Raphael and A. L. Macfie (Oxford: Clarendon Press, 1976), part 1, sec. I, ch. 1, part 1 (as it corresponds to the Glasgow Oxford edition). Emphasis ours. Although Smith's ethical theory first and foremost attaches conscience to emotion and empathy, as this quotation emphasizes, it is hardly divorced from considerations of reason. Thus, human beings extend sympathy to those who not merely suffer, but suffer unfairly.

16. This section relies heavily upon, and the authors acknowledge their great in-

debtedness to, Richard G. Stevens, "Conscience and Politics," *Teaching Political Science* vol. 11, no. 4 (Summer 1984), pp. 171–81.

17. According to Aristotle, practical wisdom consists in knowledge about affairs that change,—that is, human affairs. Ethics and politics are subjects that admit practical knowledge. See Aristotle, Nicomachean Ethics, tr, H. Rackham (Cambridge, MA; Harvard Univ. Press, 1968), pp. 5–9.

18. Stevens, p. 173.

19. Explaining how this has happened would require its own treatise.The rise of Protestantism (with its emphasis upon individual conscience) and the individualistic anti-religious teachings of modern political philosophy are key. Professor Rahe emphasizes the importance of John Locke's discussion of the seemingly harmless but ultimately subversive reduction of conscience to mere opinion vastly inferior to dictates of reason in his *Essay Concerning Human Understanding*. See Paul Rahe, *Republics Ancient and Modern* (Chapel Hill: Univ. of North Carolina Press, 1992), pp. 307–10. In our time, the ascension of historicism, relativism, postmodernism, and psychological explanations of human behavior all deserve mention and analysis.

20. Which is to say, whereas Socrates and More relied upon interpretations of the law that would have preserved their right to believe or act in ways they believed to be fundamentally important, modern-day practitioners of civil disobedience directly aim at overturning the law. Socrates and More would be practitioners of civil disobedience according to our definition (p. 185) if they had refused to obey the law as interpreted and applied by the *government*. As in the case of all definitions, this one needs to be applied on a case-by-case basis.

21. In that respect, note Locke's understanding that "*Conscience* … is nothing else, but our own disputable Opinion or Judgment of the Moral Rectitude or Pravity of our own Actions." John Locke, *An Essay Concerning Human Understanding*, ed. Alexander Fraser (New York: Dover, 1959), I, Chapter 2, para. 7–8.

22. This follows Leiser, who distinguishes direct acts of civil disobedience (where one breaks the law that one protests against) from the indirect practice (where a person violates a law that may, standing alone, may be completely innocuous, as a means of protesting another law that he or she believes to be morally objectionable). See Leiser, pp. 355–56.

23. "The law," admittedly, refers to the law that governs the campus, not the civil law of the state or of the United States. Nonetheless, its deliberate violation on moral grounds would still qualify a person as a practitioner of civil disobedience.

24. The most common example of this kind of behavior would be opposition to a tyranny. Some thinkers (going back to such classical figures as Plato and Aristotle) would raise the question of whether a person can truly be a citizen of such a regime (in the sense that, under tyrannies, meaningful political participation is impossible). This question, while intriguing, is beyond the scope of this chapter.

25. Leiser, pp. 349–50, 361–62, 368–75.

26. There is, of course, an element of something like civil disobedience in the ordinary challenging of unconstitutional laws. That is, in order to challenge the constitutionality of a local, state, or federal law, it must first be violated (otherwise, the courts would be hesitant to hear the case). This kind of ordinary law-breaking would not constitute civil disobedience unless the testing of the law was incidental to an underlying belief that the law is immoral (as opposed to simply unconstitutional).

27. On this point, see Herbert J. Storing, "The Case Against Civil Disobedience," in *On Civil Disobedience: American Essays Old and New*, ed. Robert A. Goldwin (Chicago: Rand McNally, 1970), pp. 104–05.

28. Martin Luther King, Jr., "Letter from the Birmingham Jail," in Goldwin's *On Civil Disobedience*, pp. 67–68.

29. As argued earlier, Gandhi was a practitioner of revolutionary, not political, civil disobedience. Still, a willingness to accept the penalty is rarely compatible with revolutionary civil disobedience.

(Gandhi was an exception, both because of this and also because he was a nonviolent practitioner of revolutionary civil disobedience.) Both political and revolutionary acts of civil disobedience can be effective only in a relatively decent political regime, lest it become merely the exercise of suicide by the practitioner.

30. Thus, Martin Luther King's efforts in Birmingham were aided immeasurably by the cruel, racist tactics of Public Commissioner Bull Connor, who would loose police dogs and club-wielding law enforcement officers upon peaceful demonstrators (including children). Television publicized actions that would horrify a nation. Yet, the nonviolent protestors counted upon Connor's stupid and cruel actions in their strategy. In King's words, "To cure injustices, you must expose them before the light of human conscience and the bar of public opinion, regardless of whatever tensions that exposure generates. Injustices to the Negro must be brought out into the open where they cannot be evaded." Garrow, pp. 228. See also pp. 227–30 generally. Cf. King, p. 68.

31. This point is made by John Rawls, "The Justification of Civil Disobedience," in *Civil Disobedience: Theory and Practice,* ed. Hugo Adam Bedau (Pegasus, 1969), pp. 249–50. Cf. the Declaration of Independence's proclamation regarding revolution and revolutionary acts that "Governments long established should not be changed for light and transient causes...."

32. Rawls, in Bedau's *Civil Disobedience.* The hesitancy regarding the second prong of the requirement is ours.

33. The account of Rosa Parks's act of civil disobedience is drawn from Garrow, pp. 11–14.

34. 347 U.S. 483 (1954).

35. Garrow, p. 17.

36. Garrow, p. 58.

37. Thomas Jefferson, *Notes on the State of Virginia* (New York: Harper, 1964), p. 152.

38. King, pp. 66–67.

39. Frank T. Read and Lucy S. McGough, *Let Them Be Judged: The Judicial Integration*

of the Deep South (Metuchen, NJ: Scarecrow Press, 1978), p. 225.

40. Harrison Tweed, Bernard G. Segal, and Herbert L. Packer, "Civil Rights and Disobedience to Law," in Bedau, p. 91.

41. Fweed, Segal, and Packer, p. 91.

42. Fweed, Segal, and Packer, p. 92.

43. Another problem for this argument becomes clear once it is realized that the courts frequently render contradictory constitutional interpretations. Thus, before *Brown* v. *Board of Education* the case law was mixed, yet one could make a good argument that King and his supporters in Montgomery were violating segregation practices and statutes that had been sanctioned by earlier Supreme Court opinions.

44. For example, rules regarding prisoners. Note that King's standard assumes (but does not specify) a rough equality among adult citizens who are to be equal under law (thus, for example, ruling out defining minority groups to be made up of children).

45. Although almost all of us might well agree with King's assumption of fundamental human equality, his view does not accord with all understandings. Thus, classical political thought embodied by Plato and Aristotle might well stress human inequality (in terms of unequal ability and excellences, unequal attainment of moral virtue, an unequal right to be honored by the state, and so on), although it is unlikely that these differences would ever involve racial distinctions.

46. Here the Court cited *Employment Division, Department of Human Resources* v. *Smith,* 108 L. Ed. 976 (1990). See Chapter 9.

47. Note Lincoln's 1838 address before the Young Men's Lyceum of Springfield, Ill., on "The Perpetuation of Our Political Institutions," particularly this injunction: "Let every American, every lover of liberty, every well wisher to his posterity, swear by the blood of the Revolution, never to violate in the least particular, the laws of the country; and never to tolerate their violation by others.... Let reverence for the laws ... be taught in schools, in

seminaries and in colleges...let it be preached from the pulpit, proclaimed in the legislative halls, and enforced in courts of justice. And in short, let it become *the political religion* of the nation,..." Also see Ernest Van den Haag, *Political Violence and Civil Disobedience* (New York: Harper, 1972), pp. 11–13.

48. Although, obviously, the severity with which it may respond may well vary.

49. But Locke does allow for disobedience to law when the state legislates about matters not within its authority, by which Locke appears to mean matters that deal directly with questions of conscience (the example he provides is a law that would require citizens to join a strange religion and mandate their attendance and participation in worship services). See John Locke, *A Letter Concerning Toleration* (Indianapolis: Bobbs-Merrill, 1955), p. 48.

11

Should Prayer and Bible Reading Be Allowed in the Public Schools?

THE PROBLEM POSED

God, it seems, has been removed from the public schools. Prayer, Bible reading, and the invocation of God's name in anything resembling a religious context have usually been disallowed by the federal courts. Religious references have even been prohibited from nonclassroom activities, such as graduation ceremonies.[1] The Pledge of Allegiance survives ("one nation, under God"), but its reference to God seems something of a curiosity.

Few contemporary legal issues have stirred so much controversy as has the issue of whether religiously related references to God, including prayer and Bible reading, should be permitted in the public schools. The plea "to put God back in the schools" has not only been voiced by various Christian fundamentalist leaders, but reinstating prayer was also championed by Presidents Reagan and Bush. During his first term, Reagan proposed to the Congress a constitutional amendment that would have reinstated voluntary, nongovernmentally composed prayer in the public schools. (The amendment subsequently failed.) Opponents of the proposed amendment pointed to the disquiet that would be experienced by children of minority faiths and of no faith should such a practice be reinstated. They also noted that students were still free to pray on their own because the Supreme Court had banned only state-sponsored prayers in the schools.

The extensive national debate engendered by this issue has endured for over four decades. It reflects the great depth of emotion associated with the issue. One reason for this emotional response is historical. Prayer and Bible reading had once been a common practice in many schools throughout American history. Religious instruction was one of the primary purposes for which schools had been founded in the colonies, and even after the emergence of the public school system throughout the United States, religion in one form or another persisted in the schools well into the twentieth century.[2] This being true, a natural question arises—how and why could the Supreme Court, or any governmental institution for that matter, believe that the Constitution prohibited a practice that had been so widespread for so long a time?

In order to conclude that prayer and Bible reading constituted an impermissible governmental activity, the Supreme Court relied upon two key interpretive assumptions. The first assumption was that key provisions of the Bill of Rights, including the First Amendment's Establishment Clause, imposed a restriction upon state and local governments as well as upon the national government.[3] This step was essential, for throughout American history, the public schools have been created and administered by local government. The second assumption, maintained by the Court since the *Everson*[4] case in 1947, was that the Establishment Clause prohibited all government from not merely favoring any single understanding of religion, but from aiding or promoting religion over nonreligion.[5] These two assumptions, taken together, clearly pointed the Supreme Court to a course that ultimately led to the banning of state-sponsored prayer and Bible reading in the public schools.

Although the issue of religion in the schools has remained controversial, the intensity of the dispute has diminished in recent years. Critics who hoped for a constitutional amendment or that the Supreme Court might possibly reverse course have been disappointed. Yet their arguments remained constant. In general, these critics found nondenominational prayers and religious reference to God in the classroom to be only a slight burden to nonbelievers. Meanwhile, they argued that the advantages of such exercises were twofold. First, it was contended that it was only appropriate and right to acknowledge God's presence and power in the schools. In other words, religion should be acknowledged because it is true. Second, critics pointed to the commonly made assertion that religious acknowledgements were helpful in inculcating a common morality and promoting a sense of decency in students. Thus, religious exercises were championed because they were also seen to be useful.[6]

Critics of the Supreme Court argued that there had been a high cost associated with Supreme Court Establishment Clause decisions regarding the public schools. Yet the Supreme Court (and the lower federal courts as well) not only asserted that it was following the letter and spirit of the Constitution, but that there were also positive benefits that stemmed from its decisions. So that we might better understand the Court's reasoning, especially in light of the persistent criticisms made of the judiciary, we turn to a brief examination of five important cases.

EXAMPLE 1

Engel v. Vitale, 370 U.S. 421 (1962)

Facts: The New York State Regents, a governmental agency in charge of that state's schools, composed and recommended the adoption of a non-denominational prayer in the public schools. This so-called Regents' Prayer was designed to promote moral and spiritual training in the schools. It read: "Almighty God, we acknowledge our dependence upon Thee, and we beg Thy blessings upon us, our parents, our teachers and our country." Ten parents of public school students challenged the practice of reciting the prayer, asserting that the prayer "was contrary to the beliefs, religions, or religious practices of both themselves and their children."

Result: New York's use of its public school system to encourage prayer is a religious activity that violates the First Amendment's prohibition against religious establishment as applied by the Fourteenth Amendment.

Argument of the Case: Black, Justice. Invoking God's blessing as pre-scribed in the Regents' Prayer is a religious activity constituting "a solemn avowal of divine faith and supplication for the blessings of the Almighty." Yet the Establishment Clause creates a wall of separation between church and state that precludes government from *composing* such official prayers for recitation. Historically, the practice of establishing governmentally composed prayers for religious services was one of the reasons that colonists left England. Although belied by some state practices at the time of the Constitution's adoption, there was widespread awareness of the dangers of a union of church and state. That danger inheres in the Re-gents' prayer, and its constitutionality is saved neither by its nondenom-inational nature nor by the fact that reciting it was a voluntary act for students. An official religion has been established. Furthermore, although Establishment Clause violations (unlike those involving the Free Exercise Clause) do not require demonstrating that individual citizens have been coerced, when "the power, prestige and financial support of government is placed behind a particular religious belief, the indirect coercive pressure upon religious minorities to conform to the prevailing officially approved religion is plain."

   Douglas concurs. Although a "religion is not established in the usual sense merely by letting those who choose to do so say a prayer that the public school teacher leads," the fact that government employees (teach-ers) are paid to lead such prayers in a public institution violates the Estab-lishment Clause. *Any* government financing of religion, no matter how small, violates the Constitution.

   Stewart dissents. No establishment of religion is created by a short non-denominational prayer. The First Amendment does not mention a wall of separation between church and state, and most of the Court's historical examples are from England, the colonies, and the early states where established churches existed. Rather, the Regents' prayer is like the invocation given before the Supreme Court meets ("God save the United States and this Honorable Court") or the words "In God We Trust" on American coins. New York has not violated the Constitution; it has merely followed "the deeply entrenched and highly cherished spiritual traditions of our Nation...."

Discussion

When the Supreme Court announced this decision on June 25, 1962, it triggered a spirited national debate on the proper relationship between government and religion. To many critics, it seemed like the prohibited prayer was so inoffensive, brief, and general that the Supreme Court had done little more than attack religion. Furthermore, critics of the Supreme Court's opinion noted, those children who did not want to recite the prayer were not required to participate. What possible harm, these critics asked, could such an inoffensive prayer cause?

Justice Black admitted that the government's creation and endorsement of the prayer were "relatively insignificant" when compared to governmental encroachments upon religion two hundred years before. But then he cited Madison to the effect that it "is proper to take alarm at the first experiment on our liberties." Any governmental power exercised in the religious realm is dangerous and can easily be abused. According to Black, the danger of the government exercising power in the religious realm inspired the writing of the Establishment Clause. He observed that its first purpose was rooted in the belief that a "union of government and religion tends to destroy government and to degrade religion." Thus, when government historically allied itself with a particular religious sect, hatred and contempt of religious minorities resulted. At the same time, many people lost respect for a religion that relied upon government for its vitality. Another purpose of the Establishment Clause identified by Black was to prevent persecution; the union of religious and governmental power had too often led to this intolerant practice. Thus, Black prohibited the Regents' Prayer because he understood it to be the first small (and impermissible) step along a road that could lead to a corrupted government, a discredited religion, a growing intolerance toward minority religions, and eventual persecution. The Constitution prohibits small steps as well as large strides along that path. Douglas went even further in prohibiting any accommodation between religion and government by asserting that even a single religiously related sentence uttered by a government employee or spoken in a government building (and therefore financed by government) violated the Establishment Clause.[7] Against such staunchly separationist approaches, it became easier to make the argument that the Supreme Court was anti-religious.

Black denied this accusation. He contended that it was neither "sacrilegious nor anti-religious to say that each separate government in the country should stay out of the business of writing or sanctioning official prayers and leave that purely religious function to the people themselves and to those the people choose to look to for religious guidance." Black's critics saw the exiling of religion to be anti-religious, but Black saw the absence of religion to be merely appropriate and correct, believing that the proper role of religion should be determined by the private practice of individuals.

Black's position has received support from mainline Protestant organizations (for example, the Lutheran Council of America, the National Council of Churches, the Protestant Episcopal Church of America, the United Methodist Church, and the United Presbyterian Church) as well as Jewish organizations. Various reasons for support were given, including the belief that it was simply not the government's business to inculcate prayer (suggesting that it should be left to home, family, and church). Occasionally, it was argued that any prayer that the state could possibly promulgate would be so generic and watered-down as to be religiously ineffectual or even offensive. Thus, a state-written, generalized prayer offended not only the Constitution (according to the Supreme Court), but was also inappropriately religious for some religious groups and too weak for others.

Given the Supreme Court's ruling in *Engel,* it seemed clear to observers of the Supreme Court that Bible reading in the schools would be nearly impossible to sustain. They were right.

EXAMPLE 2

Abington School District v. *Schempp,* 374 U.S. 203 (1963)[8]

Facts: Pennsylvania law required that "[a]t least ten verses from the Holy Bible shall be read, without comment, at the opening of each public school on each school day. Any child shall be excused from such Bible reading, upon the written request of his parent or guardian." Consistent with this statute, students at Abington Senior High School voluntarily gathered in the school's radio and television workshop daily, where they read ten verses from the Bible, followed by an in-unison reading of the Lord's Prayer, and then saluted the flag prior to school announcements. This program was broadcast into all the school's classrooms through the intercom system. At different times, different versions of the Bible were read, although the school provided only the King James Version. Mr. and Mrs. Schempp had two children who attended Abington High School. As Unitarians, the Schempps thought that a literal reading of the Bible contradicted several of their most important religious beliefs. Mr. Schempp had considered requesting that his children be exempted from the religious exercises, but feared that they would be labeled as oddballs, atheists, or even communists by other students and even teachers.

Result: In the public schools, both Bible reading and reciting the Lord's Prayer constitute an impermissible establishment of religion that violates the First and Fourteenth Amendment.

Argument of the Case: Clark, Justice. Historically, the United States has been a nation that has prized both religious practice and religious freedom. Therefore, the proper stance of government toward religion(s) is neutrality; it protects all, prefers none, and discourages none. This neutrality is safeguarded by the following two-prong test: "What is the purpose and primary effect of the enactment? If either is the advancement or inhibition of religion the enactment exceeds the scope of legislative power as circumscribed by the Constitution. That is to say that to withstand the strictures of the Establishment Clause there must be a secular legislative purpose and a primary effect that neither advances nor inhibits religion."[9] Prayer and Bible reading are instruments of religion. Although the state defends these practices on the grounds that they promote moral values, contradict the materialistic trends of the times, help perpetuate American institutions and teach literature, the religious nature of these activities belies these rationales. Nor does the Court's decision create a "religion of secularism";[10] neutrality toward religion not only prohibits favoring religion but also prevents government from opposing or showing hostility toward religion. Furthermore, it is appropriate to study *about* religion (rather than teach religion); comparative religion courses are consistent with the Constitution. Finally, the Establishment Clause neutrality principle does not prohibit the majority from practicing its religion; no free exercise claims are raised by keeping the majority from imposing religious practices in the schools.

Douglas concurs. Here, the state conducts and finances a religious exercise in violation of the Establishment Clause.

Brennan concurs. Although American institutions (including public schools) reflect the firm conviction that Americans are a religious people, these institutions cannot involve religion in a way "to prefer, discriminate against, or oppress, a particular sect or religion." The Constitution prohibits religious involvement with secular institutions that (a) serves the essentially religious activities of religious institutions; (b) employs the organs of government for essentially religious purposes; or (c) uses an essentially religious means to serve governmental ends where the secular means would suffice. Thus, while the contested religious practices may improve classroom discipline, increase harmony and tolerance among students, and enhance respect for teacher authority, (c) is violated, for prayer and Bible reading are essentially religious means to a government end; furthermore, secular alternatives, are available for "[i]t has not been shown that readings from the speeches and messages of great Americans... or from the documents of our heritage of liberty, daily recitation of the Pledge of Allegiance, or even the observance of a moment of reverent silence at the opening of class, may not adequately serve the solely secular purposes of the devotional activities without jeopardizing either the religious liberties of any members of the community or the proper degree of separation between the spheres of religion and government."[11]

Goldberg and Harlan concur. Although neutrality is the proper constitutional standard for resolving controversies such as this, and although the practices of this case involve the state so significantly in the realm of the sectarian that they violate both religion clauses, still the Court must be careful not to let neutrality slip into hostility toward religion.

Stewart dissents. The Establishment Clause and the Free Exercise Clause must be reconciled. For instance, expending tax monies for a chaplain may seem to violate the Establishment Clause, yet not to do so would deprive religious soldiers (who would be left without religious guidance) of the free exercise of their religion. Therefore, it is important to recognize a central value in the religion clauses of the First Amendment, which is the safeguarding of the individual's right to exercise his or her religion. Although the state is not allowed to coerce religious beliefs from its citizens, it is permitted to act evenhandedly and noncoercively. The religious free exercise both of the majority and of minority of citizens who hold different or no religious beliefs needs to be taken into account. Since the factual record is not clear regarding this last point (whether those students who did not wish to participate were coerced), the case should be remanded for retrial.

Discussion

Although the outcome of this case was fairly easy to predict and understand, several of its opinions were both long and abstract. Furthermore, although all the Justices except Stewart found the contested school practices unconstitutional, several also differed regarding their rationale. These differing rationales were important, for they provided a clue as to how far each Justice was willing to go in terms of allowing (or disallowing) church–state accommodation. In *Schempp,* the most accommodationist Justices were Goldberg and Harlan, followed (in order) by Clark (for the Court), Brennan, and Douglas. Another interesting difference (especially for students of the Supreme Court) was the fact that two justices, Clark and Brennan, outlined different Establishment Clause tests by which they hoped future cases would be resolved. Clark's proved to be, by far, the more influential of the two approaches.[12]

Schempp's practical importance in terms of prohibiting religious prayer and Bible reading from the schools was significant, although (from the perspective of the Supreme Court) relatively uncontroversial. This meant that much of the interesting debate among the Justices focused upon more theoretical matters. Thus, Justice Stewart indirectly faulted Justice Douglas for providing an inconsistent view of the religion clauses; so strict was Douglas's Establishment Clause prohibition against financing anything remotely religious that his jurisprudence could be understood as irreligious and could, in some instances, ultimately jeopardize the free exercise rights of citizens (recall Stewart's example of chaplains). Justices Clark and Brennan attempted to avoid a possible conflict between the Establishment and the Free Exercise Clause by contending that while Free Exercise Clause cases require that individual coercion take place, Establishment Clause cases did not depend upon coercion. Thus, because state-sponsored prayer and Bible reading clearly violated the Establishment Clause for both Justices, each found it unnecessary to explore the Free Exercise implications.

Yet it is an interesting question in such cases to ask if (or to what extent) religious practices like those invalidated in *Schempp* do constitute governmental compulsion or psychological coercion upon selected students.[13] During the original *Schempp* trial, expert testimony on this question was introduced by both sides. The state's expert witness testified that the Bible was nonsectarian (by which he meant nonsectarian within the Christian faith) in that it included both the Hebrew Scriptures and the New Testament, that it was of great moral historical and literary value, and that it "conveyed the message of Christians." The Schempps' expert witness looked at the contested practice from a Jewish perspective, noting that Jewish Scriptures did not include the New Testament and that portions of the New Testament were offensive to the Jewish tradition (both because the concept of Jesus Christ as the Son of God was "practically blasphemous" and because it depicted Jews as the object of ridicule and scorn). This witness even stated that reading from the New Testament without explanation could be psychologically harmful and socially divisive to Jewish children.

Obviously, if psychological coercion was at issue, it would have its most immediate impact on students of minority faiths (for example, Jewish children, Unitarian children) or children of no or little faith.[14] As we have seen, the school in *Schempp* attempted to counter this potential problem by granting students exemptions from the contested religious practices. Excusal provisions lessen the state's coercive influence over the individual student; thus, if the state's prayer and Bible reading practices (with excusal allowances) can fairly be characterized as coercive, they probably should be regarded as indirectly coercive.[15] An interesting, related question, not simply legal in scope, is whether the state's policy of exemption from religious activities proves adequate to protect the interests and the feelings of religious minorities.

Generally, Justices in this case and other cases tended to think that the exemptions were insufficient to free students from the impermissible social pressure that stemmed from their nonconformist religious opinions (again, we would remind the reader that the case did not turn upon this issue, which tended to be considered within a free exercise context). The Court's only dissenter, Justice Stewart, observed that the excusal procedure was necessary if religious exercises were conducted during the school day. Yet even if such excusal provisions were provided "and no equally desirable alternative were provided by the school authorities, the likelihood that children might be under at least some psychological compulsion to participate would be great"; still, "we would err if we *assumed* such coercion in the absence of any evidence."[16]

Justice Brennan was more emphatic in suggesting that excusal procedures were simply ineffectual ways of promoting state religious neutrality and proved inadequate to safeguard students from compulsion or coercion. Brennan advanced the following points: there are persons in every community—some devout—to whom any version of the Judeo-Christian Bible is offensive, many devout people regard prayer as profoundly personal and believe it ought to be privately rather than publicly mandated, and commenting upon biblical passages (not allowed in the practice contested in *Schempp*) may be necessary for children who do not understand biblical terms. Excusal procedures do not solve any of these problems for Brennan, because they require a profession of disbelief or nonconformity by the student (which, by itself, Brennan believed violated the Free Exercise Clause). Such a proclamation may subject students to peer group ridicule, ultimately inhibiting them from even stating their religious reservations.

Thus, even though the constitutional question of free exercise was not directly raised by *Schempp,* the case did indirectly raise the issue of whether religious exemption creates a sufficient guarantee of religious free exercise for children with minority religious beliefs. The Justices we have examined (and most others as well) have been skeptical of the legal and practical value of excusal provisions. Of course, perhaps the need to deal with individual student exemptions could be obviated if what Justice Brennan called a common core of theology "tolerable to all creeds but preferential to none" could be fashioned.[17] Such a theology would, by necessity, be reductive (and thus appeal to the most common denominator), and Brennan was skeptical about whether such an approach would be possible. Another obstacle was *Engel* v. *Vitale,* which prevented the state from writing prayers. Nonetheless, in spite of these concerns and reservations, state efforts throughout the years have not lacked resourcefulness, as we shall see.

EXAMPLE 3

DeSpain v. *DeKalb County School District 428,* 348 F.2d 836 (1967)

Facts: The DeSpains' daughter, who attended kindergarten, was asked to recite, along with classmates in a public school class, the following verses:

> We thank you for the flowers so sweet;
> We thank you for the food we eat;
> We thank you for the birds that sing;
> We thank you for everything.

The verses were similar in form to a well-known children's prayer:

> Thank You for the World so Sweet;
> Thank You for the Food We Eat;
> Thank You for the Birds that Sing;
> Thank You, God, for Everything.

The DeSpains pointed out that they did not believe in a divine being who hears or responds to prayers. The kindergarten teacher defended the practice of reciting the verse by noting that it was spoken only after milk and crackers were passed out to her kindergarten students and was intended to foster an "appreciation for the whole world that is in front of them."

Result: The United States Court of Appeals held that the poem was a prayer and further held that its compulsory recitation violated the First Amendment's Establishment Clause as applied to the states by the Fourteenth Amendment.

Argument of the Case: Swygert, Judge. The appropriate governmental attitude toward religion is neutrality. This means that it has no power over religion and there must be a secular legislative purpose and primary effect that neither advance nor inhibit religion. Applying the test to this case, the secular purpose of the test merely supplemented its more basic religious purpose, which is to thank God. This is a compulsory prayer.

Schnackenberg dissents. The verses recited are intended to express a sense of gratitude. The word *God* has been deleted from the more traditional sound-alike prayer; therefore, the court prohibits not what the children are saying but what the children are thinking. Even if there is a technical violation of the Constitution, within the context of the school day and given its larger secular purpose, it is *de minimis* and does not constitute a reason to invalidate the contested practice.

Discussion

Here was a poem whose recitation could be justified on either secular or sectarian grounds, and which was intended to be theologically inoffensive. Yet the court ruled that the kindergarten teacher had violated the Establishment Clause. A number of interpretive disagreements or ambiguities surround the resolution of this case. Specifically, there were significant differences in interpretation regarding what had actually gone on in the classroom, whether the verses constituted a prayer, and regarding the reason that the verses had been promoted.

One unanswered question about which different answers were advanced had to do with what actually had gone on in the classroom. Mrs. DeSpain visited her daughter's kindergarten class twice. She and her daughter testified that both before and during the recitation of the prescribed verse, the children folded their hands in their laps and closed their eyes. They also testified that many children said "Amen" after the poem was recited. On the other hand, several mothers of other children and the teacher testified that they did not see the children display a reverential attitude, nor did they hear the children say "Amen" after the recitation of the verse. The appeals court found the actions and attitude of the children during recitation to be immaterial to the question of whether the required recitation of the verse was a prohibited public school activity.

This dispute pointed to a second question: Did the verse constitute a prayer? Of course, according to *Engel v. Vitale,* prayers were impermissible public school enterprises. Yet the contested verse in this case was not easily classified. It looked a lot like a prayer and invoked (at least in the minds of adults) very similar language associated with a prayer that had concluded by thanking God for "everything." Yet this verse did not explicitly thank God; it thanked "you." Was "you" God? One expert witness, a theologian, contended at trial that the "you" was addressed to someone who is thought to provide everything and that this was the common definition of God. Concluding that the verse was a prayer in form and intention, this expert witness observed that it "does not stop being a prayer when the word 'God' is removed, since the children who use it as a prayer, other than where it might have been used in the schools, use it and understand it as a prayer." Therefore, "in a common context, it is a prayer which has simply been modified, but has not lost its prayer connotation or meaning."[18]

Not surprisingly, this perspective was disputed. Most interesting was the testimony of Mrs. Watne, the teacher. Although she admitted that, in her mind, the word *you* meant God, she defended the language on secular grounds. The verses were intended to thank the "helpers who came to our house ... [to] help us do things ... like TV repairmen, the plumber, [and] the milkman...."[19]

Given this interpretation, Mrs. Watne explained that the verses were re-cited because they were secular. Hers was a "good citizenship and thankful-ness" program. She sought to instill gratitude and appreciation in her kindergarten students (prior to their eating their snack). She wished to teach them manners. By contrast, the DeSpains saw the exercise as a prayer, plain and simple. Not only were they persuaded that the "you" referred to a supreme being, but they were suspicious of Mrs. Watne's motives. The year before they brought suit, their son (one year older than their daughter) had read the same verse, with only the last line changed (it was then "We thank you, God, for everything"). Mrs. Watne had changed the last line after the DeSpains had complained to her, the superintendent of schools, the principal, and the Board of Education.

DeSpain furnishes an excellent example of how what may seem obvious (namely, what constitutes a prayer?) can occasionally be difficult to define. Both the contested verse in this case and its underlying meaning are open to different interpretations. The poem may be a prayer; it may be a generalized secular poem; its purpose may be religious or secular, or *both*. All that can be said with assurance is that the appeals court's decision in this case asserted that the Establishment Clause furnished little place for exercises that could reason-ably (but not uniformly) be interpreted as religious. Although this has been the predominant approach of the federal judiciary, it has not been its sole ap-proach, especially regarding certain well-established historical practices. Thus, it is challenging to reconcile *DeSpain* with the following case, decided some thirteen years later.

EXAMPLE 4

Florey v. Sioux Falls School District 49–5, 619, F.2d 1311 (1980)

Facts: Responding to complaints that public school Christmas assemblies were religious exercises, the school board created a citizens' committee to formulate guidelines for regulating such future activities. Among other things, these guidelines stipulated that no religious belief or nonbelief should be promoted by the school district or its employees; that toleration of others' religious views should be encouraged; that students and staff members should be excused from practices contrary to their religious beliefs unless "there are clear issues of overriding concern that would prevent it"; that a legitimate educational goal consists of advancing students' knowledge and appreciation "of the role that our religious heritage has played in the social, cultural and historical development of civilization"; that several holidays that have a religious and secular basis (for example, Christmas) may be observed; that "the historical and contemporary values and origin of religious holidays may be explained in an unbiased and objective manner without sectarian indoctrination"; that music, art, drama and so on having a religious theme or basis may be permitted "if presented in a prudent and objective manner and as a traditional part of the cultural and religious heritage of the particular holiday"; and that the use of symbols of religious holidays (for example, a cross, a creche, a Star of David) are permitted as teaching aids as long as they are displayed as examples of part of the cultural and religious heritage of the holiday and are temporary in nature. Roger Florey, on his own behalf and on behalf of his minor son, Jason, contended that the rules were unconstitutional both as written and applied.[20] Florey was a self-proclaimed nonbeliever.

Result: The guidelines were upheld as a valid exercise of the school board's power.

Argument of the Case: Heaney, Judge. The case needs to be settled by applying the *Lemon* test in order to determine if the Establishment Clause, as applied to the states, has been violated. The *secular purpose* behind the rules' adoption was to ensure that no religious exercise was part of officially sanctioned school activities. They aimed at advancing students' knowledge of their cultural and religious heritage, as well as providing them with an opportunity to perform a full range of music, poetry, and drama. Nor does it matter that an amendment to limit the observance of secular and religious holidays solely to their secular aspects was defeated by the citizens' committee and the School Board (for there are any number of reasons why this amendment might have been defeated, including its possible ambiguity of wording). The *principal effect* of the rules lies in teaching about the customs and cultural heritage of the United States and other countries.[21] They allow students to encounter a wide range of art, literature, and music originally associated with traditional holidays, but since having acquired a broader, secular significance. Nor is there *excessive entanglement* here, for the rules provide a means of ensuring that the school district steers clear of religious exercises. Finally, there is no Free Exercise Clause issue. This clause does not require deletion from the curriculum of all materials that may offend any religious group; furthermore, the guidelines provide for individual exemptions.

McMillan dissents. The *Lemon* test should be applied. There is no obvious *secular purpose,* as shown by the fact that the rules address religious and not nonreligious holidays (for example, Arbor Day, Labor Day); by the fact that the observance of religious holidays does not promote secular goals; by the fact that observing only Jewish and Christian holidays limits rather than expands students' appreciation of religious and cultural diversity; and by the fact that these secular goals can be advanced by nonreligious means. The guidelines have a *primary effect* of permitting activities that advance religion (for example, Christmas assemblies advance Christianity). The *excessive entanglement* prong of the *Lemon* test is also violated because the guidelines may well require the School Board to define religion or censor the religious content of materials as well as enmesh the school in a political divisiveness related to religious belief and practice. Finally, the excusal provisions do not solve the Free Exercise violation raised by these guidelines.

Discussion

Before the challenged guidelines were adopted, Sioux Falls's public schools maintained a number of Christmas programs that were quite religious in nature. When citizen-drafted guidelines were challenged, intense criticism directed against Roger Florey broke out in Sioux Falls. The charge was made that he was taking Christmas out of the schools. Angry letters filled the pages of the local newspaper as the "Christmas carol" case created enormous dissension and anger within the community.

As the case found its way to the federal circuit court, Florey's A.C.L.U. attorney focused upon the religious nature of Christmas carols (particularly "Silent Night"), which, under the newly adopted guidelines, could be sung during Christmas programs. Florey contended that the key to understanding the carols' significance was their words. According to Florey, they were prayers. The core of the argument was straightforward:[22]

> The evidence in this case must be viewed from the following perspective. Simply stated, if "'Silent Night' constitutes a form of prayer, then 'Silent Night' may not be performed in public school Christmas assemblies: prayers may not be performed in public schools."[23] If "Silent Night" constitutes religious instruction, then "Silent Night" may not be performed in public school Christmas assemblies: public schools must be "entirely excluded from the area of religious instruction."[24] If "Silent Night" advances religion, then "'Silent Night' may not be performed in public school Christmas assemblies": public schools are required "to be neutral in [their] relations with groups of believers and non-believers."[25]

The majority of the circuit court rejected these contentions, choosing instead to adopt the legal argument quite similar to that advanced by the school district. The court centered its attention upon determining the constitutionality of the school board's religious guidelines. Regarding Christmas carols (whose discussion was reduced to a single footnote), the court first emphasized their history and then stressed their *context*. It observed that carols were sung "with regularity on public and commercial television and ... played on public address systems in offices, manufacturing plants and retail stores in every city and village." With respect to carols with a religious theme (such as "Silent Night"), "some feel their dissemination in public degrades religion while others feel it enhances religion." Regarding this disagreement, the court offered no opinion except to note both their secular and sectarian use and to suggest that they had "achieved a cultural significance that justified their being sung in the public schools of Sioux Falls, South Dakota, if done in accordance with the policy and rules adopted by that school district."

Anchoring the court's position was the fact that the guidelines adopted by the Sioux Falls School Board prohibited the singing of "Silent Night" in a religiously oriented Christmas assembly (for the whole assembly would exceed both the guidelines and the Establishment Clause of the First Amendment) but permitted it in a program that emphasized secular songs and readings, mentioned other religious traditions and practices (intended to promote tolerance among differing beliefs), and emphasized the secular aspect of Christmas or the holiday being celebrated. Thus, the kind of program encouraged by the school guidelines might (for example) combine several religiously oriented carols such as "Silent Night" with a number of secular holiday songs ("Frosty the Snowman" and "Rudolph the Rednosed Reindeer," for instance), include one or two songs from other traditions (perhaps a Chanukah song), and possibly add several yule songs from other lands (perhaps sung in foreign languages). Thus, "Silent Night" becomes one song among many in a "Winter Festivals Around the World" type of school program—and this is precisely the kind of program envisioned by the school board guidelines. Whatever its words mean, "Silent Night" (the court seemed to argue) could not be viewed as a prayer within such a context.

Thus, the reason the appeals court upheld the guidelines was not because they endorsed religion in the school—but rather because the religion was so diluted in content that it was rendered inoffensive.[26] In this sense, the case was hardly the victory for religion that pro-religion conservatives sometimes made it out to be. Still, it should be recalled that religion was substantially watered down in a case like *DeSpain*, where the Court ruled against a religious or religious-like practice. The "prayers" invalidated in that case were similar to Christmas carols and assemblies in that each had a strong secular component. Yet, if anything, it would appear that the religious references made by some Christmas carols (and therefore the state involvement in religion) exceeded the involvement of the state in religion invalidated in *DeSpain*. In light of this, one might ask why in *DeSpain* the contested practices were invalidated while, in this case, the challenged guidelines survived judicial scrutiny.

One cannot help speculating that a tacit and perhaps unique influence upon the court's decision in the *Florey* case was the long, historical tradition occupied by such carols, not only within the larger society, but also within the schools. Christmas programs and their carols have been part and parcel of the public schools for as long as anyone can remember.[27] Furthermore, Christmas, with all its secular connotations, remains an event of critical importance within society. It may well have been that the court was reluctant to strike down such a well-established, deeply felt, and traditional practice.

Not only was *Florey* difficult to reconcile with some past religion clause cases, but it also reflected its own internal tensions. All the judges agreed that the case was appropriately settled by the *Lemon* test of the Establishment Clause. Yet the majority and dissenting judges applied it differently. Thus, even when there was good agreement regarding the proper constitutional approach that courts were to employ in law and religion cases, there was not always agreement regarding its application.

The *Florey* case provided hope that the federal courts would allow some accommodation of quasireligious practices within the schools. Yet with the passage of time it became clear that *Florey* was more the exception than the rule. *DeSpain* was the more reliable precedent. It had outlawed language that resembled prayer; in time the Supreme Court would determine if the mere suggestion of prayer by a teacher (that is, by an employee of the state) followed by no spoken language raised constitutional questions. Perhaps not surprisingly, the Supreme Court discovered significant legal problems.

EXAMPLE 5

Wallace v. Jaffree, 472 U.S. 38 (1985)

Facts: Alabama law authorized a period of silence "for meditation or voluntary prayer." The statute succeeded a statute passed three years earlier, which authorized a one-minute period of silence "for meditation." Ishmeal Jaffree was the father of three minor children; two were in second grade, and one was in kindergarten. He objected to the exercise as constituting a state support of prayer in violation of the Establishment Clause of the Constitution.

Result: Because the contested statute served no valid secular purpose, it was held to violate the Establishment Clause.

Argument of the Case: Stevens, Justice. The states have no greater power to restrain First Amendment freedoms than does the national government.[28] The applicable test of whether the Establishment Clause has been violated by any government is the *Lemon* test. This law violates the first prong of the *Lemon* test; it possesses no clear secular purpose. Alabama's purpose was to endorse religion. The sponsor of the bill—Senator Holmes—testified to this. Furthermore, the contested law's predecessor allowed for a period of silence for the purpose of meditation but did not mention prayer. The addition of the word *prayer* indicates the challenged law's purpose and renders it unconstitutional.

Powell concurs. Alabama's legislative history, and the fact that the state can advance no nonreligious reason for implementing the contested statute, means that the law fails the secular purpose prong of the *Lemon* test. The views of one legislator (Holmes) are not controlling. The *Lemon* test should be maintained, and the Court's decision in this case does not necessarily invalidate other moment-of-silence state statutes.

O'Connor concurs. Alabama's rather unusual effort to officially sponsor and endorse prayer renders the statute unconstitutional (there being no constitutional bar to either voluntary prayer in the schools or to states adopting moment-of-silence laws). The *Lemon* test should be refined but not abandoned. (*Lemon*'s purpose and effect test should be cast in terms of whether the state conveys a message of endorsing religion—which would violate the Establishment Clause.) Alabama's overall legislative history—and not simply Senator Holmes's testimony—indicates that the statute conveys a message of endorsing religion.

Burger dissents. It is ironic that the Court, which opens its session with an invocation for divine protection, has invalidated this contested statute. Focusing upon the legislative history, rather than simply upon the con-tested statute's language, "is simply a subtle way of focusing exclusively on the religious component of the statute rather than examining the statute as a whole." Contending that a moment-of-silence statute that includes the word *prayer* violates the Establishment Clause reflects hostility, not neutrality, toward religion.

White dissents. The First Amendment does not prohibit statutes autho-rizing a moment of silence, even those that provide, when initially passed, for a moment of silence for meditation or prayer. Reassessing past Estab-lishment Clause precedents would be understandable.

Rehnquist dissents. Establishment Clause law has wrongly been built upon a mistaken understanding of constitutional history that sees a separa-tion of church and state. Nor does history require the government to be neutral between religion and irreligion. Finally, nothing in constitutional history prohibits the Congress or the states from pursuing legitimate secu-lar ends through nondiscriminatory sectarian means. Therefore, contem-porary Supreme Court tests of the Establishment Clause (including the *Lemon* test) are misguided.

Discussion

It now appeared that even silent prayer had been declared unconstitutional! In fact, *Wallace* was a bit more difficult. It focused less upon what the students said to themselves and more upon what the teachers said to students. *Wallace* pro-hibited teachers from suggesting that students could use a moment of silence for the purpose of praying. It is difficult to determine precisely the extent to which the Supreme Court was influenced by the particular facts of this case (specifically by what seemed to be a concerted, rear-guard effort by Alabama to promote some form of prayer in the public schools) and to what extent it was influenced by more general principles. Did *Wallace* v. *Jaffree* outlaw all public school moment-of-silence laws, especially those that did not require or allow teachers to mention prayer as an alternative? Probably not.[29]

Wallace is a case that reflects both division and agreement among Supreme Court justices. As our discussion makes clear, the case gives rise to a renewed and spirited argument over the meaning of the Establishment Clause and what tests are appropriate for its interpretation. This reexamination was occasioned by Rehnquist's lengthy dissent, which presented an historical interpretation of the Establishment Clause and argued that the contemporary Supreme Court's efforts to interpret and apply it have been radically misguided. At the same time, a clear majority of six judges in *Wallace* voted in favor of invalidating this Alabama law. For this reason, it would seem that *Wallace* is a case which shuts the door even more firmly in the face of state sponsorship of any religious activity. Combined with *DeSpain* (not to mention *Engel* v. *Vitale* and *Schempp*), it would seem to indicate that even indirect or innocuous religious references cannot be propounded by state employees. If ever one area of the law lent itself to the characterization of being part of a wall of separation between church and state (despite Justice Rehnquist's severe reservation that this metaphor was illicit), the area of prayer and Bible reading in the public schools would seem to be it.

Yet, as we observed in *Florey,* even in an area of the law marked by such a high level of consistency[30] there have been (and remain) exceptions. Perhaps one conclusion to be gleaned from this is that even in areas of church–state law that admit defensible and seemingly clear generalizations, legal and logical complexities endure. When it comes to any analysis of this area of the law, it would seem that nothing is easy.

SUMMARY

In the past generation, perhaps no other area of the law has reflected a unified judicial approach so much as that which reconciled the Establishment Clause to prayer and Bible reading in the schools. There, with a few exceptions, the judiciary's interpretation of the Constitution has had the effect of implementing a wall of separation between church and state. Indeed, it seems that virtually all state-supported religious practices in the public schools have been invalidated by the courts.

Yet the legal rationales underlying judicial decisions affecting prayer and Bible reading in the schools have been far from unanimous. Thus, despite the fact that the judiciary's decisions have seemed to create a wall of separation between church and state, most (but not all) Justices have rejected the wall metaphor in favor of the idea of state neutrality toward religion (and at least one Supreme Court Justice—Rehnquist—has argued that the state can favor religion). Additionally, most (but not all) Justices have adopted the *Lemon* test as the appropriate First Amendment Establishment Clause test. Furthermore (as the *Florey* case demonstrates), majority and dissenting judges and Justices have even differed regarding the application of this test. Also, there have been significant and interesting differences among Supreme Court Justices regarding the relationship between the Establishment Clause and the Free Exercise Clause, the applicability of the Free Exercise Clause to cases like those discussed in this chapter, and the extent to which excusal provisions from state-sponsored religiously related practices and programs shield them from violating the Free Exercise Clause.

Therefore, although one is inclined to answer the question posed at the beginning clearly and emphatically, that prayer and Bible reading are not permitted in the public schools, the issue is not quite so simple. As we have seen, if one is inclined to regard the language of Christmas carols as prayers, then one might fault the Court for not being completely consistent in rendering all forms of prayer in the schools unconstitutional. Still, such exceptions have tended to be narrow: activities that have both a secular and religious meaning, have had a long, traditional use within the schools, and have great societal importance may be permitted under certain clearly defined circumstances. Regarding the judiciary's decisions in this area, consistency is only one controversial issue to be examined; fidelity to the intent, meaning, and purpose of the Constitution is another question of equal or greater importance.

NOTES

1. *Lee* v. *Weisman,* 112 S. Ct. 2469 (1992). Whether this case prohibits all nondenominational prayer at graduation, or just prayer given by clergy at the invitation of school officials, remains ambiguous.

2. A. James Reichley, *Religion in American Public Life* (Washington, DC: Brookings Institution, 1985), pp. 136–51. Also see Robert Miller and Ronald Flowers, *Toward Benevolent Neutrality: Church, State* and the *Supreme Court* (Waco, TX: Baylor Univ. Press, 1987), 3d ed., pp. 378–79.

3. The first case said to incorporate the Establishment Clause was *Cantwell* v. *Connecticut,* 310 U.S. 296, 303 (1940), although many experts trace its formal incorporation to *Everson* v. *Board of Education,* 330 U.S. 1 (1947). See our longer discussion in Chapter 4, p. 67.

4. 330 U.S. 1 (1947).

5. For a fuller discussion of this issue, see Chapter 4, p. 68.

6. For a thoughtful and sensitive treatment of this issue, see Stephen Carter, *The Culture of Disbelief* (New York: Basic Books, 1993), p. 184.

7. Douglas thought that not only were religious exercises in the public schools prohibited, but also were "aids to religion in this country at all levels of government," including tax exemptions for churches, religious services at federal hospitals and prisons, use of G.I. Bill benefits to pay tuition at denominational colleges, the slogan "In God We Trust" on American money, and the words "under God" in the Pledge of Allegiance. *In Carter,* p. 437.

8. Also decided by *Schempp* was the companion case, *Murray* v. *Curlett.*

9. 374 U.S. 203, 222. Later, in *Walz* v. *Tax Commission of the City of New York,* 397 U.S. 644 (1970), the Supreme Court added the requirement that there not be excessive entanglement between church and state. The purpose and primary effect test from *Schempp* and the excessive entanglement test from *Walz* made up the

famous three-pronged *Lemon* test. See Chapter 4, p. 69. Regarding an early formulation of Justice Clark's Establishment Clause test in *Schempp*, see *McGowan v. Maryland,* 366 U.S. 420, 453 (1961).

10. The Court's position on this point has endured. Furthermore, when secular works are chosen for public school classes, an unconstitutional religion of secular humanism has not been created. On this point, see *Smith* v. *Board of School Commissioners of Mobile County,* 827 F.2d 684 (11th Cir. 1987).

11. 374 U.S. 203, 281.

12. *Abingdon* v. *Schempp,* 374 U.S. 203 (1963).

13. This is discussed in terms of graduation ceremonies in the case of *Lee* v. *Weisman.*

14. It should be pointed out that not all Jewish children, or Unitarian children, or children of any minority religion (or no religion) would necessarily agree. Therefore, there have been differences among children and their parents within the same religion regarding religiously related questions of school policy.

15. For example, see Clark's discussion in 374 U.S. at 228–229.

16. *Abingdon* v. *Schempp* at 318.

17. *Abingdon* v. *Schempp* at 286.

18. 384 F. 2d at 838. A point to be considered: How did the prayer in this case differ from the public school celebration of Thanksgiving, a holiday that traditionally has thanked God for nature's bounty? Admittedly, the holiday is celebrated today in a far more secular fashion, and references to God are infrequent or nonexistent—but explicit references to God are nonexistent in this prayer as well.

19. 384 F.2d at 838.

20. Since the rules were challenged immediately after having been drafted, and no holiday season had passed with the rules have been implemented, the circuit court's review was confined to ruling upon the rules as written.

21. Nor, according to Judge Heaney, did the guidelines' stipulation that holidays with a religious and secular basis be *observed* have the primary effect of advancing religion because observing such holidays must be understood within the context of an earlier guideline provision that religion was neither to be promoted nor discouraged. 619 F.2d 1311, 1316 (1980).

22. From "Plaintiff's Summary of the Evidence," United States District Court, District of South Dakota, Southern Division, pp. 1–2.

23. *Engel* v. *Vitale* 370 U.S. 421 (1962) and *Abington School District* v. *Schempp,* 374 U.S. 203 (1963) were cited.

24. *Lemon* v. *Kurtzman,* 403 U.S. 602 (1971) was cited here.

25. Cited was *Everson* v. *Board of Education* 330 U.S. 1, 18 (1947).

26. This is the same approach the Court later used regarding religious displays on public property during the holiday season. See Chapter 8, p. 155.

27. The fact that such programs had a long history was, of course, hardly a *sufficient* reason for the Supreme court to uphold them. History, combined with the fact that they had secular significance, distinguished them from solely religious activities, such as prayers.

28. Curiously, the district court had attempted to undo the incorporation of the Establishment Clause and held that the First Amendment did not prohibit Alabama from establishing a religion within the state. Steven's opinion explicitly upheld the Court of Appeals' reversal.

29. Thus, Rehnquist, White, Burger, Powell, and O'Connor stated or implied that they were likely to uphold these laws' constitutionality.

30. At least since the 1962 case of *Engel* v. *Vitale.* A tension clearly existed in previously decided cases involving the constitutionality of released time. Cf. *McCollum* v. *Board of Education,* 333 U.S. 203 (1948) to *Zorach* v. *Clauson,* 243 U.S. 306 (1952).

12

Should Religious Beliefs Have an Impact on the Curriculum of Public Schools?

THE PROBLEM POSED

Education never exists in a moral void. Every educational system has goals that are ultimately rooted in a view of the good, and this view is always open to examination and criticism. For example, a parochial school that has as its goal the encouragement of Christian virtues (faith, hope, charity) and a battle against such vices as vanity, gluttony, and lust differs from a public school that sees as its goal the encouragement of self-esteem coupled with a battle against racism, sexism, homophobia, and environmental hazards. But both schools have a moral vision (as well as educational goals). We usually recognize the moral goals behind a parochial school; it is more difficult to see that a sense of morality (although different) pervades the public school curriculum. For example, a particular parochial school may encourage its young women to think that getting married and having children is the most important thing they can do with their lives. What could be more fulfilling for a woman than supporting her husband and raising her children? On the other hand, a public school might encourage its young women to look beyond the traditional family for fulfillment. In fact, it might warn its students against the prejudice that the family must include one male and one female parent. Who is to say that lesbian or homosexual marriages are "unnatural"? Both educational systems are founded on ideas of what is good.[1]

Therefore, curriculum choices often reflect moral choices. And curriculum decisions, like many educational decisions, involve not only inclusion but also exclusion.[2] In other words, the moral vision behind a curriculum requires that some things be excluded from the classroom because they are perceived as bad. This problem is illustrated in the play *Inherit the Wind,* which is a fictional portrayal of the famous Scopes Monkey Trial.[3] The battle lines are well drawn in the play. Brady, who represents the prosecution, argues that children will be corrupted by the introduction of Darwin into the classroom. Pointing to one student, he says, "I tell you, if this law is not upheld, this boy will become one of a generation shorn of its faith by the teachings of Godless science." Drummond, who represents the teacher accused of teaching Darwin, argues that teaching children to think for themselves does not destroy faith; it simply changes the foundation of faith. Clinging to the "old-time religion" threatens intellectual freedom: "I'm trying to stop you bigots and ignoramuses from controlling the education of the United States."

The conflict here is over a biology text, but both sides see that the curriculum decision has enormous moral implications. Our first case deals with this same issue, which did not reach the Supreme Court until 1968.

EXAMPLE 1

Epperson v. *Arkansas,* 393 U.S. 97 (1968)

Facts: A 1928 Arkansas law prohibited the teaching of evolution in the public schools or state universities. The law made it a crime for any teacher to "teach the theory or doctrine that mankind ascended or descended from a lower order of animals." It also prohibited the use of any textbook that presented this theory. In 1965 the school district in Little Rock adopted a textbook that included a section on evolution. Susan Epperson was a biology teacher in Central High School, and she sought a declaration from the Chancery Court that the 1928 statute was void. The Chancery Court held that the statute violated the freedom of speech provisions of the First Amendment, but the Arkansas Supreme Court reversed the decision and upheld the constitutionality of the law, arguing that the law was a "valid exercise of the state's power to specify the curriculum in its public schools."

Result: The law was held to violate the Establishment and Free Exercise clauses of the First Amendment as applied to the states through the Fourteenth Amendment.

Argument of the Case: Fortas, Justice. The Arkansas statute is clearly unconstitutional because it "selects from the body of knowledge a particular segment which it proscribes for the sole reason that it is deemed to conflict with a particular religious doctrine." In other words, the law is based on a "particular interpretation of the Book of Genesis by a particular religious group." The landmark case of *Everson* v. *Board of Education* is cited to demonstrate that the state and national governments must be completely neutral between religion and nonreligion. The Court respects the state's "undoubted right" to develop its own curriculum but not when this violates the First Amendment. It is clear that "fundamentalist sectarian conviction was and is the law's reason for existence."

Black concurs. There is some reason to doubt that this is a real case; an unenforced law that has "slumbered on the books as though dead" is now challenged by someone who apparently has already given up her job as a teacher and moved out of Arkansas. But assuming that a case does exist, one must be careful not to "thrust the Federal Government's long arm the least bit further into state school curriculums than decision of this particular case requires." The Arkansas law is vague and should be struck down on that ground. Justice Fortas's approach implies that a school may not remove a controversial subject from its curriculum, but this is a power that public schools should have. It is also not clear that the state is taking a "neutral" position in not favoring one religious or anti-religious view; since the biblical version of creation is not taught in the Arkansas schools, it is not obvious that a one-sided view is presented in the curriculum. The danger in Fortas's opinion is that it implies that the Supreme Court "can successfully supervise and censor the curriculum of every public school in every hamlet and city in the United States."

Harlan concurs. Justice Black is correct in suggesting that this case should never have come to the Supreme Court. However, it seems clear that the Arkansas law violates the Establishment Clause of the First Amendment.

Stewart concurs. Public schools have great latitude in determining their own curricula. A school could decide not to include astronomy or biology in its curriculum, but it is a violation of the Constitution to create criminal penalties for even mentioning the existence of "an entire system of respected human thought."

Discussion

Justice Fortas conceded that basic responsibility for curriculum and textbook decisions in the public schools lies with the state and local authorities. However, he argued that there are limits to this basic responsibility. The Court has "not failed to apply the First Amendment's mandate in our educational system where essential." But what exactly was this mandate, and when was it essential that it be applied?

Fortas sought to answer these questions by applying the neutrality principle from the *Everson*[4] case (among others): "The State may not adopt programs or practices in its public schools or colleges which 'aid or oppose' any religion." Neither the purpose nor the primary effect of the challenged law should advance or inhibit religion. When the state prohibits by means of its criminal law the teaching of scientific theory because of a religious motivation, then neutrality has been breached.

According to Fortas, the real problem was not that the Arkansas law takes a moral stand or that it supports religion in some general way, but that it sanctions a particular interpretation of a particular religion. By passing this law, Arkansas gives official preference to Christianity, and it really shows a preference for only one version of Christianity. Fortas contended that it was "clear that fundamentalist sectarian conviction was and is the law's reason for existence." Fortas's interpretation of the First Amendment was relatively uncontroversial; it well accorded with precedent and contemporary Supreme Court interpretation. But it is also good to remember that the Establishment Clause as originally understood would have allowed for a substantial relationship between church and state at the state level that was invalidated in this case.[5]

In his concurring opinion in *Epperson,* Justice Black raised one final point that indirectly challenged whether the neutrality principle invoked by the Court was truly religiously neutral. He asked "whether this Court's decision forbidding a State to exclude the subject of evolution from its schools infringes the religious freedom of those who consider evolution an anti-religious doctrine." Noting the existence of a problem "far more troublesome than are discussed in the Court's opinion," Black wondered if in the Court's vigilant protection of the Establishment Clause it had run roughshod over the Free Exercise clause. It goes without saying that one's right to free exercise does not preclude the state from passing general laws that affect religion in *any* way; that would be an impossible standard. Still, Justice Black's question was not without significance. For instance, the Court's decision in *Wisconsin* v. *Yoder*[6] four years later would suggest that some forms of secular education—no matter how benign they seemed—may even threaten the very existence of a religion. This was also Brady's fear in *Inherit the Wind.* In *Epperson,* the theory of evolution directly challenged the fundamental church doctrine of some sects. Could it not be argued that the free exercise of religion is threatened by teaching only the theory of evolution?[7] This objection is intriguing, but there was a critical difference between the two cases. The *Yoder* case did not involve the attempt to alter the curriculum by excluding certain subjects from the public schools; it simply asked if the Amish could stay away from the schools that taught what they perceived to be objectionable subjects.

The issue raised in *Epperson* has to do with the attempt by the Supreme Court to balance the constitutional independence of the states with the religion clauses of the First Amendment. The Supreme Court thought this was a relatively easy task in this case and decided it accordingly. Although the Court did not demonstrate to everyone's satisfaction that the state could remain completely neutral on the subject of religion, it did decide rather effortlessly that prohibiting the teaching of evolution provided religion with too much influence under the First Amendment. Our next case is both stranger and more fundamental than *Epperson,* although it, too, was easily decided. It asks if the very secular education promulgated by the public schools constitutes a religion of its own. In other words, does the dominance of "secular humanism" in the public schools violate the Establishment Clause?

EXAMPLE 2

Smith v. *Board of School Commission of Mobile County,* 827 F.2nd 684 (1987)

Facts: The procedural history of this case is complicated.[8] However, the main issue has to do with the claim that the public schools foster a religion of "secular humanism." The evidence focused on forty-four textbooks on the Alabama State Approved Textbook list, including books in the area of history, social studies, and home economics. The district court found that the texts violated the Establishment Clause of the First Amendment, and the court "permanently enjoined the use of the textbooks in the Alabama public schools."

Result: It is not necessary to determine whether or not "secular humanism" is a religion. The forty-four textbooks do not violate the Establishment Clause. The District Court is overruled.

Argument of the Case: Johnson, Judge. The three-part test developed in *Lemon* v. *Kurtzman* makes it clear that the textbooks do not violate the Establishment Clause. The books in question do present a nonreligious point of view, but they are not "antagonistic to theistic belief." The Board of Education is merely attempting to "instill in Alabama public school children such values as independent thought, tolerance of diverse views, self-respect, maturity, self-reliance and logical decision-making." These are entirely appropriate secular goals. The fact that some of these books may be offensive to people of particular religious backgrounds is not sufficient to render their use in the public schools a violation of the Establishment Clause.

Discussion

The issues in this case go right to the heart of the great debate over the role of religion in the public schools. The neutrality test employed in *Epperson* and virtually every Establishment Clause test employed by the Supreme Court since 1947 presumed the existence and constitutionality of a nonreligious secular realm significantly freed from the influence of, and the influence upon, religion. If this understanding did not always or exactly represent a strict separation of church and state, it surely presumed a differentiation between the two. *Smith* represented a foundational attack upon this understanding, upon precedent, and upon the very way Americans thought about law, religion, and politics. It asked this: Does the secular perspective that dominates public education itself violate the Establishment Clause?

Smith began with the premise that all moral perspectives were essentially religious, that the secular schools contained and taught a secular moral perspective, and therefore that the schools taught religion (secular humanism). It followed from this syllogism that much of secular, public school education was potentially in conflict with the First Amendment. If teaching religion was unavoidable, it would seem to follow that all moral perspectives should at least be given equal time in the classroom. The practical problem with Smith's argument was that had it prevailed, it would have completely uprooted and perhaps destroyed the American public school system. If "secular humanism" really was a religion, like all other religions, then how could the state run any educational system that did not discriminate against any religion? Or how could the state teach anything at all, given the variety of moral and religious perspectives that existed in American society? For this reason alone, it was unlikely that any federal appeals court was going to endorse Smith's position.

Smith's argument that "secular humanism" amounted to a religion also seemed curious, perhaps even preposterous. Secular humanism has no single, fundamental text that defines it; it has no set of organized beliefs; it has no formal adherents. It is difficult to see how one could "establish" anything as amorphous as this. Yet, having admitted as much, we must also admit that *Smith* did raise some interesting questions that are more difficult to resolve than the court revealed.

Consider Smith's first premise, that all moral perspectives are essentially religious. We doubt that this is really true (but we leave any extended discussion of this point to another time and other authors, for this is not a book of theology). However, we would note that the Supreme Court has come close to endorsing the precise position advanced by Smith in the conscientious objector cases.[9] We would also observe that the Supreme Court has classified secular humanism as a religion,[10] which was the precise conclusion urged upon the Court by Smith!

Smith's second premise, that the secular schools contained and taught a moral perspective, also cannot be dismissed out of hand. At the very least, his assertion raises a most interesting question. For example, one of the books in dispute is a home economics textbook. Smith alleged that the book taught that students must determine what is right and wrong based on personal experience, feelings, and "internal values." Smith's interpretation received support from the lower court, which had agreed that the book "assumes that self-actualization is the goal of every human being, that man has no supernatural attributes or component, that there are only temporal and physical consequences for man's actions, and that these results, alone, determine the morality of an action." This would appear to be a powerful point. The seemingly neutral perspective of the home economics textbook was not in fact neutral; it quietly and probably unintentionally denied that standards of morality come directly or indirectly from God.

Judge Johnson attempted to steer a course away from the sensitive issue of whether "secular humanism" was a religion, arguing instead that the issue was irrelevant. For Johnson, all that mattered was that the book was secular; what *secular* meant (and whether or not it could be construed as a religion) was simply irrelevant. That this and the other challenged books were secular was determined by applying the three-part test derived from *Lemon v. Kurtzman*.[11] Regarding the contested home economics textbooks and the allegation that they teach that students must determine what is right and wrong based on personal experience, feelings, and "internal values," Johnson applied the *Lemon* test to show that the primary effect of Alabama's choice of the textbook was secular, designed to instill and advance secular values:

> ...the message conveyed is one of a governmental attempt to instill in Alabama public school children such values as independent thought, tolerance of diverse views, self-respect, maturity, self-reliance and logical decision-making. This is an entirely appropriate secular effect.[12]

Although this was the end of the argument for Judge Johnson, it merely stated the problem for Smith. For this reason, Johnson's use of the *Lemon* test did not resolve the central issue of the case raised by Smith because Smith did not contest the fact that the Alabama public schools were presenting a secular perspective. Even the words that Johnson chose to make his point could be used as evidence to support Smith's cause. For example, the value of "independent thought" is an implicit challenge to the biblical idea that wisdom begins with fear of the Lord. From this perspective, completely independent thinking would mean turning away from God. And if Alabama was attempting to "instill values," then isn't it possible that those values undermine other values? And if it is true that one of these values is "tolerance of diverse views," then the question would be this: From a biblical perspective, should one be tolerant of all views? Moses was not tolerant of those he found worshipping the golden calf, and Jesus was not tolerant of the moneylenders he found in the Temple. The *Lemon* test assumes that there is a clear distinction between religious and secular views, but this is exactly what is being questioned by Smith.

Thus, a secular perspective is not religiously "neutral," even though Johnson tried hard to make it seem so: "the message conveyed by these textbooks with regard to theistic religion is one of neutrality: the textbooks neither endorse theistic religion as a system of belief, nor discredit it." But as we have seen, many of the values innocently promoted by secular education do challenge or even discredit theistic religion. The question that really has to be answered is whether all moral perspectives are really religious (as opposed to merely positing judgments about which religion also posits judgments) and whether secularism is a religion. Yet these were the exact questions that Johnson was anxious to avoid. But regardless of how these theoretical questions might be resolved, the practical implications for public education had Smith's position prevailed were obvious to the federal appeals court and are obvious to us as well.

One possible approach to handling the tensions between the secular and religious perspectives would be to allow all those with objections to required textbooks the opportunity to participate in alternative reading programs tailored to their beliefs. But this is a worrisome approach. Would students ever be challenged to expand or change their opinions if their readings were adapted to the beliefs with which the students entered school? This issue is presented in our next case.

EXAMPLE 3

Mozert **v.** *Hawkins County Board of Education,* 827 Fed. Rep. 2nd 1058 (1987)

Facts: In 1983 the Hawkins County (Tennessee) Board of Education adopted a series of basic reading books published by Holt, Rinehart and Winston. Parents of several students complained that a number of stories offended their religious beliefs, and they worked out an alternative reading program with their children's teachers. In November of 1983 the school board voted unanimously to eliminate all alternative reading programs. When Mozert's children refused to read the Holt series, they were suspended.

Result: The Court of Appeals held that the requirement that students read the Holt series did not create an unconstitutional burden on the free exercise of religion.

Argument of the Case: Lively, Chief Judge. It could be argued that Tennessee does have a compelling interest "in the education of its young" but that the state had made a mistake when it required that the Holt series be read "in the face of the plaintiffs' religious objections." One might consider the possibility that the state could accommodate itself to these religious beliefs "without material and substantial disruption to the educational process." But this is not required by the Constitution. As long as the schools do not violate the Establishment Clause of the First Amendment, they can mandate any secular program for all students. In other words, as long as a public school does not foster religion through its curriculum, as long as its books and lessons are secular, it does not have to accommodate itself to students whose religious beliefs are offended.

Discussion

The students in this case considered themselves to be born-again Christians, and they were offended by the teachings in the Holt series. According to the students, themes ranging from evolution to what they called "futuristic supernaturalism" and magic violated their beliefs, and they argued that it was wrong to force them to read stories with these themes. The question, then, is whether the schools violated the Free Exercise Clause when they required that students read books that offended their religious beliefs.

Judge Lively argued that the state not only has a compelling interest to educate its citizens, but also possesses wide latitude to select the means and methods by which that education takes place (as long as the schools do not foster religion). In addition, he observed that religious students could not reasonably expect to be exempted from exposure to ideas they rejected. Exposure to new ideas was essential to the development of critical reading skills and to education itself. He also emphasized in his opinion that none of the parents actually offered proof that the students were required to agree with or believe any of the ideas presented in the Holt series. There was evidence that some classes required reading aloud and that some encouraged acting out the themes in the lessons, but there was no compulsion to accept the ideas, according to the court. Students do not have a right under the Free Exercise Clause to avoid exposure to ideas they find offensive.

Although Judge Lively's comments (on the whole) seem quite reasonable and his assertion of the paramount secular interest of the state in education appears persuasive, there is still a tension here similar to that which existed in the previous case. Consider: Is it fair to say that the parents were concerned only that their children might be exposed to new ideas? Isn't something more complicated taking place here? One mother of a born-again student complained about a story featuring "thought transfer and telepathy"; these themes represent, in her opinion, more than new or challenging ideas that all students should confront. These themes indicated that the public schools were involved in introducing, teaching, and inculcating superstition, which was a basic assault on her child's beliefs. And she emphasized that the problem is not with an isolated story or two. The Holt series as a whole was an assault—however unintentional—on Christianity as she understood it. In other words, when such themes are presented to children with the power of the state behind them, then one might argue that the children are not just be exposed to new ideas; instead, they are being offered a system of beliefs that point to a comprehensive rejection of revealed religion. These parents were not trying to keep their children from becoming open-minded about alternative perspectives; they sensed that their children's beliefs could be undermined by a one-sided curriculum, one that didn't give religion a chance.

In his concurring opinion, Judge Boggs states that the court ought to recognize that the Holt series does more than expose children to new ideas; it creates a burden on their free exercise of religion: "Here, the burden is many years of education, being required to study books that, in the plaintiff's view, systematically undervalue, contradict, and ignore their religion." But Judge Boggs did not go so far as to dissent from the majority opinion. He did not believe that the burden to free exercise was unconstitutional, since the reading program was not instituted in the name of some other religious belief. He admitted that this may not be completely fair and observed that the court's opinion may discourage public schools from making what would be, in most cases, a very small effort to accommodate students with minority religious objections. As Judge Boggs says, the law allows school boards to say "my way or the highway," but they need not be so uncompromising.

Boggs was critical of Lively's assertion that "the only way to avoid conflict with the plaintiff's beliefs in these sensitive areas would be to eliminate all references to the subjects [they find offensive]." And Lively invoked *Epperson* to prove that the Supreme Court has indicated that it violates the Establishment Clause "to tailor a public school's curriculum to satisfy the principles or prohibitions of any religion." But this was not the issue here. None of the parents in this case asked that the curriculum be changed. All they requested was that an alternative reading program be available for students who felt that the Holt series offended their religious beliefs.

All this seems very reasonable, yet the principle of accommodating religious students in the public schools is problematic. In a country with tremendous religious diversity and sensitivities, it is conceivable that a single school could have a large number of students with many different and subtle religious objections to the curriculum. Would it be practical to have a number of alternative reading programs tailored to each of these individual groups? And beyond the issue of practicality, how could it be said that the instituting and maintaining of such programs must exist in order to accommodate the public sphere to the free exercise right of every student and each parent? Clearly, the state should not be permitted to favor one religion over another, and it is also clear that the state should not be permitted to launch an attack on a religion as such. But should a secular curriculum have to bow to religious objections simply because it is secular and therefore offensive to some religious groups? Could public education survive such a principle? At bottom, *Mozert* argues for the supremacy of the secular over the religious, and against the proposition that secular programs that offend religious sensibilities, sensitivities, or beliefs *must* be altered as a matter of right.

EXAMPLE 4

Ware v. *Valley Stream High School,* 551 N.Y.S. 2nd 167 (Ct. App. 1989)

Facts: The Commission of Education established regulations requiring all primary and secondary school students to receive extensive AIDS education. Ware and others are members of the Plymouth Brethren, a religious organization with approximately 35,000 followers. The members of the Brethren petitioned on behalf of their children for a complete exemption from AIDS education, saying that it "conflicts with their strictly held religious belief that followers not engage in sexual relations outside marriage and not be exposed to instruction concerning sexuality or morality other than that which is imparted by the community." The school agreed to exempt the children from part but not all of the AIDS education.

Result: The court was unable to determine whether the state's compelling interest in educating children about AIDS would be frustrated by granting a complete exemption to a religious group. The appeals court therefore reversed the lower court's "summary judgment"; in other words, it determined that the facts of the case needed more analysis and that the case could not be decided on questions of law alone. For example, the court thought that a new hearing would be necessary to determine whether the integrity of the Brethren religion would be threatened by exposure to AIDS information. And it would be necessary in a new hearing to hear from the state. Could the state really prove that granting an exemption to the Brethren would be a threat to health standards?

Argument of the Case: Kaye, Judge. The school is convinced that "education is the most powerful and important weapon against the spread of AIDS." But the argument of the parents in the Brethren is that the curriculum would "undermine the foundations of our faith and scar the moral values which have been instilled into our children from the very earliest days and could even jeopardize their place in the holy fellowship of God's Son." There is no dispute about the sincerity of the Brethren's religious beliefs, and the AIDS education would be a burden, but it is not clear how serious a burden it would be. Would it be sufficient to outweigh the compelling state interest in health? The balancing of rights against claims of the state is a difficult matter that demands full attention to the facts.

Titone dissents. The parents' claim that the AIDs curriculum would undermine their faith has not been adequately contradicted. Further, the state has not proven that the moral training provided by the Brethren to their children is not an adequate substitute for a secular education.

Discussion

The free exercise claim here by the Brethren parents was as simple as the state's counterclaim. The Plymouth Brethren is a religious group established by Irish Christians who became disenchanted with established churches in the 1820s. Their central belief is the obligation to "separate from evil." They live in an insulated community and forbid their children to socialize with children who do not share their beliefs or to even eat lunch with nonmember children at school. They do not allow television or radio in their communities, and they do not see movies or read magazines. When the public schools that their children attended began a program of AIDS education, the parents complained that the well-intentioned program would expose their children to details about sexual activity that would threaten their way of life.

The school was not unsympathetic. It allowed the children of the Brethren an exemption from the part of the program called "Prevention," but required them to attend lessons called "Practice skills in saying no," "Know ways the AIDS virus can and cannot be transmitted," and "Recognize and evaluate media messages regarding sexuality." The parents pushed for a complete exemption, arguing that the exemption would not be a threat to the state since their approach to education stresses sexual chastity. In addition, the parents promised to instruct their children about AIDS, but in their own way. In his dissent, Judge Titone admitted that the parents do have a strong case. While their children might miss some information that is stressed in the AIDS program, he points out the following:

> Given the nature of the disease and the manner in which it is spread, it seems clear that prevention depends upon a combination of personal factors, only one of which involves clinical knowledge. Equally critical are such factors as an individual's choice of life-style and sense of self-esteem —precisely the areas which the Brethren's moral and spiritual training addresses.[13]

Judge Titone cautioned against the arrogance of believing that the public schools can use information to address all social problems. Moral training and habituation such as that provided to the Brethren children may, in the final analysis, be a more powerful protection against AIDS.

Yet the claim of the state remains powerful. The state is attempting to slow down the transmission of a deadly disease, and while it may have some sympathy for the fact that the Brethren children are trained so that they will not be disposed to become "sexually active," this is not sufficient. As Judge Kaye put it, "At this point in the history of the disease, it is well recognized that education is the most powerful and important weapon against the spread of AIDS." Also, it is the responsibility of the state to educate all children. The possibility exists that some children of the Brethren may "fall short of community expectations." Since the Brethren do not completely isolate themselves from the modern world, it would not be surprising if some left the religion and succumbed to the temptations around them: "Disaffected members may leave or be expelled from the confines of the faith," and these people need to have the education that the Brethren would deny them.

The court decided not to rule on this case and called for an additional hearing to determine matters of fact. In its opinion, it was inappropriate to dismiss the claims of the Brethren that its religion would be threatened by the AIDS education. The state clearly has a compelling interest in protecting its citizens from health hazards, but the court argues that this should not be done at the expense of religious belief. But Judge Titone raised an important question in his dissent. Exactly what kind of information would settle this issue? What could be presented in the form of evidence that would prove that the Brethren religion would be threatened by the AIDS program? Would the court have to listen to "expert testimony" about Brethren beliefs and conflicting testimony calling those beliefs into question? "Will the court be called upon to decide whose position is most credible, whose views represent the true Brethren faith and, finally, what is the relative hierarchical significance of the Brethren's various beliefs and practices?" Is it possible for the court to "balance" the state's program and religious belief without making inappropriate inquiries and improper judgments about religion? Once again, and not for the last time, the secular requirements of the state and the religious beliefs and practices of its citizens conflicted, and the courts were not completely able to escape the thorny and complex legal, philosophical, and moral consequences inherent in resolving this conflict.

SUMMARY

These cases raise a number of important questions about the relationship between religion and the public schools. The missions and subjects of religion and education often overlap; both are concerned with the development of character and with presenting an approach to moral questions. Thus, religion and education (for example, choices about what will be in a library or what will be taught in the classroom) often reflect fundamental moral judgments, whether or not this is recognized or acknowledged. It doesn't seem possible to educate children without making principled decisions to include or emphasize some ideas and exclude or de-emphasize others.

It follows that the so-called "neutrality" principle articulated by the Court is, at best, a slippery concept to define and implement and, at worst, an outright fiction. If the Court allows Darwin to be taught in the schools and excludes the biblical account of creation, it is not being neutral. If the Court allows the Bible to be taught as literature but not as a sacred text, it is not being neutral. However, this does not mean that the schools should strive for true neutrality. The answer to the problem is not necessarily forcing the schools to give "equal time" to the religious perspective on every (or any) matter. True neutrality may be impossible and even undesirable. John Locke argued that religious tolerance was only possible in the context of secular dominance. In other words, he openly acknowledged that religions would suffer in a secular state. But he argued that the domination of the secular was more compatible with public peace than the domination of one religion or sect over another.

Since true neutrality in education may be impossible, the choice may well be between secular domination and sectarian domination. Despite the strong tradition of secular preeminence, there still remain pockets of support that, from time to time, advocate sectarian domination. For instance, in recent years a number of groups such as Citizens for Excellence in Education (CEE) have worked to "bring God back into the classroom." According to Robert Simonds, the founder of CEE, it is important to return the "Christian World View in the classroom." He asserts that the idea of separation of church and state is a "socialist myth," and he has vowed to take over school boards throughout the United States. Simonds has already had an impact on education, having succeeded in orchestrating changes in libraries and school curricula. In San Antonio, a CEE-dominated school board removed *Little Red Riding Hood* from a public school library because it portrayed the grandmother drinking wine. Simonds wants all books that include any "anti-biblical" language banned from the schools. The secular state may place religion at a disadvantage in the public schools, but the First Amendment should at least discourage groups like CEE from dominating American education.

But if a secular perspective dominates in the schools, how much do religious groups have to suffer? The operative principle was established in *Mozert v. Hawkins.* Religious groups cannot demand an exemption from secular education as a matter of right unless the very existence of their religion is actually threatened. This means that a public school is *not* required by law to accommodate religious students offended by books in a library or by texts in a classroom. But tension between religion and the public schools need not always be settled at the level of rights. Schools are not prohibited from reaching accommodations with religious students; they are just not required to do so by the law. Thus, domination of the secular over the religious in the public schools does not necessarily culminate in hostility toward religion.

NOTES

1. There has been great controversy over what is known as the "Rainbow Curriculum," which was introduced into the New York public schools in the early 1990s and finally was rejected in part. It recommended that the family be discussed (beginning in first grade) in a new way. Teachers were told to be aware of varied family structures, including single-parent households, gay or lesbian parents, divorced parents, adoptive parents, and guardian or foster parents. The program required that children be taught to acknowledge the positive elements of each type of household. Textbooks for the public schools included a gay and lesbian coloring book for preschoolers and books titled *Daddy's Roommate* and *Heather Had Two Mommies.*

2. This issue has also been raised with regard to public school libraries. See *Board of Education, Island Trees Union* v. *Pico,* 457 U.S. 853 (1982). In this case, the Board of Education removed several books from the school library because they were "anti-American, anti-Christian, anti-Semitic, and just plain filthy." The Supreme Court ruled that the books could not be removed from the library because its purpose is different from the classroom. The library should provide a variety of perspectives; the classroom may require a particular curriculum and need not take into account as wide a variety of perspectives.

3. See Jerome Lawrence and Robert E. Lee, *Inherit the Wind* (New York: Bantam, 1981). The actual trial took place in 1925 and featured the two legal giants Clarence Darrow and William Jennings Bryan.

4. *Everson* v. *Board of Education,* 330 U.S. 1 (1947).

5. See Chapter 4, p. 77.

6. 406 U.S. 205 (1972). See chapter 14, p. 259.

7. Not only has the Court overturned state prohibitions regarding the teaching of evolution; it has also prohibited teaching "creationism" along with evolution. See *Edwards* v. *Aguillard,* 482 U.S. 578 (1987). The question in this case was whether Louisiana's "Balanced Treatment for

Creation-Science and Evolution-Science in Public School Instruction" Act violated the Establishment Clause of the First Amendment. The Court held that this "equal time" law did violate the Constitution.

8. A district court in Alabama ruled that prayers in the classroom were not unconstitutional and that the Supreme Court had erred when it ruled that the Establishment Clause of the First Amendment prohibits the states (and not just the national government) from establishing a religion. An Alabama appeals court overruled the district court, and the Supreme Court of the United States affirmed the earlier decision in *Wallace* v. *Jaffree,* 472 U.S. 38 (1985). The case was remanded to the district court, which then ruled that if prayers were unconstitutional, then so was secular humanism.

9. See our discussion, in Chapter 4, pp. 68–71.

10. This was said explicitly for the Court in a oft-cited footnote in *Torcaso* v. *Watkins,* 367 U. S. 488 (1961) at 495. Earlier, Black had written more ambiguously in *Everson* v. *Board of Education,* 330 U.S. 1 (1947) at 16, that "...other language of the [first] amendment commands that New Jersey cannot hamper its citizens in the free exercise of their own religion. Consequently, it cannot exclude individual...Nonbelievers...or members of any faith, *because of their faith, or lack of it,* from receiving the benefits of public welfare legislation."

11. See *Lemon* v. *Kurtzman,* 403 U.S. 602 (1971). The test is as follows: (1) the law or action must have a secular purpose; (2) the primary effect of the law or action must not be to either advance or inhibit religion; (3) no excessive entanglements are allowed between religion and government. See Chapter 4 for a more complete discussion of the tests devised by the Supreme Court for religion cases.

12. 827 F.2nd at 692.

13. 551 N.Y. 2nd at 182.

13

Should Religiously Sponsored Schools (and/or Religious Educators and Counselors) Receive Financial Benefits from the State?

THE PROBLEM POSED

The debate regarding the quality of American public education rages. Defenders of the current educational system point to the increasingly difficult social environment in which the public schools must function. Especially in the inner city, broken families, poverty, gangs, teen pregnancies, violence, and drugs threaten the learning environment. Furthermore, defenders contend that the public schools, under the best of circumstances, have no easy task, for they are committed to the education of all students, including those with learning disabilities. Critics acknowledge these challenges yet disparage the public schools as increasingly concerned with perpetuating a social agenda and promoting esteem and equality at the expense of competency and achievement. The critics lament declining educational results, citing conclusions of studies such as the National Assessment of Education Progress (September 1990): "Large proportions, perhaps more than half, of our elementary, middle-, and high-school students are unable to demonstrate competency in challenging subject matter in English, mathematics, science, history and geography." Equally disturbing is the fact that "even fewer appear to be able to use their minds well."[1]

The contemporary debate over the quality of the public schools relates to an older public policy debate: Should government provide aid to private (church-related) schools or to parents or children who attend those schools? Originally, the case for providing financial aid to private religious schools

235

rested upon the advantages offered by their religious viewpoint and diversity; that is, advocates thought it would be in the public interest to have various religious perspectives presented as part of state-mandated education requirements. Lately, the ground for providing financial benefits to provide advantages to such schools has shifted. Thus, aid benefiting such schools has been increasingly championed because the schools are perceived to be making an important contribution to education. One widely believed, albeit controversial, perception is that children learn better in religiously affiliated elementary and secondary schools.[2] For this reason, the case for providing some kind of financial support has increasingly assumed a more secular rationale.[3]

Not surprisingly, the debate over adopting any program of direct or indirect aid benefiting religiously sponsored schools has persistently raised financial questions, inevitably argued in terms of fairness. For example, opponents of extending financial benefits to religiously affiliated schools (and/or families whose members attend those schools) ask why they should pay extra taxes (given the fact that their tax monies already support the public schools). On the other hand, families who choose to send their children to religiously related schools ask why they should be required to pay both public school taxes and full-fare private school tuition costs, especially because their children, by not attending public schools, will no longer be educated at public expense.

In addition to this financial dispute, a thorny and continuing constitutional controversy over this subject has also endured. Since 1947, the Supreme Court has adjudicated legal questions under the First Amendment's Establishment Clause and under the Fourteenth Amendment's Due Process Clause. It is important to recognize that never, during this time, has the Court viewed the question of religion and education *as a whole*. That is, the Supreme Court has never examined the question of whether any religious exercise could take place in the *public* schools in relation to the question of whether sectarian *private* schools could receive direct or indirect public financial benefits. For example, it is conceivable that the Court might have determined that the First Amendment's requirement regarding governmental neutrality in terms of religion required barring all religion from the public schools while permitting direct or indirect state funding for the whole gamut of church-sponsored schools for an amount not to exceed the value of the secular services rendered by the school.[4] Yet such an approach was not taken. Rather, the Supreme Court has chosen to examine the question of direct or indirect aid to religiously sponsored schools divorced from all other educational considerations and on a case-by-case basis.

The result has been chaotic. Although a few clear constitutional principles can be discerned from the Court's decisions, still the Supreme Court appears to have elevated a number of subtle and contradictory distinctions to the level of First Amendment edicts. Thus, the Court has ruled that it is constitutional under the First Amendment for the state to subsidize the cost of bus rides to and from sectarian schools as a welfare measure arising out of a public concern for children's safety, but bus rides to and from governmental, industrial, cultural, and scientific centers designed to enrich the secular studies of sectarian students were ruled to be in violation of the Establishment Clause.[5] Or, to take another example, the Court has held that the First Amendment does not prevent books approved by the public schools to be lent to children attending religiously sponsored schools, yet it has determined that similarly approved films, filmstrips, and maps cannot be lent to these same schools (leading Senator Moynihan to ask his famous question: what about atlases?).[6] Additionally, furnishing publicly funded sign-language interpreters for deaf students and providing publicly funded psychological, hearing, and speech diagnostic services when requested for students at religiously affiliated schools has been upheld; yet supplying publicly funded, on-site, remedial programs for blind, deaf, emotionally disturbed, and physically handicapped students has been invalidated.[7] Apparently, public funds can be expended so that deaf students can better understand what is taught by teachers hired by and teaching within religiously affiliated schools, yet public school counselors and teachers (with no religious agenda) cannot counsel or teach these same students within the same school. Almost as troubling as these inconsistencies was the fact that when the Court has spoken on public aid that directly or indirectly benefited nonpublic, religiously affiliated schools, it hardly ever did so in a united voice. Invariably, individual cases also offered up a confusing variety of opinions and rationales. In one particularly complex case involving a number of challenged public funding expenditures benefiting private religious-sponsored schools, a dizzying array of six different voting combinations and five different opinions were in evidence.[8] Often, when deciding these aid to religiously sponsored school cases, Supreme Court Justices not only differed in their application of constitutional principles; sometimes they even propounded different principles.[9] Furthermore, the appointment of different Judges to the Supreme Court over time has also exacerbated the instability of legal interpretation. Nor is it even evident that each Justice has adhered to a consistent Establishment Clause interpretation.[10]

Therefore, it should not be surprising that the Supreme Court adjudication in this area "comprises a body of opinion that concededly makes no sense."[11] For that reason (even more than is usually so), the cases discussed in this chapter should be viewed primarily as a means of raising important questions of law, religion, and public policy, and less as a definitive explanation of the law's underlying rationale in the area of governmental aid benefiting religiously affiliated schools.

EXAMPLE 1

Everson v. Board of Education of Ewing Township, 330 U.S. 1 (1947)

Facts: A New Jersey law permitted local school districts to make rules and contracts for the transportation of children "living remote from any schoolhouse" to and from all schools, except for-profit schools. The Board of Education of Ewing Township authorized reimbursement of public bus expenses to parents of children who rode them, which included transportation to and from a Catholic parochial school.

Result: The New Jersey ordinance serves a legitimate public safety purpose by facilitating the riding of public buses rather than having children face the hazards of walking or hitchhiking. The Establishment Clause, through the Fourteenth Amendment, does not invalidate extending essential public services to pupils.

Argument of the Case: Black, Justice. The New Jersey law serves a legitimate public purpose and therefore does not raise any Fourteenth Amendment due process problems. But does it violate the Establishment Clause by imposing taxes in support of religion? American history is reviewed, including Madison's "Remonstrance" and Jefferson's "Bill for Religious Liberty." Religious liberty partially dictates that no one shall be compelled to support any religion, although it is difficult to draw "the line between tax legislation which provides funds for the welfare of the general public and that which is designed to support institutions which teach religion." The Establishment Clause creates a wall between church and state and establishes governmental neutrality between believers and nonbelievers. Extending essential services to all pupils violates neither of these tenets (although it does go to the verge of permissible legal power).

Jackson dissents. The New Jersey law permits payment for transportation to or from public or parochial school but bars it from for-profit schools. Therefore, it is the character of the school, not the needs of the children, that informs the law. Furthermore, in Ewing Township the resolution explicitly funds only nonpublic schoolchildren who attend Catholic schools.[12] Therefore, both the law and the resolution discriminate in favor of Catholics, contrary to the Establishment Clause. Black's separationist majority opinion supports this view, even though it seems "utterly discordant with its conclusion" (making the most fitting precedent "that of Julia who, according to Byron's reports, whispering 'I will ne'er consent,'—consented").

Rutledge dissents.[13] The Establishment Clause is broadly phrased—forbidding any law *respecting* an establishment of religion—thereby intending "to create a complete and permanent separation of the spheres of religious activity and civil authority by comprehensively forbidding every form of public aid or support for religion." Madison's and Jefferson's efforts in Virginia on behalf of religious freedom are reviewed. Similarly, in this case, the state uses its taxing power for the sake of supporting religion and religious education.[14] It is not a public purpose—child safety—but the private purpose of religious training and teaching—that is furthered by this law.

Discussion

What a landmark case *Everson* is! Prior to its resolution, all that was constitutionally clear concerning the Establishment Clause (according to the Supreme Court) was that states had a right to pass compulsory education laws and parents had a right to send their children to private or parochial schools.[15] *Everson* decided some important, unsettled constitutional issues definitively, while opening a Pandora's box regarding others. Consider:

A. Before *Everson,* it was not obvious that the Establishment Clause restricted the states. Prior to the 1940s, in fact, it was persistently understood that the religion clauses limited only the national government, leaving the states free to fashion individual solutions regarding the proper relationship between government and religion. Although the Supreme Court had begun to "nationalize" the Bill of Rights in earnest by the time of *Everson,* still the Court's Establishment Clause approach was hardly predetermined by precedent.[16] Influential constitutional experts who generally accepted the idea that the Fourteenth Amendment may have made important Bill of Rights protections applicable to the states did not necessarily believe that the Establishment Clause was one of these rights.[17] *Everson* authoritatively declared that it was.

B. Prior to *Everson,* the Supreme Court had not authoritatively interpreted the Establishment Clause. Two different viewpoints had been widely championed. Advocates of an "accommodationist" interpretation emphasized religion's secular advantages for the American nation. They contended that the Establishment Clause prevented government from favoring any one religion or religious sect, but did not prohibit evenhanded government cooperation with, or indirect (or perhaps even direct) financial support of, all religions (an approach that they regarded as good). By contrast, partisans of a "separationist" viewpoint argued for a constitutional interpretation rooted in what they perceived to be the original relationship between the federal government and religion. They asserted that the Establishment Clause created a complete (or nearly complete) separation between church and state. According to this explanation, government could provide no direct or indirect financial support for religion, or even cooperate with religion. Justice Black's opinion (and indeed all the Justices' opinions) appeared to endorse a historical interpretation of the First Amendment that led to the separationist point of view, an extremely influential interpretation, given the Supreme Court's selective incorporation of the Establishment Clause against the states (point A).

C. Black's separationist opinion was written in extreme language, only some of which has prevailed. In this first, and arguably among the most influential Supreme Court interpretations of the Establishment Clause, Black wrote the following:

> The "Establishment of religion" clause of the First Amendment means at least this: Neither a state nor the Federal government can set up a church. Neither can pass laws which aid one religion, aid all religions, or prefer one religion over another. Neither can force nor influence a person to go to or to remain away from church against his will or force him to profess a belief or disbelief in any religion. No person can be punished for entertaining or professing religious beliefs or disbeliefs, for church attendance

or non-attendance. No tax in any amount, large or small, can be levied to support any religious activities or institutions, whatever they may be called, or whatever form they may adopt to teach or practice religion. Neither a state nor the Federal Government can, openly or secretly, participate in the affairs of any religious organizations or groups and *vice versa*. In the words of Jefferson, the clause against establishment of religion by law was intended to erect 'a wall of separation between church and state.'"[18]

Although its firm "wall of separation" language appeared to be clearly stated, Black's opinion still raised a number of controversial points. Did he really mean to suggest that religious practitioners could not participate in government? (For instance, would he have ruled participation by clergy in government unconstitutional?[19]) Another question: Could Black's belief that the Establishment Clause's wall of separation protected believers and nonbelievers alike from being compelled financially to support religion—later reformulated to reflect the principle that the government needed to be neutral between them—be reconciled with his opinion that the Free Exercise Clause prohibited excluding *any* believer or nonbeliever *"because of their faith, or lack of it,* from receiving the benefits of public welfare legislation"?[20] At first, there may appear to be a superficial consistency between Black's interpretation of the two religion clauses; in each case he would not treat believers differently from nonbelievers. Yet this consistency is superficial. Black's interpretation of the Establishment Clause suggests that *any* financial aid benefiting religion— even if it is nonpreferential—violates the Constitution, while his Free Exercise analysis invalidates any financial aid program adopted under the rubric of advancing public welfare that *excludes* religion. Although *Everson* is hardly ever regarded as a Free Exercise case,[21] it is important to realize that its interpretations of the Establishment Clause and the Free Exercise Clause are in tension—at least when contested legislation is enacted under a public welfare rationale.

D. Recognizing this tension is crucial and constitutes another, albeit more specific way, of stating Justice Jackson's objection to Black's majority decision—namely, that permitting reimbursement to parents sending their children to church-sponsored schools was at odds with Black's separationist analysis. This criticism is accurate, and it helps explain the basis for some of the conflicting opinions and decisions subsequently rendered by the Supreme Court in this area of law.

E. *Everson's* ruling, which upheld the state law, opened the door for subsequent accommodationist Supreme Court decisions. True, Black's public welfare rationale was hotly contested by *Everson's* dissenting Justices—they doubted that paying for bus transportation was really the same as providing police and fire protection.[22] Later, the public welfare rationale became transformed into the closely related child benefit theory, which held that public policy programs that directly assist children—irrespective of where they attended school—can be constitutionally upheld even if they indirectly benefit religious institutions. The prototype of this program was the federally subsidized hot lunch program, which traditionally was not confined to the public schools. Significantly, the child benefit theory would provide some support for several Supreme Court decisions indirectly providing benefit for religiously sponsored schools, as we will discuss later.[23] Direct aid to church-sponsored schools proved to be quite another matter and certainly found no support in Black's *Everson* opinion nor in the subsequent decisions of the Supreme Court.

EXAMPLE 2

Lemon **v.** *Kurtzman,* 403 U.S. 602 (1971)[24]

Facts: The 1968 Pennsylvania Nonpublic Elementary and Secondary Education Act declared that a crisis existed in the state's nonpublic schools due to rapidly rising costs. Intending to support financially the "purely secular educational objectives achieved through nonpublic education," the statute permitted the state's government to reimburse nonpublic schools for expenditures of teachers' salaries, textbooks, and instructional materials. Reimbursement was confined to secular subjects (mathematics, modern foreign language, physical science, and physical education); textbooks and instructional materials had to be approved by the state Superintendent of Public Instruction; and the reimbursement for teaching "any subject matter expressing religious teaching, or the morals or forms of worship of any sect" was prohibited. Nonpublic schools were required to keep an accounting of the separate cost of secular education services and were subject to government audit.

Result: The monitoring necessary to ensure secular uses of the direct payment to religiously related schools and to enforce the requirement that teachers be reimbursed only for teaching "nonideological" subjects, along with the potential for political divisiveness raised by such programs, creates an impermissible entanglement between church and state in violation of the Establishment Clause and the Fourteenth Amendment's Due Process Clause.

Argument of the Case: Burger, Chief Justice. Three tests define whether the Establishment Clause has been violated: (1) the statute must have a secular legislative purpose; (2) its principal or primary effect must be to neither advance nor inhibit religion; and (3) the state must not foster excessive entanglement with religion. The Pennsylvania program was designed to improve the quality of secular education, and procedures were implemented to ensure that the program would not advance religion. Even though church-sponsored schools "have a significant religious mission and . . . a substantial portion of their activities is religiously oriented," the Court accepts the legislature's judgment that secular and religious teachings can be separated. Still, the government monitoring required to oversee finances and ensure teacher impartiality is excessive, as is the potential for division along political lines created by such programs ("a threat to the normal political process"). Therefore, the excessive entanglement test is violated, and the program is unconstitutional.

Douglas concurs.[25] Church-related schools are religious. Everything taught in these schools is "part of the organic whole," which is to advance a particular religious understanding. Tax money cannot be constitutionally expended for this purpose.

Brennan concurs. The Establishment Clause requires that government may not employ a religious means to a secular end unless it is clearly shown that a nonreligious means will not suffice. Pennsylvania does not show that the public schools inadequately advance secular education; therefore, its program is unconstitutional.

White dissents. Sectarian schools serve both an educational and religious function. There was no proof offered in the lower court that the secular subjects were presented in a way that injected religion into the classroom. In light of this, the Court has created an objectionable "insoluble paradox" for the state and the parochial schools: "The State cannot finance secular instruction if it permits religion to be taught in the same classroom; but if it exacts a promise that religion not be so taught—a promise the school and its teachers are quite willing and on this record able to give—and enforces it, it is entangled in the 'no entanglement' aspect of the Court's Establishment Clause jurisprudence."

Discussion

Lemon is a particularly noteworthy case in several respects. First, its results proved to be particularly influential. *Lemon* established the general principle that the government cannot provide direct financial benefit to church-sponsored schools. In its wake, numerous schemes of direct financial aid were struck down. Some programs invalidated included grants for the upkeep and repair of nonpublic school facilities in low-income urban areas;[26] monies for state-mandated services, including the maintenance of health and attendance and the administration of teacher-prepared tests;[27] funds for providing on-site therapeutic, guidance, and remedial auxiliary services;[28] and expenditures funding the employment of public school instructors to teach secular subjects in church-sponsored schools.[29]

Although no generalization in this constitutional area is perfect, exceptions to the principle denying direct financial benefit to church-sponsored schools have been few and far between.[30] In those relatively few areas where any kind of aid was upheld, the court either assumed that the children and not the schools directly benefited or that the form of aid was "ideologically neutral" and could not be infused with religious meanings within the sectarian school. For example, it was on this latter basis that maps and charts (which could not be lent to the church-affiliated schools) were distinguished from books (which could) and bus rides to and from schools (including parochial schools) were upheld as a matter of public safety while bus field trips to museums or city hall were disallowed (partially because "it is the individual teacher who makes a field trip meaningful"[31]). Presumably, sectarian teachers can infuse a trip to city hall with religious meaning, but funding a student's trip to the school itself raises no such problem and therefore is constitutionally permissible.[32]

An additional reason that the *Lemon* case became important was the first-time announcement of its oft-cited three-tier test. That test superseded the wall of separation metaphor of *Everson* by seeming more precisely to define the permissible relationship between religion and government under the Establishment Clause. The three-tier test retained the staunchly separationist tone of the previous test. In that respect, Justice White was surely right; on its face, the test *appeared* to make it difficult to benefit religious institutions in any respect. The primary-effect rubric required religiously affiliated organizations to pledge or document that their publicly funded activities were not religious in character. Should the state legislature (or the courts) determine that the organization's pledge was insufficient (or should the religiously affiliated organization anticipate this might happen), documentation or state inspection was required, which immediately, or at least frequently, ran afoul of the excessive entanglement prong of the test.

Yet while the *Lemon* test appeared precise (and staunchly separationist), it was not. Interpretation of its primary-effect prong (which asked if the primary effect of the contested legislation was secular or sectarian) seemed to lie primarily in the eye of each judge. Furthermore, its excessive entanglement prong was equally confusing. As was noted, excessive entanglement had two parts. Its most obvious meaning prohibited excessive governmental regulation of church-affiliated schools (whatever that meant in light of the fact that they were already "entangled" by state compulsory education laws, state teacher certification requirements, state graduation requirements, and so on). The second part of the excessive entanglement prong—that the First Amendment sought to forestall entangling political divisions along religious lines—also proved troubling for a number of reasons, not the least of which was that such an interpretation could, in principle, eliminate all programs that could benefit religion while creating political controversy. (Not surprisingly, this aspect of the excessive entanglement test proved short-lived.[33]) Thus, although the *Lemon* test was generally accepted by the Court and relied upon widely in later Establishment Clause cases, the test was, not surprisingly, subject to widely varying judicial interpretations.[34] It was also the object of intense judicial criticism.[35] Only some twenty years after its pronouncement did its influence seem to be waning.[36]

That the *Lemon* test did not preclude all forms of financial aid to religiously oriented educational organizations was evident from the first day it was announced. In the companion case of *Tilton* v. *Richardson,* the Supreme Court applied the *Lemon* test and upheld most elements of federal aid to church-affiliated *colleges.*[37] And five years later, the Court reaffirmed its Establishment Clause interpretation.

EXAMPLE 3

Roemer v. *Board of Public Works of Maryland,* 426 U.S. 736 (1976)

Facts: A Maryland statute provided for annual noncategorical grants to private colleges, including religiously affiliated institutions, subject only to the restriction that the funds not be used for sectarian purposes.

Result: The First Amendment's Establishment Clause, applied to the states, does not bar Maryland from extending financial aid to religious institutions of higher education as long as the aid supports secular purposes and it is not extended exclusively to religiously affiliated institutions.

Argument of the Case: Blackmun, Justice.[38] When the state takes action that has an impact on religion (which is unavoidable), it must be neutral toward religion, neither advancing nor impeding it. The *Lemon* test is used (and met). The secular purpose of aiding private institutions of higher education is not challenged. The primary-effect rubric is also not violated, because the religiously affiliated schools are not pervasively sectarian.[39] They perform an important secular function. This is demonstrated by the following: they exhibit a high degree of autonomy, chapel is not required, academic freedom exists, hiring decisions are not made on a religious basis, and students are not admitted according to religious belief. Finally, excessive entanglement is not violated. Given the important secular function of these schools, on-site inspections are not required. A written affidavit suffices. Nor is there evidence of excessive entanglement passing as destructive political divisiveness; in colleges (unlike elementary and secondary schools), this danger is lessened by the fact their student body is not local "but diverse and widely dispersed."

White concurs.[40] It is sufficient that the purpose of the contested legislation and its primary effect are secular. The *Lemon* test, and especially its excessive entanglement rubric, is misguided.

Brennan dissents.[41] The fact that the colleges in question are church affiliated or church related is crucial. The funding provides general subsidies, impermissibly advancing religion and involving the state with religion. Stewart dissents. This case differs from *Tilton* v. *Richardson* because at these colleges theology courses are required and are taught chiefly by clerics of the affiliated church.

Stevens dissents. State funding of this kind may encourage religious schools to compromise their mission; this can be the price of the "disease of entanglement."

Discussion

Here is another confined area where the law of church and state has become rather clearly defined (although by narrow Supreme Court majorities). Today, it is accepted that the government can provide neutral forms of financial benefit for private, religiously affiliated colleges as part of a more generalized program of aid for all private (nontheological) institutions of higher education.

To some critics, the Supreme Court's decision to permit governmental funding of religiously affiliated higher education, while denying it to religiously sponsored elementary and secondary schools, reflected an inconsistency of principle, or at the very least a theoretical flabbiness in the formulation or application of the *Lemon* test. At the heart of the Court's distinction was the contention that these two kinds of schools and their students were simply different. College students were more mature and less impressionable than their younger counterparts. Also, the elementary and secondary schools were more closely tied, financially and administratively, to their religious benefactors than were the colleges. Additionally, the elementary and secondary schools' curricula were much more pervaded by a specifically religious point of view. According to the Court, the far more secular character of religiously affiliated colleges permitted the government in these instances to identify and subsidize secular functions within this school setting.

This criterion for distinguishing religiously sponsored elementary and secondary schools from their higher education counterparts, although accepted by a bare Court majority, was still rejected by two different groups of Justices. On the one hand, accommodationist justices such as Rehnquist and White did not focus upon the respective differences among the schools but rather upon the important secular educational purpose that each of these kinds of schools advanced. For them, the Establishment Clause was not breached if religion or religiously affiliated institutions incidently benefited from broad-based governmental programs. On the other hand, separationist judges such as Brennan and Marshall adopted precisely the opposite approach. Noting that these colleges were religiously affiliated, they objected to the expenditure of tax money that in any way advanced religion at the elementary, secondary, or college level.[42] At the heart of the debate between accommodationist and separationist judges over governmental funding of higher education was a recurring core disagreement: namely, to what extent was it constitutionally permissible to use tax money to benefit religion?

This same dispute endured in other kinds of aid-to-education cases. At least the results (if not the arguments) of the previous two kinds of cases were clear. Direct aid to elementary and secondary sectarian schools was largely out; aid to religiously sponsored colleges was largely in. Even more controversial, and far more constitutionally confusing, were programs that attempted to directly aid students and parents who chose to send their children to private, religiously affiliated schools. These programs lingered in the constitutional shadow of *Everson,* and subsequent Court decisions seemed unable to illuminate a constitutional principle for dealing with them. Let us see how they failed.

EXAMPLE 4

Mueller v. *Allen,* 463 U.S. 398 (1983)

Facts: Minnesota allows taxpayers, when calculating their state income taxes, to deduct actual expenses spent for tuition, nonreligious textbooks, and transportation up to $500 or $700 (depending upon the grade attended).

Result: The Minnesota law does not violate the Establishment Clause of the First Amendment as applied to Minnesota.

Argument of the Case: Rehnquist, Justice. The *Lemon* test, while "no more than a helpful signpost," is nonetheless applied. The state's decision to defray the cost of educational expenses incurred by parents constitutes a legitimate secular purpose. Neither does the program have the primary effect of advancing religion. This is because the educational expense deduction is one among many tax deductions and is available to all parents whose children attend any school (including nonsectarian private schools and public schools). Furthermore, the assistance is channeled through parents, minimizing governmental support of religion. Excessive governmental–religious entanglement is not an issue. Although state officials have to determine which textbooks do not qualify for deductions, this process does not differ from previously approved state actions that determined which secular books could be lent to religiously sponsored schools.

Marshall dissents.[43] The First Amendment prohibits government from subsidizing religion, either directly or indirectly. Although the statute serves a legitimate purpose ("promoting pluralism and diversity among the State's public and nonpublic schools"), it fails the *Lemon* test by impermissibly advancing religion. It does not matter that all parents are eligible for the tax deduction; parents of parochial school children (and hence parochial schools) benefit disproportionately. Nor is the form of benefit germane; tax deductions (which turn upon the amount expended) are not superior to predetermined tax credits (previously ruled unconstitutional). Finally, deductions for books are impermissible because (unlike previous cases) the books are not pre-approved by the State and can be used in religious education.

Discussion

For well over a decade, the child-benefit theory has provided the most promising legal avenue available for states that, for political, economic, or educational reasons, wished to provide financial relief to parents who paid tuition to religiously affiliated schools. Additionally, this was the theory that led the Bush Administration to advocate a voucher plan benefiting church-related schools. Yet the constitutionality of this approach was not well established. Precedents cut both ways. And the Justices themselves were sharply divided regarding their fundamental understanding and application of the Establishment Clause.

In fact, by the time *Mueller* was decided, the most obvious precedents seemed to argue against the Minnesota law being upheld. True, the child-benefit theory had been employed to explain Establishment Clause decisions like those permitting reimbursing parents for the cost of transportation to parochial schools (*Everson* v. *Board of Education,* above) and the well-established practice of permitting the lending of secularly approved textbooks to students attending religiously affiliated schools.[44] Yet the most formidable precedent cut the other way. In *Committee for Public Education* v. *Nyquist,*[45] the Court had invalidated tax credits to parents who sent their children to church-sponsored (and other nonpublic) schools. In *Nyquist,* the New York scheme was sharply progressive, strongly benefiting poorer parents who chose to pay nonpublic school tuition.[46] Thus, as the taxpayer's income rose, the amount that could be subtracted from state income taxes diminished (those who had over $25,000 in gross income could claim no benefit). Significantly, it was the taxpayer's income, not the amount of money expended, that determined the level of financial benefit awarded. This provision was not upheld because, despite its secular purpose of increasing educational choice for poorer citizens, religion still was impermissibly advanced. That taxpayers had been required to provide financial support for religiously affiliated schools outweighed the fact that the benefit was indirect; in the words of Justice Powell (who wrote the Court's opinion), "the fact that aid is distributed to parents rather than to the schools is only one among many factors to be considered."[47]

The Minnesota plan upheld in *Mueller* differed from the New York plan invalidated in *Nyquist* in two ways. First, all families received tax benefits, not only those who sent their children to nonpublic schools. Second, they received a tax deduction based upon the money they had expended, as opposed to a tax credit based upon their income. Like medical expenses and charitable deductions, these tax deductions were part of the legislature's overall effort to make the tax burden fairer.

Despite these differences, one could still sympathize with the dissenting Justices who contended that these differences were inconsequential. Marshall's dissenting opinion argued rather persuasively that the differences between the invalidated New York program and the sustained Minnesota program were far more cosmetic than real. For instance, he noted that while the Minnesota plan did permit parents of public school children to benefit from the tax deduction, there was less here than met the eye, for the public schools in Minnesota were free (as was the use of their books). Furthermore, of the children attending the nonpublic schools charging tuition, over 95% were sectarian. Marshall's conclusion was that, as in *Nyquist,* religion and religiously affiliated schools were the primary beneficiaries of the Minnesota plan.

Similarly, Marshall was properly skeptical of the distinction between tax credits and tax deductions. It was "a distinction without a difference."[48] The purpose of the Minnesota deduction was also to produce a tax benefit in exchange for encouraging an activity. In this way, the cost of nonpublic (that is, overwhelmingly sectarian) education was defrayed by a tax deduction, thus encouraging the enrollment in these schools. Furthermore, from the perspective of the religiously affiliated schools (which were indirectly benefited by both the New York and Minnesota legislative programs), there simply existed no meaningful difference between the two programs.

Presuming Marshall's criticisms were correct (that there were no meaningful differences between the program invalidated in *Nyquist* and upheld in *Mueller*), then what can be fairly concluded, other than the fact that the Supreme Court is quite capable of rendering inconsistent decisions?[49] Once again, we would emphasize that the fundamental difference between the two decisions relates to the differing ways that the Supreme Court Justices interpreted the meaning of the Establishment Clause. In *Nyquist* (June 1973), a six-person majority of the Supreme Court believed that the Establishment Clause precluded indirect, child-benefit aid if it provided significant benefit to religiously affiliated schools. Ten years later, a bare majority of the Court simply came to a different conclusion about what the Establishment Clause means. Even for Justice Rehnquist,[50] who wrote the majority opinion in *Mueller* but dissented in *Nyquist* (regarding the tax credit question), the distinctions between the two programs stressed in *Mueller* were described as consequential but ultimately could not have been of constitutional importance.

It was only because the Supreme Court sought to emphasize precedent and consistency in the law that the distinctions were presented by Rehnquist as important. One fact remained clear. Once again, the child-benefit theory had yielded no clear understanding regarding the boundaries and meaning of the First Amendment's Establishment Clause. It seemed only to have raised legal technicalities to the level of constitutional mandate.

Another related way that religious education became the center of political and legal controversy was not by the usual means of contested aid that directly or indirectly benefited religiously sponsored schools, but by generalized governmental programs that benefited religious educational agencies, organizations, and teachings. This situation has occurred when the objectives of governmental programs coincided with certain religious organizations' approaches to education and when those organizations received federal funding as part of a broad-based policy program—precisely what happened in the last case we will examine in this chapter.

EXAMPLE 5

Bowen, Secretary of Health and Human Services v. *Kendrick,* 487 U.S. 589 (1988)

Facts: The Adolescent Family Life Act (AFLA) authorized federal grants to public or nonprofit organizations or agencies (including those that were charitable and/or religiously affiliated) for services or research in the area of premarital adolescent sexual relations and pregnancy. As a condition of receiving the grant, the grantee was required to furnish certain types of services, including counseling and education regarding adolescent premarital sexual relations ("prevention services") and specific help for pregnant adolescents ("care services"). In addition, the grantee was prohibited from using the funds for specific purposes, including family planning and promoting abortion.

Result: Even though AFLA confers some benefit upon religiously affiliated organizations and their teachings, still the Establishment Clause was not violated.[51]

Argument of the Case: Rehnquist, Chief Justice. The *Lemon* test should be employed to determine if the act is facially unconstitutional under the Establishment Clause. It is not violated. The act has a clear secular purpose. It is motivated primarily, if not entirely, by the goal of mitigating the social and economic problems caused by teenage sexuality, pregnancy, and parenthood. Furthermore, the challenged act does not have the primary effect of advancing religion. A variety of recipients, "including state and local health agencies, private hospitals, community health associations, privately operated health care centers, and community and charitable organizations," have received grants. The extent to which religious organizations have been funded reflects, at most, Congress's judgment that they can help solve the problems that the act addresses. (Thus, Congress "found 'prevention of adolescent sexual activity and adolescent pregnancy depends primarily upon developing strong family values and close family ties'" and therefore has sensibly recognized "that religious organizations can influence values and can have some influence on family life....") There is no requirement that the grantee be religious; neither the services nor the approach provided under the act is inherently religious. Nor does the fact that the religious organizations' religious teachings coincide with the act's approach to teenage sexuality mean that the state advances religion. Finally, the excessive entanglement test is not breached. Although the grants require government monitoring, "there is no reason to assume that the religious organizations which may receive grants are 'pervasively sectarian' in the same sense as the Court has held parochial schools to be." Possible individual violations should be reviewed and individual remedies fashioned (such as withdrawing approval) by the district court (to which the case is remanded), for applications that violate the act and the Establishment Clause cannot be tolerated.

O'Connor concurs. The "partnership between governmental and religious institutions contemplated by the AFLA need not result in constitutional violations...." Still, *any* use of public monies that promotes religious doctrines violates the Establishment Clause, and *extensive* violations—should they be proven—would be relevant in helping shape appropriate remedies.

Kennedy concurs.[52] Even if certain organizations are to be "pervasively sectarian," government neutrality (awarding grants to religious and nonreligious applicants alike) exists. Therefore, the real question is how the religious organization spends the grant.

Blackmun dissents.[53] Congress enacted legislation that has facilitated and encouraged religious instruction. Thus, the law has the primary effect of impermissibly advancing religion because it requires teaching and counseling "on matters inseparable from religious dogma." Excessive entanglement is also violated; the religious organizations benefited are as sectarian as church-sponsored schools, and like them a high level of monitoring is required, raising entanglement concerns.

Discussion

This complex case appropriately ends our chapter. As in the first case we examined (*Everson*), once again we find the Supreme Court quite divided regarding the meaning and application of the Establishment Clause. At stake here was a piece of social welfare legislation with rather unobjectionable ends (mitigating the effects of teenage pregnancy) through a somewhat more controversial means (which excluded family planning or abortion counseling). There were at least two religiously controversial parts of the program. First, the conservative political approach encompassed in the Adolescent Family Life Act paralleled the approach toward teenage sexuality (that is, abstinence) advocated by a number of religious sects, most notably the Roman Catholic Church. An additional concern was that some of the organizations that were awarded federal grants because they performed specified education and counseling duties were religious agencies. Under such circumstances, could the federal government ensure (through minimal monitoring) that religion was not being taught at these agencies? This question became even more important because evidence of some abuses had been entered into the record at the district court level.

These questions can be answered at two interrelated levels: constitutional principle and legal precedent. From the perspective of constitutional principle, the most accommodationist approach was that of Kennedy and Scalia. For them, it did not matter if the benefited organization was religious or nonreligious. It was sufficient that the First Amendment required neutrality between government and religion (and nonreligion) and that the federal government funded a wide variety of nonprofit organizations. So the affiliation of the organization receiving the funding made no difference to Kennedy; all that mattered was its teaching (that is, ensuring that it was not essentially religious). The reasonably accommodationist Rehnquist opinion expressed concern about both the teaching and the character of the religious organizations receiving grants but assumed that these organizations were not "pervasively sectarian" (while instructing the district court to review and provide remedy for individual instances where religion was taught in violation of the act and the Constitution). By contrast, the four dissenters propounded a far more separationist interpretation of the Establishment Clause. The fact that some recipient organizations were sectarian and the fact that some appeared to have taught religion were sufficient to prove that the Establishment Clause had been violated. At the heart of the dissenters' argument was an understanding of the Establishment Clause formulated in staunchly separationist terms that precluded significant cooperation between government and religion. We would note that this question of the Establishment Clause's true meaning and limits was precisely the matter that had been addressed (and obviously not settled) in *Everson* more than forty years earlier.

The dissenters had good legal weapons when they resorted to legal precedents in support of their position. Essentially, their argument began with the observation that the religiously affiliated organizations and agencies that had received governmental grants to dispense educational and counseling services were, by definition, religious and therefore akin to religiously sponsored schools. Thus, Blackmun referred to the example of St. Ann's, a grant recipient that was a home for unmarried pregnant teenagers operated by the Order of Daughters of Charity, owned by the Archdiocese of Washington, D.C. Blackmun contended that this agency at one time had selected teaching materials that were emphatically religious and that had not been already selected and approved for use in secular contexts.[54] Of course, such teaching materials by themselves were objectionable, but Blackmun believed that religiously affiliated organizations also were inherently infused with religion, and therefore should be excluded for funding by the Establishment Clause.

Previously, when the Supreme Court had formulated the law regarding aid to religiously related elementary and secondary schools, it had declared as much. As we have already observed in our discussion of the *Lemon* case, the Court had persistently disallowed direct aid to these schools. The Court had found them to be "pervasively sectarian" institutions and had held that aid to them impermissibly had the primary effect of advancing religion. According to Blackmun, the religiously associated funded agencies resembled sectarian elementary and secondary schools. They, too, had institutional ties to religious denominations, obeyed their requirements, and followed (and did not contradict) their doctrines. They acted, or in some cases were inspired by, religious dogma. Under similar circumstances, sectarian teachers and counselors could not be paid. The similarity to sectarian schools furnished Blackmun with an analogy founded in precedent that provided another argument for overturning the contested statute.

How did the Court's majority deal with the sectarian school precedents? It did so by distinguishing the religiously affiliated agencies and organizations funded under AFLA from parochial schools. According to Rehnquist, these entities were not really like sectarian elementary and secondary schools at all. Rather, they far more closely resembled the religiously affiliated liberal arts colleges whose funding had been previously sustained by the Court. Therefore, asserted the Court, they were not "pervasively sectarian." In those scattered instances where they might be, Rehnquist ordered the district court on remand to formulate remedies (which no doubt would have disallowed funding).

The Court did not furnish much explanation for its reliance upon the higher education precedents, and the dissenters were not much impressed. They worried that teaching had great potential to breach the Establishment Clause. Constitutionally, it was an inherently "dangerous" activity, far more likely to be infused with religion than were other aspects of social welfare services. Thus, Blackmun observed that the "risk of advancing religion is much greater when the religious organization is directly engaged in pedagogy, with the express intent of shaping belief and changing behavior, than where it is neutrally dispensing medication, food, or shelter."[55] Although the Supreme Court had not raised a similar objection to public funding in the higher education cases, the dissenters also noted that the education in those cases was wholly secular. The dissenters worried that the education funded in *Bowen* was both secular and sectarian. They thought that religion was at the core of the subsidized activity, affecting the way the service was dispensed. Precisely for that reason, "on a continuum of 'sectarianism' running from parochial schools at one end to the colleges funded by the statutes upheld in ... *Roemer* at the other, the AFLA grantees described by the District Court clearly are much closer to the former than the latter."[56]

Blackmun was probably right, that from the perspective of precedent, the contested act should have been ruled unconstitutional (probably on its face and certainly as it applied to certain religiously affiliated agencies and organizations). Whether he was "right" from the perspective of the Constitution and the Establishment Clause posed another, more difficult question. Today, in the area of education there are some practical issues that have been more or less settled by the Supreme Court's interpretation of the Establishment Clause. Yet regarding broad public policy areas, as with the child-benefit theory, the application of Establishment Clause principles remains conflicting and uncertain.

SUMMARY

Since 1947 and the *Everson* case, there has been little doubt that the Establishment Clause applies to the states. Thus, whatever is meant by the clause, its restrictions apply not only against the federal government but also against the states. Furthermore, whatever programs and policies the Constitution permits or prohibits against the federal government it also permits or prohibits against the states.

In one area, where educational organizations and institutions have been defined as essentially sectarian, a separationist interpretation of the Establishment Clause has prevailed. The Supreme Court has repeatedly held in this area that the Establishment Clause disallows almost all forms of direct financial aid.

In other areas, however, the Supreme Court has interpreted or applied the Establishment Clause in a more accommodationist fashion (which is not to say that an accommodationist understanding has always prevailed). This has been particularly true where public policy has been justified by a secular rationale and where its implementation only incidentally benefits religion and religiously affiliated institutions. This, too, is the logic behind broad-based public safety and child-benefit rationales that the Court has, from time to time, upheld. Additionally, in the realm of certain forms of aid to religiously affiliated colleges, an accommodationist disposition has prevailed. Thus, the Supreme Court has emphasized these colleges' secular function and relative independence.

In areas where accommodation between government and religion has been upheld, the law has often appeared unstable. Cases have been decided by the barest of majorities, and the law has sometimes seemed outright contradictory (especially in cases involving the child-benefit rationale). Even the tests that usually have been employed to interpret the Establishment Clause (usually the *Lemon* test but less frequently the idea of neutrality—normally applied to governmental aid distributed among religious and nonreligious institutions and individuals[57]) have been applied differently. And, as we noted earlier, the *Lemon* test no longer enjoys the unanimous consent of all Justices. Evidently, in the area of taxes and governmental funding indirectly benefiting religiously affiliated organizations, further constitutional surprises await.

NOTES

1. Cited in Chester Finn, Jr., *We Must Take Charge: Our Schools and Our Future* (New York: Free Press, 1991), p. 5.

2. This remains a controversial claim in some quarters. To the extent it is believed, the superior academic results of private, church-affiliated schools are generally explained by church related schools' higher level of discipline and the greater interest of parents and students in education. Defenders of the public schools point out that they are required to deal with a greater variety of students and more problem students. The counterargument is provided by the researchers of one study:

Consider the possibility that inner-city parochial schools which enrolled relatively [educationally] advantaged students might be providing a desirable public service by enhancing the achievement of capable students whose achievement otherwise might suffer if they were placed in the dysfunctional educational environment typical of inner-city public schools or by making it possible for supportive families unwilling to send their children to public schools to continue living in or near the inner city.

The quotation is from the study of Levine, Oxman, Lachowicz, and Tangeman, "The Home Environment of Students in a Highly Praised Inner-City School, and a Nearby Public School" cited in Peter Schotten, "The Establishment Clause and Excessive Governmental–Religious En-

tanglement: The Constitutional Status of Aid to Nonpublic Elementary and Secondary Schools," *Wake Forest Law Review,* vol. 15, no. 2 (April 1979), p. 243.

3. Some evidence for this can be seen in the large percentage of non-Catholic students—many of them minority students—who over the past two decades have attended parochial schools in inner cities such as Chicago.

4. One of the influential interpretations of the Establishment Clause is that it requires governmental neutrality (See Chapter 4). The last part of the formulation was proposed by Jesse Choper in an influential law review article, "The Establishment Clause and Aid to Parochial Schools," *California Law Review* 56 (1968), pp. 260, 265–66.

5. Cf. *Everson* v. *Board of Education,* 330 U.S. 1 (1947), to *Wolman* v. *Walter,* 433 U.S. 229 (1977).

6. Cf. *U.S.* v. *Allen,* 392 U.S. 236 (1968), and *Wolman* v. *Walter,* 433 U.S. 229 (1977).

7. This distinction follows from *Wolman* v. *Walter,* 433 U.S. 229 (1977). Diagnostic services were debatably distinguished from therapeutic services partially on the ground that public professionals performing the former services would have "only limited contact with the child, and that contact involve[d] chiefly the use of objective and

professional testing methods to detect students in need of treatment." *Allen* at 244. However, in 1993 the Supreme Court held that a publicly employed sign language interpreter could be provided to a deaf student enrolled in a sectarian school, arguing that the Individuals with Disabilities Act under which the service would be provided was a general governmental program that neutrally distributed benefits to all qualifying children, so the Establishment Clause was not violated. See *Zobrest* v. *Catalina Foothills School District*, ___ U.S. ___ (1993).

8. *Zobrest v. Catalina Foothills School District*, __ U.S. __(1993).

9. See our discussion in Chapter 4. Also, it might be noted that while these cases have constantly been considered to raise Establishment Clause concerns, there have been hints that denying aid to students who choose to attend religiously affiliated schools may raise Free Exercise Clause issues. (Hence Justice Rehnquist in *Thomas* v. *Review Board*, 450 U.S. 707, 724 n. 2 [1981], comments that "[i]t might be argued that a State may not deny reimbursement to students who choose for religious reasons to attend parochial schools.") Also note our discussion of *Everson* below.

10. For example, see Schotten, pp. 213, 247.

11. This 1978 opinion was offered by Antonin Scalia. It is quoted in Schotten, p. 210.

12. But note Black's comment: "Although a township resolution authorized reimbursement only for parents of public and Catholic school pupils, appellant does not allege, nor is there anything in the record which would offer the slightest support to an allegation, that there were any children in the township who attended or would have attended, but for want of transportation, any but public or Catholic Schools." Schotten, p. 4, n. 2.

13. Justices Frankfurter, Burton, and Jackson join this opinion.

14. On Rutledge's (and Black's) misuse of history regarding James Madison's effort in Virginia, see Jonathan Van Patten, "Standing in the Need of Prayer? The Supreme Court on James Madison and Religious Liberty," *Benchmark* III, nos. 1 & 2 (Jan.-Apr., 1987), pp. 59–69; and Edward Corwin, "The Supreme Court as National School Board," *Law and Contemporary Problems* 14 (Winter 1949), pp. 9–16.

15. *Pierce* v. *Society of the Sisters of the Holy Names of Jesus and Mary*, 268 U.S. 510 (1925).

16. Although *Cantwell* v. *Connecticut*, 310 U.S. 296 (1940) at 303, is often thought to have decided the matter, the issue was not firmly settled until *Everson*.

17. Thus, Corwin held in "The Supreme Court as National School Board" (p. 14) that "the principal importance of the [first] amendment lay in the separation which it effected between the respective jurisdictions of state and nation regarding religion, rather than in its bearing on the question of the separation of church and state" and further observed that "the Fourteenth Amendment does not authorize the Court to substitute the word 'state' for 'Congress' in the ban imposed by the First Amendment on laws 'respecting an establishment of religion.' *So far as the Fourteenth Amendment is concerned, states are entirely free to establish religions, provided they do not deprive anyone of religious liberty.* It is only *liberty* that the Fourteenth Amendment protects" (p. 19). According to Corwin, both the Establishment Clause of the First Amendment and the Fourteenth Amendment's guarantee of liberty had been illegitimately expanded by the Court.

18. Corwin, pp. 15–16.

19. For a discussion of this point, see Chapter 5, p. 88.

20. *Everson*, at 16. For a discussion of the Founders' view of religion (which has important applications to Black's belief that the secular state needs to be neutral between religion and nonreligion), see our discussion in Chapter 2.

21. Although contrary to the reigning perception, it may well be that the case was decided on these grounds.

22. Jackson emphasized the alleged discriminatory aspect of the program (which excluded nonreligious private school students and, presumably, non-Catholic religiously affiliated school children) while

Rutledge pointed to the fact that the private welfare of Catholic schools and not the public welfare was advanced by the contested governmental actions. *Everson,* at 25–26, 50–51. Another problem with Black's analogy is that there is one police and fire department available to all citizens much in the way that there is one public school system available free to all citizens. Interpreted this way, Black's analogy fails to persuade.

23. For example, in *Board of Education* v. *Allen,* 392 U.S. 236 (1968), and *Wheeler* v. *Baretta,* 417 U.S. 402 (1974). *Bowen* v. *Kendrick,* 108 S. Ct. 2562 (1988), is discussed later.

24. This case was decided with the companion Rhode Island case of *DiCenso* v. *Early.*

25. This opinion was joined by Justice Black.

26. *Sloan* v. *Lemon,* 413 U.S. 825 (1973); *Committee for Public Education & Religious Liberty* v. *Nyquist,* 413 U.S. 756 (1973).

27. *Levitt* v. *Committee for Public Education,* 413 U.S. 472 (1973).

28. *Meek* v. *Pittenger,* 421 U.S. 349 (1975).

29. *Grand Rapids School District* v. *Ball,* 473 U.S. 373 (1985); *Aguilar* v. *Felton,* 473 U.S. 402 (1985).

30. One limited exception: support for the using and scoring of state-mandated standardized tests in *Wolman* v. *Walter,* 433 U.S. 229 (1977).

31. *Wolman* v. *Walter,* 433 U.S. 229 at 253 (1977).

32. These sorts of metaphysical distinctions have delighted critics of the Supreme Court's jurisprudence; note Justice Rehnquist's comments regarding the incoherence of the Court's jurisprudence in his dissenting opinion in *Wallace* v. *Jaffree,* 472 U.S. 38 at 110–11:

The results from our school services cases show the difficulty we have encountered in making the Lemon test yield principled results.

For example, a State may lend to parochial school children geography textbooks that contain maps of the United States, but the State may not lend maps of the United States for use in geography class. A State may lend textbooks on American colonial history, but it may not lend a film of George Washington, or a film projector to show it in history class. A State may lend classroom workbooks, but may not lend workbooks in which the parochial school children write, thus rendering them nonreusable. A State may pay for bus transportation to religious schools but may not pay for bus transportation from the parochial school to the public zoo or natural history museum for a field trip. A State may pay for diagnostic services conducted in the parochial school but therapeutic services must be given in a different building; speech and hearing 'services' conducted by the State inside the sectarian school are forbidden... but the State may conduct speech and hearing diagnostic testing inside the sectarian school.... Exceptional parochial school students may receive counseling, but it must take place outside of a parochial school, such as in a trailer parked down the street.... A State may give cash to a parochial school to pay for the administration of State-written tests on secular subjects. Religious instruction may not be given in public school, but the public school may release students during the day for religion classes elsewhere, and may enforce attendance at those classes with its truancy laws.

33. Regarding criticisms of this part of the excessive entanglement test, see Schotten, pp. 221–28.

34. For instance, cf. the opinion of Justice Powell and Chief Justice Burger (dissenting) regarding the secular effect section of the *Lemon* test in *Committee for Public Education & Religious Liberty* v. *Nyquist,* 413 U.S. 756 (1973) at 780–90 and 804–806.

35. For instance, see Justice Rehnquist's dissenting opinion in *Wallace* v. *Jaffree,* 472 U.S. 38 (1985) at 110–12.

36. Although the test had been ignored in some Establishment Clause cases (for example, *Marsh* v. *Chambers,* 463 U.S. 783 [1983]), its absence was conspicuous in the Court's opinion in the school graduation prayer case *Lee* v. *Weisman,* 112 S.C. 2649 (1992). Particularly telling was Justice Scalia's concurring opinion in the 1993 case, *Lamb's Chapel* v. *Center Mociches Union Free School District,* where he noted that five of the nine Supreme Court Justices had abandoned the *Lemon* test and chided the majority for relying upon it: "[l]ike some ghoul in a late-night horror

movie that repeatedly sits up in its grave and shuffles abroad, after being repeatedly killed and buried, *Lemon* stalks our Establishment Clause jurisprudence once again, frightening the little children and school attorneys...."

37. 403 U.S. 672 (1971).

38. Blackmun's judgment for the Court was joined by Chief Justice Burger and Justice Powell.

39. In this sense they differed from religiously affiliated elementary and secondary schools.

40. This opinion is joined by Justice Rehnquist.

41. Justice Marshall joins this opinion.

42. In this regard, note Justice Douglas's mostly applicable comment in his dissenting opinion in *Tilton v. Richardson*: "The facilities financed by taxpayers' funds are not to be used for 'sectarian' purposes.... Money not spent for one purpose becomes available for other purposes. Thus the fact that there are no religious observances in federally financed facilities is not controlling because required religious observances will take place in other buildings." 403 U.S. 672 at 693.

43. Justices Brennan, Blackmun, and Stevens join in this opinion.

44. The practice had been upheld in *Board of Education* v. *Allen,* 392 U.S. 236 (1968); *Meek* v. *Pittenger,* 421 U.S. 349 (1975); and *Wolman* v. *Walter,* 433 U.S. 229 (1977).

45. 413 U.S. 756 (1973).

46. In fact, the progressive nature of the plan was even more progressive than the discussion indicates. The poorest parents could take advantage of a limited plan providing tuition reimbursements. The tax-credit provision of the law was available for parents who did not qualify for this program.

47. *Committee for Public Education* v. *Nyquist* at 781.

48. *Mueller* v. *Allen*, at 411.

49. Evidently, Justice Powell held a contrary opinion since he (and he alone) was a member of both the *Nyquist* and *Mueller* majorities. Significantly, Powell held the key to the Court's five-person majority. Rehnquist, Burger, and White had all previously dissented in *Nyquist*. A pro-accommodationist vote was also cast by Justice O'Connor, who replaced Justice Stewart, who had voted against the New York tax credit plan in *Nyquist*. One might speculate that *Nyquist* was distinguished, and not overruled, as the price of obtaining Powell's vote.

50. As well as for Chief Justice Burger and Justice White.

51. Despite the fact that the act was ruled constitutional, still the Court was concerned with possible individual violations. Therefore, it instructed the district court (which it had reversed) to examine the administration of the act and fashion appropriate remedies for violations consistent with the act and the Establishment Clause. Specifically, the Court was troubled that there might be individual instances where the teaching of religion was funded by taxpayer money.

52. Justice Scalia joins this opinion.

53. The dissent is joined by Justices Brennan, Marshall, and Stevens.

54. *Bowen* v. *Kendrick* at 635, n. 7.

55. *Bowen* v. *Kendrick* at 641.

56. *Bowen* v. *Kendrick* at 623.

57. Neutrality has often, but not always, accompanied the *Lemon* test; in these instances it has acted as a kind of constitutional synonym for that test. Regarding neutrality, the early accommodationist thesis that neutrality represented a pro-religion stance that allowed government to favor religion and barred it only from favoring any single religion has garnered limited support from the Court.

14

✤

Should the State Exempt Some Religious Groups from Compulsory Education?

THE PROBLEM POSED

We commonly think of education as a right, as something that the political community must provide to us for our benefit.[1] But education also serves the needs of the political community. Popular governments depend on their citizens for their survival, and unless they possess certain skills, it may be difficult for them to endure. For example, citizens must be able to read and write reasonably well in order to keep informed; unless they can read the newspapers and use the library, their representatives will not be restrained by appropriate scrutiny. Citizens should also have a basic understanding of how the government is structured so that they can follow the political process and can know when and where they have access to it. Beyond this, citizens should develop the basic skills necessary to live and prosper. For instance, everyone should know enough mathematics to be able to manage his or her household.

Finally, education serves the needs of the political community by instilling what have been called "democratic values." In other words, it is not sufficient to give citizens a certain amount of information and then send them on their way; popular government depends on citizens who have certain habits of action and who hold certain beliefs in common. For example, it is crucial that citizens be able to control themselves if they are going to be able to control the government; hence, a capacity for self-restraint is necessary.[2] Citizens should also be willing to contribute to the common tasks of the community. They must learn to sacrifice their short-term interests to the common ends of the people from time to time. Consequently, they need to develop some attachment to, as well as some understanding of, the basic political principles of the community in whose name they may be asked to make sacrifices. As the famous American philosopher John Dewey has pointed out,

> A society which makes provision for participation in its good of all its members on equal terms and which secures flexible readjustment of its institutions through interaction of the different forms of associated life is in so far democratic. Such a society must have a type of education which gives individuals a personal interest in social relationships and control, and the habits of mind which secure social changes without introducing disorder.[3]

Citizens living in a democracy need more than just information if they are to live together successfully; they need to respect those with whom they disagree. They need to know how to listen, how to plan, and how to cooperate with one another without resorting to violence.

The Supreme Court has confirmed that these are legitimate state goals. The Court has asserted that public schools are important "in the preparation of individuals for participation as citizens" through "inculcating fundamental values necessary to the maintenance of a democratic political system." The Court has gone even further:

> Today, education is perhaps the most important function of state and local governments. Compulsory school attendance laws and the great expenditures for education both demonstrate our recognition of the importance of education to our democratic society ... It is the very foundation of good citizenship. Today it is a principal instrument in awakening the child to cultural values.[4]

This passage is taken from the famous *Brown* v. *Board of Education*. In striking down laws that established dual school systems for blacks and whites, the Court stressed the significance of public education. Education was made more difficult when the two races were separated: "separate is inherently unequal." By separating the races within the public school system, the state was teaching harmful lessons about what human beings are. The state was harming both blacks and whites by making it more difficult for them to accept one another as equals in a democratic society.

Considering the importance of education to the state, what should be done with a group that believes that its religion is threatened by the very "cultural values" that the community (through its school board and school administrators and teachers) has said should be inculcated? How should the state respond to a group that wants to divorce itself from the "very foundation of good citizenship"? If the Court argued in *Brown* that separation *within* the public school system is problematic, how much more problematic is it for a religious group to want a separation *from* public education or any other education monitored by the state? This is the problem raised by our first example.

EXAMPLE 1

State of Wisconsin v. *Yoder,* 406 U.S. 205 (1972)

Facts: Wisconsin's compulsory school attendance law required that children attend public school (or a private school that met state standards) until they reached the age of sixteen. Several members of the Old Order Amish religion withdrew their children from school after they completed the eighth grade (when they were fourteen and fifteen years old). They based their actions on their right to free exercise of their religion, arguing that they would endanger their salvation and that of their children if they allowed them to continue in school. The children were not enrolled in private school and so did not clearly appear to qualify for the usual exemption from compulsory public school attendance.

Result: Wisconsin's compulsory education law, as applied to Amish children age fourteen and older, violates the First Amendment's Free Exercise Clause as applied to the state by the Fourteenth Amendment. Thus, the Amish children were granted an exemption from compulsory school attendance.

Argument of the Case: Burger, Chief Justice. Expert testimony was offered that explained that the Amish believe in de-emphasizing material success and rejecting the competitive spirit; this belief requires that they isolate themselves from the modern world in order to devote themselves to a simple, Christian life. Another feature of Amish life is its devotion to a harmony with nature that comes from working with the soil. Consequently, the Amish have particular objections to attending public education beyond the eighth grade. The "values" taught in high school are "in marked variance with Amish values and the Amish way of life," tending to emphasize competitiveness and a worldly success that stems from individualism. But the problem with high school attendance is not only the "values" taught; even mere attendance is harmful because it takes the children away from their community during crucial formative years when they should be working on the farms. Expert witnesses argued that attendance in high school would cause great psychological harm to the Amish children and would threaten the very existence of the Amish community. The state argued that there were two main defenses of compulsory education: (1) that citizens need to be well enough educated to participate effectively in our political system and (2) that people living in modern society need to be self-reliant and self-sufficient. However, it does not appear that these goals are well realized when the state requires education beyond the eighth grade for Amish children in place of the informal vocational education that naturally occurs in their community. (In other words, while education must prepare children for life in the political community, the Amish "learning-by-doing" agrarian life does adequately prepare the Amish for life in *their* community.) In order to resolve the case, a balancing test must be applied to see if the state's interest in compulsory education is "of sufficient magnitude" to override the religious free exercise right of the Amish. Only a state interest "of the highest order and those not otherwise served can overbalance legitimate claims to free exercise of religion." Because the state's rationale is weak and because the Amish's free exercise claim is strong (for the Wisconsin law requires the Amish to either abandon their beliefs and way of life under threat of criminal sanction or leave the state in search of a more tolerant environment), the Constitution requires that a limited exemption (beyond the eighth grade) be granted to the Amish. Other considerations enhance this conclusion, including the arbitrary standard of age sixteen in Wisconsin's compulsory education law (perhaps tied to concerns about improper child labor) and the unique nature of the Amish, whose long history and religious–vocational way of life establish their religious sincerity and limit future religious-based group exemptions.

Stewart concurs.[5] It is important to understand that this case does not involve a conflict between Amish parents who want to deny their children the right to a full public school education and Amish children who are asserting that right (despite Justice Douglas's dissent). Amish children retain the right to attend public school, and if a parent were to refuse to allow his or her child that right, then the Court would have to rule on the issue.

White concurs.[6] Had the claim of the Amish been that their children should be excused from public school (or a state-certified alternative) completely, then perhaps a different ruling should have been made. But since the exemption requested is slight and since these Amish children have already attended school through the eighth grade, it seems unlikely that they would be incapable of making their way as citizens of a modern society if they so chose.

Douglas dissents in part. This case is problematic because it focuses on the legal rights and obligations of the parents rather than the children. If the parents succeed in obtaining an exemption for their children, they will, in effect, be guilty of imposing their religious views on their children.

Discussion

The Supreme Court re-emphasized its well-established position that public education is extremely important, but it argued that it had to balance the state interest against other "fundamental rights and interests." Chief Justice Burger, writing for the majority, stated that it was always dangerous to allow "an exception from a general obligation of citizenship on religious grounds." However, he argued that exceptions are still appropriate under some circumstances. In this case, Burger stressed the importance of the Amish way of life: "Amish society emphasizes informal learning-through-doing; a life of 'goodness' rather than a life of intellect." The goal of Amish education is not to prepare the child for life in modern society, but to lead him or her to become part of a "separated agrarian community that is the keystone to the Amish faith." The Amish accepted the necessity of formal schooling for their children through the eighth grade, but they believed that schooling beyond this point "tends to emphasize intellectual and scientific accomplishments, self-distinction, competitiveness, worldly success, and social life with other students." The problem, then, was recognized by the Court as a religious one: compulsory attendance could destroy the entire Amish community. This threat was confirmed by expert witnesses.

The Court imposed a very high standard of proof upon the state; the Free Exercise Clause required government to demonstrate that imposing compulsory education for Amish children past the eighth grade was a compelling interest.[7] Burger decided that the state's interest in education was not sufficiently compelling when balanced against the religious harm it caused, including its interference with parents' right to direct the religious rearing of their children as well as the possible destruction of a religious community. One might question whether the courts really have a greater ability or even more of a legal obligation to attempt this kind of balancing than do state legislatures, which could write into the laws exemptions from compulsory education requirements for religious groups. But more relevant to the issues here is the question of whether (or to what extent) school attendance through the ninth grade, as Wisconsin required, would be more subversive of the Amish community than requiring eighth grade attendance only, as did the Supreme Court. Does the ninth grade place significantly more emphasis on intellectual and scientific accomplishments than the eighth grade does? Are students taught to be cooperative in the eighth grade and turned in the direction of competitiveness only in the ninth? But even leaving these matters aside and accepting the basic constitutional issue raised by this case, the question still remains: What should be done?

In its broadest context, the Amish claim seemed to be that the Free Exercise Clause gives them the right to withdraw themselves significantly from mainstream American life. This claim was one that many other Americans may find disturbing. However, Burger cautioned against succumbing to this feeling: "A way of life that is odd or even erratic, but interferes with no rights or interests of others, is not be condemned because it is different." Burger's idea is important; after all, the Founders intended that the United States allow for great diversity among its citizens, a group that included a multiplicity of interests and religious sects. In this large republic, must there not be a place for real diversity?

Yet the argument of the state authorities also seemed persuasive. State compulsory education laws had almost always been upheld by the courts, both in the abstract and as applied to religious groups that had requested exemptions. The state suggested that the requested exemption was not simply a claim in the name of diversity, but rather an assertion of a right to withdraw from full citizenship. Compulsory education, the state argued, exists to "prepare citizens to participate effectively and intelligently in our open political system."

The state was not persuaded by the idea that the Amish were not interested in participating in that system. And if we take the principle implied by the Amish claim, it does lead in disturbing directions. To what extent do religious groups have a right to isolate themselves from the very education that is designed to integrate them into the full life of the broader American community? Could not this idea lead well beyond a healthy diversity and into a balkanized country, a nation divided into separate, suspicious, and semi-autonomous religious groups? Is this really what the Founders had in mind?[8]

On the other hand, Burger contended that the Amish have been good citizens. "Its members," he says, "are productive and very law-abiding members of society." Burger's contention revealed a minimalist view of citizenship. Isn't it true that we usually think of citizenship as involving some positive participation in the political life of the nation, not just a negative form of participation (that is, not disobeying the law)? Can it really be said that *meaningful* citizenship is simply being born in one's native land (or naturalizing) and not violating the rights of others?[9]

Although Burger's view of citizenship is widely held today, others might argue that as a prerequisite for meaningful citizenship it is necessary that Americans share some fundamental ideas and that they be one nation in a very real sense: *e pluribus unum.* Perhaps diversity is not incompatible with the idea that citizens should share a common core of fundamental ideas and beliefs. In *Wisconsin* v. *Yoder,* the Court made an unusual ruling because it wanted to allow for decent accommodation for a decent people. Whether this accommodation, provided in the form of an exemption from mandatory state education laws, was warranted remains a controversial question.

EXAMPLE 2

T.A.F. and E.M.F., Juveniles, v. *Duvall County,* 273 So 2d 15 (1973)

Facts: The parents of two children in Jacksonville, Florida, refused to enroll their children in public school because they objected to "racial mixing" there. In their opinion, racial mixing was sinful and contrary to their religious beliefs. Because they were violating compulsory education laws, the children were then put under the supervision of a court juvenile counselor. The parents claimed to be educating the children in a private school within the home and wanted their children to be returned to their educational supervision, but the home school did not meet state requirements. The County Juvenile Court ruled against the parents, and they appealed to the District Court of Appeal.

Result: The District Court of Appeal ruled that the parents were not protected by the Free Exercise Clause.

Argument of the Case—Per Curiam: The parents of these two children claimed to be educating them in the Ida M. Craig Christian Day

School, but the only regular instructor there was the mother, and she had not been certified as a teacher by the state and did not meet any state requirements for a private tutor. However, the parents claimed that the home school was a legitimate parochial school under the aegis of the Covenant Church of Jesus Christ, where the father of the children is an ordained minister. In spite of this, the Court held that two main factors prohibited it from ruling in favor of the parents. First, parochial schools in the United States are never beyond minimal state control in the form of state requirements for teachers. Second, the church that supposedly supports the parochial school was not a recognized church in the state.

Discussion

The father of these children stated that the main tenet of his religion is that "Blacks and Orientals" (as he refers to them) were "conceived through the copulation of Eve and Satan, who was disguised as the serpent in the Garden of Eden." In his opinion, it is therefore sinful to associate with these people. The Ida M. Craig Christian Day School taught these beliefs. It existed under the supervision of the Covenant Church of Jesus Christ, but the church apparently held no services for anyone and was not registered with the state.

This case did not raise serious legal issues for the court, which adopted the usual one approach: religious exemptions from educational requirements are seldom given, and even religiously affiliated schools are required to meet state accreditation standards. This conclusion was based upon the recognition that for many years, the courts have argued that the free exercise of religion meant absolute freedom to believe anything one chooses to believe. Thus, a church could be founded on the doctrine that the Earth is really flat and that all evidence to the contrary has been manufactured by the CIA. A church could even be founded on a racist doctrine, as was the Covenant Church of Jesus Christ. But could a religiously sponsored school be established and run according to some racist doctrine? The court did not need to decide this question.[10] Instead, it steadfastly maintained the more limited doctrine—that the state could never relinquish its authority to set minimal standards for teacher qualifications and for curricula. However racist the parents might have been was not at issue here, for there was no doubt that the state could still demand that they have a certain amount of education and/or training. This case was decided narrowly according to the uncontroversial proposition that certain standard subjects may not be neglected if they are required by the state. This approach *seemed* to excuse the courts from examining the content of religious beliefs and also accorded well with precedent, for the Supreme Court has emphasized that state requirements cannot stifle religious distinctiveness. Religiously sponsored schools may not be brought under "strict governmental control" or given "affirmative direction concerning the intimate and essential details of such schools."[11]

Still, one cannot help wondering if it was really the case that the parents in this case were treated less sympathetically by the court because of their pernicious and unpopular religious beliefs, especially compared to those more appealing beliefs held by the Old Order Amish in *Yoder.*[12] After all, in *Yoder* the Amish children had been *totally* excused from certain state educational requirements. (Thus, while the Court did refer to the continuing parentally supervised vocational education inherent in the Amish way of life, that "education" did not imply any formal schooling, so it did not have to meet state accreditation requirements.) True, the Supreme Court admitted that such exemptions could not be granted lightly. Thus, Burger wrote in *Yoder* that the "court must move with great circumspection in performing the sensitive and delicate task of weighing a religious claim for exemption from generally applicable educational requirements."[13] Still, the question arises of how *Yoder* can be distinguished *in principle* from this case (and the great majority of cases that have been similarly decided).

In *Yoder,* Burger said of the Amish (indicating why they, as opposed to other groups, should be granted exemption): (1) that they, for three centuries, had been an identifiable religious sect; (2) that the sincerity of their religious beliefs was clear for all to see; (3) that their religious beliefs informed the Amish way of life; (4) and that their religion and way of life were threatened by the state compulsory education laws. Yet the family in the Jacksonville case certainly fits most of these criteria. Was there any doubt that this family sincerely held to its racist religious beliefs, that the beliefs influenced their life, or that attending integrated schools—one of whose objectives was to promote citizenship by fostering a respect for all peoples—would fundamentally threaten those beliefs? True, the family did not amount to a community in the larger, Amish sense and likely was not almost completely segregated from the remainder of American life. And it was also true that the Amish religion was older and clearly recognized by all to be a religion; however, it is not obvious why the age of a religion should determine its appropriateness for exemption.[14] Furthermore, even if the beliefs promulgated by the Ida M. Craig Christian Day School seem unusual (and offensive), was it obvious that they were not as religious as the Amish religious beliefs? Finally, the children in the Jacksonville case were unwilling to attend any public school classes (as opposed to the Amish, who wished exemption only after the eighth grade). This is something of a difference between the two cases. Still, a legal exemption is a legal exemption, and the Amish were granted it by the courts while virtually no other sects are. The controversial question remains: Are the religious differences between the Amish and the students of the Ida M. Craig Christian Day School so profound that they merit different treatment by the state, or are the Amish merely more admirable people?

In this case the court commented on the fact that the Covenant Church of Jesus Christ did not hold services and was not registered with the state, but this is not a determining factor in the case. The court might have its suspicions about the legitimacy of a church, but the church-affiliated school would still have been considered as a fair alternative to public schools if it had met state requirements. In other words, the real issue addressed by the court was not how odd or troubling this religion might be, but whether the children in the school are getting a basic education as defined by the state. But what would happen if a religious group claimed that the state requirements themselves were an imposition on their free exercise of religion? Our next case examines this issue.

EXAMPLE 3

Johnson v. Charles City Comm. Schools Bd. of Ed., 368 N.W. 2nd 74 (Iowa 1985)

Facts: Pastor Randy Johnson and fellow members of the Calvary Baptist Christian Academy organized a parochial school in Charles City, Iowa. The members of the church school refused any state oversight whatsoever. Pastor Johnson would not agree that teachers in the school should be certified or approved by the state, and he denied that the state could establish even minimum standards for the curriculum in a religious school. He also refused to submit to any state reporting requirements. Johnson challenged the state educational requirements and also applied for relief under the state "Amish exception." The curriculum of the school was called the Accelerated Christian Education Program and was not challenged as inadequate by state authorities.

Result: Society has a duty to educate its children, and it can establish minimum educational standards for private religious schools. Also, the "Amish exception" is not to be granted.

Argument of the Case: Harris, Judge. The right to establish private religious schools is important, and the concern of Pastor Johnson and his church parents is legitimate. If the state establishes comprehensive educational standards, it can destroy the distinction between public and private education. However, the Supreme Court has long established the right of the state to regulate all schools in a reasonable way; the state may set standards for teachers and require basic matters to be covered in the curricula of private schools. In addition, the Calvary school does not qualify for the "Amish exception" because the members of the Calvary Baptist Church, unlike the Amish, do not separate themselves from modern life. Their children are expected to "live, compete for jobs, work, and move about in a diverse and complex society."

Schultz dissents. The Calvary Baptist Christian Academy should be granted the "Amish exception." Any religious group that maintains "unusual principles that clash with the state's philosophy of education" should receive this exemption.

Carter dissents. The court's decision is misguided; its narrow interpretation of the Iowa "Amish exception" statute would deny the statute any meaningful application.

Discussion

Pastor Johnson's claims here are far more extreme than those made by the Amish. On the one hand, he would take advantage of the exemption accorded them by the Supreme Court. But, more extremely, he directly raised the question of whether the state had *any* legitimate authority over education, a question far more radical than that raised by the Amish in *Yoder.*

Here, the court agreed that parents had a right to educate their children in a private religious school. The problem was that they were "unwilling to submit to any state inquiry" into standards for teachers and curriculum. The parents and the pastor did submit a letter giving some information about the orientation of the school, but that was all. For example, this letter stated that "all subjects were presented from a biblical point of view without apology; there was no need or any opportunity for any assistant to present a subject from a so-called 'secular point of view.'" The pastor asserted that his judgments about hiring teachers and fixing the curriculum were made "after prayer and after learning of God's will." Because of this, he argued that "his selection of a teacher (or a particular course) is God's selection ... and that a mere state can have no part in either approving or disapproving or controlling or having any influence or licensing or certifying authority" at his church school.

From the standpoint of religious belief, Johnson's perspective is understandable. How can secular authorities specify the requirements for teachers or curricula if in fact these requirements imply a rejection of the biblical perspective? What, after all, makes a teacher truly qualified? Is an English teacher qualified if he or she has strong training in and experience with secular literature? But what if this literature was seen to be unworthy of study because of its secular foundation? In this case, a teacher familiar with the Bible might be more qualified to teach literature than someone conversant with secular literature. Johnson asserted that "since God created everything including truth, all learning or education involves education in God's truths and that education and religion are therefore one and the same."

Johnson argued that since his school and his church were fully integrated, the state had no power to regulate the school; it was simply part of the church. In addition to this, he made the point that the Bible granted no educational authority to the state; hence, the state has no authority over education. The court rejected these arguments completely, saying that the right to use alternative education in the United States does not include the right to stand completely apart from state supervision. The very case that established the right to alternative education, *Pierce* v. *Society of Sisters,* assumed as much:

> No question is raised concerning the power of the state reasonably to regulate all schools, to inspect, supervise, and examine them, their teachers and pupils; to require that all children of proper age attend some school, that teachers shall be of good moral character and patriotic disposition, that certain studies plainly essential to good citizenship must be taught, and that nothing be taught which is manifestly inimical to the public welfare.[15]

In other words, the state has the power of "reasonable regulation." What is reasonable? Here, the court admitted that it was possible for state power to go too far in attempting to control private education. (Thus, in *State* v. *Whisner*[16] an Ohio court ruled that the state's educational regulations were excessive; the state may not establish regulations that are so comprehensive that the distinction between public and private education is abolished.) On the other hand, the court made it clear that it would not be sufficient for a state to test children in private schools at regular intervals: "To merely test the children ... does not satisfy the state's rightful role." The state has a responsibility to establish "basic parameters for curriculum and teacher qualifications." The court argued that this power of the state is derived from the existence of the social contract:

> When such standards are set in place, compliance with them falls within the ambit of the fundamental contract between the citizen and society. It need scarcely be said that each of us, in order to enjoy membership in an organized social order, is pledged to adhere to a number of minimum norms. Of these, one of the most central is society's duty to educate its children.[17]

In other words, education exists to serve individuals, but it also exists to serve the legitimate needs of the state, and individual needs must always be modified in civil society by regulations that are designed to serve the public good. As the court put it, "a citizen must submit to them, persuade society to change them, or join a society without them."

As was noted earlier, Johnson also suggested that his school be granted what he called the state's "Amish exception," but the court found that this legitimate exemption from compulsory education laws was not designed for every church group that wanted to provide its children with a religiously oriented education. Once again, the court pointed out that the facts in *Wisconsin* v. *Yoder* were so unusual that the precedent was difficult to apply. Most importantly, the court contended that the children in Johnson's school were not living isolated lives: "plaintiff's children, for all the distinctive religious convictions they will be given, will live, compete for jobs, work, and move about in a diverse and complex society. Considering these facts, Johnson cannot claim that complying with minimal state regulations will pose a threat to the existence of his religious community."

EXAMPLE 4

Duro* v. *District Attorney, Second Judicial District of North Carolina, 712 F.2nd 96 (1983)

Facts: Duro and his wife and five school-age children are Pentecostalists. Duro refused to send his children to public school or to the only private school in the county, the Cabin Swamp Christian School, operated by the

Church of Christ. His complaints against the public schools are that they foster what he called "the unisex movement," encouraging boys and girls to become like one another instead of maintaining their distinctive sexual characteristics. He also objected to the teaching of secular humanism and the use of physicians, which he believed was a violation of his religious view that God heals any problem. Duro's children were taught in his home by his wife, who used the Alpha Omega Christian Curriculum, a "self-teaching" program that is also used in the Cabin Swamp Christian School. North Carolina attempts to give its private or parochial schools great leeway in developing their own approaches to education, but it still has compulsory education laws, requires that disease immunization records be kept for all children, and requires the administration of standardized tests at various intervals during the school year.

Result: The U.S. Court of Appeals held that Duro must comply with North Carolina's compulsory education laws.

Argument of the Case: Hall, Judge. The facts of *Wisconsin* v. *Yoder* make it applicable only in rare cases. Duro was keeping his children out of the public schools, but he admitted that he expected them to "go out and work in the world" when they turned eighteen. In the Amish case, the parents made it clear that their children were not supposed to leave their isolated religious community. In *Wisconsin* v. *Yoder* the Court found that the particular focus of education after the eighth grade challenged the entire way of life of the Amish and that requiring the Amish children to attend public schools could pose a threat to the existence of the entire Amish community. No such threat exists for Duro's religion. The Pentecostalist community does not face extinction; in fact, the religion does not require that children be taught at home or even in parochial schools. The majority of the Pentecostalist children attending the Duros' church attend public schools. Since *Yoder* has a different factual basis, the court ruled against Duro.

Sprouse concurs. Judge Sprouse was really concerned only with the implications of one footnote in the majority opinion that stressed the importance of considering the rights of the Duro children. He did not want this case to establish a precedent that would allow children to have rights against their parents in educational matters.

Discussion

This case raises the issue of "home education." Duro refused to send his children to the public school or to the only private school in town. His problem seems real; one can imagine any number of circumstances under which both the public school and the private schools available might be unacceptable. What would a Muslim family do if it objected to the public schools and then discovered that the only accessible private school was a Catholic school? Home education seems to be an important alternative to public and private education, and it has received legal sanction. In *Hinrichs* v. *Whitburn*,[18] a federal court considered the issue of a Catholic woman who considered herself employed as a teacher of her own children and who therefore refused to comply with a state requirement under the Aid to Families with Dependent Children program that she attend an educational session to assist her with job training and job searching. She argued that she was employed in the home and that it was a violation of her religious freedom to demand that she begin a job training program in order to keep her monetary benefits as a participant under Aid to Families with Dependent Children. The court accepted the concept of home education and stated its willingness to protect the woman's benefits under some circumstances. Duro's case failed because he attempted to win an exemption from compulsory education laws by appealing to *Wisconsin* v. *Yoder.* The court was reluctant—as most courts have been—to grant an exemption unless all the requirements of that case are met. Since the existence of Pentecostalism was not threatened by public education and since Duro's family and children did not lead lives of isolation from modern life, the "Amish exception" could not be granted.

The real problem with Duro's case is not that he wanted his children educated at home, but rather that his wife did not seem to the state to be a qualified educator. For example, the mother in the *Hinrichs* case was approved by the state. Like church-sponsored schools, home education depends upon a variety of laws and regulations in the various states. The laws attempt to ensure that irrespective of religious orientation, children receive a competent education. The federal courts have constantly upheld this state power.

The requirement that home school teachers be approved by the state seems quite reasonable, but it can have serious consequences for families of minority religions in small communities. Using the example once again of the Muslim family in a community with a Catholic private school, the difficulty is clear. Unless someone in the family can obtain approval from the state, the children will have to attend a public school that presents a secular perspective to its students or a private school with a strong Christian orientation. This quandary seems irresolvable, one of the many issues that grow out of the tension between private religious belief and the state's strong interest in providing a sound education for all of its young.

SUMMARY

The main issue raised by these cases is an important one for any country: How much diversity can be tolerated? Any country that places a value on freedom will not want to force all of its citizens to think the same thoughts or believe in the same gods. However, can any country survive if its citizens share nothing except pursuing their own interests?

In *Wisconsin* v. *Yoder* the Court seemed to establish a limited religious right for a group to separate itself from the very education that is designed to bring us together as a nation. The Amish argued that public education was a threat to the existence of their community, but some critics of *Yoder* have also argued that the religious right established in the case is potentially a threat to the larger political community—not because the Amish themselves would act in any improper or illegal fashion, but because the principle articulated by the Court could open the door to religious exemptions for others. The theoretical problem inherent in a "right to separation" was examined by U.S. Representative Barbara Jordan in her Keynote Address to the Democratic National Convention in 1976. Representative Jordan was the first black woman to give a Keynote Address at a national political convention, and she chose this occasion to talk about the tension between diversity and community:

> But this is the great danger America faces—that we will cease to be one nation and become instead a collection of interest groups: city against suburb, region against region, individual against individual—each seeking to satisfy private wants. If that happens, who then will speak for America? Who then will speak for the common good? This is the question which must be answered.... Are we to be one people bound together by a common spirit sharing in a common endeavor, or will we become a divided nation?[19]

America champions respect for differences, but the principle (admittedly applied in a limited fashion in *Yoder*) asks if there can come a point at which certain differences undermine the nation.

It must be recognized that the problematic principle articulated in *Wisconsin* v. *Yoder* has been rarely applied in court. In the cases examined in this chapter, all the courts held that the specific facts of the Amish case made it almost unique. Thus, an unregulated "right of separation" seems to be a right only under rare circumstances. In constitutional law, *Yoder* is the exception, and the state's authority to regulate education for the welfare of its people is the rule.

NOTES

1. However, it is important to note that the Supreme Court has not held that public education is a fundamental constitutional right. See *San Antonio Independent School District* v. *Rodriguez*, 411 U.S. 1 (1973).

2. Harry Clor, *Obscenity and Public Morality* (Chicago: Univ. of Chicago Press, 1969), pp. 186–190, 201–202.

3. John Dewey, *Democracy and Education* (New York: Macmillan, 1916), p. 115.

4. The quotations are all from *Brown* v. *Board of Education*, 347 U.S. 483 (1954).

5. Justice Brennan joins this opinion.

6. Justices Brennan and Stewart join this opinion.

7. Later, in *Employment Division, Oregon Department of Human Resources* v. *Smith*, 494 U.S. 872 (1990) at 881, n. 1, the Court attempted to distinguish *Yoder* from other free exercise cases in order that it might impose a lower (reasonable rather than compelling) state interest test. *Smith* argued that Yoder was decided *both* on the basis of the Free Exercise Clause and upon the right of parents to direct the religious upbringing of their children (affirmed by the Court in the 1925 case of *Pierce* v.

Society of Sisters). Not surprisingly, *Smith's* interpretation of *Yoder's* holding remains controversial. The test in *Smith* was effectively rejected by Congress when it passed the Religious Freedom Restoration Act.

8. This problem is discussed thoughtfully in *The Disuniting of America: Reflections on a Multicultural Society*, by Arthur M. Schlesinger, Jr. (New York: Norton, 1992), p. 43. He says that "the ethnic upsurge (it can hardly be called a revival because it was unprecedented) began as a gesture of protest against the Anglocentric culture. It became a cult, and today threatens to become a counter-revolution against the original theory of America as 'one people,' a common culture, a single nation."

9. However, one should note that Burger's assumptions about citizenship agree with those of the Constitution, which does not distinguish citizens from noncitizens on the basis of their participation in, or contribution to, the political order, but merely on the basis of their birth.

10. Whether such religiously affiliated schools, founded upon the declared doctrine of racial discrimination, could gain state accreditation was problematical (in that such a regulation violates declared public policy) and may well turn in part upon the court interpretation of *Bob Jones University* v. *United States*, 461 U.S. 574 (1983). See Chapter 9, pp. 165–67.

11. *Farrington* v. *Tokushige,* 273 U.S. 284 (1927).

12. Since this case accords with the legal rule by which such cases have been decided, and *Yoder* proves to be an exception, perhaps it might be better to ask if the Court was overly influenced by its positive view of the benign Amish way of life.

13. 406 U.S. at 235 (1972).

14. Although such a test might deter practitioners of fraudulent religions from seeking legal exemption from the law.

15. 268 U.S. 510 (1925) at 534.

16. *Ohio* v. *Whisner,* 351 N.E. 2d 750 (1976).

17. 351 N.E. 2d 750.

18. *Hinrichs* v. *Whitburn,* 975 F.2nd 1329 (7th Circuit 1992).

19. Keynote Address to the Democratic National Convention, July 12, 1976.

PART IV

Religion and Medical Care

15

How and Why Does Religion Affect Abortion Policy?

THE PROBLEM POSED

The modern state has traditionally been understood to protect a sphere of privacy from public intrusion. The doctrine of natural rights, which provides the theoretical foundation for the modern state, presents the rights of the individual as primary and the powers of civil society as derived from the individual's basic and original autonomy. A fundamental problem for the modern state is that private rights and public power must be balanced. If all our actions are completely free and privately chosen, then we are back in the state of nature where rights are absolute but insecure, a state that Hobbes described as "solitary, poor, nasty, brutish, and short." In other words, the attempt to live together requires that we give up the absolute freedom that we have outside of civil society. On the other hand, if all our actions are directed by public power, then we are in a state of tyranny. The success of the modern state can turn on its ability to distinguish between the private and the public spheres of life.[1]

The issue of abortion revolves around this fundamental problem. People seem to sense that the resolution of this tension between the private and the public will have ramifications for the way in which all other issues are addressed in our society. The controversy over abortion has been serious, and it has often been ugly. Proponents of abortion believe that liberty itself is at stake when abortion clinics are picketed, while opponents of abortion believe that human life and civilization are compromised when liberty is allowed to decline into license. And the conflict over abortion has turned violent. Doctors who perform abortions have been under assault around the country.[2] Nor have such acts of violence been the final word on this issue. Some abortion opponents argue that such violence is mild compared to the violence of the million-plus abortions that are performed each year in the United States. Meanwhile, the government has acted, passing in 1994 a Freedom of Access to Clinic Entrances bill, intended to halt attempts by anti-abortion protestors to limit or block entrance to abortion clinics. Finally, the Supreme Court, in a limited decision, held that anti-abortion protestors can be sued under RICO (Racketeer Influence and Corrupt Organizations) law. Although anti-abortion protestors are nonprofit and do not extract money through coercion from unwilling victims (the way a loan shark might), they do cause the loss of significant sums of money as a result of such protests and therefore fall under the purview of this law.[3]

At the core of the controversy is what is for many a religious question: What is life? Most of those who advocate abortion on demand deny that the fetus is alive, or at least argue that the fetus is not a human being or person in the complete sense; abortion is therefore a medical procedure that a woman can choose for her own reasons. By contrast, most of those who oppose abortion believe that because the fetus is alive, or that because the fetus is from the time of conception a live human being, abortion is therefore murder. The question for the courts has been how to resolve the political issue without taking a stand on the religious issue. Our first case illustrates the difficulty the courts have had.

EXAMPLE 1

Roe v. *Wade,* 410 U.S. 113 (1973)[4]

Facts: Jane Roe (a pseudonym for an unmarried pregnant woman) challenged a Texas abortion law that allowed for abortions only when they were necessary to save the mother's life. She based her claim on several grounds (equal protection, due process), including the right to privacy. A district court ruled that the Texas law was unconstitutional.

Result: Since the right to privacy includes the woman's abortion decision, the Texas law limiting abortions to those "procured or attempted by medical advice for the purpose of saving the life of the mother" violates the liberty protection safeguarded by the Fourteenth Amendment and is therefore unconstitutional.

Argument of the Case: Blackmun, Justice. Restrictive abortion laws are of relatively recent origin. The main argument against abortion is that the state has an interest in protecting prenatal life. While this is true, it has to be balanced against a woman's right to privacy. The state cannot ban abortions under all circumstances where the mother's life is not in danger.

Nor is a woman's right to an abortion absolute; she cannot obtain an abortion "at whatever time, in whatever way, and for whatever reason she alone chooses." A woman's right to privacy does include the abortion decision, but this right has to be balanced against the state's interest in protecting the life of the mother and protecting "potential life." Blackmun argues that the state's interest becomes stronger as the pregnancy continues. Drawing on "the light of present medical knowledge," he says that pregnancy can be divided into three parts. In the first trimester, the abortion decision is left the woman and her doctor; the state may not interfere. During the second trimester, the state may regulate abortion procedures, but it may not prohibit abortion. For example, it could set standards for the kind of clinic that would be allowed to perform abortions. The state's interest becomes compelling at the end of the second trimester, when the fetus reaches "viability"—that is, when it becomes more likely that the fetus could survive outside the womb: "Subsequent to viability, the state in promoting its interest in the potentiality of human life may, if it chooses, regulate, and even proscribe, abortion except where it is necessary, in appropriate medical judgment, for the preservation of the life or health of the mother...."

Burger concurs. The Texas law impermissibly limits abortions under the Fourteenth Amendment. The Court's opinion does not allow for abortion on demand.

Stewart concurs. The Fourteenth Amendment prohibits the "broad abridgment of personal liberty worked by the existing Texas law." The state's interest in protecting potential human life and the life of the mother allows for significant regulation and even prohibition of abortion in the later stages of pregnancy, but the Texas law goes far beyond this.

Rehnquist dissents. The abortion decision cannot be protected by the "right of privacy." There are constitutional limits to the state's power to regulate behavior. However, the Fourteenth Amendment does not state that such personal liberty is "guaranteed absolutely against deprivation, only against deprivation without due process of law." The traditional test of whether or not such a law has followed due process is whether the law has a "rational relation" to a valid state objective. The Texas law does meet this test.

White dissents.[5] Nothing in the language or history of the Constitution supports the Court's decision; the Court simply fashions and announces its judgment.

Discussion

The right to privacy is not mentioned explicitly in the Constitution. It was first recognized by the Supreme Court in 1965 in *Griswold v. Connecticut*,[6] a highly controversial birth-control plurality opinion decision written by Justice Douglas. In *Griswold*, Douglas made the argument that "specific guarantees in the Bill of Rights have penumbras, formed by emanations from those guarantees that help give them life and substance." He contended that "various guarantees create zones of privacy" that were unnamed but that could be extrapolated from the emanations of named rights. In his dissent, Justice Black stated, "I like my privacy as well as the next one, but I am nevertheless compelled to admit that government has a right to invade it unless prohibited by some specific constitutional provision." The issue in *Griswold* was whether Connecticut could forbid birth-control assistance (and the *use* of contraceptives!) to married couples. Everyone on the Court seemed to agree that the law was uncommonly foolish (although it was also a law that had not been enforced for many years). But Justice Stewart said, "We are not asked in this case to say whether we think this law is unwise, or even asinine. We are asked to hold that it violates the United States Constitution. And that I cannot do." Over Black and Stewart's vigorous opposition, a generalized right to privacy—one not tied to a specific provision of the Constitution—was established in *Griswold*.[7]

Roe vastly expanded individual privacy protection by attaching it to the woman's decision whether to continue her pregnancy and by holding that the fetus (and, of course, the embryo) was not a person in a legal sense and that it, for this reason, could not claim legal or constitutional protection. At the heart of *Roe* was the attempt to balance the right of a woman to an abortion against the legitimate state interest in protecting the life of the mother and the "potential" life of the embryo/fetus. Blackmun began his discussion in this way:

> Texas urges that, apart from the Fourteenth Amendment, life begins at conception and is present throughout pregnancy, and that, therefore, the State has a compelling interest in protecting that life from and after conception. We need not resolve the difficult question of when life begins. When those trained in the respective disciplines of medicine, philosophy, and theology are unable to arrive at any consensus, the judiciary, at this point in the development of man's knowledge, is not in a position to speculate as to the answer.[8]

But the fact is that Blackmun did provide something of an answer to this question. If human life begins at conception, then abortion at any stage of pregnancy is clearly the taking of a human life. By dividing pregnancy into trimesters and allowing abortion on demand through the second trimester, Blackmun silently assumed that human life begins not at conception, but at what he termed "viability." Until that point, the fetus is not a human life; it is merely "potential life":

> With respect to the State's important and legitimate interest in potential life, the "compelling" point is at viability. This is so because the fetus then presumably has the capability of meaningful life outside the mother's womb. State regulation protective of fetal life after viability thus has both logical and biological justification.[9]

But all that "viability" means is strength or independence. It is a tautology to note that a fetus can survive in the womb only until it is strong enough to survive outside the womb. Thus, Blackmun's explanation did not settle the more difficult philosophical (or religious) question of when life or personhood begins. Life itself (or personhood) cannot be defined by strength or independence, for there are many children born at full term who cannot survive on their own. Furthermore, as Justice O'Connor would repeatedly point out, viability is hardly a fixed concept; improvements in technology make the age of viability much earlier (a fact at odds with *Roe*'s rigid trimester system). In the end, such considerations did not matter, for the fetus's viability, according to Blackmun, did not preclude its abortion; Blackmun allowed the states the authority to proscribe third-trimester abortions but did not demand that they do so. Thus, although Blackmun had attempted to circumvent the difficult question of when life begins by focusing on "viability," without admitting it, he ultimately provided the Court with a controversial and not altogether satisfactory answer to the philosophic or theological question that he had claimed the Court should not attempt to answer.

In his dissent, Justice Rehnquist focused on the technical issue of whether the Court has the authority to make decisions of this kind. He argued that since the Constitution does not address the problem of abortion rights, then the "rational relation" test ought to be applied. This means that the only question the Court should ask is whether there is a rational relation between the law in question and a valid state objective:

> ...[the] Court's sweeping invalidation of any restrictions on abortion during the first trimester is impossible to justify under that standard, and the conscious weighing of competing factors that the Court's opinion apparently substitutes for the established test is far more appropriate to a legislative judgment than to a judicial one.[10]

In other words, Rehnquist believed that the democratic political process ought to sort out the problem of abortion. But leaving the abortion question with state legislatures would not have been a satisfactory solution for Blackmun, who would accuse Rehnquist of abandoning fundamental rights to majority vote, something the Constitution was designed to prohibit.

Rehnquist's allusion to the democratic process was an important reminder that the Court's opinions do not take place in a vacuum. In the next case, we examine the attempt by Congress to limit abortions by refusing to fund them.

EXAMPLE 2

Harris **v.** *McRae,* 448 U.S. 297 (1980)

Facts: In 1965, Title XIX of the Social Security Act created the Medicaid program, which was designed to make federal aid available to states that reimburse some costs of medical treatment to the needy. Since 1976, an amendment (called the "Hyde Amendment" after Representative Hyde) limited the use of federal funds that were used to pay for abortions under Medicaid. Cora McRae sued in federal district court on behalf of all indigent women to stop enforcement of the Hyde Amendment on the grounds that it violates both the Due Process Clause of the Fifth Amendment (and its implicit guarantee of equal protection) and the religion clauses of the First Amendment.

Result: The federal government does not have a constitutional obligation to fund abortions.

Argument of the Case: Stewart, Justice. Even though the Hyde Amendment creates financial obstacles to abortion for some women, the government does not have an obligation to remove all obstacles that are not the creation of government: "It does not follow that a woman's freedom of choice carries with it a constitutional entitlement to the financial resources to avail herself of the full range of protected choices." The Due Process Clause cannot be read to require that Congress must subsidize abortions. Nor is the Establishment Clause violated by the simple fact that opposition to abortion happens to be a religious tenet of the Roman Catholic Church. The Free Exercise Clause is also not violated by the Hyde Amendment; McRae did not prove that she sought an abortion under compulsion of religious belief.

White concurs. The right to an abortion, first articulated in *Roe,* "was the right to choose to undergo an abortion without coercive interference by the government." *Roe* did not guarantee that the government would make all abortions financially feasible. In this case the government is not trying to impose a "coercive restraint."

Brennan dissents.[11] The state must "refrain from wielding its enormous power and influence in a manner that might burden the pregnant woman's freedom to choose whether to have an abortion." The Hyde Amendment clearly intrudes upon this private decision. It is clear that the Hyde Amendment is an attempt to circumvent the constitutional right established in *Roe.*

Marshall dissents. The Hyde Amendment cuts off federal funding for abortions that might be medically necessary to avert harm to the mother. Justice Stewart's argument "studiously avoids" the fact that denial of federal funding under Medicaid "is equivalent to denial of legal abortion altogether" for the poor. The natural result of this argument will be to send poor women to "back-alley butchers."

Blackmun dissents. The Hyde Amendment is unconstitutional because it "punitively impresses upon a needy minority its own concepts of the socially desirable, the publicly acceptable, and the morally sound."

Stevens dissents. This case effectively revokes the right to an abortion established in *Roe.* Once the government set up Medicaid for the purpose of alleviating some of the hardships of poverty, "the government must use neutral criteria in distributing benefits." The Hyde Amendment does not provide such neutral criteria.

Discussion

Stewart argued that the abortion right was not violated by the Hyde Amendment. He drew on *Maher* v. *Roe*, which concerned a Connecticut welfare regulation that allocated Medicaid payments for childbirth but not for abortion.[12] In that case, the court held that the state may attempt to make childbirth a more attractive alternative to abortion in order to influence a woman's decision. The fact that some women may be too poor to pay for an abortion does not mean that the state has placed obstacles in the path. There was a "basic difference between direct state interference with a protected activity and state encouragement of an alternative activity." The Hyde Amendment was like the Connecticut welfare regulation in that it placed no direct obstacles in the way of a woman's right to an abortion. Stewart pointed out that the Hyde Amendment left an indigent woman with the same range of choices that she would have had if Congress had not chosen to subsidize any health care costs. Furthermore, the fact that a right exists does not require that it be funded. (For example, a citizen has a right to travel, but the government is not required to fund travel. It may be regrettable, but it is of no constitutional consequence, that wealthy people are more able to afford to travel than are poor people.)

The Establishment Clause and Free Exercise Clause claims of McRae were handled rather easily. McRae's first argument was that the Hyde Amendment violates the prohibition against religious establishment because it "incorporates into law the doctrines of the Roman Catholic Church concerning the sinfulness of abortion and the time at which life commences." But Stewart argued that the Hyde Amendment meets the three-part *Lemon* test. The amendment did have a secular purpose, its primary purpose was neither to advance nor inhibit religion, and it encouraged no excessive entanglements between religion and government. Nor did it follow that a law is unconstitutional simply because it happened to coincide or harmonize with a religious principle. "That the Judaeo-Christian religions oppose stealing does not mean that a State or the Federal Government may not, consistent with the Establishment Clause, enact laws prohibiting larceny," contended Stewart. The claim that religious free exercise was violated was not even dealt with by Stewart because of an important technical problem: none of the women actually claimed that they sought abortions for religious reasons, and "it is necessary in a free exercise case for one to show the coercive effect of the enactment as it operates against h[er] in the practice of h[er] religion."[13]

In *Harris,* Stewart relied upon the "rational relation" test that Rehnquist, in dissent, had advocated in *Roe.* The government had a legitimate interest in protecting potential life, and all that Congress had done was advance its legitimate interest through funding. Stewart criticized the lower court for using a "balancing" test to rule against the Hyde Amendment: "In making an independent appraisal of the competing interests involved here, the District Court went beyond the judicial function." Indeed, such "decisions are entrusted under the Constitution to Congress, not the courts." Like Rehnquist, Stewart showed deference to the political branches of government. His opinion allowed Congress to succeed in limiting the number of abortions performed under the right established in *Roe.*

This type of analysis frustrated the dissenting Justices. Justice Blackmun contended that the legislative process had not adequately represented the interest of poor women, and Justice Marshall emphasized that those women were from minorities in disproportionate numbers. Stevens noted that *Roe* had placed the abortion decision, prior to viability, squarely in the hands of a woman and her doctor. Only "valid health regulations" may be imposed in the second trimester. Stevens argued that *Roe* had made it clear that the government may not pursue its valid interest in protecting potential life until viability occurs; therefore, the Hyde Amendment was unconstitutional.

This closely decided case made it clear that the Supreme Court recognized the right of Congress to make public policy choices based on moral standards. Congress can support childbirth over abortion with its funding, even if it cannot outlaw abortion. But how far can Congress go to enforce its morality-based decisions? The next case illustrates that the power of the purse—Congress's appropriation power—can have profound ramifications.

EXAMPLE 3

Rust v. *Sullivan,* 111 S. Ct. 1759 (1991)

Facts: In 1970 Congress passed Title X of the Public Health Service Act, which provides federal funds for family services. These funds were to be distributed with an important limitation: section 1008 stipulated that "[n]one of the funds appropriated under this subchapter shall be used in programs where abortion is a method of family planning." The Secretary of Health and Human Services interpreted this to prohibit counseling about the use of abortion for family planning and to prohibit abortion referrals. There were also other directives from the Secretary that are not directly relevant to this case (for example, a prohibition against lobbying for abortion by clinics receiving funds). Dr. Irving Rust worked at a clinic that received federal funds under this law. He went to court to argue that the law violated the First and Fifth Amendments of the Constitution. A federal district court ruled in favor of the Secretary of Health and Human Services, and this ruling was affirmed by a court of appeals. Dr. Rust appealed to the Supreme Court.

Result: The Title X restrictions on abortion do not violate either the First or the Fifth Amendments of the Constitution.

Argument of the Case: Rehnquist, Chief Justice. First of all, Rehnquist acknowledges that the law is ambiguous. The wording of section 1008 does not clearly require the prohibition of abortion counseling. However, the Secretary's interpretation is permissible; his "construction of Title X may not be disturbed as an abuse of discretion if it reflects a plausible con-

struction of the plain language of the statute and does not otherwise conflict with Congress' expressed intent." While it is true that this Secretary's
interpretation represents a break with previous interpretation, this new
interpretation was an attempt to respond to critical reports of the General
Accounting Office, stating that the administration of the law "failed to
implement properly the statute." Taking this into consideration, the law is
clearly constitutional. The government may, "without violating the Constitution, selectively fund a program to encourage certain activities it believes to be in the public interest, without at the same time funding an
alternate program which seeks to deal with the problem in another way."
A woman's right to an abortion is not violated by this law.

Blackmun dissents.[14] Until today, the Supreme Court has never upheld
"viewpoint-based restrictions of protected speech." It is disturbing that
this law goes well beyond the prohibition of certain lobbying activities to
a whole range of "communicative conduct." It manipulates the content of
doctor-patient dialogue. Since the suppressed speech contains "truthful
information regarding constitutionally protected conduct...one can
imagine no legitimate governmental interest that might be served by suppressing such information."

Stevens dissents. The new interpretation of the law was "an assumption
of policymaking responsibility that Congress had not delegated to the
Secretary." The Secretary did not change the application of the law: he
created a new law.

O'Connor dissents. The language and the history of the legislation do
not allow for the Secretary's interpretation. Congress, rather than the courts,
should clarify its intention or accept the consequences if it fails to act:
"We should not tell Congress what to do before it has chosen to do it."

Discussion

Again drawing on the precedent set in *Maher*, Rehnquist says that "the Government has not discriminated on the basis of viewpoint; it has merely chosen to
fund one activity to the exclusion of another." This is something that the government does every day. Rehnquist points out that Blackmun's objections to
Title X would have to lead him to object to a number of government programs:

> When Congress established a National Endowment for Democracy to
> encourage other countries to adopt democratic principles, it was not con-
> stitutionally required to fund a program to encourage competing lines of
> political philosophy such as Communism and Fascism. Petitioners' asser-
> tions ultimately boil down to the position that if the government chooses
> to subsidize one protected right, it must subsidize analogous counterpart
> rights.[15]

Rehnquist's analogy was not perfect; the government's choosing to fund
the spread of democracy (as opposed to the spreading of Fascism) is not exactly the same as when Congress acts deliberately to discourage the exercise of
a right that had previously been declared to be fundamental. Still, Rehnquist's

point was clear: the government does not have to make "value-free" political choices. It can even try to limit the effectiveness of *Roe* without violating the Constitution. The political process allows the political branches leeway in the promulgation of public policy, a fact that was emphasized when the Clinton Administration eliminated the restrictive administrative interpretation of Article X.

Opposing Rehnquist's argument for the Court, Justice Blackmun (one of the dissenting Justices) based his argument on another case, *American Communications Association* v. *Douds*.[16] In that case, the Court said, "to deny an exemption to claimants who engage in certain forms of speech is in effect to penalize them for such speech.... The denial is 'frankly aimed at the suppression of dangerous ideas.'" This kind of regulation is "intrusive" and "ideologically based." In other words, it violated the private sphere of communication (between doctor and patient) that the Constitution was designed to protect. Blackmun observed that "liberty, if it means anything, must entail freedom from governmental domination in making the most intimate and personal of decisions."

But this argument makes sense only if one assumes (as Blackmun no doubt did) that abortion does not involve the taking of a human life. Thus, the fundamental, underlying issue that many people saw as religious remained unsettled: What is life? If abortion involves murder, as most opponents of *Roe* and defenders of *Rust* believe, then the state is under no obligation to respect the decision that leads to that act, for no political community can allow its citizens to commit murder as the result of a private decision. On the other hand, if abortion is a medical procedure that eliminates only a "potential life" or a pre-personhood entity (as many supporters of *Roe* and opponents of *Rust* have contended), then it seems that the government should respect the private decision and communication that lead to that act. In such a case, the modern state should not concern itself with the decisions that a woman makes about the direction of her own life. However, in either instance, the problem is that the Court has rendered decisions that impact or even reflect current religious views.

Harris and *Rust* dealt with two instances where Congress sought to limit the ultimate scope of *Roe* v. *Wade*. Our next case continues to address the way in which the strictly political branches of government revise and define constitutional rights as defined by the Court. In this case we consider what kinds of regulations of and limitations on abortion can be introduced by state legislatures.

EXAMPLE 4

Planned Parenthood* v. *Casey, 112 S. Ct. 2791 (1992)

Facts: The Pennsylvania Abortion Control Act of 1982 required that a woman seeking an abortion give her informed consent prior to the procedure and that she be given certain information at least 24 hours before the abortion was performed. (Her physician was to inform her about the risks of abortion as well as the risks of carrying the fetus to term. Another section of the law required a physician or counselor to provide information regarding paternal child support and state-funded alternatives to abortion.) The law also required that minors seeking an abortion inform at least one parent (although there is a judicial bypass process for minors who do not wish to obtain or cannot obtain parental consent). Under the law, married women seeking abortions must sign a statement indicating that they have informed their husbands (with some exceptions—for example, when the husband is not the father or when informing the husband might result in bodily harm to the woman or to some other individual). The law did allow exceptions to all of the above requirements in the case of medical emergencies. Finally, the law required that facilities that perform abortions keep detailed records of the procedures, although the identity of each woman was to remain confidential. Before any of these provisions took effect, five abortion clinics and one independent doctor went to court to enjoin the provisions' enforcement on the grounds that they were unconstitutional. The district court ruled that all the provisions were unconstitutional, but the court of appeals upheld all the provisions except for the requirement that husbands of women seeking abortions be notified.

Result: There is nothing wrong with the informed-consent provisions of the law, even if it means that there will be a 24-hour waiting period for most abortions. The one-parent consent requirement for minors seeking abortions is constitutional. The husband notification provision is an undue burden and is invalid. The record-keeping provision of the law is constitutional.

Argument of the Case: O'Connor, Justice.[17] The question of abortion revolves around the meaning of "liberty" under the Fourteenth Amendment. A woman's right to an abortion is derived from this idea of liberty; there is a private sphere of belief and conduct that cannot be touched by the state, except under extraordinary circumstances. The ruling of *Roe* v. *Wade* is reaffirmed. But protecting *Roe* is also important because of *stare decisis* (the judicial principle that courts should attempt to adhere to precedent). In addition, *Roe* has had such an impact on society that overruling it would create significant societal problems: "The ability of women to participate equally in the economic and social life of the Nation has been facilitated by their ability to control their reproductive lives." The Supreme Court must under these circumstances "exercise that same capacity which by tradition courts always have exercised: reasoned judgment." Medical advancements since 1973 have advanced viability to a point earlier in pregnancy, but this fact does not invalidate the central principles of *Roe*. Whenever viability occurs, this is the point at which the state's interest in protecting the life of the mother and potential life becomes compelling. Following from the principles of *Roe*, an "undue burden" standard should be applied. A law or a provision of a law is invalid if it places "substantial obstacles in the path of a woman seeking an abortion." Taking all of this into consideration, *Roe*'s rigid trimester framework is rejected although the main principles of *Roe* are reaffirmed. Some "pre-viability" regulation is allowable, as long as no undue burden is placed on a woman's right to an abortion. The informed-consent, one-parent consent, and record-keeping provisions of the law are constitutional; the husband notification provision places an undue burden upon the woman and is unconstitutional.

Stevens concurs in part and dissents in part. *Roe* should be reaffirmed today, especially because of the importance of *stare decisis*. However, the trimester framework of *Roe* is not as problematic as O'Connor argues. If the state's interest is secular and begins with the recognition that the fetus is not a person under the law, then the interest is legitimate. However, the state's interest is "not grounded in the Constitution." It is a combination of humanitarian and pragmatic concerns. This limited interest of the state is not strong enough to allow for significant pre-viability encroachment on a woman's decision to have an abortion. The mandatory 24-hour waiting period is therefore wrong and unconstitutional: "The mandatory delay thus appears to rest on outmoded and unacceptable assumptions about the decisionmaking capacity of women," and it and the counseling provisions of the law are unconstitutional. The husband notification provision of the law is also unconstitutional for the same reasons.

Blackmun concurs in part and dissents in part. It is important that a woman's right to reproductive choice and "bodily integrity" has been reaffirmed here, but all the provisions of the Pennsylvania law are unconstitutional. Also, the trimester system established in *Roe* is still workable.

Rehnquist concurs in part and dissents in part.[18] *Roe* v. *Wade* was wrongly decided, and it should (consistent with the importance of *stare decisis*) be overruled. The concept of liberty that is guaranteed by the Fourteenth Amendment is not broad enough to include the abortion decision: "One cannot ignore the fact that a woman is not isolated in her pregnancy, and that the decision to abort necessarily involves the destruction of a fetus." All the provisions of the Pennsylvania law should be upheld. Even using the standards of *Roe*, these provisions should be upheld, because they do not prohibit abortion; they merely regulate the practice. Also, the "undue burden" standard applied in this case is simply an invitation to courts everywhere to apply their personal standards of right and wrong under the guise of "reasoned judgment."

Scalia concurs in part and dissents in part.[19] The states may permit abortion on demand, but they are not required to do so by the Constitution. In a democracy, issues like this one are to be decided by voting. Many laws intrude on liberty in the absolute sense. For example, laws against bigamy intrude on choices that men and women make about whom to marry. The issue is not whether to power to abort a fetus is a "liberty"; the issue is whether that liberty is a protected liberty.

Discussion

This case returns to the fundamental issue of whether there exists a constitutional right to an abortion. It also raises the secondary question of what limitations upon that right can be permitted, and it reveals the deep division within the Court about this issue. In her opinion, Justice O'Connor attempted to alleviate some of the problems with *Roe* by abandoning the trimester system and redefining the standards that should be used in abortion cases, but she was unable to resolve the problems in any satisfactory way. She pointed out that "men and women of good conscience can disagree, and we suppose some always shall disagree, about the profound moral and spiritual implications of terminating a pregnancy, even in its earliest stages." This underscores the problem of *Roe*: the question of when life or personhood begins cannot be answered in a way that will lead to consensus. Of course, it does not follow that the truth of any matter is measured by consensus, but it does remind us of the fact that there will always be disagreement about this basic issue.

But O'Connor did not seem to understand the full implications of her own point. She says: "the underlying constitutional issue [regarding pregnancy] is whether the State can resolve these philosophic questions in such a definitive way that a woman lacks all choice in the matter...." But we have already seen in our discussion of *Roe* that allowing women to choose abortion implies a definite answer to the question of when life or personhood begins just as much as prohibiting abortion implies an answer. O'Connor more or less maintains the standard of "viability" here. She defined it in this way: it is "the time at which there is a realistic possibility of maintaining and nourishing a life outside the womb, so that the independent existence of the second life *can* in reason and all fairness be the object of state protection."[20] By arguing that pre-viable fetuses cannot "in reason and all fairness" be protected by the state, O'Connor decided the very issue that she claimed could not be decided. Modern liberalism teaches that we should respect the right of individuals to make choices, but even John Stuart Mill argued that choices that lead to the physical harm of others cannot be allowed. (His standard was that society cannot punish people to protect moral standards as such, but coercion may be used to prevent physical harm.[21]) So the question remains: Do abortions cause physical harm to "others"—to other living human beings? This issue cannot be resolved by general praise for the goodness of choice. Regardless of one's personal position on the issue of abortion, it is important to analyze the continuing, complex, and unresolved problems that the Court has had in attempting to articulate the principles behind abortion rights.

The test that Justice O'Connor used and pressed for acceptance as a means to measure the constitutionality of the Pennsylvania law was the "undue burden" test. In other words, procedures and practices that unduly burden a woman's freedom to choose an abortion are unconstitutional. This test led O'Connor to reject the provision of the law that requires spousal notification (as distinguished from permission). Her argument was that many women would face consequences from notification severe enough to effectively prohibit them from obtaining the abortions that they have a right to obtain. The law did allow for exceptions to spousal notification, but these were not seen as sufficient. A woman who feared bodily harm from her husband did not have to notify him of the abortion, but O'Connor rightly pointed out that women can be subjected to severe psychological harm as well. A woman might also fear that her husband would harm her other children if she informed him of her desire for an abortion, and this possibility was not covered by the law. All this is true, but some asked an interesting question: Does the husband have no right to be involved in the abortion decision, even to the extent of being informed?

By way of providing an answer, O'Connor made a rather odd argument. She said that after a child's birth, the interest of the mother and the father is equal, but "before birth, however, the issue takes on a very different cast." She further contended that it "is an inescapable biological fact that state regulation with respect to the child a woman is carrying will have a far greater impact on the mother's liberty than on the father's." The reason is that the Constitution protects the rights of individuals, married or otherwise. Individuals should be free from unwarranted governmental intrusion into their privacy. Before birth, the woman is disproportionately affected by pregnancy, even if both the mother and father are equally affected after birth.

A couple of interesting side issues emerge here. If husbands have no right to be involved in the abortion decision, then what responsibilities should they have for the child after its birth? For instance, should a divorced man be able to refuse to pay child support on the grounds that he did not have the opportunity to be involved in his former wife's decision of whether or not to carry the child to term? Another ambivalence surrounding O'Connor's presumption of virtual individual autonomy of the pregnant woman (at least during the early stages of her pregnancy) arises when one compares O'Connor's approach to other presumptions in the law. For instance, in Minnesota, a man who attacks or through negligence causes harm to a pregnant woman's fetus can be charged with taking a life. Thus, in *Minnesota* v. *Merrill,* Sean Merrill was found guilty of first-degree and second-degree murder of Gail Anderson and second-degree murder of her unborn child, a 27-day-old embryo.[22] Fetal homicide is a crime in seventeen states, but Minnesota is one of only four states that create criminal liability for "pre-viable" fetuses. In other words, under *Roe,* Gail Anderson could have chosen to abort her fetus because it is not a person under the law, but Sean Merrill can be charged with murder for terminating the life of the same fetus. Apparently, a woman choosing an abortion is an autonomous individual carrying only "potential life" within her, but she is a mother with child if her fetus is killed by another.[23]

In his dissent, Rehnquist did not point to this problem. Still, he was as unhappy with O'Connor's "undue burden" standard as he was with the Supreme Court's earlier rationale in *Roe* v. *Wade.* He contended that the undue burden standard was "created largely out of whole cloth." Once again, he recommended a "rational relation" test whereby the Court would simply limit itself to determining whether the law has a rational relation to a valid state objective. Rehnquist believed that the "undue burden" test was too subjective. It was an invitation to the Justices to substitute their own moral views for those of elected officials. Legislatures can make moral choices without necessarily being right, but the courts should limit themselves in any way they can to avoid imposing their moral standards on the people. Rehnquist's approach had a certain appeal, but many observers wondered if the Court could really wash its hands and turn away from an issue that remains so important to American society.

SUMMARY

In spite of deep divisions in the Court, the right to an abortion has been reaffirmed. The basic principles of *Roe* continue to inform the Court. The right of privacy is understood to include the abortion decision, but that right has never been described as absolute; it must be balanced against the legitimate state interest in protecting potential life, an interest that becomes compelling at the point of fetal viability. Until then, the state can administer only regulations that do not create an "undue burden" on a woman's right to make her own decision about abortion. The Court continues to work to honor both life and liberty.

There are three main areas of controversy inherent in the abortion decisions. First is the generalized right to privacy that was initially revealed in *Griswold* v. *Connecticut*. For some, the contentious nature of *Griswold* leaves all the abortion decisions under a cloud. Second, every decision since *Roe* has been based on an unacknowledged and extralegal view of when life and/or personhood begins. The Court has emphasized that it cannot resolve this question, but it has acted as if the question were in fact resolved. Finally, the particular tests employed by the Court have provided legislators with very little guidance as to what regulations can be placed on abortion. The Court itself has been inconsistent regarding many of the specific rules and regulations surrounding this issue. Nor does the latest effort at clarification, by Justice O'Connor—the undue burden test—seem destined to solve this problem. What is "undue"? What is a "burden"? More litigation will follow *Casey* until acceptable parameters for legislative actions are firmly fixed.

The particular sensitivity of the abortion issue has led to a dynamic interplay between the courts and the political branches. The cases in this chapter illustrate how Congress and the state legislatures have worked to limit the applicability of *Roe*. And President Clinton joined this process by marking the twentieth anniversary of *Roe* by not only eliminating the prohibition against abortion counseling in federally funded family planning clinics but also by proposing a budget that included a change from previous administrations in that he restored federal funding for abortion services to Medicaid recipients.[24] Clinton also initiated a federal study of the controversial pill RU-486, known as the French abortion pill. If the study yields positive results, he has promised to lift the current ban on the drug's importation. But the push and shove nature of politics has failed to resolve the fundamental issues first raised in *Roe*. Where does the private sphere of life end and the public sphere begin?

NOTES

1. See our discussion of John Locke in Chapter 1, pp. 13–16.

2. In March 1993, Dr. David Gunn was murdered in Florida by an angry opponent of abortion, and in August of 1993 another doctor in Kansas was shot. Shortly thereafter, Rev. David Trosch tried to place a newspaper ad that described the murder of doctors who perform abortions as "justifiable homicide." See *Newsweek*, August 30, 1993, p. 59. Nearly a year later, also in Florida, a former minister and anti-abortion zealot, Paul Hill, murdered two people, one of whom was a doctor who performed abortions. Hill argued that such action was "a fulfillment of the commandment of Christ." See "Is Murder 'Justifiable Homicide'?" in *Newsweek*, August 8, 1994, p. 22.

3. The case is the *National Organization of Women* v. *Schiller*, 114 S. Ct. 798 (1994). The free speech ramifications of both Congress's law and the above decision have yet to be determined.

4. This case was decided with the companion case of *Doe* v. *Bolton*, 410 U.S. 179 (1973).

5. Justice Rehnquist joined in this opinion.

6. 381 U.S. 479 (1965).

7. For an excellent discussion of the transformation of the right to privacy, see Ralph Rossum and Alan Tarr, *American Constitutional Law* (New York: St. Martin's, 1983), pp. 701–11. They argue that limited privacy rights were originally place-oriented and property-based. These were extended to legally protected for example, relationships (marriage) in the 1960s and ultimately became rooted in the individual in *Griswold*.

8. 410 U.S. at 159 (1972).

9. *Roe* at 163.

10. *Roe* at 173.

11. This opinion was joined by Justices Marshall and Blackmun.

12. *Maher* v. *Roe*, 432 U.S. 464 (1977).

13. Cf. *Abington School District* v. *Schempp*, 347 U.S. 203 (1963).

14. This opinion was joined by Justices Marshall, Stevens, and O'Connor.

15. *Rust* v. *Sullivan*, III S.CT.1759 (1991).

16. 339 U.S. 382 (1950).

17. This opinion was joined by Justices Kennedy and Souter.

18. This opinion was joined by Justices White, Scalia, and Thomas.

19. This opinion was joined by Chief Justice Rehnquist, Justice White, and Justice Thomas.

20. Note: *can* and not *must*. Emphasis ours.

21. See John Stuart Mill, "*On Liberty*," in *Utilitarianism, Liberty and Representative Government* (New York: Dutton, 1951), pp. iii–v.

22. 450 N.W. 2nd 318 (1990). For a related discussion of this issue, see Chapter 16, p. 298.

23. One might try to reconcile this conflict by saying it is not the fetus that is being protected, but merely the woman's past choice (to continue her pregnancy) and future right to choose. But this reconciliation would be satisfying only to some. Others would retort that it is not clear why the status of the fetus should turn on how its mother chooses to regard it or how any other person chooses to regard it. Another question is why it is the process of choosing, rather than the moral worth of the choice, that is so important. For example, those who champion a woman's unlimited right of choice on the basis that her autonomy and dignity demand no less would surely be unhappy with a number of women who—for whatever reason—

choose abortion as a means of sex-selecting their children, especially when they disproportionately choose to abort female fetuses.

24. This would, in effect, repeal the Hyde Amendment. The estimated cost of funding Medicaid abortions in one year is between $62 million and $75 million to pay for approximately 312,000 abortions. See *Congressional Quarterly Weekly Report*, April 3, 1993, p. 839. Clinton's proposal was not adopted by Congress in the 1993–94 session.

16

Should Lifesaving Medical Care Be Imposed on Those with Strong Religious Objections?

THE PROBLEM POSED

Both the Judeo-Christian tradition and United States law emphasize the value and sanctity of human life.[1] The religious foundation of this belief is almost self-evident; it stems from the recognition that life is a precious gift from God that requires from us nurture, respect, and, above all, protection. This religious belief at least partially explains why murder is commonly regarded as the most serious of crimes. More striking yet is the fact that in many jurisdictions, attempted suicide is against the law. These statutes have been profoundly influenced by the religious convictions of those legislators who drafted them. Little wonder then, if one were searching for a statement of common morality, a formulation designed to demonstrate the primacy and universality of religiously inspired moral values, that one could conceive of no clearer formulation than the principle that it is morally wrong to deprive another person arbitrarily of his or her life. Presumably, all decent human beings should be able to agree to this moral precept, be they religious or not.

Yet the perceived importance of human life does not depend solely upon religious authority. The Declaration of Independence, drafted by Thomas Jefferson, declares the protection of natural rights, most notably the right to life, to be the logical end of government.[2] It is important to recall that the Declaration was rooted in the secular natural-rights philosophy of such seventeenth-century thinkers as Thomas Hobbes and John Locke, whose political philosophy derived not from God, but from the claim to have understood human nature accurately.[3] Thus, Hobbes argued that no desire or passion was as strong in human beings as the drive for self-preservation. Therefore, no right was as important as the right to self-preservation, a right so fundamental that its securing gave government its very reason for existence.

Thus, both a strong religious tradition and strong secular tradition support the idea that government possesses the general power to safeguard the life, health, and welfare of its citizens.[4] This generalized authority is called the police power and, under the American system of government, is thought to rest primarily with the states. An important example of the police power occurred in 1905, when the Supreme Court (in *Jacobson* v. *Massachusetts*[5]) upheld the right of the states to require all citizens to be vaccinated against smallpox. The contagious nature of smallpox, coupled with government's great authority to protect citizens' lives and health, overrode general individual objections to vaccination. But what if the state's interest was less, because the threat to citizens' lives did not stem from a contagious disease? Furthermore, what if citizens wanted to decline medical treatment in the name of religious objections raised under the First Amendment's Free Exercise Clause? More specifically, given the strong religious and secular beliefs within society in favor of choosing (and protecting) life, what happens when individuals choose to risk their lives because of unorthodox religious convictions? Such questions pose profound moral and legal tensions for a society that prizes the sanctity of life yet also treasures personal liberty. As troubling and difficult as these choices may be, however, they cannot be avoided, as the following cases reveal. All of them involve involuntary blood transfusions. The first focuses upon a controversial court order issued by a circuit court judge.

EXAMPLE 1

Application of President & Directors of Georgetown College, Inc.,
331 F.2d 1000 (1964)[6]

Facts: Mrs. Jesse Jones was a 25-year-old mother and a Jehovah's Witness. She and her husband interpreted the Bible's teaching that blood should not be ingested as prohibiting blood transfusions. Mrs. Jones was brought to the hospital when a ruptured ulcer caused her to lose two-thirds of her blood supply. The doctors believed that, without blood transfusions, she would die. However, the doctors thought that with blood transfusions there was a better than fifty-percent chance that she could be saved. When death appeared imminent, attorneys for the hospital applied for a court order, which was denied by the district court judge. They appealed. Before deciding on a course of action, Circuit Court Judge Wright consulted with Mrs. Jones's husband (who refused to approve the transfusion), Mrs. Jones's doctors (who all strongly recommended it), and Mrs. Jones (whose only audible reply was "Against my will").

Result: A court order was issued mandating a blood transfusion.

Argument of the Case: Wright, Judge. Signing the emergency order saving Mrs. Jones's life was necessary to preserve the *status quo* and prevent the legal issues from becoming moot (as they would have should she have died). Mrs. Jones's mental condition was much like that of a child in that she was unable to decide what to do. Nor did her husband have a right to deny medical treatment that could save her life. In addition, Mrs. Jones is the mother of a seven-month-old child, and the state, as *parens patriae,* will not allow voluntary child abandonment. (Allowing Mrs. Smith to die would be tantamount to this.) Furthermore, refusing blood transfusions looks a great deal like attempted suicide, which is commonly against the law. Honoring Mrs. Jones's request would expose the hospital and attending doctors to criminal and civil liability. But the most decisive consideration was that of life itself: "The final, and compelling reason for granting the emergency writ was that a life hung in the balance."

Discussion

This is a classic case. It pits, in stark terms, the right of the individual to hold and act upon religious convictions against the power of the state to act in order to preserve human life. Here, the conflict is resolved in favor of the state's interest in preserving human life. Despite the fact that this has been the most common approach of the judiciary, it is also worth noting that there exists a great deal of judicial discretion in this area of the law and that there have been conflicting rulings by other federal, state, and municipal courts.[7]

Motivating Judge Wright was the value of human life. Of course, preserving Mrs. Jones's life was the prerequisite for any extended consideration by the courts of the issues in this case. But for Judge Wright, preserving life was arguably the most important responsibility of government. But note that what motivated Mrs. Jones was a religious belief more fundamental than life itself. And just as the state could no longer litigate the case if transfusions were not administered, so it was also the case that after transfusions had been administered, they could not be undone. The damage to Mrs. Jones's religious convictions was irreversible. At this level, the case seemed impossible to resolve. In order to decide what to do, Judge Wright balanced the state's interest in preserving life against the importance of Mrs. Jones's religious beliefs. Here, the court sided with the state and with its obligation to preserve human life.

Once Judge Wright got past affirming the value of human life, his other reasons were relatively less important and also less persuasive. Regarding Judge Wright's assertion that Mrs. Jones's plight was similar to that of a child, in terms of being incapable of deciding what to do, there is good reason to resist Wright's analogy. First, even in her weakened physical and mental state, Mrs. Jones's preference was nonetheless clearly and unambiguously stated (her utterance "Against my will" would seem to be clear enough). Furthermore, her statement was entirely consistent with her previously stated opposition to blood transfusions.[8] Finally, the fact that Jones was taken to a hospital and sought medical attention (and, in Judge Wright's words, "did not want to die") did not necessarily diminish the force of Jones's opposition to blood transfusions. Mrs. Jones's position was undoubtedly that she generally favored life over death (and for that reason sought medical assistance), but she did not favor applying *any* form of medical attention in order to stay alive. Specifically, she rejected procedures and remedies that violated her understanding of Scripture, blood transfusion being one of the prohibited practices.

Furthermore, Judge Wright's observation that Mrs. Jones's choosing admission to a hospital furnished proof that she did not want to die was in tension with his suggestion that declining medical treatment was akin to attempted homicide. One either wishes to kill oneself or one does not; there would not seem to be a reasonable middle ground. Rather more persuasive was Wright's concern that Mrs. Jones's death would be akin to child abandonment, leaving her seven-month-old baby motherless. By this argument, Wright immediately established the immediate and significant interest of another person in Mrs. Jones's life, and thus emphasized that Mrs. Jones's life-and-death decision had immediate consequences for others. Yet even this point proved problematical. For instance, do Wright's comments indicate that if Mrs. Jones had no child, her desire to avoid blood transfusions would have carried more legal weight? Can the existence of immediate dependents, and not the will and religious beliefs of the individual, ever be the most important factor in a case like this? If not, precisely how important is this factor? Finally, while it is undeniable that Mrs. Jones's death would cause her child significant psychological harm, are there not other factors to consider? As one legal commentator has observed about cases like this, "there is a contrary argument of some moment, namely that the parent refusing medical treatment is providing the child with a most important lesson: that there are some moral and religious principles more important than physical life itself."[9]

Thus, the core issue involving forced blood transfusions inevitably involves choosing between respecting a person's life and his or her faith. We would note that a similar issue often arises in euthanasia cases, when the patient is critically ill and wants to die (or is so fundamentally impaired that loved ones want to make the decision for the individual). In these conflicts, too, the state's interest in preserving life is weighed against not the patient's religious beliefs but the patient's dignity and right to choose.[10] In each instance, what is at stake is the state's interest in preserving and affirming life. The question is this: Do religious convictions, any more than a person's dignity or self-determination, tilt the balance in favor of the individual and diminish the state's interest in life? If this question is difficult to answer, there is another conclusion easier to discern: the state's interest in safeguarding life is even greater for minors than for adults. Let us see why.

EXAMPLE 2

Jehovah's Witnesses in the State of Washington et al. v. King County Hospital No. 1 (Harborview), 278 F. Supp. 488 (1967)

Facts: A Washington law directed that children found to be dependent (partially defined as a person under eighteen who was "grossly and willfully neglected as to medical care necessary for his well-being") were to be turned over to the state court, which "shall make such order for the care, custody and commitment of the child as the child's welfare in the interest of the state requires." This provision was widely interpreted to permit the state to order blood transfusions for minors, even over the objections of parents. Certain Jehovah's Witnesses sued as a part of a class action against a variety of state defendants.[11] The Jehovah's Witnesses denied that the state possessed the authority to remove children from their family's authority and make them wards of the state. Again, they also argued that blood transfusions violated their religious beliefs[12] and advanced statutory and constitutional arguments to that effect (including a free exercise claim).

Result—Per Curiam: In that the right to practice religion freely does not include the liberty to expose children to ill health or death, the state may intervene in the name of health and welfare for their benefit and authorize blood transfusions, even over parents' objections.

Argument of the Case: Precedent dictates upholding the constitutionality of the challenged laws. Controlling is the Supreme Court case of *Prince* v. *Massachusetts,*[13] which examined the extent and limits of parental authority of parents over minors and concluded that the "right to practice religion freely does not include liberty to expose ... the child ... to ill health or death."[14] The Court acknowledged that the construction of the state statutes was still open to some controversy, and their final construction would be left to the state courts.

Discussion

This federal circuit court case makes clear one important fact. The state's interest in preserving citizens' lives is substantially stronger in the case of children than it is for adults (even when that adult is the parent of an infant child or children). The reason for this situation is clear and has been commonly acknowledged. The law generally presumes that children have not the maturity of judgment to govern their own lives successfully; in John Stuart Mill's words, they are sufficiently lacking in reason that their lives cannot be improved by free and equal discussion.[15] For this reason, parents possess the legal authority to act on behalf of their children and their best interests, while children (depending, of course, upon their age) are often excused from full legal liability for their acts.

Although parents can exercise broad authority over their children, *Prince* made clear that their authority was hardly absolute. The state can impose requirements upon children in spite of parents' wishes.[16] Under its *parens patriae* power, it can require school attendance, regulate the conditions and hours of children's work, and require children to receive compulsory health treatment (such as smallpox immunizations). *Prince* was (and remains) consistent with the broad range of state court decisions that upheld the power of the state to prosecute parents who deliberately denied medical aid to children (often relying instead upon prayer), especially when their refusal resulted in the death of their offspring. In the words of one of the most oft-cited early state precedents,[17] parents have the responsibility to protect children, who "when born into the world, are utterly helpless, having neither the power to care for, protect, or maintain themselves."[18] However, the court went on to note that when a parent rejects this responsibility for any reason, including religious beliefs, then the state is legally entitled to intervene on behalf of the child or, alternatively, to punish the parent if the child has suffered harm and intervention is no longer possible or desirable.

This rule has been commonly adopted, and the law appears to be reasonably clear in such cases. Not only does the state interest in preserving a child's life clearly outweigh a parent's authority to determine a child's best welfare, the cumulative body of case law suggests that the state's interest is stronger when it intercedes on behalf of a child, as opposed to an adult. Furthermore, in either instance, religious belief seems to provide little protection from state intervention. For example, in cases like the one above, parents claiming exemption from medical care for their children because of religious reasons generally have not been given any greater consideration than were parents claiming exemption for any other reason.[19]

In the first two cases, we examined cases in which courts overrode religiously based desires to decline medical care. In the first instance, a woman chose to endanger her own life; in the second case, parents had made the same decision regarding their child. But what might have been decided in the case of a pregnant woman? Presumably, a pregnant woman's plea for exemption from the imposition of lifesaving medical care would carry more weight than that of a nonpregnant woman because the state's interest would seem to be both in her life as well as in the health of the fetus. On the other hand, according to the landmark case of *Roe* v. *Wade*,[20] a woman's right to an abortion (in all but the last trimester) always outweighs society's interest in the life of the fetus. Therefore, a pregnant woman's claim for exemption would be indistinguishable from that made by a nonpregnant woman. Noting these complex questions, we are moved to inquire as to what extent is there a general societal interest in the life of the mother *and* the fetus? Therefore, it is to a third Jehovah's Witness blood transfusion case that we now turn our attention.

EXAMPLE 3

Raleigh Fitkin–Paul Morgan Memorial Hospital and Ann May Memorial Foundation in the Town of Neptune, New Jersey v. *Willimina and Stuart Anderson,* 201 A.2d 537 (1964)

Facts: Mrs. Anderson was more than 32 weeks pregnant. She informed the hospital that a blood transfusion violated her religious beliefs. The evidence suggested that without a transfusion, it was probable that both she and her unborn child would die. The mother left the hospital against the advice of her doctors. Still, both the mother and the hospital asked the court to determine the issues, for the issue was likely to rise again.

Result—Per Curiam: The court ordered that a special guardian be appointed for "the infant"; that the guardian be substituted for the Andersons as plaintiffs in the case; that the guardian be ordered to consent to such blood transfusions as were necessary to preserve the life of the mother and the child; and, finally, that the mother be directed to submit to such blood transfusions and that the father be restrained from interfering.

Argument of the Case—Per Curiam: Significantly, it was the need to protect the life of the infant child that provided the clearest rationale for the court to order blood transfusions. Indeed, "[t]he more difficult question is whether an adult may be compelled to submit to such medical procedures when necessary to save his life." Nonetheless, the case need not be settled in broad terms because "the welfare of the child and the mother are so intertwined and inseparable that it would be impracticable to attempt to distinguish between them...." Therefore, the blood transfusions (including those made necessary by the delivery) may be imposed to save *either* the life of the child or that of the mother.

Discussion

In this case, the court vigorously defended the obligation of the state to intervene in order to protect life. Interestingly, it viewed the fetus as an infant and regarded the court's obligation to preserve the fetus's health to be more important than its obligation to preserve the mother's life. Nonetheless, the fact that both the mother's life and the fetus's life are intertwined gave the court the maximum incentive for ordering transfusions over the objections of Mr. and Mrs. Anderson.

Although there are conflicting precedents, the *Fitkin Memorial Hospital* case still generally represents good law. It is important to note that it was decided some nine years before *Roe* v. *Wade.* What is striking about the opinion is the strength of the court's interest in the life of the fetus. Although courts today (post-*Roe*) often come to the same legal conclusion (that is, allowing governmental intervention by ordering blood transfusions to preserve the fetus's health), the following two considerations are relevant in terms of attempting to define the state's interest primarily in terms of the embryo or fetus:

A. According to *Roe,* a woman has a virtually unlimited right to an abortion during the first two trimesters of pregnancy. During the third trimester (roughly correlated with viability), a state, if it desires, can proscribe most abortions. Therefore, the state's interest in the life of the fetus increases dramatically during the third trimester of pregnancy, although even then its interest is not automatically determinative. (*Roe* made clear that while the state could outlaw third trimester abortions, it could not prohibit them in situations in which an abortion was necessary for the preservation of the life and health of the mother.) Therefore, to the extent that *Roe* afforded states a choice in how they would deal with third trimester abortions (a situation that, in theory at least, existed before *Roe*), it has limited effect in helping judges decide whether to order blood transfusions for the unborn. In situations where states have chosen to ban third trimester abortions, state abortion laws would be consistent with the *Raleigh Fitkin-Paul Morgan Memorial Hospital* decision. However, when a state permits third trimester abortions (choosing to favor the mother's right of choice over the life of the unborn), a tension exists. Requiring blood transfusions to save the life of the unborn child over the mother's objection (even if it means that the mother will lose her life) is hard to reconcile with a law that grants complete discretion to a woman over the course of her pregnancy.

We should also note that in the earlier stages of pregnancy, *Roe's* impact is greater. In such instances, *Roe* and subsequent decisions have clearly favored the woman's health and right of choice as the primary good to be protected against state intervention. In such instances when the state intervenes to impose lifesaving medical aid against the mother's wishes, *Roe* contradicts the *Raleigh Fitkin-Paul Morgan Memorial Hospital* decision (to the extent that decision can be applied to include a larger class of pregnant women). For second trimester pregnancies, the logic of *Roe* allows the state to permit abortions only when it is necessary to preserve the mother's life (not the situation here), and it does not allow government to contravene the woman's right to choose whether to end her pregnancy. This tension between the two cases makes clear why *Roe's* three trimester test is increasingly viewed as arbitrary and why decisions like *Raleigh Fitkin-Paul Morgan Memorial Hospital* have become more problematical of late.

B. Although *Roe's* impact on a case like this one is not simple, it is not the only kind of law that poses potential conflicts for court rulings that require blood transfusions for the unborn. In some instances (and according to some laws) a state can protect the right of the unborn child, irrespective of its stage of development. For example, Minnesota has a number of statutes that prohibit crimes against "unborn children" (defined as "the unborn offspring of a human being conceived, but not yet born").[21] The rationale of these laws, adopted after *Roe,* seems to intend the protection of both embryos and fetuses, and (as subsequently interpreted by the courts) the law does not even depend upon the mother or perpetrator being aware of her pregnancy.[22] From the perspective of protecting the unborn, the seeming tension with *Roe* is not hard to miss: *Roe* permits the mother substantial leeway in aborting an embryo or a fetus, yet Minnesota law punishes substantially the same act when performed by another person. According to the Minnesota Supreme Court, however, the conflict is more apparent than real, for the "defendant who assaults a pregnant woman causing the death of the fetus she is carrying destroys the fetus without the consent of the woman."[23] Thus, the life of the embryo or fetus is not so much protected as is the woman's right of choice regarding the unborn child's future.[24] The Minnesota approach essentially makes the following statement: as long as a woman maintains her pregnancy by taking no action to end it, the law assumes that she wishes to be pregnant and will punish those who harm the fetus or terminate the pregnancy.

Reconciling the logic of such unborn-children statutes to a case like *Raleigh Fitkin-Paul Morgan Memorial Hospital* is not easily done. The main problem is that the Minnesota laws protect the mother's autonomy in determining the outcome of her pregnancy and punish those who would interfere with or restrict her choice, yet when the court imposes a blood transfusion in order to save the life of the unborn child it elevates the state's interest in *not* terminating the woman's pregnancy over the woman's wishes. Clearly, a woman's choice and the life of the unborn can sometimes be competing goods protected by different aspects of the law. Furthermore, both the Minnesota laws and *Roe* v. *Wade* are grounded in the secular rationale of maximizing a woman's liberty—that is, her freedom of choice. Some may question if the adoption and elevation of such a secular rationale, coupled with the rejection of the religious rationale for refusing medical intervention in *Raleigh-Fitkin Paul* (and in the previous cases examined in this chapter), reflect a bias against religion by the state.

Despite the pervasiveness of such questions and the existence of troubling complexities regarding the legal and moral status of the unborn, it is perhaps reflective of the complex factors raised by such cases that the one conclusion which seems relatively clear actually contradicts the court's language in *Raleigh-Fitkin Paul*. Despite the court's assertion there, what matters most in such cases is the state's interest in preserving the mother's (and not the unborn child's) life. In the final analysis, whether the woman is pregnant or not, or has an infant son or daughter or not, probably matters less than the fact that her life hangs in the balance. In such instances, the state's interest in preserving *her* life governs, despite her religious convictions.

SUMMARY

The three cases analyzed in this chapter all deal with individuals who refused medical treatment because of their religious convictions. In these cases, the courts upheld mandatory blood transfusions against the claims of a mother, the claims of parents speaking on behalf of their children, and the claims of a pregnant woman. Since the cases presented here represent the way that the courts have normally decided these cases, it is probably reassuring to note that the courts' decisions are consistent on this general issue.

However, difficulties in viewing these cases consistently can easily arise if the courts were more inclined to honor the religious beliefs and assertions of those refusing lifesaving medical procedures. Assimilating what the courts have said, one might be inclined to conclude that the state's strongest interest in preserving its citizens' lives can be ranked as follows (going from strongest interest to weakest): minors, adults, and unborn children (embryos and fetuses). Given the cases discussed in this chapter, the following questions arise for those who are inclined to allow the individual greater latitude in refusing lifesaving medical treatment. If the state should honor some or all religious-based refusals of lifesaving medical treatment, which requests should be respected? Should the state defer in each kind of case mentioned in this chapter? If not, does the state really have a stronger interest in protecting the lives of children than adults, and adults more than the unborn, and are all unborn equal in dignity and equally deserving of protection? Furthermore, according to what principle should the state intervene in some cases and defer in others? For instance, what does it say about the state's respect for religious belief when it contravenes such belief to impose lifesaving measures for the sake of the unborn but accepts a secular rationale for abortion? These, of course, are not simple questions. But the central question raised in this chapter is itself far from simple. It addresses the most fundamental issues of religious belief and the purpose of the state. Such matters can be, quite literally, questions of life and death.

NOTES

1. There is general agreement upon this point, but note Peter J. Riga's comment that the idea of sanctity of life "has always been difficult to express, and perhaps after *Roe* v. *Wade* it is no longer a viable legal concept." See Peter J. Riga, "Compulsory Medical Treatment of Adults," *Catholic Lawyer* 22 (Spring 1976), p. 134. Riga's discussion is provocative, and a number of points discussed in his article are also raised in this chapter.

2. This does not mean that a person can never be deprived of life. Rather, it means that government has an obligation to preserve and safeguard its citizens' lives and can never arbitrarily deprive them of their lives.

3. On the incompatibility of natural rights and divine revelation, see Walter Berns, "Religion and the Founding Principle,"

in *The Moral Foundations of the American Republic*, ed. Robert H. Horwitz, 3d ed. (Charlottesville, VA: Univ. of Virginia Press, 1986), pp. 215–28.

4. The government acts by enforcing the *criminal* law. This idea is the focus of this chapter. Increasingly, however, such cases have been the subject of civil lawsuits. The front page of the August 20, 1993, Minneapolis *Star-Tribune* carried an account of a $5.2 million judgment awarded by a jury to the natural father of an 11-year-old boy who died of diabetes when his Christian Scientist mother did not seek medical treatment. Seven defendants, including the boy's mother and several Christian Scientist associations (one of them a Christian Science church) and representatives, were assessed damages. According to the *Star-Tribune*, this was the

first civil case to go trial on the issue of whether a reasonable person (and not a reasonable Christian Scientist) could rely on prayer when treating illness. According to the testimony of one medical expert, the boy would have had a 99% probability of being cured if appropriate medical care had been sought. The jury later awarded an additional $9 million in punitive damages to the father.

5. 197 U.S. 11 (1905).

6. For the appeals court opinion denying a petition for rehearing, and particularly for the provocative dissenting opinions of Justices Miller and Burger, see the Feb. 3, 1964, appeals court decision, 331 F.2d 1010 (1964).

7. For example, judgments that have upheld a patient's limited right to refuse treatment for religious and other reasons are various and include *Erickson* v. *Dilgard*, 44 Misc. 2d 27, 252 N.Y. S. 2d 705 (Sup. Ct. Nassau County 1962); and *In re Estate of Brooks*, 32 Ill. 2d. 361, 205 N.E. 2d 435 (1965). It is noteworthy that Brooks was a single woman who had no dependents.

8. Riga, p. 124.

9. Riga, p. 124.

10. Admittedly, there is a real question of whether the right to choose represents a meaningful concept in American law. It frequently arises as a synonym for privacy rights akin to those identified in *Roe* v. *Wade*, 410 U.S. 113 (1973).

11. Defendants included the State Attorney General, other state governmental officials, individual physicians, superior court judges and officials of the superior court, and individual members of hospital staffs within the state of Washington.

12. The biblical passages relied upon by the Jehovah's Witnesses include Acts of the Apostles, Chapter 15, verse. 20 ("Hence my decision is not to trouble those from the nations who are turning to God, but to write to them to abstain from things polluted by idols and from fornication and from what is strangled and from blood") and Leviticus, Chapter 17, verse 10 ("As for any man of the house of Israel or some alien resident who is residing as an alien in your midst, who eats any sort

of blood, I shall certainly set my face against the soul that is eating the blood and I shall indeed cut him off from among his people").

13. 321 U.S. 158 (1944).

14. *Prince* v. *Massachusetts* at 442.

15. Regarding his simple principle (that the sole ground under which society can interfere with individual liberty is selfprotection), Mill observed that "[i]t is, perhaps, hardly necessary to say that this doctrine is meant to apply only to human beings in the maturity of their faculties. We are not speaking of children, or of young persons below the age which the law may fix as that of manhood or womanhood. Those who are still in a state to require being taken care of by others, must be as protected against their own actions as well against external injury." John Stuart Mill, *On Liberty* (Chicago: Henry Regnery, 1955), p. 14. A controversial (and everchanging) exception to this dictum has been some court decisions involving abortion that have overturned parental notification laws.

16. A somewhat different approach is to identify three interests at stake: (1) the parents, who have the right to raise a child according to their beliefs; (2) the best interest of the child, for which the court substitutes its judgment for the child's; (3) and the state, motivated by its obligation to preserve the life and welfare of its citizens along with the ethical integrity of the medical profession. Generally, courts employing this analysis have come to the same conclusion, arguing that (2) and (3) outweigh (1). See Mathew J. Marcus," Note, State Intervention When Parental Decision Based on Religious Beliefs Threatens Child Held Constitutional—In re *McCauley*, 409 Mass. 134, N.E. 2d 411 (1991)," *Suffolk Law Review* vol. XXV (1991), pp. 813, 814–17.

17. *People* v. *Pierson*, 68 N.E. 243 (1903).

18. *People* v. *Pierson* at 246.

19. See Deborah Sussman Steckler, "A Trend Toward Declining Rigor in Applying Free Exercise Principles: The Example of State Courts' Consideration of Christian Science Treatment for Children, "*New*

York Law School Law Review, vol. 36 (1991), pp. 487–519.

20. 410 U.S. 113 (1973).

21. These include the murder of an unborn child in the first degree, the second degree, the third degree; manslaughter of an unborn in the first degree and in the second degree; assault on an unborn child in the first degree and in the second degree; injury or death of an unborn child in the commission of a crime; criminal vehicular operation resulting in death to an unborn child, or resulting in injury to an unborn child; and criminal vehicular homicide and injury resulting in death to an unborn child. There are a few other kinds of applications of state laws (not discussed here) that raise similar kinds of problems discussed in this section; these are laws that protect the unborn child from abuse by its mother and can be used to prosecute mothers who engage in alcohol or drug abuse prior to the child's birth.

22. *State of Minnesota* v. *Merrill,* 450 N.W. d 318, 323 (Minn, 1990).

23. *State of Minnesota* v. *Merrill* at 321.

24 . Whether the status of the unborn *ought* to depend upon the wishes and desires of the mother is an intriguing philosophical question beyond the scope of this chapter.

PART V

Religious, Employment,
and Civic Obligations

17

How Can the Religious Beliefs of Employers and Employees Affect Their Work?

ˋ THE PROBLEM POSED

Religion in the workplace constitutes a much litigated aspect of the American law of church and state. We have already encountered similar examples of religiously related claims. In Chapter Six we observed how a Mormon-owned gymnasium was permitted, by an Congressional exemption to the 1964 Civil Rights Act upheld by the Supreme Court, to discriminate in favor of hiring employees who shared its religious faith.[1] In Chapter Nine the important case of *Employment Division, Department of Human Resources* v. *Smith* was discussed, and we noted that when individuals were fired from their jobs for violating the law (even though their illegal action was undertaken for a religious reason), the Supreme Court held that unemployment compensation could be legally withheld.[2] Finally, in Chapter Ten, we noted the moral predicament of FBI Special Agent Ryan, whose firing was upheld by the federal courts, even though his refusal to carry out an assignment was made on the basis of his religious beliefs.[3]

The questions raised by such cases make up only a small sample of the many workplace and business-related issues that arise in the law. In this chapter we explore these issues and the questions that they raise somewhat more systematically.

EXAMPLE 1

Tony and Susan Alamo Foundation v. *Secretary of Labor,* 471 U.S. 290 (1985)

Facts: The Alamo Foundation is a nonprofit religious organization created "to establish, conduct and maintain an Evangelistic Church; to conduct religious services, to minister to the sick and needy, to care for the fatherless and to rescue the fallen, and generally to do those things needful for the promotion of Christian faith, virtue and charity." The Foundation derives its income from the operation of a number of commercial businesses (service stations, clothing outlets, hog farms, and so on). The businesses are staffed largely by "associates" who are former drug addicts, derelicts, or criminals, all in the process of rehabilitation. They are unpaid but receive food, clothing, shelter, and other benefits. The Secretary of Labor alleged these workers were compensated in violation of minimum wage, overtime, and record-keeping provisions of the Fair Labor Standards Act. Among other things, the Foundation argued that the application of this act violates rights protected by the Free Exercise and Establishment Clauses of the First Amendment.

Result: Applying the Fair Labor Relations Act to the Alamo Foundation violates neither religion clause of the First Amendment.

Argument of the Case: White, Justice. The Foundation's businesses constitute a business within the meaning of the Fair Labor Relations Act, and the Alamo Associates are also covered by its provisions, for they are employees who receive compensation. Neither the act's language nor its legislative history anticipates exceptions for religious, nonprofit organizations. The Free Exercise Claim, that the minimum wage and record-keeping requirements violated the associates' religious beliefs,[4] creates no burden upon religious belief. The legislative act classifies compensation broadly to include "the reasonable cost...of furnishing [an] employee with board, lodging, and other facilities"; therefore, they are covered, and their religious beliefs against accepting wages are not compromised. Nor does the act's record-keeping provision violate the Establishment Clause by having the primary effect of inhibiting religious activity or by excessively entangling the government with religion. The record-keeping provisions are of modest scope, apply only to commercial activity, and do not require ongoing governmental surveillance.

Discussion

The Alamo Foundation was no ordinary employer, and the associates it aided were no ordinary employees. Therefore, the case's inclusion in this chapter emphasizes the wide variety of religiously related cases that arise in the workplace. Furthermore, while for some purposes religiously affiliated organizations are treated differently under the law (for example, they can favor employees of their own religious persuasion without standing accused of violating civil rights laws), this case makes clear that in other (indeed most) areas of the law they are treated the same as for-profit, nonreligious, commercial businesses.

This case was decided on fairly narrow grounds by a unanimous Supreme Court. The nature of the decision probably precludes broad generalizations regarding the case's significance. Nonetheless, it can be fairly stated that the Supreme Court was quite content to leave questions about the rules, regulations, and exceptions pertaining to religiously affiliated businesses for Congress to settle. Thus, not only did the Constitution not demand any single approach in this legal area, but there was also a variety of legislative approaches that it did not preclude.

EXAMPLE 2

Braunfeld v. *Brown,* 366 U.S. 599 (1961)

Facts: A 1959 Pennsylvania criminal statue prohibited the Sunday sale of a large category of items. Braunfeld is an Orthodox Jewish merchant engaged in the sale of clothing and home furnishings (goods prohibited from Sunday sale by the statute). His religion requires him to honor the Sabbath and close his store from sundown Friday to sundown Saturday. He contends that the statute penalizes his religion by placing him at a serious economic disadvantage, therefore burdening his religious practice because Braunfeld will have to keep his store closed both Saturday for religious reasons and Sunday for secular reasons.

Result: The Pennsylvania law poses only an indirect burden on religious practice that does not violate the Free Exercise Clause of the First Amendment (as applied to the states by the Fourteenth Amendment).

Argument of the Case: Warren, Chief Justice.[5] Freedom of religious beliefs is absolute; freedom of religiously related practice is not. Yet the contested law does not directly outlaw any religious practice; it imposes only an indirect financial burden upon religiously motivated actions while not intending any invidious discrimination against religion or any particular religion. Striking down such legislation would unduly restrict the legislature. Nor does the Constitution require that an exemption be made for those disadvantaged by their religious convictions. Whether such an exemption is wise is another matter; the Court's obligation is to evaluate the legislation's constitutionality, not its wisdom. Additionally, such an exemption might economically advantage people like Braunfeld (and tempt others to claim religious motivations), for being open on Sundays when competitors are closed would likely afford economic advantage.

Frankfurter, with Harlan, concurs. The secular interest (guaranteeing a day of rest "which assures to the community a time during which the

mind and body are released from the demands and distractions of an increasingly mechanized and competition-ridden society") must be weighed
against the economic disadvantage to the religiously oriented enterpriser.
The former tends to predominate.[6]

Brennan dissents. Since Braunfeld may well lose his business, this case
poses the question of whether the state can require such an individual to
choose between his business and his religion. The correct First and Fourteenth Amendment standard dictates that the judgment of this case be
reversed. (When legislation is challenged on these constitutional grounds,
the government must not merely show that the legislation was reasonable,
as it has done in this case, but it also must demonstrate that a restricting of
rights is justified by a grave and immediate danger to the interests that the
state may lawfully protect.)

Stewart dissents. The state cannot constitutionally compel a citizen to
choose between religious faith and economic survival.

Douglas dissents. The contested law places minorities at a serious economic disadvantage and amounts to state interference with their free exercise of religion.

Discussion

It seems difficult today to believe that, as late as 1960, forty-nine out of fifty
states maintained some kind of restriction upon Sunday commercial activities.
The small number and influence of such laws today provide further evidence
(if further evidence is indeed needed) of the increased secular pressure upon
American life and of the ever-increasing influence of commerce and business.
Only in the restrictions placed upon the Sunday sale of alcohol by an ever-di-
minishing number of states can we today find remnants of Sunday observance
laws.

The stated purpose behind the enactment of these laws was the state's interest in helping ensure a shared day of rest for its citizens. Only two kinds of
business establishments were usually allowed to conduct business on Sunday:
recreational and sporting organizations (baseball teams, amusement parks) and
businesses that sold necessities (grocery stores, drugstores).

Although Sunday closing laws were commonly justified by a secular purpose, these laws also contained a strong religious flavor. Two religious aspects
of these laws combined to make them susceptible to legal challenge. First,
their origin (and earlier practice in American colonies and states) could be directly traced to the Fourth Commandment:

> Remember the sabbath day to keep it holy. Six days shalt thou labour, and
> do all thy work: But the seventh day is the sabbath of the LORD thy
> God: in it thou shall not do any work, thou, nor thy son, nor thy daugh-
> ter, thy manservant, nor thy maidservant, nor thy cattle, nor thy stranger
> that is within thy gates. For in six days the LORD made heaven and
> earth, the sea, and all that in them is, and rested the seventh day: where-
> fore the LORD blessed the sabbath day and hallowed it.[7]

Second, the particular day singled out by these laws (Sunday) coincided with the Christian Sabbath. Although Sunday represented the official day of rest for Protestants and Catholics, it was not the Sabbath for certain religious minorities such as Seventh-day Adventists and Jews, who believed that the Sabbath should be observed on Saturday. Therefore, Sunday observance laws were potentially open to two kinds of attack. First, they favored religion over nonreligion, imposing a day of rest upon all citizens, even those whose religious or nonreligious opinions did not require or desire one. Second, the laws seemed to prefer (or at least rely upon) the interpretation of one religious tradition and therefore favored that tradition.

These issues were resolved by the Supreme Court in four cases decided the same day, one of which was *Braunfeld* v. *Brown*. The Sunday day-of-rest state laws were contested on Establishment Clause grounds in two of the cases, and *Braunfeld* was one of two cases that challenged the Sunday observance laws on Free Exercise Clause grounds.[8] In all the cases, the constitutionality of the challenged state laws was upheld. Against the contention that the state had advanced religion by legislating an official, Christian day of rest, the Supreme Court conceded that while this may have been the main purpose of such laws, it no longer was—a secular purpose of providing a shared day of rest now predominated. These days of rest "have become part and parcel of... great governmental concern wholly apart from their original purposes or connotations."[9] What about the fact that the government's concern for the health and welfare of its citizens was manifested by prohibiting commercial activity on Sunday, the Christian Sabbath? The Court, referring to the laws' secular purpose, noted that the "present purpose and effect of most of them is to provide a uniform day of rest for all citizens; the fact that this day is Sunday, a day of particular significance for the dominant Christian sects, does not bar the State from achieving its secular goals." Indeed, to "say that the States cannot prescribe Sunday as a day of rest for these purposes solely because centuries ago such laws had their genesis in religion would give a constitutional interpretation of hostility to the public welfare rather than one of mere separation of church and state."[10] Justice Frankfurter furnished some additional support of this position in his concurring opinion, observing that a day of rest needed to be common (not individually determined); that letting individual enterprisers choose different days of rest would disrupt families whose members were differently employed; and that disallowing Sunday (while requiring another day, Monday or Tuesday, for instance) was unreasonable. He further contended that designating Sunday as a day of rest conformed to the moral temper and sense of community in a way that no other day could.[11]

The staunchest opponent of these arguments was Justice Douglas, whose dissent encompassed all four cases. Douglas emphasized the continuing religious connotations inherent in Sunday as a day of rest. Repeatedly, he made the point that the law's familiarity blinded people to its religious importance as well as to the burden it placed upon religious minorities. Douglas's argument is provocative and should be considered:

The issue of these cases would therefore be in better focus if we imagined that a state legislature, controlled by orthodox Jews and Seventh-Day Adventists, passed a law making it a crime to keep a shop open on Saturdays. Would a Baptist, Catholic, Methodist or Presbyterian be compelled to obey that law or go to jail or pay a fine? Or suppose Moslems grew in political strength here and got a law through a state legislature making it a crime to keep a shop open on Fridays. Would the rest of us have to submit under the fear of criminal sanctions?[12]

Nor were the questions of whether the Sunday closing laws are religiously motivated or discriminatory the only controversial ones raised by these cases. Another somewhat related issue posed by *Braunfeld* v. *Brown* posits the following theoretical and legal question: Assuming that the Sunday closing laws can be upheld on secular grounds, to what extent does fairness (and the Constitution) require exemptions for individuals who have unintentionally been harmed by the law? Legally, the Court held that exemptions were not constitutionally mandated, which meant that they were left to the states to adopt or reject. Theoretically, the question of fairness simply admits no obvious answer. There is no doubt that Braunfeld is economically disadvantaged because of his religion; he is obligated to close his store two days rather than one. On the other hand, as the Court pointed out, granting him an exemption would likely have afforded him a competitive advantage. His would have been one of few stores open on Sunday, and it would be fair to assume that his Sunday business would have exceeded his Saturday sales. Given this realization, would some people falsely claim a religious belief in order to gain financial advantage? Would the government be obligated to examine the sincerity of the religious beliefs of those who applied for exemption? What about the employees? Would they have to be of the same religion? And, if so, would this not necessitate religious discrimination in hiring in order to mitigate the social and religious effects on the employees of the exempted business?[13]

The Sunday day-of-rest cases are therefore interesting for a number of reasons, not the least of which is that they illustrate the practical difficulty that surrounds the elimination of all advantage or disadvantage for those who are burdened by the passage of laws that unintentionally affect their private religious beliefs and practices. This problem is common to almost all religious disputes in the workplace. Although Sunday rest laws are relatively rare today, and although most of these disputes tend to involve employees rather than owners of businesses, fairness questions are never far below the surface of even routine religiously related workplace disputes. Let us examine a far more routine dispute.

EXAMPLE 3

***Rasch* v. *National Railroad Passenger Corporation*,** No. 90-0913 (JHG), 1991 U.S. Dist. Lexis 14431 (D.D.C. 1991)

Facts: Stephen Rasch is a practicing member of the Worldwide Church of God. His religious beliefs precluded him from working from sundown Friday until sundown Saturday, as well as from working on certain religious holidays. Rasch worked as an assistant conductor for Amtrak. He had low seniority, and under the labor contract seniority provided the basis for making work assignments. Shortly after being hired, Rasch informed his supervisor about his religious beliefs (he had not noted them in his job application). Initially, for a brief period of time, Rasch's supervisor accommodated his religious beliefs. However, fellow, more senior employees soon began complaining that the labor contract was not being followed and that they were being required to work trips for which Rasch had been scheduled. From February 6, 1988, until June 4, 1988, he was charged with thirty-two absences (causing his employer to replace him, or try to replace him). Additionally, from April 1987 to November 1988, he was unavailable for work some 123 times. Eventually, he was fired from his position.[14]

Result: Amtrak did not religiously discriminate in violation of Title VII of the United States Civil Rights Act when it failed to accommodate Rasch's religious beliefs, for accommodating Rasch would have placed too great a hardship upon Amtrak.

Argument of the Case: Green, Judge. The law is as follows: in order to prove that the anti-religious discrimination provision of the 1964 Civil Rights Act was violated, Rasch must show (1) that he subscribes to a bona fide religious belief that conflicts with an employment requirement; (2) that he has informed the employer of his belief; and (3) that he was disciplined or discharged for failure to comply with the employment requirement. Once these requirements have been established, then Amtrak assumes the burden of proving either that it had made a good-faith effort to accommodate Rasch or that it would have been impossible to accommodate him without undue hardship. Since such accommodation is impossible, and since there is no factual disagreement between the parties, summary judgment in favor of the railroad company was granted.[15]

Discussion

The *Rasch* case is included here because it is typical of the many religiously motivated conflicts that occur in the workplace. First, this is a district court case. Although religiously motivated work disputes claiming a violation of federal law or the Constitution all begin in such courts, often these disputes are ignored, for it is only circuit court or Supreme Court cases and opinions that are generally read or studied. Second, it is noteworthy that the case is pressed under Title VII of the 1964 Civil Rights Act, which prohibits religious discrimination in private employment.[16] Thus, most workplace disputes that become litigated do not assert that a real, potential, or past employer has violated the Constitution, but rather that the employer has violated the 1964

Civil Rights Act. Third, the case is typical of a number of these kinds of religiously motivated disputes because it describes a workplace that is more complicated than we are first likely to imagine. Recall that Rasch's supervisor initially was sympathetic and accommodating, granting Rasch the days off he requested. Only when Rasch's fellow workers complained did problems arise. Nor was it mere petty jealousy that motivated their complaints. The company had a comprehensive labor agreement with the United Transportation Union that governed a number of thorny and complex work assignment issues. It was hardly irrelevant that the agreement was seemingly violated by the informal agreements made between Rasch and his immediate supervisor.

Finally, this case is typical in that it represents a rather routine example of the manner in which federal law has been applied by the courts in these kinds of cases.[17] Note that although the burden of proof is initially put upon the individual (to show that he was disciplined or dismissed for acting according to a bona fide religious belief that conflicted with a work requirement about which the employee had informed his employer), the burden of proof very quickly shifts to the employer. Furthermore, the courts' application of federal law has emphasized accommodation and cooperation in the workplace. Thus, if an employer cannot accommodate an employee, it must clearly demonstrate that to do so would have caused undue hardship. This requirement imposes a rather high level of proof upon the employing company or corporation, no doubt with the intention of encouraging settlements of religiously motivated workplace disputes at an informal level, before they become litigated. Thus, the federal law encourages accommodation as a kind of rough and approximate proxy for fairness in the workplace.

But accommodation between employer and employee is not always possible. *Rasch* reveals as much. But what happens if no accommodation can be reached, and the employee quits or is dismissed for actions motivated by religious reasons? Is such a person entitled to unemployment insurance as a constitutional right? This question is explored below.

EXAMPLE 4

Thomas v. Review Board of Indiana Employment Security Division, 450 U.S. 707 (1981)

Facts: Thomas, a Jehovah's Witness, was originally hired by the Blaw-Knox Foundry and Machinery Company to work in a roll foundry that fabricated sheet steel for a variety of industrial uses. Approximately a year later, the roll foundry closed. Thomas was transferred to a department that fabricated turrets for tanks. Thomas also discovered that all remaining departments of Blaw-Knox were engaged in weapons production. Alleging that the direct production of weapons violated his religious beliefs, Thomas quit his job and applied for unemployment compensation under Indiana law. He was denied benefits. Indiana's law requires that unemployed workers be compensated for "good cause" unemployment (that is, through no cause of their own) but that people unemployed voluntarily for personal reasons not be eligible. Thomas argued that Indiana's denial of unemployment benefits violated the Free Exercise Clause of the First Amendment.

Result: Indiana's denial of unemployment benefits cannot be justified as the least restrictive method of achieving a compelling state interest and therefore violates the Free Exercise Clause of the First Amendment as applied to the states through the Fourteenth Amendment.

Argument of the Case: Burger, Chief Justice. Determining what constitutes a religious belief or practice is "a difficult and delicate task" that should not turn upon a judicial perception of the particular belief or practice in question...." Religious beliefs "need not be acceptable, logical, consistent, or comprehensible to others in order to merit First Amendment protection." Thomas's beliefs are protected by the First Amendment. A person cannot be forced to choose between exercising a First Amendment right and participating in an otherwise available public program. To force this choice is impermissible coercion. Such a practice can be permitted only if it is the least restrictive means of achieving some compelling state interest. The state's interest is twofold. First, it wishes to avoid widespread unemployment and the consequent burden to the unemployment fund if workers were allowed to leave jobs for personal reasons; second, the state would prefer avoiding detailed investigations by employers into employees' religious beliefs. Yet the number of people terminating employment for religious reasons is sufficiently small to make neither rationale sufficiently compelling to withstand constitutional scrutiny. Finally, a particular religion is not established by acknowledging Thomas's religion and extending him unemployment benefits; this appearance is just a consequence of the tension between the two religion clauses.

Blackmun concurs without opinion.[18]

Rehnquist dissents. The tension between the Establishment Clause and the Free Exercise Clause is largely created by the Court. The Court has unduly expanded the Free Exercise Clause by invalidating legislation that only indirectly penalizes religious beliefs and practices. By so doing, the Court requires Indiana to provide direct financial assistance to persons solely on the basis of their religious beliefs. This violates the Court's own (*Lemon*) Establishment Clause test. The religious exemption proviso would serve a religious *purpose*, would have the *effect* of advancing religion by facilitating the exercising of religious belief, and would excessively entangle the state in religion. Indiana may choose to grant a religious exemption; for the Supreme Court to do so distorts the Constitution and creates an unnecessary conflict between the two religion clauses of the First Amendment.

Discussion

Chief Justice Burger began by addressing an unavoidable question: Was Thomas really motivated by a true religious conviction? As we have noted, this kind of question cannot be avoided (as was considered in Chapter Six). Burger discussed this question in detail and decided in favor of minimal governmental evaluation of and interference with Thomas's proclaimed religious convictions.

The Indiana State Supreme Court had expressed doubt regarding Thomas's religious beliefs. It had concluded that Thomas made a personal philosophical choice, not a religious one. Why? According to that court, Thomas's "reasons for quitting were described as religious, [yet] it was unclear what his belief was, and what the religious basis of his belief was." Evidence for this conclusion was revealed by the fact that Thomas had admitted to struggling with his religious beliefs, that he had been unable to articulate them precisely, that Thomas's stated opinion that he could work at a job producing steel, some of which could end up in armaments, but could not work at a job that directly produced steel for armaments was at odds with his stated opposition to participating in the production of armaments, and that Thomas's Jehovah's Witness coworker did not hold similar reservations about producing steel. Burger found this evidence unconvincing and concluded that the Indiana Supreme Court's effort to examine the form and substance of Thomas's religious convictions was misguided. That Thomas was struggling with his religious views, or that his beliefs were not articulated with the consistency and precision "that a more sophisticated person might employ," gave the courts no reason to dissect a person's religious opinions.[19] Nor was it consequential that Thomas's coworker interpreted his Jehovah's Witness religion differently. In Burger's words, "Interfaith differences of that kind are not uncommon among followers of a particular creed, and the judicial process is singularly ill equipped to resolve such differences in relation to the Religion Clauses."[20] In the end, Burger upheld Thomas's simple statement of religious opposition. "I really could not, you know, conscientiously continue to work with armaments," Thomas had originally testified. "It would be against all of the ... religious principles that ... I have come to learn...."

Given the Court's acceptance of Thomas's religious opposition to armaments production, Burger's next point followed rather quickly. Indiana's law had unconstitutionally coerced Thomas by forcing him to choose between the free exercise of his religion and unemployment insurance. This is precisely the point of disagreement between Burger and Rehnquist (dissenting). For Rehnquist, Indiana's law imposed only an indirect (and therefore permissible) burden upon religion and religious belief. It did not outlaw or prohibit either; it simply made the practice of religion more costly. In Rehnquist's words, when "a State has enacted a general stature, the purpose and effect of which is to advance the State's secular goals, the Free Exercise Clause does not ... require the State to conform that statute to the dictates of religious conscience of any group." Rehnquist believed that there were very few instances in which the Constitution mandated (as opposed to merely permitted) a state to grant religious exemptions.

At stake in the debate between Burger and Rehnquist was the following question: When is the burden upon individual religious practice and belief so substantial that the Constitution is violated? Burger's point that the choice between job and religion raised in *Thomas* is so onerous as to create a kind of psychological coercion seems quite persuasive. However, Rehnquist's rebuttal also raises important concerns. Rehnquist pointed out that the Court's interpretation of the religion clauses (necessary to establish the idea of an impermissible governmental coercion) is itself inherently contradictory because it requires exemptions favoring religion under the Free Exercise Clause while denying religious favoritism under the Establishment Clause. Rehnquist attributed the growing instances of Establishment/Free Exercise Clause tensions to three primary causes. First, the growth of social welfare legislation during the last half of the twentieth century affected the individual in almost every area of life (including the workplace), thus significantly expanding the potential for religious conflict, litigation, and inconsistent court interpretations. Second, using the First Amendment against the states by means of the Fourteenth Amendment also greatly expanded the potential for religiously rooted litigation and thus increased the potential for tension between the two religion clauses. However, the final reason was arguably the most important one for the persistent tension between the two clauses. The potential for litigation coincided with the Supreme Court's expansion in meaning of both the Establishment Clause and the Free Exercise Clause. Given that expansion, and given increasing litigation, Rehnquist believed that conflict was inevitable.

If *Thomas* in 1981 represented an example of the new, broader interpretation of the Free Exercise Clause (a movement dating back to 1963[21]), Rehnquist believed that the Supreme Court's opinion in *Braunfeld v. Brown* had stood for a more traditional, restrictive, and sounder interpretation of that clause.[22] Although Rehnquist did not specifically elaborate upon the inconsistencies between the two cases, he certainly was correct to note their existence. We would observe that there are at least three important ways that the two cases are difficult, if not impossible, to reconcile.

First, the results of the two cases differ substantially. In *Braunfeld,* the Orthodox Jewish enterpriser did not prevail, for the Supreme Court did not grant him an exemption. In *Thomas,* the Supreme Court insisted that the Free Exercise Clause demanded such an exemption.

Second, the Supreme Court employed different constitutional standards in these two cases for determining whether a violation of the Free Exercise Clause had occurred. In *Braunfeld,* Chief Justice Warren accepted the proposition that a state could pass reasonable legislation for the public good. What was important was that the statute did not directly harm a religious practitioner. Thus, a state legislature, if it so chose, might grant an exemption to compensate those who were disadvantaged by general legislation, but it was not obligated to do so (for such an obligation would unduly restrict it). In *Thomas,* Burger employed a far more restrictive free exercise test in order to establish religious-based exemptions as a matter of constitutional right. In order to deny religious-based exemptions, Indiana had to demonstrate that its policy of compensating workers only for being unemployed due to no fault of their own, and not for personal reasons (including religious reasons), was the least restrictive means to achieving a compelling state interest. While in *Braunfeld* the burden of proof rested upon the individual to show some kind of direct (and significant) harm resulting from the contested legislation, in *Thomas* the state assumed the heavy burden of proof (laws restricting freedom of religion, as defined by the Court, were presumed unconstitutional). Little wonder that neither of Indiana's legal justifications for excluding personal religious reasons for unemployment benefits—its interest in safeguarding state funding and its concern for limiting employer probes of employees' religious beliefs—proved sufficiently compelling to withstand judicial scrutiny.

There was a third notable difference between the two cases. In *Braunfeld* the Court implied that one reason why the legislature, rather than the Court, should be charged with the granting of exemptions had to do with the overall complex social policy effects that such exemptions would have upon others. Permitting Braunfeld (and others like him) to work on Sundays would likely have provided him with a comparative advantage over his competitors (because fewer competitors would be open on Sunday, thus affording Braunfeld a much greater market share of available business). By means of this discussion, Chief Justice Warren managed to illustrate in *Braunfeld* both the limits of any judicial solution as well as the legal and theoretical difficulty of ensuring complete fairness under law among citizens with vastly different beliefs and understandings regarding religion. Warren indicated that granting Braunfeld an exemption would have economically harmed a large number of citizens who obeyed the law, which presumably included those with conventional Christian religious beliefs (as well as everyone else, believer or nonbeliever, who simply was bound to obey the law). A similar problem occurred in *Thomas,* although the question did not pit those with different religious beliefs against one another, but rather only contrasted those acting from religious convictions against citizens who resigned or been terminated from their jobs for other, personal reasons. Recall that the effect of the Court's opinion in *Thomas* was to require Indiana to grant an exemption to Thomas (and others like him who were motivated by religious beliefs) when they applied for unemployment compensation. Other employees who resigned for nonreligious, personal reasons were not entitled to any such exemption. Therefore, the personal religious reasons of those who had discounted employment for religious reasons were favored; their motivation was simply worth more than that of others who left their positions for nonreligious personal reasons (for example, disagreement with corporate policies, excessive stress). It may well be true that the Constitution, through the Free Exercise Clause, elevates religious reasons above other personal reasons and requires such favoritism. Yet it is also worth noting that while the Court in *Braunfeld* concerned itself extensively with the potential for religious favoritism inherent in the granting of exemptions, the Court in *Thomas* was not nearly so concerned, for it simply assumed that such bias was constitutionally necessary.

One final point regarding the *Thomas* case should be emphasized. It is perhaps easy to dismiss Justice Rehnquist's dissenting opinion as the unhappy complaining of a Justice who could find no support among his colleagues. Of course, it would be unfair to dismiss the *substance* of Rehnquist's opinion simply because of its singular nature. In American constitutional law, as in philosophy generally, it is the argument, not the number of people who advocate a position, that ultimately earns respect.[23] In this respect, it is interesting to note that less than a decade after *Thomas* (in 1990), Rehnquist, now Chief Justice, joined in an opinion for the Court's majority in the controversial *Smith* case, which outlawed unemployment compensation to those who broke the law. In that opinion, Justice Scalia made a number of constitutional points for the majority that Rehnquist had initially made as a lone dissenter in *Thomas*. Most notably, Scalia discarded the compelling state interest test as the constitutional standard for gauging Free Exercise Clause violations. Scalia, like Rehnquist, was clear on the point that he would make it far more difficult for employees to assert successful claims of free exercise violations. If *Thomas* was inconsistent with *Braunfeld*, *Smith* was not. Thus, in time, Justice Rehnquist's minority position in *Thomas* would be vindicated. But it would not endure for long, because in 1993 the Rehnquist—-Scalia position would be reversed once again—this time by Congress in the Religious Freedom Restoration Act, which restored the compelling justification test in free exercise cases.

Congress notwithstanding, the Supreme Court's interpretation of the Free Exercise Clause has been inconsistent and confusing. Might the need for judicial intervention and interpretation have been avoided or minimized if state legislatures had simply been more sensitive to the rights of religious minorities? What would have happened if the legislatures had attempted, as a matter of policy, to maximize each individual's free exercise claim? Although this idea may seem promising, it would not necessarily be able to withstand judicial scrutiny, as we shall see.

EXAMPLE 5

Estate of Thornton v. *Caldor,* 472 U.S. 703 (1985)

Facts: This case was originally brought by Donald Thornton, who died while his appeal was pending before the Supreme Court of Connecticut. (The administrator of Thornton's estate continued the suit on behalf of the estate.) Thornton worked for Caldor Inc., a department store. For a while, he managed the men's and boys' clothing department in the Waterbury, Connecticut, store; later, he worked in Caldor's Torrington store. When Connecticut law was changed and permitted Caldor to stay open on Sundays, Thornton, like all other similarly situated managers, was required to work every third or fourth Sunday. Thornton complied with this requirement for over two years. Subsequently, Thornton informed his employer that, as a Presbyterian, he could no longer work on Sunday (his Sabbath). Caldor offered to transfer him to a management position in

Massachusetts (which did not allow such businesses to be open on Sundays) or to a nonsupervisory position in the Torrington store at a lower salary. (The prevailing collective bargaining agreement for nonsupervisory employees provided that they were not required to work on Sundays if this was contrary to their religious convictions.) Thornton rejected both offers. He was then transferred to a clerical position in Caldor's Torrington store, from which he promptly resigned. Thornton filed a grievance with the State Board of Mediation and Arbitration, alleging he was discharged from his manager's position in violation of a Connecticut law which proclaimed that "[n]o person who states that a particular day of the week is observed as his Sabbath may be required by his employer to work on such day. An Employee's refusal to work on his Sabbath shall not constitute grounds for his dismissal."

Result: The Connecticut law, which safeguards the Sabbath observance of each employee, violates the Constitution's Establishment Clause because it has the primary effect of advancing religion by favoring Sabbath religious concerns over all secular interests in the workplace.

Argument of the Case: Burger, Chief Justice. The *Lemon* test must be employed in order to determine if the Establishment Clause has been violated. Therefore, the contested statute must have a secular purpose, it must have a primary effect that neither advances nor inhibits religion, and it must avoid excessive government–religion entanglement. The contested Connecticut law declared that those who, for religious reasons, observe a Sabbath on any day of the week must be granted that day off, no matter what burden or inconvenience is imposed upon an employer or fellow workers. The law imposes upon employers the absolute duty to conform their business practices to an employee's religious practices. There is no exception for special circumstances and no consideration whether employers have attempted special accommodation. Thus, the statute impermissibly advances a particular religious practice in violation of the Establishment Clause.

O'Connor and Marshall concur. The state statute gives Sabbath observers special and absolute protection, thus conveying the message of state endorsement of religion in violation of the Establishment Clause. The state cannot advance religion, yet this does not suggest that the religious accommodation provisions of the Civil Rights Law, which attempt to effect a reasonable accommodation between employees and private employers, are unconstitutional.

Rehnquist dissents with no opinion.

Discussion

This is another seemingly straightforward case that contains unanticipated legal and theoretical complications. After Connecticut's Sunday closing law had been declared by its state courts to be unconstitutionally vague, the state, in 1976 and 1978, unsuccessfully attempted to fashion a Sunday closing law that could withstand challenges to its constitutionality. The contested statute guaranteeing employees an absolute right not to work on their Sabbath was passed in 1976, along with a revised formulation of the Sunday closing law. Although the 1976 Sunday closing law revision was subsequently invalidated by the state courts, the law guaranteeing Sabbath worship was not challenged. Therefore, it successfully escaped legal scrutiny until it was ultimately invalidated in the *Caldor* case.

Thus, when the Supreme Court reviewed the Sabbath guarantee law in isolation, it did so within a different context than when the law was originally passed. Because the contested Sabbath guarantee law was originally passed along with a revised Sunday rest law, it could have been fairly regarded as a exemption to that statute—a guarantee of religious free exercise to (a) traditional Christian employees who were among those employed by a limited number of businesses allowed under the 1976 law to remain open and (b) other religious practitioners whose Sabbath fell on a different day. Essentially, what Connecticut did in 1976 was to say that (a) most businesses should be closed on Sundays, although (b) some businesses may remain open, and (c) if either (a) or (b) imposes a hardship on any citizen's religious beliefs or practices, then, as a matter of law, this citizen can be exempted from such a law.

The Connecticut state legislature had good reason for thinking it had passed a constitutional law. In *Braunfeld* the Supreme Court had declared that while the Constitution did not mandate religious exemptions from secular obligations arising from Sabbath closing laws, it did permit them (this matter being appropriately left to the legislative branch). Furthermore, in cases regarding unemployment compensation, the Supreme Court had emphasized the fundamental importance of religious free exercise at the same time it had overturned state laws that required citizens to choose between their religious convictions and their economic well-being (here defined in terms of their ability to obtain unemployment compensation[24]).

What, then, happened in *Caldor*? Why did the Supreme Court invalidate the statute? First, as we have noted, by the time *Caldor* was argued and decided, the Sabbath guarantee law stood alone, Connecticut's day of rest law having previously been invalidated by state courts. Second, the case was treated by the Supreme Court not as a guarantee of individual religious free exercise, but as an instance of religious establishment.[25] This allowed Chief Justice Burger, for the Court, to characterize its absolute protection of a citizen's right to practice the Sabbath of his or her choice as placing an absolute and unqualified burden on employers, rather than portraying the law as providing an absolute and unqualified guarantee of religious liberty to citizens. Admittedly, Connecticut's statute imposed a heavier economic burden upon employers than did legislation such as the anti-religious-discrimination provisions of the 1964 Civil Rights Act. But until *Caldor* was decided, it was by no means clear that this was an impermissible burden or that a state legislature was not free to balance the religious beliefs of its citizens against the potential economic harm to businesses and employers in reasonable ways as it saw fit.

Many would argue (and therefore agree with Rehnquist's dissent as well as his opinions in other, related cases) that opinions like those written by Chief Justice Burger in *Caldor* (disallowing a state's favoring individual religious free exercise because of the Establishment Clause) and *Thomas* (requiring the state to acknowledge religious free exercise on the basis of the Free Exercise Clause) are hard to reconcile. Although these two cases clearly pose problems of consistency, other interpretations are possible. Thus, some observers may focus upon individual differences between the two cases or see an inherent, and perhaps irreconcilable, tension between the two religion clauses that places a heavy or perhaps even impossible responsibility upon the Supreme Court. In any case, we would emphasize points that have gained general agreement: that the Constitution requires both a deference toward individual religious convictions in the workplace while it prohibits favoring any particular religion. How significant a deference is constitutionally mandated or even permitted, especially when religious belief and practice are unintentionally burdened by neutral, secular work practices or especially by secularly motivated laws, remains a rich area for litigation and continuing controversy.

SUMMARY

The Supreme Court's interpretation of the Establishment and Free Exercise Clauses of the United States Constitution, as well as the application of the relevant provisions of the 1964 Civil Rights Act, makes clear one practical principle of the law: in the workplace, reasonable efforts must be made to accommodate individual religious belief and practice while not irreparably harming employers. In different ways, *Rasch* and *Caldor* both clearly stand for this principle.

There are a few other practical conclusions that follow from judicial scrutiny of conflicts over religion in the workplace and that emerge from a study of the cases included in this chapter. Although religious or religious-related employers may be exempted from certain neutral governmental regulations, there are many that they have to obey. Similarly, owners of businesses who may be indirectly and unintentionally disadvantaged by secular laws because of minority or unusual religious beliefs are still bound to obey these laws unless the legislature specifically exempts them. And as we have noted, within the workplace the laws of the United States attempt to foster an accommodation between employee and employer. Should that accommodation fail, government cannot withhold unemployment benefits from those who lose or have resigned jobs for religious reasons.

Behind the general impetus of United States law to encourage accommodation in the workplace lies a range of thorny theoretical constitutional issues, especially having to do with the relationship and compatibility (or lack thereof) between the Establishment Clause and the Free Exercise Clause. With the *Lemon* Establishment Clause test under increased judicial criticism[26] and the free exercise compelling state interest test having been significantly restricted or abandoned by the Rehnquist Court, this area remains a fertile area of analysis and dispute among Supreme Court Justices and constitutional experts alike. For the present, we would note only the clear tension that exists between the Supreme Court's resolution of free exercise disputes in *Braunfeld* (and, later, in *Department of Human Resources* v. *Smith*) on the one hand and the Court's resolution of the *Thomas* case on the other (although, as we have seen, Congress eventually sided with the Court's approach in *Thomas*). Another area of confusing and perhaps conflicting constitutional interpretation exists between (a) *Thomas's* recognition and protection of religious beliefs from state intrusion in the name of free exercise and (b) *Caldor's* invalidation of state recognition and protection of religious beliefs in the name of avoiding the establishment of religion. We do not suggest that resolving these tensions is simple. Rather, we are content only to suggest that there are few areas of the law of religion and government that have led to clearer practical guidelines and more confused theoretical constitutional formulations than those which deal with questions that arise from religious practices in the workplace.

NOTES

1. See pages 111–16.

2. See pages 167–72.

3. See pages 195–96.

4. The court (ft. 26) cited associates' testimony, such as the following, which had been introduced at trial:
And no one ever expected any kind of compensation, and the thought is totally vexing to my soul. It would defeat my whole purpose. (testimony of Ann Elmore)

I believe it would be offensive to me to even be considered to be forced to take a wage.... I believe it offends my right to worship God as I choose. (testimony of Bill Levy)

5. The Chief Justice carried with him only three other Justices; Black, Clark, and Whittaker.

6. However, in *Braunfeld*, Frankfurter (but not Harlan) would have sent the case back to the lower court for reargument (contending that a technical error had been committed).

7. Exodus 20:8–11.

8. See the Establishment Clause cases of *McGowan* v. *Maryland*, 366 U.S. 420 (1961) and *Two Guys from Harrison-Allentown, Inc.* v. *McGinley*, 366 U.S. 582 (1961); the other free exercise case besides *Braunfeld* v. *Brown* was *Gallagher* v. *Crown Kosher Super Market*, 366 U.S. 617 (1961).

9. *McGowan* v. *Maryland*, 366 U.S. 420, 445.

10. *McGowan* v. *Maryland* at 445.

11. *McGowan* v. *Maryland* at 506.

12. *McGowan* v. *Maryland* at 565.

13. These points are made both by Chief Justice Warren (for the Court) at 608–609 and by Justice Frankfurter in *McGowan* at 514–21.

14. Rasch was eventually reinstated and informed that a position was available in Salisbury, North Carolina, for which Rasch possessed sufficient seniority to allow him to observe his Sabbath. He held this position at the time of his suit. Presumably, the problems originally encountered when Rasch worked at the far more popular Washington, D.C., base could happen again, whence explaining the Court's interest in resolving the case.

15. Summary judgment simply means that where there are no factual disagreements between the parties, the court renders a legal opinion and decides the case.

16. Specifically, the amended act states that "It shall be an unlawful employment practice for an employer (1) to fail or refuse to hire or to discharge any individual, or otherwise to discriminate against any individual with respect to his compensation, terms, conditions, or privileges of employment, because of such individual's race, color, religion, sex, or national origin."

17. It is also generally consistent with Supreme Court case law. See *Trans World Airlines, Inc.* v. *Hardison,* 423 U.S. 63 (1977).

18. Blackmun joined in all aspects of the Court's opinion, except that which dealt with the relationship between the Establishment Clause and the Free Exercise Clause.

19. A point to think about: Was the kind of logical inconsistency of which the "unsophisticated" Thomas was accused (where he agreed to participate in the general making of steel, some of which might be used for weapons of war, while proclaiming an opposition to the making of weapons of war) any more inconsistent than the kind of contradiction Justice Rehnquist accuses the presumably more sophisticated Supreme Court of committing, namely unintentionally establishing religion partially by an expanded reading of the Free Exercise Clause?

20. 450 U.S. at 715.

21. In *Sherbert* v. *Verner,* 374 U.S. 398. This opinion was reaffirmed in *Hobbie* v. *Unemployment Appeals Commission of Florida,* 480 U.S. 136 (1987).

22. 450 U.S. at 722–723. Significantly, Chief Justice Rehnquist's 1990 opinion for the Court in *Employment Division,*

Department of Human Resources of Oregon v. *Smith* returned to the *Braunfeld* standard and reestablished the more traditional Establishment Clause test.

23. In that regard, all one has to do is recall Justice Harlan's lone dissent in *Plessy* v. *Ferguson,* 163 U.S. 537 (1896).

24. In fact, the Connecticut law would substantially obviate the need for any Connecticut citizen to collect unemployment insurance under such a circumstance, for it would protect that individual from losing his or her job and thus needing unemployment benefits.

25. The Court's ignoring of the Free Exercise Clause is striking. Only in one sentence at the beginning of Section II (Section I having described the facts of the case) does Burger make even indirect reference to it, and then only in the briefest possible manner: "Under the Religion Clauses, Government must guard against activity that impinges on religious freedom, and must take pains not to compel people to act in the name of any religion. In setting the appropriate boundaries in Establishment Clause cases,…" 472 at 708.

26. Rehnquist's attack on the *Lemon* test can be clearly discerned in his lengthy dissenting opinion in *Wallace* v. *Jaffree* 472 U.S. 38, 91. Further attacks upon the *Lemon* test can be seen in Justice Scalia's opinion in *Edwards* v. *Aguillard,* 473 U.S. 578, 636–640 (1987); Justice O'Connor's opinion in *Aguilar* v. *Felton,* 473 U.S. 402, 426–430; and Justice White's opinion in *Roemer* v. *Maryland Board of Public Works,* 426 U.S. 736, 768–769 (1976). By 1994, the *Lemon* test no longer commanded a majority of the Court.

18

✤

Should the State Exempt Some Religious Groups from the Obligation to Salute the Flag?

THE PROBLEM POSED

All nations expect their citizens to be loyal—to share an appreciation of their nation's history, traditions, institutions, and government. Patriotism involves both a feeling of affection and a willingness to sacrifice, uniting citizens concerned about their nation's well-being. Patriotism is a bond among citizens, a feeling of common destiny, and an attachment that citizens have to their nation's past and its principles.

Although such feelings can arise naturally, it is the case that governments do not leave the development of such attachments to chance. As James Madison noted in *The Federalist Papers,* even "the most rational government will not find it a superfluous advantage, to have the prejudice of the community on its side."[1] Different governments promote patriotism to vastly varying degrees and employ significantly different means to do so, but all governments, in the end, make the effort. Although the American Founders wanted to encourage a multiplicity of opinions, passions, interests, and religions in the new republic, they also sought to perpetuate a singular reverence for the principles of liberty and equality that were articulated in the Declaration of Independence and the Constitution. This is the problem of patriotism in the United States: the nation cannot survive without patriotism, yet the nation exists to honor a freedom that transcends patriotism. How does one balance the need for patriotism with the value we place on freedom?

Our particular focus is, of course, on religious freedom. To what extent does the state's interest in encouraging patriotism limit religious freedom? How far can a nation go towards asking its citizens for allegiance before it imposes upon the private allegiances that its citizens have for their religions? The following cases look at this problem from a variety of perspectives.

EXAMPLE 1

Minersville School District **v.** *Gobitis,* 310 U.S. 586 (1940)

Facts: Lillian Gobitis and her brother William (ages twelve and ten, respectively) were expelled from the Minersville, Pennsylvania, public schools for refusing on religious grounds to salute the American flag and to say the Pledge of Allegiance. The children were Jehovah's Witnesses and were raised to believe that offering allegiance to flag and country was forbidden by Scripture. The parents had to place their children in private school and sued in order to gain readmittance for their children to the public schools, arguing that they should not have to bear the additional expense of private school.

Result: The Court ruled against the Gobitis family; the First and Fourteenth Amendments did not prohibit the state from encouraging patriotism in the public schools with the flag salute and the Pledge of Allegiance.

Argument of the Case: Justice Frankfurter. The Court acknowledged the sensitivity of this issue and recognized that the purpose of the First Amendment was to guarantee religious freedom and to avoid the religious strife that was characteristic of the centuries preceding our nation's founding. The affirmative pursuit of one's convictions is therefore protected, and the right to propagate one's belief or disbelief is also protected. The Constitution ensures "generous immunity" from penalties to those who might offend others in the pursuit of their beliefs. But there are times when one's beliefs lead to actions that come into conflict with the secular interests of one's fellow citizens. The Court pointed out that "no single principle can answer all of life's complexities." The right to follow one's conscience is fundamental to our political community, but no right is absolute. The religious liberty that our Founders sought to protect with the First Amendment was not designed to exclude legislation "of a general scope not directed against doctrinal loyalties of particular sects." Families that disagree with the perspectives offered in the public schools do have the freedom to choose alternative private education, but the state has a legitimate interest in the public schools of fostering the loyalty of its citizens. The Court did express some reservations about the approach taken by the state of Pennsylvania, but stated that even an unwise law is not necessarily unconstitutional. The Court has no particular competence to determine what approach to fostering patriotism might be better than the one chosen by the Pennsylvania state legislature. The flag salute and the Pledge of Allegiance may be required by the state.

Justice Stone dissents. The Pennsylvania law violates the right to free exercise of religion as guaranteed by the First Amendment. The Gobitis children have not exhibited any disloyalty to the United States; they are simply being punished for following their religious beliefs, which no one doubts are sincere. It is true that no right is absolute, but the state may not use its power to compel belief through public affirmations that violate religious scruple. There should be "reasonable accommodation" between the interests of the state and private rights, and since the state has other means at its disposal to encourage patriotism that do not impose on religious freedom, this law is unacceptable.

Discussion

The Court's decision reflects the understanding of free exercise that was first articulated in *Reynolds* v. *U.S.*,[2] that there is no religious right to an exemption from valid secular law. The Pennsylvania law had as its purpose the secular goal of inculcating patriotism, especially during the formative years. Therefore,

> Conscientious scruples have not, in the course of the long struggle for religious toleration, relieved the individual from obedience to a general law not aimed at the promotion or restriction of religious beliefs. The mere possession of religious convictions which contradict the relevant concerns of a political society does not relieve the citizen from the discharge of political responsibilities.[3]

Frankfurter pointed out that a free society depends on the "binding tie of cohesive sentiment," and in this respect he happened to agree with Abraham Lincoln, who stated the following:

> ...in this and like communities, public sentiment is everything. With public sentiment, nothing can fail; without it nothing can succeed. Consequently he who moulds public sentiment, goes deeper than he who enacts statutes or pronounces decisions. He makes statutes and decisions possible or impossible to be executed.[4]

In other words, a free society rests on something elusive, something nonrational. The very religious freedom that the Gobitis family treasured depends upon an inculcation of patriotism that is a precondition of religious freedom. Frankfurter referred to the importance of that "unifying sentiment, without which there can ultimately be no liberties, civil or religious."

But no matter how important this "unifying sentiment" seems to be, is it really right for the power of the state to be used in the schools to enforce beliefs that some find offensive to their religions? In his lone dissent, Justice Stone contended that the problem with the law in question is that it "seeks to coerce these children to express a sentiment which, as they interpret it, they do not entertain, and which violates their deepest religious convictions." In his opinion, the purpose of the religion clauses of the First Amendment is to keep this type of abuse from happening. He did not question the general power of the state to control the education of its citizens, but when that general power comes into conflict with specific guarantees of the Constitution, there must be an accommodation. The public schools may instill patriotism in a number of ways. Civics courses may be taught. History courses may be taught. These subjects will inspire patriotism in ways that do not violate the free exercise of religion.

Yet Frankfurter's eight-person majority decision justified its position by insisting that the limitations on free exercise were relatively mild. Frankfurter reminded us that we have the right to private education in the United States; those of us who want our children raised with fundamentally different sentiments can avail ourselves of the opportunity to send our children to private schools. This is true, yet it means that those who want their children to be protected from the "unifying sentiment" that the public schools seek to instill have to bear the extra expense of private education. Critics asked this: Is it fair to require people with unpopular religious views to pay this kind of price in order to live according to their principles? Isn't this choice too harsh except for the most affluent? Isn't Frankfurter saying that people of modest means will simply have to accept what amounts to an assault on their children's religious beliefs?

Frankfurter's final point relates to an important debate within the field of constitutional law, and while the details of this debate are not our primary concern, a short explanation is necessary for understanding this case. Frankfurter argued that the Supreme Court cannot rule on the wisdom of a state law such as this. Frankfurter himself remarks that the law may not be wise:

> Even were we convinced of the folly of such a measure, such belief would not be proof of its unconstitutionality. For ourselves, we might be tempted to say that the deepest patriotism is best engendered by giving unfettered scope to the most crotchety beliefs. Perhaps it is best, even from the standpoint of those interests which ordinances like the one under review seek to promote, to give to the least popular sect leave from conformities like those here in issue.[5]

In other words, Frankfurter likely believed that it would have been wiser for the Pennsylvania legislature to have offered exemptions for religious groups whose scruples did not allow them to say the Pledge of Allegiance. Frankfurter also believed that an unwise law could still be constitutional. This is sometimes a very difficult point to comprehend; indeed, Frankfurter essentially accused Justice Stone of failing to understand this. The crucial issue for the case must be whether the First Amendment has been violated (as applied to the states through the Fourteenth Amendment), not whether the Pennsylvania legislature wrote a bad law. Although the issues raised in this case seemed settled, surprisingly, they were not. Only a little later did the Supreme Court agree to a flag-salute case that raised the same legal questions.

EXAMPLE 2

West Virginia State Board of Education **v.** *Barnette,* 319 U.S. 624 (1943)

Facts: Following the *Gobitis* decision, the West Virginia legislature changed its statutes to require all the public schools in the state to teach courses in history, civics, and the Constitution, and it also required the flag salute and the Pledge of Allegiance as a regular part of the schools' activities. Students who refused to participate were considered "insubordinate" and were subject to expulsion, with readmission possible only upon compliance. While these students were out of school, they were considered "unlawfully absent" and their parents were subject to criminal prosecution, with a maximum fine of $50 and a jail term of up to 30 days. Walter Barnette, a Jehovah's Witness, claimed that the flag salute and Pledge of Allegiance compelled his children to violate their religious prohibition against worshipping graven images.

Result: Overruling *Gobitis,* the enforcement of the West Virginia regulations is enjoined as a violation of the First Amendment's Freedom of Speech and Press provision as applied to the states by the Fourteenth Amendment.

Argument of the Case: Jackson, Justice. The rights claimed by the Barnette family did not bring them into collision with rights claimed by any other individual. Additionally, there was no claim by the state that the Barnette children's behavior was disruptive or a challenge to peace in or out of the classroom: "The sole conflict is between authority and the rights of the individual." The state has the legal authority to encourage patriotism by teaching about the politics and history of the country, but West Virginia exceeds its authority: "Here, however, we are dealing with a compulsion of students to declare a belief." Yet West Virginia does not have the authority to compel a belief under the First Amendment unless it is facing a clear and present danger that would make this necessary. The Court stated that the question of free exercise of religion and the matter of religious exemption were really secondary to this consideration. The purpose of public education would be compromised if schools were not "faithful to the ideal of secular instruction and political neutrality." State power cannot "prescribe what shall be orthodox" in politics or religion.

Black and Douglas concur. Although the Constitution must not be used rigidly to prohibit states from regulating conduct threatening to the public welfare, the Court must rule that religious scruples that prohibit saluting the flag and saying the Pledge of Allegiance pose no such threat. If the Court were convinced that the salute and the pledge were "imperatively necessary to protect society as a whole from grave and pressingly imminent dangers," then religious scruples would provide no excuse from following the state requirement.

Murphy concurs. The free exercise of religion is so important that only a threat to what is "essential to the maintenance of effective government

and orderly society" would be sufficient to warrant a limitation on freedom of conscience. Free exercise means no state compulsion to "affirm
what is contrary to one's beliefs."

Roberts and Reed dissent. They adhere to the *Gobitis* decision without
opinion.

Justice Frankfurter dissents. The right to free exercise is a guarantee of
"freedom from conformity to religious dogma, not freedom from conformity to law because of religious dogma." The state would have no right to
compel anyone to accept a religious dogma or proclaim allegiance to a
particular god, but the state law in West Virginia attempts only to promote good citizenship, and this is within the power of the state. It may
not be a wise law, and it may not be the best way to promote good citizenship, but it is a law that violates no clause of the First Amendment.

Discussion

The decision in *Minersville School District* v. *Gobitis* was eight to one, but in
only three years the Court had changed its mind dramatically. Frequent criticism by legal scholars and widespread violence against Jehovah's Witnesses
since the *Gobitis* decision have been suggested as factors that may have contributed to the change.[6] Additionally, two members of the Court's majority
had been replaced (Justices Jackson and Rutledge having succeeded Justices
Hughes and McReynolds), and Justices Black and Douglas had already re-
nounced their votes in the case. Justice Murphy would also change his mind.

The Jackson opinion in the *Barnette* case approached the Pledge of Allegiance question in a different way than had any of the Justices in *Gobitis*. Jackson asked whether the state had the power in the public schools to compel
students to declare a belief. The Court considered this question by borrowing
one of its tests from free speech cases and applying it here. According to Justice Jackson, neither speech nor silence can be compelled by the state unless it
faces a "clear and present danger" of the kind it is empowered to prevent: "To
sustain the compulsory flag salute we are required to say that a Bill of Rights
which guards the individual's right to speak his own mind, left it open to public authorities to compel him to utter what is not in his mind." The principle
that stands behind Jackson's judgment is that conscience must be respected by
the state unless the state is facing an immediate danger to its authority and
functioning. In other words, the state must be prepared to prove to the satisfaction of the courts in every particular case that conscience cannot be honored. In its decision, the Court was echoing the sentiments of John Stuart
Mill when it praised "intellectual individualism" and a "rich cultural diversity" as significant advantages stemming from the freedom guaranteed by the
Constitution. The Court also observed that "eccentricity" and "abnormal attitudes" are a small price to pay for such benefits, at least when such attitudes
are arguably harmless to others and to the state. The principle that stands behind the decision here was enunciated by Jackson and reveals a popular view
of the nature of the American regime:

If there is any fixed star in our constitutional constellation, it is that no official, high or petty, can prescribe what shall be orthodox in politics, nationalism, religion, or other matters of opinion or force citizens to confess by word or act their faith therein. If there are any circumstances which permit an exception, they do not occur to us.[7]

This view is popular, but not beyond challenge, especially since it rests on a view of freedom and the state that emerged well after the founding of the American regime.[8] Jackson rejected the more traditional view that even a nation devoted to freedom must be based on some common opinions, a minimal set of shared political ideas that serves as a prerequisite for popular government.[9] This was the view that Frankfurter had maintained for the Court in *Gobitis* and now defended in his dissenting opinion in *Barnette*.

Frankfurter called attention to the fact that, as a Jew, he belonged to "the most vilified and persecuted minority in history" and was therefore sensitive to the freedoms guaranteed by the Constitution. But he said that "it would require more daring than [he] possess[es] to deny that reasonable legislators could have taken the action" of requiring a flag salute and Pledge of Allegiance. No one is required by this act to profess allegiance to a religion; if profession of allegiance to civil society is offensive to some religious groups, then they must adjust to the needs of civil society: "That claims are pressed on behalf of sincere religious convictions does not of itself establish their constitutional validity." Frankfurter reminds us that the case deals with the public schools, not society at large. He makes it clear that he would oppose a loyalty oath imposed on citizens. But he asserts that the state does have the authority (as long as private education is an option) of inculcating patriotism, especially since children and their parents are still free to express their disagreement with the pledge and make serious criticisms of the regime in speech and in print.

Frankfurter also pointed to the amazing religious diversity that existed; the United States contained more than 250 different religious denominations. According to Frankfurter, 120 of these denominations were in Pennsylvania and 65 in West Virginia! He argued that secular law would be at the mercy of this diversity if religious exemptions were allowed as a matter of right. And there was a further problem: "If religious scruples afford immunity from civic obedience to laws, they may be invoked by the religious beliefs of any individual, even though he holds no membership in any sect or organized denomination." Anyone claiming to have religious scruples of one kind or another could claim exemption from secular law.

But Frankfurter's position in his dissent did not prevail; the Court reversed its earlier position and established, over Frankfurter's protest, the right of students to refuse participation in the flag salute and the Pledge of Allegiance. Later, the federal courts expanded upon the principle of *Barnette* by overturning laws requiring students who refused to recite the Pledge of Allegiance to stand or to leave the room.[10] The issues raised in *Gobitis* and *Barnette* continued to be important to the nation, as our next case reveals.

EXAMPLE 3

Sherman v. *Community Consolidated School District of Wheeling,*
785 F. Supp. 1244 (N.D. Ill. 1991)

Facts: Roger Sherman and his son Richard are atheists and claimed that
the Illinois statute that requires the daily recitation of the Pledge of Allegiance in the public elementary schools violates the Establishment Clause
and Free Exercise Clause of the First Amendment (as well as other constitutional provisions). The court indicated that the school district did not
require Richard to recite the pledge or even to stand while it was being
recited; however, the pledge was recited in his presence.

Result: The Illinois statute did not violate the Establishment Clause or
Free Exercise Clause of the First Amendment (or any other constitutional
provision).

Argument of the Case: Williams, Judge. The court applied the three-
part Establishment Clause test from *Lemon* v. *Kurtzman* and held that (1)
the Illinois law had the secular purpose of instilling patriotic "values" in
elementary school students; (2) the primary purpose of the statute was
neither to advance nor inhibit religion, even though one (and only one)
of the sponsors of the bill had mentioned his interest in returning prayer
to the public schools; and (3) no excessive entanglements between religion and the state were created by this statute. With regard to free exercise, the court held that since Richard was not required to say the Pledge,
his free exercise was not harmed in any way.

Discussion

Unlike previous cases, Richard Sherman did not object to having to say the
Pledge of Allegiance or being required to act or refrain from acting in predetermined ways during the reciting of the pledge. (That is, the issue raised by
the case was not how the pledge affected a student who was required by the
law to somehow respond—recite its language, stand, and so on.) Rather, part
of Sherman's objection seemed to be that pledge was said by others in school.
The Shermans also alleged that Richard had been disciplined for his refusal to
say the pledge, but the court found no evidence that such punishment had
happened.

  This case reaffirms the authority of the state to inculcate patriotism in its
citizens through the public schools. In evaluating Sherman's claim that the
practice violated the Establishment Clause, the court relied upon the *Lemon*
test. Its conclusion that the purpose and primary effect of the law were secular
was supported by the court interpretation of the legislative debates that led to
its passage. The sponsors of the bill stated several times that "the purpose of
the law was to instill patriotic concern and knowledge of American ideals in
elementary school students." In order to accomplish this, the law required not
only the flag salute and the Pledge of Allegiance but also that students be

"taught and tested on the principles enunciated in the American Declaration of Independence, the U.S. Constitution and the Constitution of the State of Illinois."

The district court also denied that the phrase "under God" in the pledge constituted establishment of religion.[11] The court stated that "any religious references therein are incidental and expressive only of the faith which as a matter of historical fact has inspired the growth of the nation." But does this argument really stand up to scrutiny? The Pledge does not present itself as a history lesson, as something to inform us about a faith that may once have been important to the founding and development of the country. It states that we are one nation under God, and by saying this it teaches elementary school students about what the country is and what it should be. This is something more than a mere "historical" or "incidental" reference to religion. Still, the *Lemon* test prohibits only a law that has as its *primary* purpose advancing or inhibiting of religion, and it is clear that the primary purpose of the Pledge is not religious.

The free exercise claim made by Richard Sherman was interesting because both he and his father admitted that they were atheists. Here, the court assumed and therefore implicitly followed the Supreme Court's previous understanding that atheism was protected by the Free Exercise Clause.[12] Given this assumption, the court relied upon *Barnette* as its primary precedent. In fact, the court indicated that the only legitimate question was whether the law demanded that all students say the pledge. The state law used the word *shall* in establishing the flag ceremony requirements, but the court held that this was not sufficient to rule the law unconstitutional since no student (including Richard) had ever been forced to salute the flag or say the Pledge. Apparently, Richard Sherman had faced some unpleasantness from his classmates, but this was never condoned by school officials. Although atheists have free exercise rights, they must be concretely and adversely affected by the state for the Constitution to be violated.

In each of these three cases we have analyzed cases involving the rights of students. But what about teachers? Does their situation differ because they choose their employment and (unlike students) are not required to attend classes because of compulsory state education laws?

EXAMPLE 4

Palmer v. Board of Education of Chicago, 603 F.2nd 1271 (1979)

Facts: Joethelia Palmer, a Jehovah's Witness, was a probationary kindergarten teacher in the Chicago public schools. Shortly after she was hired but before her first classes began, she told her principal that she would be unable to teach any subjects having to do with love of country, the flag, or other "patriotic matters." For example, she said that she would consider teaching about Abraham Lincoln and why his birthday is celebrated to be idolatry. She asked the court to allow her a religious exemption to the general curriculum requirements.

Result: Her dismissal from her job did not violate the Free Exercise Clause and was upheld by the court.

Argument of the Case: Wood, Judge. Ms. Palmer has the right to her own freedom of religion, but in this case she would be imposing her beliefs on others who have a right to expect a good education: "Plaintiff's right to her own religious views and practices remains unfettered." There is a "compelling state interest in the choice and adherence to a suitable curriculum for the benefit of our young citizens and society." The courts have never denied the authority of the state to inculcate patriotism.

Discussion

In this case, a U.S. Court of Appeals balanced the teacher's right to protect her religious beliefs against the state's interest in promoting patriotism, and it found in favor of the state. According to the court, there were several key factors that tipped the balance in the state's direction. First, it was not that the teacher objected only to one exercise, such as the saying of the Pledge of Allegiance. Rather, she objected to a whole range of activities. Taken as a whole, these activities made up an integral part of the school's curriculum. And, according to the court, there existed a compelling state interest to adhere to a state-mandated curriculum.

A related concern focused on the teacher's job. The flag ceremony, the patriotic songs, and the recognition of celebration of holidays made up a significant part of her teaching duties. Thus, her claim for exemption compared unfavorably to that of another teacher who had been dismissed from her job for refusing to say the Pledge of Allegiance and who had won her case before the Supreme Court in 1973.[13] In that case, Susan Russo was not the senior instructor in the class; she was an art teacher who stood silently and respectfully at the side of the room while the pledge was being led. As the Court pointed out,

> Her job was not to teach patriotic matters to children, but to teach art. The court carefully indicated that through its holding it did not mean to limit the traditionally broad discretion that has always rested with local school authorities to prescribe curriculum.[14]

But Ms. Palmer's job on behalf of the state of Illinois was to teach the very things that her religious scruples forbade her to teach. Her failure to participate in what was central to her job makes her case different from that of Susan Russo.

In addition to this, Ms. Palmer's actions had a substantial impact on others. The court stated that her failure to teach about national heroes and holidays as well as her failure to lead flag ceremonies "would deprive her students of an elementary knowledge and appreciation of our national heritage." Worse yet, systematically excluding such sources of national pride would present her students with a distorted and unbalanced view of our country's history: "It cannot be left to individual teachers to teach what they please." The court emphasized that Ms. Palmer's right to her own religious convictions and practices "remains unfettered." But her refusal to teach these subjects and lead these ceremonies goes well beyond personal freedom. It is an imposition upon the rights of others: "she has no constitutional right to require others to submit to her views and to forgo a portion of their education they would otherwise be entitled to enjoy." In the court's opinion, the results of such a neglectful and unbalanced view could be consequential:

> In this unsettled world, although we hope it will not come to pass, some of the students may be called upon to defend and protect our democratic system and constitutional rights, including plaintiff's religious freedom. That will demand a bit of patriotism.[15]

Thus, the court seemed to suggest that balancing the teacher's religious convictions with the state's interest in education was addressed by two factors: how central to a teacher's job responsibilities was his or her refusal to participate in religiously offensive activities and what the impact of that refusal was upon students. Each criterion requires judicial interpretation. Consider the hypothetical case of how the court would have ruled had Palmer only refused to lead and participate in the flag ceremonies (choosing a student to do so instead) and had chose not to lead her class in celebrating one or two national holidays. The court would have had to interpret and apply how central this refusal was to the teacher's responsibilities and the extent to which students would be negatively affected. Furthermore, there are subtle considerations that the court did not consider in *Palmer.* For instance, it would not be hard to make the argument that students are not very deprived in such a situation. In fact, one could argue that the teacher would be providing an important civics lesson by setting the highest example of the meaning of free exercise of religion in refusing to join them in the flag salute and the Pledge (and by modestly refraining from other activities). Clearly, any teacher who refused on religious grounds to carry out a substantial number of his or her responsibilities is in a difficult situation (and that is the point of *Palmer*), but the case sets only the broadest guidelines for determining the more fundamental issue of the rights of teachers to follow their religious scruples.

SUMMARY

Since 1943, the courts have consistently affirmed two basic principles: (1) that the states may pass laws that require flag ceremonies as a regular part of public school activities and (2) that no one can be compelled to participate in these ceremonies. The flag salute and the Pledge of Allegiance are one way that the states have attempted to promote patriotism among their young students.

Constitutional problems arise only when these activities unintentionally infringe upon a person's religious (or at least sincere) beliefs. When this happens, the courts have attempted to balance the interest of the state in promoting patriotism with the right to free exercise of religion. When the law has required something of the believing student, the free exercise of religion has almost always taken precedence over the secular interests of the state. The *Barnette* case was decided during World War II, and even this fact was not sufficient to tip the scales of the state's interest. Contrasting with the legal rights of students, teachers are in a more problematical legal position. Under some circumstances, they can refrain from participating in flag ceremonies, although court decisions in this legal area ultimately turn on a number of subtle issues.

Even though the *Gobitis* decision has been reversed, its argument poses an important theoretical (and controversial) challenge to prevailing law. Can civil society survive and flourish without the undefined feeling we call patriotism? And in a country as diverse as ours, to what extent can patriotism be encouraged if those with religious objections (or at least sincere objections) have a legal right to exemption from the public school ceremonies designed to instill that patriotism? Frankfurter argued that this feeling, which encourages a national unity and cohesion transcending individual interests and differences, lies at the very foundation of everything we hold dear: "The preciousness of the family relation, the authority and independence which give dignity to parenthood, indeed the enjoyment of all freedom, presuppose the kind of ordered society which is summarized by our flag."[16] Still, most people are not persuaded. For many, individual freedom remains the highest value. True religious freedom demands exemption from flag ceremonies. But others wonder: Can the impulse to protect all freedom ultimately lead to freedom's diminution or even to its ultimate extinction?

NOTES

1. Alexander Hamilton, John Jay, and James Madison, *The Federalist*, (New York: Modern Library), No. 49, p. 32.

2. 98 U.S. 145 (1878). See Chapter 9, p. 161.

3. 310 U.S. at 595–596.

4. Abraham Lincoln, "First Joint Debate," Ottawa, August 21, 1858, in *The Lincoln–Douglas Debates*, ed. Robert Johannsen (New York: Oxford Univ. Press, 1965), p. 65.

5. *Minersville* at 598.

6. Robert T. Miller, and Ronald B. Flowers, *Toward Benevolent Neutrality: Church, State, and the Supreme Court* (Waco, TX: Markham Press Fund, 1987), 3d ed., p. 57.

7. 319 U.S. at 642.

8. See Walter Berns, *The First Amendment and the Future of American Democracy* (Washington, DC: Gateway, 1985), pp. 185ff.

9. This older view is described by Arthur Schlesinger, Jr., in *The Disuniting of America* (New York: Norton, 1992), pp. 24–28.

10. *Lipp v. Morris*, 579 F.2d 834 (1978); *Goetz v. Ansell*, 477 F.2d 636 (1973).

11. The phrase "under God" was not part of the original pledge of allegiance, which was introduced by President Benjamin Harrison on October 12, 1892, and amended slightly when it was formally established on June 14, 1924. The phrase

"under God" was added in 1954 by a joint resolution of Congress.

12. See Chapter 4, pp. 68–71.

13. *Russo* v. *Central School District*, 411 U.S. 932 (1973).

14. *Russo* v. *Central School District*, 411 U.S. 932.

15. *Palmer* v. *Board of Ed.* at 1274.

16. 310 U.S. at 586.

19

Should Houses of Worship, Religiously Owned Property, and Religious Representatives Be Taxed?

THE PROBLEM POSED

Today, in an era of tight federal and state budgets and widespread budget deficits, raising adequate revenue to run government can pose a taxing challenge. Before taxes can be collected, however, sources of revenue must be identified. Who should pay for government? Everyone, it might initially be answered. But do we really believe this? There would seem to be exceptions. Certainly, as a society, we do not think that poor people, who barely earn enough money to survive, should be required to pay. Nor do we require a wealthy person who derives all income from tax-free municipal bonds to pay income taxes. In every state, certain not-for-profit organizations are exempted from many forms of taxation. Therefore, while initially we might respond that everyone should pay taxes, our society routinely identifies and may even exempt certain kinds of "special" cases. The question posed in the chapter is this: As a nation (at all levels of government—federal, state, and local), should we impose taxes upon religious organizations and their representatives?[1]

Although religiously employed clergy are required to pay income taxes like any other American citizen, they may be eligible for tax-advantaged housing deductions.[2] Religious organizations are also exempted from sales tax (along with other not-for-profit organizations) and from property taxes (provided that the organizations are not used for commercial purposes or profit). Are such exemptions fair? Further questions beckon. If an exception to taxation is made, isn't government assisting religion? And if this is truly a form of government assistance, is it acceptable under the religion clauses of the Constitution?

Property tax exceptions are particularly widespread and well-established. The constitutions, laws, or court opinions of every state command or permit the exemption of religiously owned property from property taxes. These exceptions trace their history back to post-colonial times and the tax immunity enjoyed by property owned by established churches within the states.[3] Unlike general charities, which were similarly exempt from state taxation but which performed both a sectarian and public function (so, had they not existed, governmental action would likely have been required), tax exemptions for religion, its buildings (for example, churches), and its property did not advance any quasi-public function. Thus, eighteenth- and nineteenth-century tax exemptions directly benefited the religious activities of religion and made no pretense of promoting any sort of distinct, secular public interest. Initially, then, tax exemptions for church property often grew out of a union of church and state at the state level, likely developed in accordance with the view that encouraging religion was a positive good (for its own sake); then, in the twentieth century, these arrangements were defended solely as a means of advancing public morality and virtue.[4]

In terms of twentieth-century jurisprudence, the problem was that none of these three rationales was consistent with post–World War II interpretations of the Establishment Clause by the Supreme Court as applied to the states through the Fourteenth Amendment. Therefore, the source of conflict was occasioned by the fact that history was in conflict with constitutional interpretation. Later, we will observe how this conflict was addressed by the Supreme Court. First, however, we note that early Supreme Court examinations of religious taxation initially arose not within the context of assessing tax exemptions for religiously owned property, but over the matter of imposing taxes upon the actions of religious representatives. Indeed, one example of these early cases was a famous Jehovah's Witnesses case, one of more than eighty legal disputes in which this controversial religious sect challenged state laws before the Supreme Court in the name of basic American freedoms, especially freedom of religion.

EXAMPLE 1

Murdock v. *Pennsylvania,* 319 U.S. 105 (1943)

Facts: Jeannette, Pennsylvania, required a business license for those selling door to door. The license was to be purchased from the city, paid by a tax whose amount varied with its length of use. Petitioners, who were Jehovah's Witnesses (and who also were ministers, for all baptized Jehovah's Witnesses are considered ministers), sought contributions. They did so by going door to door, handing out religious literature, and asking for contributions. The city regarded their actions as soliciting for the purpose of persuading people to "purchase" religious books and pamphlets. Nonetheless, the Jehovah's Witnesses did not apply for a business license.

Result: The town violates the First Amendment's Free Exercise Clause as applied to the states when it requires Jehovah's Witnesses to purchase business licenses.

Argument of the Case: Douglas, Justice. A tax laid on the free exercise of religion or on preaching would be unconstitutional, yet "the license tax imposed by this ordinance is in substance just that." Petitioners, as missionary evangelists, follow their religious beliefs (for example, Paul, in Acts 20:20, admonishes to teach publicly from house to house). The Witnesses preach and distribute literature, and this is a form of protected free speech and press as well as religious liberty (for it "occupies the same high estate under the First Amendment as do worship in the churches and preaching from the pulpits"). It is of no consequence that the literature is "sold" just as it is of no consequence for the freedom of press provision that books are sold. Selling is incidental to the main object of preaching (it is like passing the collection plate). Nor does it matter that the tax is nondiscriminatory (affecting religious and nonreligious solicitation alike); religious belief is still adversely affected. Jehovah's Witnesses (and all religious sects) are not exempt from all forms of taxation, nor are they exempt from all strictures of law. But other forms of taxation are not here contested, and there is no contention that the peace has been breached. It is of no moment that Jehovah's Witness literature is provocative; this is precisely the kind of literature that the First Amendment was designed to protect.

Reed dissents.[5] The Constitution does not forbid general occupation taxes. Furthermore, neither church nor press must be free from the financial burdens of government. The law in question is reasonable and nondiscriminatory and does not aim at destroying religion or imposing prior restraint (for example, censorship) on the press. Furthermore, distributing literature is more than preaching, and charging for it "destroys the sacred character of the transaction," making the evangelist "a book agent." Spiritual rites are protected by the First Amendment—for example, prayer, mass, sermons, and sacraments—but commercial sales are not. This law unduly limits the state legislature and wrongly overturns precedent.

Frankfurter dissents.[6] The Witnesses do not contend that the tax unjustifiably curtails their right to communicate their views; rather, they claim an outright immunity from taxation. But this immunity cannot be sustained because they are engaged in religious activities or because they exercise a constitutional right. A clergyman is also a citizen who shares in his nation's benefits (traffic safety, health protection, and so on) and its obligations (that is, taxes). Such a person is taxed for these benefits. Since the tax works no hardship upon religion, it is not an abuse of power, for the "fact that a power can be perverted does not mean that every exercise of the power is a perversion of the power."

Discussion

One of the dissenters, Justice Reed, was indisputably correct about one thing. *Murdock* clearly reversed precedent. Less than a year before, in the case of *Jones* v. *Opelika*,[7] the Court, by a bare majority, had ruled the other way. It upheld a tax upon the distribution of literature on the ground that the tax was nondiscriminatory, not disadvantaging religious practitioners over other salespeople. The Court also declared that the First Amendment did not require government to extend a fiscal exemption to help subsidize religion. Nor was the theoretical or legal path direct and straightforward after *Murdock*. A year later, in *Follett* v. *McCormick* (another Jehovah's Witness case), the Court did bolster its *Murdock* line of reasoning by determining that a person whose sole source of income came from selling religious books could be exempted from a flat business and license tax on bookselling. Yet, as we shall see later in this section (specifically in the case of *Texas Monthly, Inc.* v. *Bullock*[8]), much of the logic of *Murdock* would not endure. Thus, *Murdock* has proven to be both unstable and controversial. Let us see why.

Understanding *Murdock* begins with the recognition that, for the Supreme Court's liberal majority, the Jehovah's Witnesses were precisely the kind of group the First Amendment was intended to protect. Small, unorthodox, intensely controversial, the sect's opinions and methods were constantly under scrutiny and debated. This group cooperated neither with government nor with other religions. Thus, Jehovah's Witnesses routinely refused civic obligations (voting, jury duty, military duty, saluting the flag,[9] and so on). Furthermore, they frequently appeared hostile toward other religious groups, particularly Roman Catholics. Finally, their fervent door-to-door evangelism (where they gave away their publications *Awake!* and *Watchtower* and then asked for contributions) and occasional aggressive use of sound trucks frequently annoyed residents and sometimes led them to adopt restrictive ordinances designed to curb the Witnesses' proselytizing activities.

For the Court's majority, it was key was that the Witnesses were undertaking constitutionally protected activities. Indeed, the Court viewed this case as a generalized First Amendment dispute. It mentioned, almost interchangeably, the Free Exercise Clause, the Free Press Clause, and the Free Speech Clause. All came together when the Jehovah's Witnesses evangelized door to door. In this case, the rights of a group to practice religion, to publish religious literature, and to disseminate ideas all merged. Justice Douglas declared as much for the Court, noting that with this decision, "we can restore to their high, constitutional position their religious beliefs and the tenets of their faith through distribution of literature."[10]

More precisely, Douglas rested *Murdock*'s rationale upon two interrelated constitutional foundations. Douglas examined exactly what the Jehovah's Witnesses did. They went from house to house, distributing their literature and then asking for contributions to pay for their expenses. Was this activity "religious or purely commercial"? (Commercial activity is entitled to a far lower level of constitutional protection.) The answer Douglas seemed to suggest was that the Witnesses' activity was an example of religious free exercise *and* protected free speech and press; therefore, it could not be seen as purely commercial. The Witnesses' activity was religious (and not commercial) in the sense that passing the collection plate in church does not transform the church service from a religious exercise into a commercial service. Nor was the "right to use the press in expressing one's views ... to be measured by the protection afforded commercial handbills"; after all, added Douglas, "It should be remembered that the pamphlets of Thomas Paine were not distributed free of charge."[11] Thus, it would seem that the Jehovah's Witnesses' activities retained their protection, either under the rubric of protected religious free exercise or as protected speech and press. In Douglas's words,

> But an itinerant evangelist, however misguided or intolerant he may be, does not become a mere book agent by selling the Bible or religious tracts to help defray his expenses or to sustain him. Freedom of speech, freedom of the press, freedom of religion are available to all, not merely to those who can pay their own way. As we have said, the problem of drawing the line between a purely commercial activity and a religious one will at times be difficult. On this record it plainly cannot be said that petitioners were engaged in a commercial rather than a religious venture.[12]

Douglas differed from the dissenters in a key respect. The dissenters stressed the secular purpose and general application of the tax. Justice Reed pointed out that the tax was nondiscriminatory. It affected all salespeople and did not single out for taxation religious representatives (who were considered by the law to be simply one kind of salesperson). Justice Frankfurter emphasized that this broad-based tax was a means by which government raised money to provide essential public services for all citizens, including Jehovah's Witnesses. For each of the dissenters, the key was that the tax was primarily secular and only worked an incidental, remote, or indirect hardship upon religious practice. Balancing the governmental interest against the religious infringement created by the act, the dissenters opted for the governmental interest and upheld the tax.

Their approach differed from that of Douglas, who began by defining the disputed action as essentially religious (with free speech and press overtones). Not only was asking for contributions similar to passing the collection plate around a church; the dissemination by a Jehovah's Witness of material in another's home was akin to delivering a sermon. Perhaps other, less direct, religiously related activities could be taxed, but Douglas contended that Murdock's house-to-house proselytizing could not. Furthermore, once Murdock's religious (and speech and press) rights had been properly identified, the First Amendment afforded him maximum protection and therefore needed to be accorded great weight. In any balancing process, these rights were in a preferred position, not merely when compared to other rights, but also when weighed against the exercise of governmental powers.[13]

Interestingly, when the Supreme Court considered whether Murdock's religious actions were entitled to broad First Amendment protection, there was no consideration of the Establishment Clause. That constitutional provision had not yet become an issue for the Supreme Court. It had not been applied to the states (and would not be until 1947, in the case of *Everson* v. *Board of Education*).[14] Thus, *Murdock* presented one straightforward issue—namely, whether Murdock's religious and free speech rights had been compromised by the tax imposed by the local township. By determining that they had, Douglas presented the Supreme Court as championing an unpopular religious minority whose First Amendment rights had been jeopardized. However, whether the Court's interpretation improperly favored religion over irreligion (which was the type of question inevitably posed in Establishment Clause cases) was not disputed or even discussed. This issue would be addressed later.

Although it was not considered in the *Murdock* case, the effect of the Establishment Clause *did* prove to be an issue in a second important case decided by the Supreme Court regarding the extent to which religion, religious representatives, and religiously owned property could be exempted from governmental taxation. This controversy did not involve Jehovah's Witnesses' proselytizing efforts, but rather examined the extent to which places of worship and religiously owned property could be exempted from routine property taxes. Both for what it decided and for the legal tests it employed, it would prove to be a noteworthy case indeed.

EXAMPLE 2

Walz v. *Tax Commission of the City of New York,* 397 U.S. 644 (1970)

Facts: The New York Constitution allowed exemptions from taxation of real or personal property "used exclusively for religious, education or charitable purposes as defined by law and owned by any corporation or association organized or conducted exclusively for one or more of such purposes and not operating for profit."

Result: Extending tax exemptions to church property does not require taxpayers to make a contribution to a religious body in violation of the Establishment Clause and the Fourteenth Amendment; therefore, the exemption is constitutional.

Argument of the Case: Burger, Chief Justice. Those who wrote the religion clauses of the First Amendment prohibited religious establishment where it "connoted sponsorship, financial support, and active involvement of the sovereign in religious activity." This understanding of the Establishment Clause must be reconciled with the Free Exercise Clause. A neutral course must be followed between the two clauses, for they tend to clash if extended to their logical extremes. That course begins by recognizing that here no one church or churches have been singled out for exemption by the state. Rather, the state "has granted exemption to all houses of religious worship within a broad class of property owned by nonprofit, quasi-public corporations which include hospitals, libraries, playgrounds, scientific, professional, historical and patriotic groups." Such organizations have "a beneficial and stabilizing influence in community life...." Therefore, this is a permissible state accommodation with religion. Sponsorship does not exist because the government does not transfer part of its revenue to churches. Excessive entanglement, which would also violate the Establishment Clause, is also avoided; government would, in fact, become more entangled with religion if property taxes were collected. Churches are also exempt from federal income taxes and uniformly exempt from state property taxes. Both practices (particularly the latter) have a long history and are instructive.

Brennan concurs. His criteria for Establishment Clause violation have not been breached: (1) The exemptions do not benefit the essentially religious activities of religious organizations; their principal effect is secular, intending to encourage public service activities and a pluralistic society. (2) The organs of government are not employed for an essentially religious purpose, for government does not foster these activities by exempting them from taxation—at most, it merely leaves them untouched. (3) Neither do the exemptions amount to an essentially religious means to serve governmental ends where secular means would suffice, for there is no nonreligious substitute for religion.

Harlan concurs. The tax exemption does not endanger the essential values of the religion clauses. It undermines neither neutrality (among religions and between religion and nonreligion) nor volunteerism, and it does not give rise to religiously based political divisiveness.

Douglas dissents. The New York statute exempts from taxation real property of a corporation owned exclusively for religious purposes and used exclusively for such purposes. Yet nonbelievers who own property are taxed. Therefore, religion is advanced and nonbelievers are not, so the Establishment Clause is breached.

Discussion

New York has exempted some, but not all, nonprofit corporations from paying property tax. The key characteristic shared by these entities was their dedication to the cultural or moral improvement of citizens or their performance of certain "good works" that government might otherwise have to undertake. (On these grounds, they were distinguished from nonexempted, nonprofit entities owning property, including political parties, labor unions, social clubs, and chambers of commerce.) Included among the exempted entities were churches and other houses of worship. At first glance, New York's classification scheme may have seemed unobjectionable. Most people would readily agree that religious entities intend the moral improvement of their parishioners and also that such organizations often undertake quasi-public services (for example, family counseling, child care, and aid to the elderly). Yet, unlike the other exempted entities, houses of worship do not exist *primarily* for these secular purposes; participation in the worship service is, clear and simple, the primary purpose for their existence. Any moral improvement or quasi-public services they render constitute, at best, an indirect effect. Thus, to look at a specific example, a church (or synagogue or mosque) differs from a museum by being primarily religious, although each has both secular and religious aspects (for example, a museum displays religious art) and the law treats them equally (by exempting each of them from property taxes). Museums also differ from such nonexempted entities as labor temples because, as the rationale behind the contested legislative classification scheme seemed to suggest, museums exist primarily for the cultural enjoyment and improvement of citizens while a labor temple essentially exists to serve the "partisan" interest of its sponsoring labor union. (However, it would not be wrong to point out that labor unions, too, sometimes undertake quasi-public activities—for example, involvement in charitable fund drives and other community activities.) If one were to examine the reasonableness of New York's method of classifying non-profit organizations in order to confer tax-exempt status, one could, in simple language, ask if a church was more like an exempted museum or a nonexempted labor temple. Or, perhaps, were religious entities different from both—in a class by themselves?

That New York's classification scheme had to make sense at all, and that it required an independent secular rationale to sustain tax-exempt status upon houses of worship, was a product of a dilemma that no Justice in *Walz* discussed directly. The problem was alluded to at the beginning of this chapter and is extraordinary important to recognize. Since before the Constitution was adopted, American colonial and state history not only had provided support for religion and religious institutions; it had specifically allowed (and in some cases required) the kind of tax exemptions challenged in this case. However, this pro-religious history was at odds with the contemporary Supreme Court interpretation of the Establishment Clause. As applied to the states, it stipulated a separation of church and state, and/or church–state neutrality, and/or that the state pass legislation that had neither the purpose nor primary effect of advancing or harming religion. In brief, what the Supreme Court had to reconcile in *Walz* was a pro-religious history with interpretations of the Establishment Clause that precluded such a pro-religion stance by government.

It is intriguing to note how the various Justices attempted to resolve this core dilemma. For the Court, Burger avoided the problem by focusing on what would have happened if New York had not exempted religious property from taxation. To that end, he offered a wide variety of arguments intended to demonstrate that taxing religious establishments would reflect an impermissible hostility toward religion (not endorsed by history or permitted by the Supreme Court's prior interpretation of the Establishment Clause). Burger's most original contribution was the announcement of the excessive entanglement test (which would later be explicitly incorporated as part of the influential *Lemon* test[15]). His argument was that the Establishment Clause limited entanglement between government and religion, that tax exemptions diminished entanglement while taxation increased it, therefore that tax exemptions were more consistent with the Establishment Clause than were taxes. By focusing upon avoiding both governmental hostility to religion and excessive governmental-religious entanglement, Burger managed largely to ignore the tension between the Supreme Court's previous Establishment Clause language and the nation's pro-religious history, a problem perhaps exacerbated by what was commonly considered to be a pro-religion decision in *Walz*.

The concurring Justices addressed this problem in different ways. Brennan resolved the tension between history and previous Court Establishment Clause language by suggesting that the state interest was advanced by the "good works" undertaken by various religions and by the state's interest in promoting religious diversity. Harlan asserted that as long as the property tax exemption "includes groups that pursue cultural, moral, or spiritual improvement in multifarious secular ways, including, I would suppose, groups whose avowed tenets may be antitheological, atheistic, or agnostic, I can see no lack of neutrality in extending the benefit of the exemption to organized religious groups."[16] Both Brennan's and Harlan's arguments proved unenlightening. Brennan's accommodationist application of his Establishment Clause principles, which required only evenhanded treatment of religions and which saw secular benefits deriving from the very existence of diverse religious institutions, had been largely rejected by the Court since *Everson* and would be repeatedly rejected by Brennan in later cases. For instance, Brennan thought that the Establishment Clause prohibited the government from providing financial benefits (through direct grants) to religiously sponsored schools and colleges, despite the fact that the money was not earmarked for any one religion, and despite the fact that the elementary and secondary schools, and certainly the colleges, were far less religious in character than the houses of worship exempted from taxation in *Walz*.[17] Similarly, Harlan's point that tax exemption was religiously neutral because anti-religious groups as well as religious entities would also be benefited by the New York taxation scheme was less than stunning, for as Justice Douglas contended, "with all respect, there is not even a suggestion in the present record that the statute covers property used exclusively by organizations for 'antitheological purposes,' 'atheistic purposes' and 'agnostic purposes.'"[18]

Justice Douglas may correctly have detected the weakness in Harlan's Establishment Clause argument, but his dissent had its own difficulties. Douglas pointed to a number of cases that suggested both that religion could not be directly benefited and that religion could not be favored over nonreligion to bolster his argument that the logic of the Establishment Clause precluded direct subsidies to religious establishments. But what about history? What about the clear record of state aid to religious establishments? Douglas's answer was concise and to the point:

> In affirming the judgment the Court largely overlooks the revolution initiated by the adoption of the Fourteenth Amendment. The revolution involved the imposition of new and far-reaching constitutional restraints of the States. Nationalization of many civil liberties has been the consequence of the Fourteenth Amendment, reversing the historic position that the foundations of those liberties rested largely in state law.[19]

In other words, the tension between history and constitutional theory needed to resolved in favor of constitutional theory. The Supreme Court's nationalizing of the Bill of Rights (and the Establishment Clause[20]) may have been right or wrong (Douglas thought it was right), but it was the law of the land, irrespective of the extent to which it conflicted with past or current practice. Not Douglas nor any of the other Justices was able to provide a persuasive rationale in *Walz* that successfully reconciled the established Supreme Court's religiously neutral Establishment Clause interpretation with favorable state government practices, such as New York's providing property tax exemptions for religiously owned property.

As the Supreme Court applied the Establishment Clause to the states, it continued to have reason both to re-examine pro-religion state practices and to look at its own past opinions. That this was no easy task becomes clear as we turn to our next case.

EXAMPLE 3

Texas Monthly v. *Bullock,* 489 U.S. 1 (1988)

Facts: A Texas statute exempted from sales and use tax periodicals "published or distributed by a religious faith ... consist[ing] wholly of writings promulgating the teachings of the faith and books ... consist[ing] wholly of writings sacred to a religious faith." Other publications were not exempted.

Result: The Establishment Clause, as applied to the states, prohibits a sales tax exemption that solely benefits publications that are exclusively religious.

Argument of the Case: Brennan, Justice.[21] The Establishment Clause prohibits legislation that endorses one religious sect or religion generally (as this statute does). The Constitution does not prohibit legislation where religion incidentally benefits; thus, in *Walz* the property tax exemption sustained applied to religious property and to property owned by a wide array of nonprofit organizations. Here only religious periodicals are exempted. The law exists for a religious purpose. Taxpayers are forced to become indirect donors to these periodicals' publication and dissemination. Furthermore, impermissible state entanglement with religion is more advanced by the law than by its repeal (for state officials are required by the law to determine which publications are entitled to exemption). The Free Exercise Clause does not require individualized exemptions to taxation laws. To the extent that the ruling is in tension with language in previous free exercise opinions such as *Murdock* v. *Pennsylvania,* that language is now overturned.

White concurs. The Texas law discriminates on the basis of a publication's content, and this is forbidden by the Free Press Clause of the First Amendment.

Blackmun concurs.[22] This case requires reconciling the Establishment Clause, the Free Exercise Clause, and the Free Press Clause (the first two being particularly challenging, since the Free Exercise Clause requires special exemption for religious books while the Establishment Clause forbids it). Generally, the state might satisfy these constitutional requirements by writing "a tax-exemption statute consistent with both values: for example, a state statute might exempt the sale not only of religious literature distributed by a religious organization but also philosophical literature distributed by nonreligious organizations." *Texas Monthly* should be decided narrowly by avoiding the free exercise problems (inherent in cases such as *Murdock*) and only by deciding that a tax exemption limited to the sale of religious literature by religious organizations violates the Establishment Clause.

Scalia dissents.[23] History and widespread practice (in at least 45 states) support laws like this. So do precedents (especially *Walz*). They make clear that religion can be accommodated under the Establishment Clause (even though such action is not required by the Free Exercise Clause). Sometimes, when religion is incidentally benefited by the law, the breadth of coverage rationale is employed (that is, that both religious and certain nonreligious entities are benefited), but it is not the only basis by which contested legislation can be sustained under the Establishment Clause. Even when religion is solely benefited by the contested legislation—if, for example, the state legislature would have found that the absence of such laws would reflect a hostility toward religion—such a statute can still be sustained under the Establishment Clause.

Discussion

Here we encounter a situation that politely can be called (for lack of a more scientific term) a fine legal mess. The Justices in this case disagreed about virtually everything. They disputed the results, disagreed about precedents (especially the two, *Murdock* and *Walz*, that we have already reviewed), and seemed mired in an continuing argument about precisely how the two religion clauses related to each other. Before examining these disputes in greater detail, we would point out that with the *Bullock* decision, the law in this area became hopelessly muddled, perhaps even outright contradictory.

The broad question of this chapter is whether religious property and religious representatives exclusively performing religious tasks should be taxed. In *Murdock,* the Court gave an emphatic no as an answer, defending, on First Amendment grounds, the right of a Jehovah's Witness minister to "sell" his publications without paying a local license tax. In *Texas Monthly* v. *Bullock* the Court denied the legality of the sort of tax exemption for religious materials that it had seemed to accept in *Murdock.* As has been suggested, one key difference is that the Court in *Bullock* accepted the legal proposition it had not considered in *Murdock,* that the Establishment Clause affects the states. The Establishment Clause seemed to limit the extent or manner to which the state might afford legal exemption to general taxation, lest it be accused of fostering an establishment of religion (on the grounds of favoring religion or favoring one religion).

The Court's solution to these seemingly conflicting cases was to read the *Murdock* precedent narrowly. Brennan, for the Court, suggested a reconciliation in lukewarm terms: although the two cases were different to the extent that *Murdock* imposed a restraining occupation tax (and not a sales tax), they could be reconciled if *Murdock* could be read to mean that "equal treatment of commercial and religious solicitation *might* result in an unconstitutional imposition of religious activity warranting judicial relief, particularly where that activity is deemed central to a given faith … and where the tax forbidden is far from negligible."[24] The protected activity in *Murdock,* absent in *Bullock,* was the Jehovah's Witnesses' religious proselytizing. However, Brennan emphasized that the *Murdock* precedent should not be interpreted too broadly. In fact, "[t]o the extent that our opinions in *Murdock* … suggest that the States and the Federal Government may never tax the sale of religious or other publications, we reject those dicta."[25]

Scalia, dissenting, was skeptical of Brennan's attempted reconciliation of precedent. He noted that *Murdock* should have suggested that tax exemption for religious literature was permissible, perhaps even required.[26] Furthermore, a sales tax was not readily distinguishable from a license tax; both burdened religion. Nor was the religious proselytizing of the missionaries and the literature they distributed readily distinguishable from the message or importance of the religious periodicals exempted in *Bullock*. Scalia would have distinguished *Murdock* from *Bullock* on the ground that while religious exemption was required in *Murdock,* it was only permitted in *Bullock:* "The proper lesson to be drawn from the narrow distinguishing of *Murdock* … is if the exemption comes so close to being a constitutionally required accommodation, there is no doubt that it is at least a permissible one."[27]

If *Murdock* was a disputed precedent, *Walz* became the focal point of an outright judicial donnybrook. This was, in the words of the Brennan plurality opinion, "the case most nearly on point." For Brennan, *Walz's* tax exemption for religious properties provided an adequate model for the kind of legal program the Court ought to uphold, a broad secular program that limited governmental involvement with religion. He believed that the Texas program overturned in *Bullock* differed significantly because there religion *alone* was exempted from taxation.

Scalia was neither impressed nor mollified by this explanation. On the contrary, he contended that *Walz* required that the Texas tax exemption law be upheld. "Nineteen years ago … we considered and rejected an Establishment Clause challenge that was in all relevant respects identical," began his analysis of this precedent. The tax exemption upheld in *Walz* was shown to be compatible with the *Lemon* test, had a long history, and was recognized in all fifty states. Regarding Brennan's notion that *Walz* had been upheld as part of a general governmental program of exempting certain nonprofit organizations, Scalia noted that the Supreme Court's "finding of valid legislative purpose was not rested upon that, however, but upon the more direct proposition that 'exemption constitutes a reasonable and balanced attempt to guard against' the 'latent dangers' of government hostility towards religion…."[28] In support of his interpretation, Scalia observed that *Walz*'s holding explicitly relied upon the citing of federal legislation that *alone* had exempted religion (remitting duties paid on the importation of plates for printing Bibles). Furthermore, the Court's *Walz* opinion gave no reason why religious property was included with other nonprofit entities exempted; in fact, the majority opinion specifically denied that religious property was exempted for social services or "good works." According to Scalia, religion had been exempted by the Court on the basis of accommodation (which was a legitimate Establishment Clause principle). In *Walz,* the Court "did not approve an exemption for charities that happened to benefit religion; it approved an exemption for religion *as* an exemption for religion."[29]

Irrespective of these arguments over precedents, what really separated Scalia from Brennan in *Bullock* was a fundamental disagreement over the Establishment Clause's meaning. For Brennan, the Establishment Clause meant that government could not directly favor religion and could accommodate it only when religion benefited indirectly and incidentally from a generalized governmental program (and then not always). For Scalia, the Establishment Clause did not prohibit government from nondiscriminatory accommodation of religion, especially when to withhold benefits would work a hardship upon religion. Both Brennan and Scalia could cite precedents on behalf of their Establishment Clause interpretation. In favor of Brennan's interpretation was that it was most consistent with the language (and arguably the holding) of the Supreme Court's interpretation of the first Establishment Clause case, *Everson,* and with recurring Supreme Court language to the effect that government cannot aid religion. In favor of Scalia's position was that the application of his constitutional interpretation better accorded with widespread contemporary practice, that its application had extensive historical support, and that his Establishment Clause interpretation was easier to reconcile with an interpretation of religious free exercise, which also permitted latitude for individual religious exemptions under the Free Exercise Clause.[30]

Justice Blackmun detected this last problem, although his interpretation was somewhat different. To his mind, Brennan's *Bullock* opinion had ignored the Free Exercise Clause and associated precedents while Scalia had dispensed with settled Establishment Clause interpretations and associated precedents by favoring religious belief over disbelief. But how could both settled Establishment Clause interpretation and the Free Exercise Clause be reconciled? Blackmun had an idea, and he made it by way of suggesting to Texas (and other states) how such a law might be written:

> Perhaps it is a vain desire, but I would like to decide the present case without necessarily sacrificing either the Free Exercise value or the Establishment Clause value. It is possible for a State to write a tax-exemption statute consistent with both values: for example, a state statute might exempt the sale not only of religious literature distributed by a religious organization but also of philosophical literature distributed by nonreligious organizations devoted to such matters of conscience as life and

death, good and evil, being and nothing, right and wrong. Such a statute, moreover, should survive Press Clause scrutiny because its exemption would be narrowly tailored to meet the compelling interests that underlie both the Free Exercise and Establishment Clauses.[31]

But, unfortunately, Blackmun's solution was no solution at all. Rightly or wrongly, Scalia was no doubt right about one thing; the purpose of the Texas tax exemption statute was to benefit (or at least not to harm) religion. Whether the belief of the Texas legislature originally was that religion (and religious publications) should not be taxed or disadvantaged because it was true or because it was socially useful, we need not decide or even know. What we do know is that there was no independent rationale for additionally exempting philosophical publications from taxation except to legitimate (in Blackmun's eyes) the validation of the original religious exemption. And determining precisely which publications qualified for the exemption, under Blackmun's expanded criterion, seemed to present something of an administrative nightmare. For these reasons, Blackmun's proposed resolution to the seeming conflict between the religion clauses created more problems than it solved.

Yet, despite the sad state of legal affairs in *Bullock,* all was not lost. In the last case we will examine in this chapter, the Supreme Court not only decided unanimously the relevant legal questions it faced, but went some distance in resolving some of the ambiguities and contradictions in the law apparent after *Bullock.* Let us see how this happened.

EXAMPLE 4

Jimmy Swaggart Ministries v. *Board of Equalization of California,* 493 U.S. 378 (1990)

Facts: Jimmy Swaggart Ministries was a religious organization incorporated as a Louisiana nonprofit entity and was recognized by the IRS as such. (According to its charter, it was organized "for the purpose of establishing and maintaining an evangelistic outreach for the worship of Almighty God.") From 1974 to 1981, Swaggart conducted numerous crusades in California, sold recordings of these services as well as books, tapes, and records, and published a monthly magazine (*The Evangelist*) that was sold in California and nationwide by subscription. Swaggart was subject to California's sales and use tax. The sales tax requires retailers to pay for commercial transactions of tangible personal property, and the use tax is imposed upon state residents who buy that same kind of property out of state. California's law allows no religious exemptions, although Swaggart argued that the religion clauses ought to require California to exempt his purely religious activities and products from both taxes.

Result: California's sales tax and use tax violate neither the Establishment Clause nor the Free Exercise Clause as applied to the states by the Fourteenth Amendment.

Argument of the Case: O'Connor, Justice. The Free Exercise Clause does not permit legislatures to restrain freedom of religion. Furthermore, even neutral regulations that place a substantial burden on a central religious belief or practice violate the Free Exercise Clause unless they are supported by a compelling governmental interest. Swaggart relies heavily upon *Murdock* (and *Follett* v. *McCormick*); *Murdock* held that "spreading one's religious beliefs or preaching the Gospel through distribution of religious literature and through personal visitations is an age-old type of evangelism with as high a claim to constitutional protection as the more orthodox types." Yet the type of tax imposed in each case is significant; the flat license tax in that case operated as a restraint upon religious liberty. To that extent, *Murdock* and *Follett* are limited as precedents. Furthermore, there is no evidence that the collection and payment of the taxes violate the religious beliefs of Swaggart or his organization. Nor is the amount of the tax onerous; it does not crush religion. Thus, the Free Exercise Clause argument fails. So does the Establishment Clause argument. The taxes do not excessively entangle religion and government. Contrary to Swaggart's claim, the collection and payment of the taxes do not impose a serious accounting burden, much less an unconstitutional burden. Nor does excessive entanglement arise from the fact that Swaggart's organization must bear the cost of collecting and remitting the taxes; there is no continuing governmental surveillance. Finally, imposing the taxes does not require the government to examine the religious beliefs of the organization, also freeing it from excessive entanglement.

Discussion

Jimmy Swaggart is best remembered as a prominent "televangelist"—a fundamentalist Protestant minister whose sexual misbehavior eventually caused his downfall. But, as this case makes clear, Swaggart also headed a large-scale commercial business (for instance, in less than seven years his Louisiana-based corporation sold to California residents alone more than $1,700,000 worth of merchandise in mail-order sales). Finally, Swaggart has also gained a limited sort of constitutional notoriety by litigating a case whose resolution seems to have brought about an uneasy truce on a Supreme Court that had been bitterly divided upon the question of taxing religious properties and activities.

The unanimous (!) resolution of the *Swaggart* case accomplished two primary tasks for the Court. First, it integrated the *Murdock* (and *Follett*) precedents into the main body of American constitutional law. It did this by further limiting their applicability. According to the Court in *Swaggart,* the constitutional problem of the laws challenged successfully in those cases was not that they taxed religious activities, or that the tax they imposed was unduly harsh and abusive, but rather that the form the tax assumed was impermissible. A flat license tax, neither apportioned nor related to the taxed activity, served to restrain and suppress religious activity. The challenged business licenses in Jeannette, Pennsylvania, in 1943 (when *Murdock* was decided by the Supreme Court) cost $1.50 per day, $7 per week, $12 per two weeks, and $20 for three weeks. Yet the amount of the tax was not the point. Rather, because the tax was a precondition of doing business, it might inhibit poorer practitioners (Jehovah's Witnesses in this case) from even undertaking their religious activities. Sales taxes, like those challenged in *Swaggart,* did not have such a chilling effect on religious free exercise.

In addition to disposing successfully of troubling precedents, the Court, with the pronouncement of its *Swaggart* opinion, accomplished a second goal by presenting something close to a coherent, integrated view of the Establishment and Free Exercise clauses. After *Swaggart,* one might summarize the Court's position as follows: the Free Exercise Clause hardly ever compels government to exempt religion from general taxation—except in those rare instances when a tax serves to inhibit the free exercise of protected religious activity. Already the Court had, by something less than a clear majority, put forward an Establishment Clause rule in *Bullock* that government could not exclusively aid religion, religious property, and publications; any benefit had to be part of a more general governmental program. (*Bullock* was the reason why Swaggart's Establishment Clause attack upon California's taxes focused upon an excessive entanglement claim, an argument that was rather easily rejected by the Court.) Thus, in the vast majority of cases in this area of the law, the Constitution, as interpreted by the Supreme Court, appeared to approach a famous test for reconciling the two religion clauses, namely "that the freedom and separation clauses should be read as a single precept that government cannot utilize religion as a standard for action or inaction because these clauses prohibit classification in terms of religion either to confer a benefit or confer a burden."[32]

SUMMARY

By 1990, the Supreme Court seemed to have restored some degree of order and predictability to the area of the law regarding religious tax exemptions. The road leading up to this uneasy consensus grew out of a number of conflicts, notably between common state practice and a long history favoring tax exemptions benefiting religion, and the First Amendment theory pronounced by the Supreme Court, which increasingly suggested that the Constitution could not favor (or disfavor) religion. An additional, complicating factor was that early Supreme Court decisions in this area were litigated solely under the Free Exercise Clause, the Establishment Clause being applied against the states only later. The result of this early litigation (in cases like *Murdock*) tended to provide broad exemptions to religion and religious practice, case law that later proved to be something of a legal embarrassment for the Court.

In the aftermath of some fifty years of confusing and contentious court opinions, a clearer legal pattern emerges. The Supreme Court now suggests that the religion clauses prevent government from exempting religion and religious representatives from taxation, except as part of a generalized governmental program benefiting similar organizations, publications, and/or properties, or where the tax has the effect of inhibiting protected religious exercise. The religion clauses require governmental neutrality between religion and nonreligion. Religion can be exempted from taxation under the Establishment Clause, or taxed in spite of religious beliefs and practices under the Free Exercise Clause, just as long as religion is not singled out for favoritism (in the first case) or penalized (in the second). Only when broad-based government programs directly chill essential religious activities (or perhaps when neutral governmental programs directly contradict central religious beliefs) does the Free Exercise Clause demand that religion be singled out and exempted. When such exemption is demanded, it presumably cannot be argued that the Establishment Clause is breached, for treating religious activities and property differently from nonreligious activities and property by exempting them from taxation restores religious neutrality. This should not constitute religious establishment; rather, it merely promotes religious survival.

Yet, having suggested that something approaching a coherent interpretation of the Constitution has emerged in this area of taxing religious property and activity, we must also point out that there remains sharp disagreement on the Court regarding a variety of issues. Judges still read precedents differently, occasionally even interpreting their facts differently. Some Justices would still permit government to offer nondiscriminatory support to religion. Therefore, the judicial controversy endures. But it is also safe to say that after more than fifty years of heated litigation, there is substantially more agreement today than there was in the past.

NOTES

1. This question is discussed in Chapter 6, p. 116, but within the context of what happens when religion is used as a pretext for claiming exemption from taxation. Also discussed in that chapter is the extent to which religiously owned activities may be exempted. See p. 111.

2. Regarding the question of fraud in so far as it relates to claiming these exemptions, see Chapter 6.

3. In certain key respects, this introduction builds upon observations made by Arvo Van Alystyne, "Tax Exemption of Church Property," *Ohio State Law Journal,* vol. 20 (1959), pp. 461–507.

4. This was especially true as it became clear that the religion clauses affected both the states and the federal government and that a new rationale was required to sustain tax exemptions in the light of broader constitutional restrictions.

5. This opinion was joined by Justices Roberts, Frankfurter, and Jackson.

6. Justice Jackson joined this dissent.

7. 316 U.S. 584 (1942). *Jones v. Opelika* (II) was reargued along with *Murdock* and hence constitutes a *per curiam* opinion explaining this fact.

8. 489 U.S. 1 (1988).

9. See Chapter 18.

10. *Murdock* v. *Pennsylvania* at 117.

11. *Murdock* v. *Pennsylvania* at 111.

12. *Murdock* v. *Pennsylvania* at 111.

13. For identification of Douglas's position in terms of the beginning of the Supreme Court's acceptance of the First Amendment's preferred position doctrine, see Robert T. Miller and Ronald B. Flowers, *Toward Benevolent Neutrality: Church, State, and the Supreme Court* (Waco, TX: Markham Press Fund, 1987), 3d ed., p. 57.

14. 330 U.S. 1 (1947).

15. For a discussion of this test, see Chapter 13, p. 241.

16. *Murdock* v. *Pennsylvania* at 664.

17. For a discussion of this issue, see Chapter 13, p. 237.

18. *Walz* v. *Tax Commission* at 700.

19. *Waltz* v. *Tax Commission* at 701.

20. See our comment, Chapter 13, p.239.

21. This opinion was joined by Justices Marshall and Stevens.

22. Justice O'Connor joined this opinion.

23. Chief Justice Rehnquist and Justice Kennedy joined this opinion.

24. *Texas Monthly* v. *Bullock* at 23. Emphasis ours. Note Brennan's lack of clarity about whether the Court would uphold *Murdock*.

25. *Texas Monthly* v. *Bullock* at 24.

26. *Texas Monthly* v. *Bullock* at 30–31.

27. *Texas Monthly* v. *Bullock* at 42.

28. *Texas Monthly* v. *Bullock* at 36.

29. *Texas Monthly* v. *Bullock* at 38.

30. Although both Justices would allow special treatment for religion or those practicing religion, Brennan's view would go further than Scalia's in upholding an individual free exercise claim against state government; to that end, compare their opinions in *Employment Division, Department of Human Resources of Oregon* v. *Smith,* 494 U.S. 872 (1990). As such, Brennan's libertarian free exercise interpretation is more difficult to reconcile with his Establishment Clause views than is Scalia's, whose free exercise interpretation may permit, but does not require, religious exemptions from the law.

31. *Texas Monthly* v. *Bullock* at 27–28.

32. The test is Philip Kurland's, offered in "Of Church and State and the Supreme Court," Vol. 29 University of Chicago Law Review, p. 1.

20

Should the Government Allow for Religious Exemptions from Military Service?

THE PROBLEM POSED

Issues of war and peace are central to every religion and to every political community. Jews and Christians share the Commandment that states "Thou shalt not kill,"[1] yet governments everywhere act as if it is within their authority to demand that their citizens take up arms, either to defend the country or to serve the national interest. What happens when the perceived demands of religion to avoid killing come into conflict with the demands of the political community to have its citizens fight in a war?

In the United States, the term *conscientious objector* has been used to describe someone who refuses on religious grounds to serve in the military or in combat. From the earliest days of the Republic, legislative attempts have been made to accommodate conscientious objectors who were conscripted[2] into the armed forces.[3] By the time of the Civil War, federal law established exemptions from military service for them. But do those with religious objections to war have a *right* to an exemption from military service? Even if one believes that no such right exists, one could still contend that decent societies ought to respect religious objections to war as much as is practical, reserving for themselves the authority to revoke these exemptions whenever they deem it necessary.[4]

And a further problem emerges as we consider this issue. Although there are religious sects for which pacifism has long been a well-recognized tenet— Quakers and Mennonites, for instance—claims for exemption from military service or combat have not been confined to them. What exactly distinguishes "conscientious" objections to war from other objections? If "conscientious" objections are religious objections, then how does one define religion so as to exclude nonreligious objections to war? It seems important to distinguish the two, because maintaining any kind of military would be very difficult if anyone wishing an exemption for personal reasons could obtain it. The problem is that religion is a very difficult thing to define;[5] on the one hand, a narrow definition seems to exclude many nonwestern or simply unfamiliar religions; on the other hand, a broad definition seems to include what normally could be called philosophic or simply "moral" views that are usually considered nonreligious.

These are the two basic questions that arise. First of all, do those with conscientious objections to war have a right to an exemption from military service? Second, how do we define "conscientious objections" (and their precise relationship to religion)? Our first case illustrates the traditional way in which the Supreme Court has attempted to resolve these issues.

EXAMPLE 1

Hamilton v. *Regents of the University of California,* 293 U.S. 245 (1934)

Facts: Two students applied for admission to the University of California and at the same time applied for an exemption from the required course in military science. Their petition was denied, and they were suspended from the university with readmission contingent upon their willingness to take the course in military science. The course (designed for the Reserve Officer Training Corps, or R.O.T.C.) included instruction in marksmanship, combat principles, and the use of automatic rifles, but the students were both members of the Methodist Episcopal Church and both of their fathers were ordained ministers. They believed that "war, training for war and military training [were] immoral, wrong and contrary to the letter and spirit of His teaching and the precepts of the Christian religion." The Supreme Court of California found in favor of the University of California, and the students appealed to the Supreme Court.

Result: The University of California may require a course in military science, and no rights under the Fourteenth Amendment are denied by this requirement.

Argument of the Case: Butler, Justice. The states have the authority to train their citizens to prepare them should it be necessary to call upon them to defend their country in the military. The military science course at the University of California falls under this authority of the states. The students at the university are not actually placed into the military; they are merely required "to develop fitness" for the military. It is important to remember that the students are not required by law to attend the university. They are seeking the education that the state of California can provide for them and at the same time are asking for an exemption from a required course solely on religious grounds. But while Congress has granted some exemptions from actual military service to conscientious objectors, this exemption is a privilege and not a right, and it is derived from an act of Congress rather than the Constitution. Citizens owe a duty to their government to "support and defend" it against all enemies, and there is no right against the authority of the state governments to an exemption from the military science course. "Liberty" as defined by the Fourteenth Amendment is not denied by the states exercising this authority.

Cardozo concurs. The principle advanced by these students is destructive because of the way it exalts personal views over the authority of the state. If such a principle were accepted, then those with religious objections might refuse to pay taxes to support an offensive or defensive war: "The right of private judgment has never yet been so exalted above the powers and the compulsion of the agencies of government." Congress has generously agreed to grant exemptions from military service to those with religious objections, but these exemptions are not constitutional rights. And the military science course does not involve any actual military service.

Discussion

The sincerity of the students objecting to war was uncontested. They belonged to a Christian sect that had announced its opposition to war in several official church documents shortly before the two applied to the University of California. In the General Conference of the Methodist Episcopal Church in 1928, the church declared that "we renounce war as an instrument of national policy." And as a result of this official church position, the Conference called for "the United States Government to grant exemption from military service to such citizens who are members of the Methodist Episcopal Church, as conscientiously believe that participation in war is a denial of their supreme allegiance to Jesus Christ." In addition, the Conference discussed the issue of military training, calling for moral support for those who "hold conscientious scruples" against such training. The sincerity of the students' belief was measured by their participation in a recognized church that had issued official pronouncements on military service and training. In other words, there was proof that the religious scruples of the students were not invented for the sake of avoiding civic responsibilities, and the scruples were not simply the result of personal reflection.

But sincerity was not sufficient. The authority of the state governments was also considered:

> The States are interested in the safety of the United States, the strength of its military forces and its readiness to defend them in war and against every attack of public enemies. Undoubtedly every State has authority to train its able-bodied male citizens of suitable age appropriately to develop fitness, should any such duty be laid upon them, to serve in the United States army or in state militia....[6]

In the light of this authority, the claim of the students could not be maintained. Congress had created by law certain exemptions from actual military service, but because these exemptions were a matter of privilege and not of right, the principle behind the military service exemptions did not need to be extended to military training in the states. As Butler observed,

> The conscientious objector is relieved from the obligation to bear arms in obedience to no constitutional provision, express or implied; but because, and only because, it has accorded with the policy of Congress thus to relieve him.... The privilege of the native-born conscientious objector to avoid bearing arms comes not from the Constitution but from acts of Congress. That body may grant or withhold the exemption as in its wisdom it sees fit....[7]

The argument here is very clear. No country can exist without a military, and no military can survive unless it has the authority to compel military service from its citizens. In another case that is quoted here by Butler, the authority of the government to compel service is stressed: the citizen "may be compelled, by force if need be, against his will and without regard to his personal wishes or his pecuniary interests, or even his religious or political convictions, to take his place in the ranks of the army."[8] It follows that conscientious objectors have no right to withhold their service but that Congress may allow them an exemption as a matter of public policy if it is convenient. However, that exemption can be withdrawn at any time for reasons of policy. In his concurring opinion, Justice Cardozo goes so far as to use a religious term to emphasize the point that no right to exemption exists. Cardozo says that the Congressional exemptions are "act[s] of grace."

This case introduces us to the traditional approach taken by the courts. Since the 1930s, the Supreme Court and lower courts have struggled with these issues again and again, and the approach they have taken has changed dramatically in recent years (most notably in the 1960s, when the courts confronted a number of cases growing out of conscription for the Vietnam War). Our next case reflects this change and deals with a person who made a claim for exemption from military service but whose religious views were somewhat unorthodox.

EXAMPLE 2

United States v. *Seeger*, 380 U.S. 163 (1965)

Facts: Daniel Seeger was convicted in district court[9] for refusing to submit to induction into the armed forces. The request that he had made for conscientious objector status indicated that he was opposed to war in any form by reason of his "religious belief"; however, he stated that he was unsure about whether he believed in a supreme being. This skepticism about the existence of a supreme being, which was required by the

Selective Service Act, was the sole reason that his request for conscientious objector status was rejected. The appeals court reversed the district court decision.

Result: The Supreme Court affirmed the appeals court decision, holding that it was an improper interpretation of Congressional intent to confine conscientious objector status only to those who believe in a traditional God; the phrase "supreme being" has a broader meaning.

Argument of the Case: Clark, Justice. In 1948 Congress amended the language of the statute dealing with conscientious objector status to explain that eligibility was reserved for those whose "religious training and belief" led them to oppose war in any form. Congress defined "religious training and belief" as "an individual's belief in a relation to a Supreme Being involving duties superior to those arising from any human relation, but [not including] essentially political, sociological, or philosophical views or a merely personal moral code." Clark stated that it was significant that Congress replaced the older references to "God" with the phrase "Supreme Being." This change indicated that Congress wanted to broaden eligibility to include a wide variety of beliefs. In other words, Clark argues that the phrase "Supreme Being" includes "all sincere religious beliefs which are based upon a power or being, or upon a faith, to which all else is subordinate or upon which all else is ultimately dependent." This interpretation is supported by references to such contemporary theologians as Paul Tillich, who defines religion in very broad terms. For these reasons, Clark offers a broad interpretation of the statute and allows for Seeger's eligibility.

Douglas concurs. If the statute under examination were interpreted to include only those religions that define themselves in terms of a Supreme Being, then it would violate the Free Exercise Clause of the First Amendment and the Equal Protection Clause of the Fourteenth Amendment. In other words, the statute would be enforcing "discrimination." Douglas discusses the basic beliefs of Hinduism and Buddhism in order to show how minority religions (which do have a small but significant following in the United States) would not be included in a restrictive interpretation of the statute.

Discussion

This is a remarkable case because Clark manages to interpret the phrase "Supreme Being" to mean religious belief, whether or not it relates to a Supreme Being! Justice Douglas comes very close to admitting that the Court is willfully misinterpreting the statute to keep it from being applied in what he regards as an unfair manner. Douglas says that, in this case, the Court has done "no more so than other instances where we have gone to extremes to construe an Act of Congress to save it from demise on constitutional grounds." The fact was that Congress attempted to distinguish religious from nonreligious belief by using the "Supreme Being" standard, but the Supreme Court was not satisfied that such a standard would include minority religions and therefore transformed its meaning through its interpretation in *Seeger*.[10]

As we observed earlier, Congress had allowed for exemptions from combat or military service from the earliest days of the Revolution, and it had asserted federal control of the standards for exemption since the Civil War. Originally, exemptions were made available to those who were members of denominations opposed to the use of arms and whose articles of faith clearly stated the grounds of opposition. However, in 1940 Congress broadened its standard for eligibility to include those who did not actually belong to a denomination that formally espoused pacifist doctrine. Congress recognized that "one might be religious without belonging to an organized church." This was, of course, true, but it caused some difficulty for military authorities who attempted to determine whether someone attempting to obtain conscientious objector status was truly religious. It removes from the requirements what was a fairly objective test.

Clark devised a new test to be used in determining eligibility. A person must have "a sincere and meaningful belief which occupies in the life of its possessor a place parallel to that filled by the God of those admittedly qualifying for the exemption ... within the statutory definition." In other words, religious beliefs are meaningful (moral) beliefs that act like religious beliefs; this is a definition of religion that is no definition at all. Clark's test focuses on the completely subjective issue of how important and honest a belief is to an individual, rather than on the content of the belief.[11] And any person can be sincere about his or her beliefs, whether they are based on any thought or whether they make any sense. Clark here explicitly cited Paul Tillich, but also followed in the trail set by the eighteenth-century French philosopher Rousseau, who sought to weaken the influence of revealed religion by replacing faith in God with mere sincerity in the profession of faith. Such a transformation was and is significant, for it has the effect of elevating the importance of the individual and the manner in which he or she believes at the expense of what is believed in—that is, at the expense of the power and majesty of God.[12]

A further problem with Clark's revised test of religion is self-deception; people can delude themselves into believing they are sincere when faced with the prospect of serving in combat. The realization that one might face death can easily serve as an incentive to change one's views about the desirability of war and to believe in the new views immediately. But Clark's new interpretation of the statute did "not distinguish between externally and internally derived beliefs." Clark's formulation had the practical effect of vastly expanding the number of people who could successfully claim conscientious objector status. His sincerity standard made it extremely difficult for the military to deny someone this status. Clark says that "their task is to decide whether the beliefs professed by a registrant are sincerely held and whether they are in his own scheme of things, religious." But how does one impugn someone's sincerity, and if the only real standard is the registrant's "own scheme of things," then how can any test measure that?

But can one avoid these problems? Is Clark's sincerity test of religion insufficient, or does it simply reflect the complexity of the subject? Justice Douglas spent a great deal of time in his decision describing the Hindu and Buddhist religions in order to prove that important minority religions are not organized around a traditional Western notion of a Supreme Being. Douglas seems to be saying that the diversity of religion in America requires the acceptance of a broad definition of religion. But this leaves us with a problem: either we reject the old objective test (which appears too narrow) or we embrace the new subjective test (which is so broad that it is no test at all).

Once the old objective test was rejected, new challenges to the laws defining conscientious objector status emerged. If the only real standard is the registrant's "own scheme of things," then how could the military demand someone prove that he or she is opposed to all war in order to be granted conscientious objector status (as Congress had stipulated)? This problem is analyzed in our next example.

EXAMPLE 3

Gillette v. *United States,* 401 U.S. 437 (1971)[13]

Facts: Two cases were decided together here. Guy Gillette refused to be inducted into the military because of his "humanist" view that the Vietnam War was unjust. He did not object to war in any form, but he did not think that he could in good conscience fight in the Vietnam War. The second case involved Louis Negre, who was a Catholic subscribing to the traditional distinction in his religion between just and unjust wars. Since he believed the Vietnam War to be unjust, he applied for conscientious objector status only after he finished boot camp and received his orders for Vietnam duty. Could Congress limit eligibility for conscientious objector status to those who refuse to participate in all wars? Also, would limiting eligibility in such a way violate the religion clauses of the First Amendment?

Result: Congress may limit conscientious objector status to those who object only to all wars. Such a limitation does not violate the religion clauses of the First Amendment.

Argument of the Case: Marshall, Justice. The sincerity of the beliefs held by Gillette and Negre is not questioned. But the statute defining conscientious objector status clearly indicates that eligibility is reserved for those who object to "participation in war in any form." This does not violate the Establishment Clause, because there is no design to discriminate against any particular religion, and the claim that there is *de facto* discrimination is also rejected by Marshall. This requirement reflects valid secular purposes. In other words, the requirement is "neutral" with regard to religion. The Free Exercise Clause is not violated because the issue here is not the right to hold beliefs but the limited right to act on one's beliefs.

Douglas dissents. With regard to the *Gillette* case, Douglas argues that "the law as written is a species of those which show an invidious discrimination in favor of religious persons and against others with like scruples." There is no reason that a person with conscientious objections to unjust wars should be forced to serve in the military (at least in combat roles) simply because his reasons are "humanist." The *Negre* case also illustrates that the current law is discriminatory. Catholic doctrine clearly teaches that one must make a distinction between just and unjust wars. Negre's beliefs are sincere, and to force him to serve in Vietnam would violate the First Amendment.

Discussion

This case follows only one year after the Supreme Court had heard *Welsh* v. *United States*,[14] a case concerning a conscientious objector who denied that his beliefs were religious in any sense. In fact, when filling out his form requesting conscientious objector status, Welsh had struck the word "religious" and had later emphasized that his objection to war was derived from his readings in history and sociology. In spite of this, Justice Black argued that Welsh was eligible to be a conscientious objector. After *Welsh*, it was not clear that there were any real limits to eligibility. The *Gillette* case seems to be a kind of response to concerns that arose naturally from a reading of *Welsh*.

Here, Justice Marshall upheld Congress's power to confer conscientious objector status upon only those who objected to all wars and suggested that if Gillette and Negre were allowed to receive conscientious objector status, then almost anyone could receive it. Marshall noted that "a virtually limitless variety of beliefs are subsumable under the rubric, 'objection to a particular war.'" This is true, but the real question is how can the Congress—or the Supreme Court, or anyone—distinguish authentic religious belief from unauthentic belief on the basis of conscientious objection to all wars as opposed to an objection limited to unjust wars? Marshall thought it appropriate to distinguish between "those whose dissent has some conscientious basis from those who simply dissent." In other words, from Marshall's perspective, people who objected to all war were *conscientiously* objecting, while those who objected only to unjust wars were more likely to be objecting *without* conscience.[15] But how could this distinction make sense, especially after *Seeger* had created an essentially subjective formulation of religion? Marshall's argument was especially confusing when one considers the *Negre* case, because he was basing his opposition to the Vietnam War on traditional Catholic doctrine. Was Negre's opposition any less conscientious than, let us say, Seeger's?

But Marshall was adamant about the fact that Congress could limit conscientious objection eligibility to those who opposed all war. He argued that this limitation did not violate either the Establishment Clause or the Free Exercise Clause. Yet, upon reflection, each of these conclusions proves troubling.

The Establishment Clause demands "governmental neutrality in matters of religion, and this is not contradicted by the Congressional standard."[16] Although requiring a belief that all war is wrong explicitly identifies no single religion, such a standard does differentiate among religious beliefs, disadvantaging those (like Roman Catholicism) where there exists a tradition of classifying wars and rendering only some unjust. In this way, the standard allows people with one kind of religious objection to be exempted from military service, while it forces those with different religious objections to serve against their principles. Gillette and Negre assert that the statutory standards work "a de facto discrimination among religions." Marshall's response to this claim was to emphasize the practical problem faced by Congress. He contended that such discrimination would not be sufficient to make the statute unconstitutional "so long as an exemption is tailored broadly enough that it reflects valid secular purposes." This makes a certain kind of sense. Congress does not want everyone to have a legal right to an exemption from military service, so it needed to find some way of limiting eligibility (a problem exacerbated by the judiciary's previous constitutional interpretation). However, can it be denied that the way Congress chose to do so has the effect of granting exemptions to some religious groups and not to others, based primarily on differences of religious doctrine? Marshall says that the government limited eligibility to those who oppose all war because it has an "interest in maintaining a fair system." He emphasized that the government needed to implement "fair, evenhanded, and uniform decisionmaking." But is such a system fair and evenhanded? Marshall's argument about the Establishment Clause is problematic.

The Free Exercise discussion is also a bit troublesome. Marshall's main point seems to be that the Congressional standards are not "designed to interfere with any religious ritual or practice, and do not work a penalty against any theological position." But both Gillette and Negre claim that their desire to be exempted from military service comes from a theological position. Can one state with assurance that no theological position distinguishes one kind of war from another (especially given the way the Supreme Court had defined notions akin to "theological position" in cases like *Seeger* and *Welsh*)? Marshall turned to a balancing test to complete his point: "The incidental burdens felt by persons in petitioners' position are strictly justified by substantial governmental interests that relate directly to the very impacts questioned." This kind of balancing test heavily favors the government's authority to regulate conscription, an authority that previously was rendered problematic in *Seeger* and *Welsh,* when the Court rewrote and transformed Congress's law in this area. Outside the context of a cramped legalism, it is difficult to understand how the Court could champion the *religious* claims of Seeger and Welsh and deny those of Gillette and Negre.

In spite of the problems with the specific argument that Marshall presents, it does seem fair to say that the free exercise claim raised in *Gillette* and *Negre* is weaker than the Establishment Clause claim. If the law is a valid secular law (that is, if it does not violate the Establishment Clause), then it would seem to follow that an unintentional and minor effect of the law on a religious group's actions (rather than on its beliefs) should be allowable under the Constitution.

EXAMPLE 4

Reiser v. Stone, 791 F. Supp. 1072 (1992)

Facts: Dr. Lynda Reiser attended college under an R.O.T.C. scholarship and became a second lieutenant when she graduated, owing the Army four years of service. She sought and received a deferment in order to attend medical school at the Army's expense. By attending medical school, she reduced her required years of service from four years to three. After graduating from medical school, she received another deferment from the Army to begin a medical internship, although the Army was willing only to grant her a one-year deferment, a shorter time than she requested. During the course of her internship, Dr. Reiser made arrangements to take a three-year fellowship in anesthesiology that would begin at the end of her one-year deferment. At this point, she advised the Army that she wanted a discharge for reasons of conscientious objection. The Army denied her request.

Result: Dr. Reiser should be granted her request for conscientious objector status.

Argument of the Case: Pollak, Judge. Even though Dr. Reiser does not belong to any church and "does not subscribe to formal religious beliefs or direction in formulating her views about war," her views must be classified as religious. Although Army regulations demand that a person's opposition to all war come from "deeply held moral or ethical (not political, philosophical, or sociological) beliefs," Pollak suggests that these distinctions are merely "semantic." Also, her views are sincere. Pollak rejects the Army's claim that her sincerity ought to be questioned because her request for conscientious objector status surfaced at exactly the moment when she would have been called upon to repay her country with active duty.

Discussion

This case illustrates the way in which the principles in *Seeger* have been extended. Pollak addresses two main questions that must be answered in order to know whether conscientious objector status should be granted: What does the law consider "religious," and what does the law consider "sincere"? Both of these questions point to the more basic issue: What makes an objection "conscientious"?

Pollak states that there is no doubt that "the views expressed by Dr. Reiser constitute views which are of a moral and ethical weight, and which are, for the purposes of this inquiry, as strong and consequential as religious views of a conventional sort." What evidence is there to support this? One of the most compelling experiences in Dr. Reiser's life was her reading of Kurt Vonnegut's *Slaughterhouse Five* and her viewing of Oliver Stone's *Born on the Fourth of July.* These "helped her to put into perspective the military principles of war and were particularly influential to her decision to seek separation from the Army."[17] It is important to recognize just how distant these experiences are from the ones first accepted by the government as grounds for granting conscientious objector status. Belief in Oliver Stone has replaced belief in God. And when Justice Clark in *Seeger* celebrated the extension of eligibility to minority religions that do not have a Supreme Being as central to their beliefs, did he have Oliver Stone in mind? The military board of review indicated that it did not believe that Dr. Reiser presented sufficient evidence that she had "a convictions methodology that is comparable to the rigorous means by which traditional religious convictions are formulated." Considering the importance of popular novels and movies to her thinking, this is an understatement. But Pollak rejected the board's criticisms as unfounded.

The other question that dominates this case was whether Dr. Reiser was sincere. The Army board pointed out that Dr. Reiser was an R.O.T.C. scholarship student from 1983 to 1986, and a member of the Army Reserve from 1986 to 1990; she relied on the sponsorship of the military for her entire education and never sought to be released from service. It was only when her medical career would be disrupted by military service that she developed objections to service. On the other hand, Dr. Reiser claims that she always had misgivings about military service, but that her views "did not mature into a fixed conviction of hostility to violence, implying a hostility to military service in any form" until recently. However, in spite of the uncontested fact that Dr. Reiser never sought to be released from military service before, Pollak accepts her story and criticizes the military board for failing to make a real case against her sincerity. He says that "something more tangible than suspicion is needed to support a finding of insincerity." This is important because, in his view, we need to remember that "conscientious scruples may flower at any time."

The question that Pollak does not answer and that lies at the heart of this case (as it does for all of the cases in this chapter) is a philosophic or theological one: What is the conscience? And while a full inquiry into the nature of conscience is beyond the scope of this chapter, some clarity about the subject is necessary.[18] The original notion of conscience is still evident in the literal meaning of the word: "to know along with others." Today, we tend to think of the conscience as a completely personal or subjective sense, but the conscience was originally thought to be a kind of knowing that was shared with others. In other words, one's private or subjective sense of right and wrong was not reliable on its own terms; it had to be confirmed by an agreement with first principles.[19] This process of confirmation was thought to require both study and moral training. Otherwise, the conscience would be corrupt, or easily corrupted. St. Thomas Aquinas alerts us to a passage from Titus 1:15 that states, "To the pure all things are pure, but to the corrupt and unbelieving nothing is pure: their very minds and consciences are corrupted."[20] There are two important points to be made here. First of all, the original view of conscience was that it was a type of knowledge, not a mere feeling. Second, it was a type of knowledge that was derived from objective truths, truths beyond the individual rather than inside the individual. As Hadley Arkes points out,

If the conscientious objector presents us with claims based wholly on his inner feelings, then he offers a claim whose worth and validity we cannot really know. For the same reason, we cannot know that his feelings deserve to be treated with a respect that we do not confer on other kinds of feelings.[21]

To state the matter baldly: Why should our personal feelings about war be any more respected than our personal feelings about the taste of food? The traditional view of conscience was that it was rooted in something greater than ourselves, whereas the contemporary view of conscience (as illustrated by this case) transforms it into a kind of taste. The courts have come to accept in an uncritical manner the modern view of conscience, as they previously had accepted the contemporary, subjective view of religion.

SUMMARY

No case in this chapter decides the issue of whether there is a constitutional right to refuse military service in the name of religion. In fact, the Supreme Court has never directly ruled upon this question.[22] Statutes have provided exemptions from the time of the Civil War, and all the cases we have examined attempt to determine the status of rights under those laws. Justice Marshall referred to the claims for conscientious objector status as claims for "nonconstitutional" rights. This in no way is meant to suggest that there might not be what was formerly called a natural right to refuse service in the name of higher obligations or even of self-preservation. But this kind of right transcends the authority of the Constitution and of ordinary statutes, and it cannot be granted to us by human action.

The cases we have considered address a lower form of right, a legal right, and this kind of right can be defined by a legislature in the way that a natural right cannot. So the cases in this chapter are examined as laws to see if the provisions of these laws are consistent with the Constitution. Once statutes have created a legal right to conscientious objection, the issue becomes one of definition: which objections are conscientious and which are not.[23] This has been a difficult issue for the courts, and there has been a dramatic change in the way in which this term has been defined. In the earliest cases, the courts related conscientious objection to established and familiar religions and reserved exemptions from military service for those who could document active involvement with recognized, nonviolent sects. But in an attempt to avoid religious discrimination, the courts have come to identify the conscience as a subjective feeling; it then becomes difficult to distinguish—in the words of Marshall—conscientious dissent from any other kind of dissent. It also becomes difficult to deny exemptions to those who make their claims for exemption on nonreligious grounds.

The only substantial limitation on eligibility for conscientious objector status is that one's objection must be against all wars, not just against particular wars. But this requirement seems to institutionalize discrimination against religions or sects that teach that killing is justified under some circumstances. Why is such a teaching less "conscientious" than a teaching that all killing is unjustified? Only a philosophic or theological inquiry can resolve this issue, and such an inquiry remains beyond the competence of our courts.

NOTES

1. There is, of course, great controversy over the exact meaning of this Commandment. Is all killing prohibited, or is the commandment a prohibition against murder alone? The Bible seems to allow both for capital punishment and for the waging of war, under some circumstances.

2. The United States does not currently have a military draft, but cases are still heard on these issues (see *Reiser* v. *Stone* in this chapter). Also, these issues are central to gaining a full understanding of the relationship of religion and politics.

3. See the history of conscientious objection exemptions in *U.S.* v. *Seeger* (discussed as Example 2 in this chapter). They date back to the Continental Congress in 1775 but were not always national; sometimes the national government left their possible adoption to the states (whose responsibility it was to raise militia).

4. See Hadley Arkes, "Conscientious Objection," in *First Things* (Princeton, NJ: Princeton Univ. Press, 1986), p. 191.

5. See Chapter 6.

6. 293 U.S. 245, 260 (1934).

7. *Hamilton* v. *Regents* at 264. Butler's observation itself was a quotation from *United States* v. *Mcintosh*, 283 U.S. 605 (1931).

8. This quotation is from *Jacobson* v. *Massachusetts*, 197 U.S. 11 (1905).

9. A number of different cases were consolidated by the Supreme Court in *U.S.* v. *Seeger* so that the issues could be analyzed together. Our focus here is on Seeger's case alone.

10. Not surprisingly, after *Seeger*, Congress responded by amending the Selective Service Act, removing the Supreme Being clause while retaining the language that excluded "essentially political, sociological or philosophical views...." This language was subsequently ruled unconstitutional by several district judges (see, for example, *United States* v. *Sisson*, 297 F. Supp 902, 906 D., Mass. [1969]). The Supreme Court chose not to overturn this provision, but rather (like *Seeger*) chose to interpret its provision very loosely.

11. Note our remarks in Chapter 4 on the changes in the definition of religion.

12. See Allan Bloom, *Love & Friendship* (New York: Simon & Schuster, 1993), p. 75. Bloom follows Arthur Melzer's excellent analysis of Rousseau in *The Natural Goodness of Man: On the System of Rousseau's Thought* (Chicago: Univ. of Chicago Press, 1990), p. 280. Bloom's comment on this point is quite insightful:

Faith means belief in another, in the mysterious God who exists objectively. Sincerity puts the onus on the subjective certainty of the self without reference to further authority. The shift in focus is reflected in our parlance when we say we have faith in someone as opposed to saying we are in good faith. The primacy of the latter reflects the dignity and legislative power of the individual. It is a proud affirmation of the dignity of the self rather than the pious annihilation of the self before a higher dignity.

The Supreme Court's definition of religion, according to a very influential Law Note, is based upon Paul Tillich's understanding of religion as the "ultimate experience." Thus:

The meaning of the term "ultimate" is to be found in a particular human's experience rather than in some objective reality. Tillich's thesis, then, is that the concerns of any individual can be ranked and that if we probe deeply enough, we will discover the underlying concern which gives meaning and orientation to a person's whole life. It is of this kind of experience, Tillich tells us, that religions are made; consequently each person has a religion.

This phenomenological definition, stressing the function which a belief plays in a individual's life, brings within the ambit of religion much which is not conventionally understood as religion."

Note, "Toward a Constitutional Definition of Religion," *Harvard Law Review*, vol. 191 (1978), p. 1067.

13. This case was decided with *Negre* v. *Larsen*, which is referred to in the *Gillette* summary.

14. 398 U.S. 333 (1970).

15. See Arkes, pp. 179ff.

16. Refer to Chapter 4 for a full discussion of different interpretations of the Establishment Clause.

17. Dr. Reiser also stated that she had some conversations with friends about her emerging attitudes. She also was disturbed while living in Philadelphia by seeing patients who had been shot. Note that none of these experiences rises to the level of systematic testing of one's beliefs against a body of knowledge or a system of ethics.

18. For further discussion of this point, see Chapter 10, p. 183.

19. For a detailed and thoughtful treatment of this issue, see Richard Stevens, "Conscience and Politics," in *Teaching Political Science*, Volume 11, Number 4 (Summer 1984), pp. 171-181. We are indebted to his analysis for our treatment of the problem.

20. *Stevens*, p. 172.

21. Arkes, p. 190.

22. See Justice Douglas's remarks in *Gillette*: "The question, Can a conscientious objector, whether his objection be rooted in 'religion' or in moral values, be required to kill? has never been answered by the Court."

23. See Chapter 6 for a discussion of the way in which government is drawn into the job of defining religion. The discussion of *U.S.* v. *Ballard* is particularly relevant to the issues raised in this chapter.

Afterword

Religion in America: Triumphs and Challenges

How are we, as a nation, doing religiously? Has the United States truly solved the problem of religion and politics? That is, has our nation managed to make this a haven for free religious worship and practice as well as a nation whose politics is freed from religiously inspired discord? Briefly, we want to reflect upon and try to assess the contemporary religious–political health of the United States while also examining the challenges that lie ahead. In order to do this, we will briefly summarize three thoughtful, if somewhat different, critiques of the interrelationship between religion and politics in American life.

OVERVIEW

To understand our contemporary religious–political circumstances, we need to remind ourselves of where we, as a nation, have been. Where we have been and where we are going have been decisively influenced by the theoretical and constitutional beliefs of those who founded the American nation. Recall that the United States was fashioned against the immediate background of European religious persecution and warfare. Throughout much of the sixteenth and seventeenth centuries, outright religious hostility reigned in Europe. The human suffering and political instability caused by this persecution and warfare were among the most important political influences on our nation's Founders. Even after the actual violence in Europe had diminished, prejudice and discrimination still endured. In southern Europe (France, Italy, Portugal, and Spain), Protestant minorities suffered; in northern Europe (Britain, Germany, Holland, and Scandinavia), Catholic minorities were singled out. The American colonies were largely founded by Protestants of one sect or another, many of whom had escaped European persecution. Still, having gained political power, they did not eschew religious favoritism. And although the colonies generally became more tolerant of religious minorities with the passage of time (especially after the Revolutionary War), the strong and potentially dangerous link between church and state continued.

The new nation, created by the Constitution, decisively broke with the European tradition and with early colonial practices. It established self-government for the purpose of securing individual natural rights, not for the purpose of implementing God's truth. Thus, religious oaths, traditionally a precondition for holding political offices, were barred, not required. Religion was to be largely privatized. The attitude of the Founders toward religion was nicely communicated by James Madison in *Federalist* 37. After suggesting that astonishment was the appropriate human reaction to the fact that the Constitutional Convention surmounted unprecedented difficulties by producing a Constitution to which the Convention had given its unanimous support, Madison discreetly suggested that it was impossible "for a man of pious reflection not to perceive in it, a finger of that Almighty hand which has been so frequently and signally extended to our relief in the critical stages of the revolution." Those pious individuals inclined to see God's intervention in human affairs were also likely to see it at the Constitutional Convention (which was hardly the same as saying that God did intervene). For everyone else (and especially the nonpious), there simply was no reason to believe that the Constitution was anything but the product of human reason, written for the purpose of advancing secular, not religious, goals. "When the Almighty himself condescends to address mankind in their own language," Madison had noted earlier in the same *Federalist* paper, "his meaning, luminous as it must be, is rendered dim and doubtful, by the cloudy medium through which it is communicated." Even had God's voice been heard at the Convention, it would not necessarily have been understood.

The Constitution's aim of securing citizens' natural rights, including religious freedom, from the menace of religious zealotry, persecution, and warfare has proved remarkably successful. By European standards, American religious relations almost immediately became tranquil. Since its founding, the United States has been a nation without inquisitions, religious warfare, or widespread religious persecutions.

Still, it would be a mistake to believe that America automatically became and remained a nation without religious tensions and conflicts. From its first colonial days through the nineteenth century, self-proclaimed atheists were occasionally ridiculed or even placed at a disadvantage under the civil law. Furthermore, Catholics, Jews, and Mormons have also encountered considerable religious prejudice in the United States.[1] Something of a high-water mark of prejudice against Catholics in the United States took place in the mid-nineteenth century, when anti-Catholic literature (containing lurid tales of nuns and monks who had abandoned their faith because of torture, mental brutality, and sexual abuse) were widely disseminated. These tales both fueled and reflected widespread anti-Catholic bias; Protestant fears and prejudices fanned by such perverse literary tales led to riots in Boston, New York, Philadelphia, St. Louis, and elsewhere. Frequently, physical attacks upon seminaries, convents, and churches (such as the burning of the Ursuline Convent of Charlestown in Boston in 1834 and of the St. Michael's and St. Augustine's churches in Philadelphia in 1844) accompanied the riots. Also in the mid-nineteenth century, in Boston, Philadelphia, and New York, great battles raged over the public schools as Catholics protested against the predominant Protestant textbooks and Bible (the King James version, from which prayers were commonly read). Politically vehement anti-Catholic associations (for example, the American Protestant Association, the Christian Alliance, the American and Foreign Christian Union, the American Protective Association, and the American Alliance) and anti-Catholic political parties (such as the Native American parties of the 1840s, the Know-Nothing Party of the 1850s, and, to some extent, the Republican Party of the 1850s and 1860s) combined to intimidate individual Catholics and diminish Catholic political influence.

Later in the nineteenth century (and into the early twentieth century), both Catholics and Jews occasionally found themselves the objects of acts of violence committed by such groups as the Ku Klux Klan. Like Catholics earlier, Jews in the later part of the nineteenth century also found themselves portrayed in unflattering terms in the literature of the day. The works frequently used offensive, stereotypical terms, picturing Jews as influential, money-grubbing, and unscrupulous. Into much of the twentieth century, quotas in the most prestigious colleges and universities were enforced. Many of the most expensive hotels refused to rent rooms to Jews as a matter of policy. During this time, Jews also encountered significant discrimination in the rental and purchase of houses.

Finally, Mormons, too, have encountered much religious prejudice, discrimination, and violence. The historical record is not pretty:

> From the founding of the Mormon Church in 1830, Mormons were subject to harassment and persecution. The governor of Missouri stated in 1838, "The Mormons must be treated as enemies and must be exterminated or driven from the state, if necessary, for the public good." And in several states, mainly in the South, they were. Joseph Smith and his brother were jailed and then killed by a mob in Illinois in 1844; four Mormon missionaries were killed by a mob in Cane Creek, Tennessee, in 1884; and numerous others became victims of beatings, tar-and-featherings, and other acts of violence.[2]

It is important to recognize that shameful as this religious record is, it has two relatively positive aspects. First, we would reiterate that despite this embarrassing and distressing record of religious bigotry, by the traditional standard of the modern nation–state, America's record of accommodating religious diversity was successful. Second, it is worth mentioning that the kind of religious strife and intolerance described in the above paragraphs have become largely absent from American society. In contemporary America, the evidence appears overwhelming that religious conflict, not to mention religious bigotry and intolerance, has significantly diminished. The following observation seems to us to be correct: "When we look all around the social and political landscape, we see a general harmony among the traditional faiths of the United States; by and large, Protestants get along well with Catholics, Christians get along better with Jews, and even the small number of religious cults are more of a curiosity than a source of widespread resentment and antagonism."[3]

If this perception is true, and religious persecution and prejudice have greatly diminished within the American nation, does this mean that the Founders' vision of a peaceful nation of religious diversity, comprising a multiplicity of religious sects, has finally been achieved? Are there any political–religious questions of great importance facing our nation today? Significantly, there are, and they grow out of the very success of the American nation's solution to the political–religious problem.[4] Perhaps it seems surprising that thoughtful observers tend to agree on the broad outlines of the most important political–religious question currently facing the American nation. Still, their agreement exists only at the most general level, where they hold that the American nation (and its culture, politics, and political and philosophical assumptions and principles) has overwhelmed privately held, religious based beliefs and their public influence. In order to understand this critique more completely, we will examine and summarize differing perspectives by briefly examining three of the most prominent and persuasive (if somewhat conflicting) interpretations of this contemporary American religious–political predicament. Each interpretation is rooted in a book that has garnered considerable attention and controversy, and each presents an important point of view regarding the most important religious–political question that faces the United States today. We now turn our attention to each of them:

A. *The Naked Public Square*,[5] by Richard John Neuhaus. Neuhaus's title is revealing. The business of American democracy is conducted without regard to religion. In the American secular state, religion and religiously grounded values are excluded from the conduct of the public's business. Secularism, the belief in the value and (the ever-changing) values of a secular society, has become the prevalent belief in America. Additionally, Neuhaus thinks that the authority and influence of the mainline Protestant churches that have long defined cultural norms in America are in the process of an inevitable decline. A moral vacuum has occurred, and contending forces from the far right evangelical movement to secular humanists all aspire to fill the vacuum.

Militant religiosity contains risks, but so does militant secularism. Religious persecution and wars are well-known; on the other hand, the "case can be made that the great social and political devastations of our century have been perpetuated by regimes of militant secularism, notably those of Hitler, Stalin and Mao."[6]

Therefore, avoiding fanatical religiosity *and* fanatical secularism while advancing a true public morality should be society's goal. Our society, like all societies, is founded on a vision of how the world is and how it ought to be (a matter about which Neuhaus has some definite ideas). But a major problem is "that a public ethic cannot be reestablished unless it is informed by religiously grounded values."[7] In the United States, religion legitimizes moral values. And moral values are necessary, because human nature is fundamentally flawed. (For Neuhaus, human beings are radically imperfect and sin is an ever-present fact of life.) Yet the relatively new idea of secularism (secular humanism) denies the authority and legitimacy of religion in the public life of the nation. By undermining moral authority, it potentially undermines public morality and the consensus about what is right and just, leaving the state and its laws grounded in nothing but raw power. And in the place of religion it has substituted nothing.

The inevitable result of the naked public square is that decadence replaces virtue.[8] Deprived of its moral anchor, the American ship of state increasingly founders, open to every impulse or influence tossed about by every moral fad, by every passion, and by every influence. Furthermore, religion, too, has been decisively enervated. Faith once provided the moral anchor for America. In fact, at "first it simply called itself Christianity, then evangelical Christianity, and then, much later, mainline Protestantism"; this is what culturally defined the morally permissible boundaries of politics. But no longer. Religion and religious organizations have become confused about their very reason for being. Once, religion and politics shared a common moral foundation. But no longer. And therein lies the contemporary crisis of American religious–political relations.

B. *Habits of the Heart,*[9] by Robert Bellah *et al.* Although *Habits of the Heart* is not a book exclusively, or even primarily, devoted to defining the relationship between religion and politics, it has important and intriguing things to say about this subject. Robert Bellah and his fellow researchers asked white, middle-class Americans a series of questions during the 1980s.[10] How ought we to live? How do we think about how to live? Who are we, as Americans? What is our character? These questions all pointed to a unifying concern. "The fundamental question we posed, and that was repeatedly posed to us," noted the authors, "was how to preserve or create a morally coherent life."[11] At bottom, this is a political question; the moral character of a people is fundamentally related to the nature, organization, and governance of a particular political community. For Bellah, religion (like the family and political participation) is one of the habits of the heart (or what Tocqueville called the mores)—habits that help form the character of a people. Mores can influence and be influenced by the political community.

Mores (like religion) also can aid or combat the most powerful tendencies of the age. According to Bellah, the most powerful tendency in America is individualism, the elevation and celebration of the self. But Bellah believes that individualism is dangerous. It cuts citizens off from each other and has become so pronounced that it has become "cancerous." For that very reason, the dominance of individualism is the chief American political problem in need of solution. It threatens community; it is correlated with competition, selfishness, and greed; and it corrupts character while producing unfulfilled, empty lives:

> Clearly, the meaning of one's life for most Americans is to become one's own person, almost to give birth to oneself. Much of this process, as we have seen, is negative. It involves breaking free from family, community, and inherited ideas. Our culture does not give us much guidance as to how to fill the contours of this autonomous, self-responsible self....[12]

Bellah and his associates believe that citizen character is best fulfilled, and citizen happiness simultaneously best maximized, by participation in the political community. "Getting involved" expands private, self-oriented perspectives and turns them into a concern for the public welfare—in Bellah's words, "a commitment to the public good." Although that commitment may have originated in a desire to help others, or even in self-interest, it still constitutes the essence of citizenship. Consider Bellah's admiration for Mary Taylor, one of the people whom Bellah and his researchers interviewed (and whose comments are summarized in a section titled "From Volunteer to Citizen"). According to Bellah, Taylor respects others' points of view and advocates fair procedure yet is not without her own political point of view or commitment to others:

> In our conversations with Mary Taylor, a member of the California Coastal Commission, we found a civic-minded professional who was able to move from the cosmopolitan value of relativistic tolerance toward the kind of commitment to the common good that is necessary to assure the integrity of a community. A housewife married to a literature professor, Mary became involved in politics by volunteering in the League of Women Voters and has since moved on to work in a number of organizations concerned with a broad range of environmental issues in California, particularly Friends of the Earth.[13]

According to Taylor and to Bellah, Mary Taylor's commitment to public life crystalized when she fought to implement the provisions of a state law requiring mixed-income housing in coastal areas. While fighting to "provide access to public processes to those usually excluded and unable to take part," she became unhappy with the "incestuous relationship between political leaders and economic interest groups."[14] Because of her political involvement, she has come to prize long-term over short-term interests and continental interests over narrower state interests. Out of her political involvement has come not simply a good feeling, but something yet more profound—"a generosity of spirit":

> Generosity of spirit is thus the ability to acknowledge an interconnectedness—"one's debts to society"—that binds one to others whether one wants to accept it or not. It is also the ability to engage in the caring that nurtures that interconnectedness. It a virtue that everyone should strive

for, even though few people have a lot of it—a virtue the practice of which gives meanings to the frustrations of political work and the inevitable loneliness of the separate self. It is a virtue that leads one into community work and politics is sustained by such involvements. As Mary Taylor seems to recognize, it is a virtue that goes against the grain of much of the American cultural tradition....[15]

So what does this commitment to others, a sense of community, and a generosity of spirit have to do with religion? Bellah's first sentence in his chapter on religion speaks directly to this issue: "[r]eligion is one of the most important of the many ways in which Americans 'get involved' in the life of their community and society."[16] For Bellah, religion is important to the extent that it fosters involvement in the larger political society. The mainline church—whether it be liberal or conservative—does not teach this. It is essentially inward-looking and self-oriented. The liberal church speaks in the language of modern psychology, specifically in terms of growth and self-esteem; the conservative church preaches traditional God-based morality. Both are directed toward advancing an individualistic morality. What is needed is a new church, one where individual commitment translates into religiously inspired community action. Martin Luther King's "I Have A Dream" speech ("I have a dream that every valley shall be exalted and every hill and mountain shall be made low.... This will be the day when all of God's children will be able to sing with new meaning 'My country 'tis of thee, sweet land of liberty, of thee I sing'") combines the language of the Prophets with the dream of America and thus captures the essence of this religious commitment. It is an oration that presents the "classic strand of the American tradition that understands the true meaning of freedom to lie in the affirmation of responsibility for uniting all the diverse members of society into a just social order."[17]

Bellah understands religion in political terms.[18] The political (or politicized) religion he advocates is not reflected by piety to God or grounded in revelation; rather, it is championed because of its salutary results. It is advocated not because of its truth but because of its usefulness. Its usefulness is defined by its capacity to improve human welfare on this earth by promoting community and a sense of human belonging. The role of religion is to help bring the individual out of isolation and, via political action and involvement, create a generous spirit and a sense of community.

Comparing Neuhaus and Bellah. Both Neuhaus and Bellah see a common problem plaguing the United States: a public life shorn of those fundamental, agreed-upon beliefs and values that provide a moral foundation for human well-being, virtue, and community. The danger associated with such a religious lacuna is significant. For Neuhaus, the direction of politics is shaped by culture, and culture "is shaped by our moral judgments and intuitions about how the world is and how it ought to be." For the great majority of Americans, such moral judgments and intuitions are the product of a religious belief that is systematically excluded from American life. Community and moral consensus are simultaneously undermined, for "it is the dynamic of religion that holds the promise of binding together (*religare*) a nation in a way that may more nearly approximate *civitas*.[19] Like Neuhaus, Bellah notes a similar association between religion and the national decline of community and consensus, observing that while the tension between private interest and the public good can never be completely resolved, still, "in a free republic, it is the task of the citizen, whether ruler or ruled, to cultivate civic virtue in order to mitigate the tension and render it manageable." The tragedy of contemporary times, Bellah notes, is that as "the twentieth century has progressed, that understanding, so important through most of our history, has begun to slip from our grasp."[20]

Despite their similar concerns about the influence and status of religion in contemporary America and the correlative lack of a moral community in the United States, there are still differences that fundamentally divide their two approaches. We will focus upon two of those differences, one obvious, one rather subtle, but each interrelated. The most obvious difference that divides the two authors is that they simply have different understandings of religion. Neuhaus has an orthodox understanding of religion. Religion (and specifically Christianity) still has everything to do with God, with revelation, and with the salvation of the human soul. Thus, religion is a serious concern, a matter of profound importance. Still, religion can and must inform politics and the public realm. Neuhaus believes that one should not be hesitant to proclaim positions based upon religious understandings, yet the arguments made in favor of public positions cannot be made on the basis of the private, religious truth of the believer and must be presented in terms of the reasoned defense of a policy or program of secular importance to society.[21] Traditional religion can and must inform politics, but these positions must always be debated and defended in terms of their public impact.

By contrast, Bellah and his colleagues maintain a rather more flexible understanding of religion. The content of their interviews shows that religion and God are far more amorphous concepts for them; a person is religious if that individual believes that he or she is religious. The most extreme of these people interviewed is a woman named Sheila Larson. Larson reflects both religion in America and what is wrong with religion in America:

> Today religion in America is as private and diverse as New England colonial religion was public and unified. One person we interviewed has actually named her religion (she calls it her "faith") after herself. This suggests the logical possibility of over 220 million American religions, one for each of us. Sheila Larson is a young nurse who has received a good deal of therapy and who describes her faith as "Sheilaism." "I believe in God. I am not a religious fanatic. I can't remember the last time I went to church. My faith has carried me a long way. It's Sheilaism. Just my own little voice." Sheila's faith has some tenets beyond belief in God, though not many. In defining "my own Sheilaism," she said: "It's just try to love yourself and be gentle with yourself. You know, I guess, take care of each other. I think He would want us to take care of each other."[22]

Sheila is an extreme version of the American mainline religion, which both reflects and reinforces the destructive individualism inherent in all aspects of life in America. Such a religion fails to give to persons what individual religious belief should provide—namely, a meaning to life and love of others that make the public world of competitive striving in America bearable.[23] Bellah's solution to this problem is to affirm a greatly expanded idea of religion that merges spirituality, ethics, political action, and commitment to others for the purpose of advancing an egalitarian political community. Lauding their effort to "recover our social ecology" and contending that this effort draws upon our biblical tradition, Bellah praises the following individuals (in his chapter on "transforming the American Culture"): (1) Cecilia Dougherty, a single mother of four teenagers who after her husband's death became active in politics and was particularly active in organizing tenants (through her active membership in the Campaign for Economic Development); (2) Mary Taylor, the environmental activist whom we encountered earlier; (3) Ed Schwartz, a former Philadelphia City Council representative and the leader of the Institute for the Study of Civic Values, which helps create "local institutions of self-help in poor and working-class neighborhoods that draw previously uninvolved citizens not only into the politics of community, but into the larger arena of interest politics on the citywide level and beyond as well";[24] and (4) Minister Paul Morrison, who labors in his Episcopal Church to create a sense of community and caring, and who "often speaks in his sermons about people, not only in the United States but in Central America or southern Africa, who are on the margins and the edges and how the church must stand with them."[25]

Reading these summaries, it might be concluded that the individuals admired by Bellah are those who refocused their spiritual energy upon affairs of this world (and not upon the next) and have involved their energies in advancing liberal, activist political programs. This recognition brings us to the second disparity between Neuhaus and Bellah. They differ profoundly on the question of human nature. Neuhaus accepts the traditional Christian understanding that human beings, by nature, sin. He comments that even conservative "revivalists" too often ignore sin and blame moral corruption and decadence upon secular humanists, television, or on the larger culture. In Neuhaus's words, "As some secular liberals believe man to be innocent and perfectible, if only the injustices of inequality and ignorance can be remedied, so moral majoritarians come close to suggesting that innate human righteousness would flourish in the absence of the decadence purveyed by television and other elite-controlled institutions."[26]

Although no moral majoritarian, Bellah is, arguably, one of the secular liberals who believes human nature to be innocent and perfectible. Not surprisingly, his writing displays a socialist bent, and in many respects he is a follower of Rousseau.[27] Believing that social structures corrupt a benign or malleable human nature, he speaks not of sin, decadence, or human vice but of cooperative, communitarian political involvement that can liberate human beings from cutthroat economic competition. For Neuhaus, imperfection and failure can be traced to human beings; for Bellah, these go back to social institutions. Little wonder that these two authors differ on the meaning and role that religion can and should play in modern-day America. The larger form that this disagreement frequently assumes in contemporary America is analyzed in our third and final work, below.

C. *Culture Wars*,[28] by James Davison Hunter. Hunter does not discuss religion explicitly. One searches in vain for it in his book's table of contents. Still, he has much to say about the influence of religion in contemporary America. Let us see why.

Hunter's work is more descriptive than analytical. His judgment is that there exists within the United States a fundamental split over culture; Americans have profoundly different opinions and judgments regarding the purpose of the nation's most important institutions, including the family, education, media and the arts, law, and politics. Gay rights, prayer in the schools, abortion, flag burning—these are a few of the more common battles waged in our arenas. This nature of this widespread public disagreement is primarily moral (and often emerges as political conflict). Thus, regarding the purpose and proper functioning of the most important public and private institutions in America there exist profoundly different moral perspectives that today fundamentally divide the United States.

Yet accompanying this religiously related conflict is, paradoxically, an increasing religious toleration and acceptance among citizens within American society. Clearly, we are not experiencing a revival of religious conflict or warfare. Yet, according to Hunter, a new type of religious warfare has emerged. It defies traditional categories and therefore is especially difficult to describe. The social and political conflict that makes up the culture war that Hunter details is rooted in different and competing moral understandings and world views *within* traditional religious sects. These conflicting world views are not always sharply defined but are best understood as polarizing tendencies within American culture.

Hunter believes that underlying the moral conflict currently being experienced in America are two different moral perspectives; one is the impulse toward orthodoxy, and the other is the impulse toward progressivism. Again, each of these impulses cuts across religious denominational lines. Thus, both the impulse toward orthodoxy and the impulse toward progressivism can be found in all sects of Christianity and within Judaism.

The defining element of an impulse toward orthodoxy "is the commitment on the part of adherents to an external, definable, and transcendent authority."[29] This belief in something like a traditional notion of God provides "a consistent, unchangeable measure of value, purpose, goodness, and identity, both personal and collective." Furthermore, it fulfills the purpose of telling "us what is good, what is true, how we should live, and who we are."[30] By contrast, progressivism posits a moral authority defined by the spirit of the modern age, specifically by "a spirit of rationalism and subjectivism."[31] Both scientific rationalism and personal experience become the most important measure of value; within a particular religious tradition, the progressivist impulse desires to transform that tradition and bring it up to date. What is most important about the progressive perspective is that it posits that moral judgments should accord with what we know (or think we know). Hunter argues that what "all progressivist world views share in common is the tendency to resymbolize historic faiths according to the prevailing assumptions of contemporary life."[32] In general, adherents of the progressivist point of view reject Scripture, papal pronouncements, or Torah as possessing an exclusive or even a predominant binding power over their lives. For this reason, most secularists or secular humanists tend to fall in the progressivist camp.

Those who exhibit the impulse toward orthodoxy can be fairly called cultural conservatives while those who advance the impulse toward progressivism are, by and large, cultural liberals. Each is engaged in a theoretical disagreement and a political struggle over the meaning and direction of America. Each wishes its favored opinion of America to prevail. This situation has led to new political alliances across religious lines and a fractionalizing within religious sects.

Hunter believes that an individual's political persuasions are partially or largely determined by his or her attitude toward culture, and at the root of a person's attitude toward culture lies a specific faith. Hunter defines faith broadly, both in terms of traditional theisms (Protestantism, Catholicism, Judaism, and Islam) as well as being made up of secular beliefs (such as Marxism, fascism, and humanism). Such faiths may differ profoundly, but they share a core concern: each makes a claim to truth about the world. Thus, the "struggle for power (which is the essence of politics) is in large part a struggle between competing truth claims, claims which are by their nature 'religious' in character if not in content."[33]

Faith plays an essential role in the lives of citizens. It explains how the individual relates to community and nation, and how the individual should relate. That is, such "belief systems explain why some people are rich and others poor, why some people suffer and others do not, why some people are loved and appreciated and others despised or ignored, why there is injustice, why there is tyranny, why there is war—explanations for the issues that all individuals and communities confront in their experience at various times and in various ways." Furthermore, these same belief systems specify political action, for they prescribe "what should be done, if anything, to help the poor, to alleviate suffering, to pursue justice and peace in the larger order."[34] Just as important is the fact that faiths define the moral significance of different social and political institutions. The moral and social importance of the family, education, law, and government can be variously defined by differing faiths rooted in radically different understandings of the divine. Thus, the most deeply held beliefs of right and wrong, good and bad, just and unjust—standards of reason and sources of profound passions—grow out of the differing faiths of citizens. In this sense, cultural conservatives and cultural liberals simply often disagree about the moral purpose and effective functioning of such institutional arrangements. And, Hunter argues, the evidence of that disagreement is present every day in the culture war that currently dominates politics in America.

CONCLUDING THOUGHTS

It is likely that the seriousness of the religious–political challenges facing the United States has been significantly transformed and tamed by the Founders' successful effort to found a nation for the purpose of securing private individual rights (and not for the end of advancing religious truth). Still, the relationship between politics and religion in the United States today is far from perfect. However, it is significant that observers vigorously disagree about the precise form that such a challenge assumes. According to Richard John Neuhaus, American politics and public discourse have increasingly been conducted and impoverished by a moral and political discourse divorced from any relationship to God and religion. Robert Bellah agrees; American politics and political discourse are woefully inadequate. Yet Bellah's religious prescription for political health differs markedly from Neuhaus's. Bellah champions a revitalization of religion that eschews individualism and selfishness and encourages Americans to subordinate their private interests and pursue the advancement of a true national community. Finally, according to James Davison Hunter, America is divided by citizens (and by political associations and organizations made up of citizens) who split along lines in most respects not very different from the positions advocated by Neuhaus and Bellah, respectively.

If Hunter is correct, the nature of American religious struggle has become an indirect and pale imitation of the religious conflicts that had been part of European history and that remain a source of tension among different groups and within nations around the world. Contemporary American religious practice remains a private concern. This fact is largely consistent with the Founders' vision, although they probably did not anticipate the extent to which religion would eventually be excommunicated from the public realm. Yet although religion has been subordinated as a direct vehicle for political action, its influence has hardly vanished. Today, privatized traditional religion forms the basis of many citizens' cultural and political perspectives. For other citizens, beliefs rooted not in God but in some foundational, secular core maxim furnish the basis for those who adhere to a significantly different moral perspective. Today, religious battles are usually no longer explicitly fought in the name of religion. Nor are they fought primarily between religions, or among religious believers.

Yet traditional religious belief remains a potent cultural, social, and political force in the United States, even as it lurks beneath the surface. It endures for many as the source of life's meaning and as a moral imperative for political life. Thus, religion, as a source of potential societal conflict, has been domesticated but not totally suppressed. On the other hand, religion, as the instructor of agreed-upon moral behavior, has also weakened, and its postulates seem increasingly controversial as the United States approaches the twenty-first century. It would appear that theistic religion, frequently proclaimed as the source of both truth and strife in the Western world, today possesses diminished influence upon good and evil in the United States. Still, any careful analysis of religion and politics cannot help but conclude that religion still retains some of its past influence in the arena of American public life.

NOTES

1. The following discussion borrows and builds upon an analysis by James Davison Hunter, *Culture Wars: The Struggle to Define America* (New York: Basic Books, 1991), pp. 35–41. We acknowledge our dependence upon this work.

2. Hunter, p. 39.

3. Hunter, p. 41.

4. As discussed in detail in Chapter 2.

5. Richard John Neuhaus, *The Naked Public Square: Religion and Democracy in America* (Grand Rapids, MI: William B. Eerdmans, 1984).

6. Neuhaus, p. 8.

7. Neuhaus, p. 21.

8. Neuhaus, pp. 75, 101.

9. Robert Bellah, Richard Madsen, William Sullivan, Ann Swindler, and Steven Tipaton, *Habits of the Heart: Individualism and Commitment in American Life* (Berkeley: Univ. of California Press, 1985).

10. Bellah, *et al.* ask the following questions on p. vii

11. Bellah *et al.*, p. vii.

12. Bellah *et al.*, pp. 82–83.

13. Bellah *et al.*, p. 192.

14. Bellah *et al.*, p. 193.

15. Bellah *et al.*, pp. 194–95.

16. Bellah *et al.*, p. 219.

17. Bellah *et al.*, p. 249.

18. This political religion (so to speak) differs from Bellah's earlier description of a civil religion, which traced the use of religious symbols, beliefs, and rituals in American political discourse for the purpose of building or maintaining community. See Robert Bellah, "American Civil Religion," in *Beyond Belief: Essays on Religion in a Post-Traditional World* (New York: Harper, 1970), pp. 175–76.

19. Neuhaus, p. 60.

20. Bellah, *et al.*, pp. 270–71.

21. This is the basis of Neuhaus's disagreement with the Christian, right-wing political movement. See Neuhaus, p. 19.

22. Bellah *et al.*, pp. 220–21.

23. This point and the discussion that immediately follows are based on Bellah *et al.*, p. 292.

24. Bellah *et al.*, p. 216.

25. Bellah *et al.*, p. 242.

26. Neuhaus, p. 105.

27. These points and many other good insights and arguments are presented by Bruce Frohnen, "Robert Bellah and the Politics of 'Civil' Religion," *The Political Science Reviewer,* vol. XXI (Spring 1992), pp. 148–218.

28. James Davison Hunter, *Culture Wars: The Struggle to Define America* (New York: Basic Books, 1991). Hunter has further developed his understanding of contemporary American culture in so far as it is reflected in the abortion debate in the United States in *Before the Shooting Begins: Searching for Democracy in America's Culture War* (New York: Free Press, 1994). We have chosen to discuss Hunter's first book because it is seminal.

29. Hunter, p. 44. Italics in the original have been deleted.

30. Hunter, p. 44.

31. Hunter, p. 44.

32. Hunter, pp. 44–45. Italics deleted.

33. Hunter, p. 58.

34. Hunter, p. 58.

Index

Cases